Land and Desire in Early Zionism

THE SCHUSTERMAN SERIES IN ISRAEL STUDIES

The Schusterman Series in Israel Studies publishes original scholarship of exceptional significance on the history of Zionism and the State of Israel. It draws on disciplines across the academy, from anthropology, sociology, political science, and international relations to the arts, history, and literature. It seeks to further an understanding of Israel within the context of the modern Middle East and the modern Jewish experience. There is special interest in developing publications that enrich the university curriculum and enlighten the public at large. The series is published under the auspices of the Schusterman Center for Israel Studies at Brandeis University.

For a complete list of books in this series, please see www.upne.com

Boaz Neumann
Land and Desire in Early Zionism

Anat Helman
Young Tel Aviv: A Tale of Two Cities

Nili Scharf Gold
Yehuda Amichai: The Making of Israel's National Poet

Itamar Rabinovich and Jehuda Reinharz, editors
Israel in the Middle East: Documents and Readings on Society, Politics, and Foreign Relations, Pre-1948 to the Present

Land and Desire in Early Zionism

Boaz Neumann

TRANSLATED BY HAIM WATZMAN

Brandeis University Press

Waltham, Massachusetts

Brandeis University Press
An imprint of University Press of New England
www.upne.com

Manufactured in the United States of America
Designed by Katherine B. Kimball
Typeset in Quadraat by Integrated Publishing Solutions

University Press of New England is a member of the Green Press Initiative. The paper used in this book meets their minimum requirement for recycled paper.

Library of Congress Cataloging-in-Publication Data
Neumann, Boaz, 1971–
[Teshukat ha-halutsim. English]
Land and desire in early Zionism / Boaz Neumann ; translated by Haim Watzman. — 1st.
p. cm. — (The Schusterman series in Israel studies)
Includes bibliographical references and index.
ISBN 978-1-58465-967-9 (cloth : alk. paper) —
ISBN 978-1-58465-968-6 (pbk. : alk. paper) —
ISBN 978-1-61168-015-7 (ebook)
1. Zionism. 2. Halutzim—History. 3. Pioneers—Israel—History. 4. Palestine—Emigration and immigration—20th century. 5. Hebrew language—Israel—History. 6. Palestine—History—1799–1917. 7. Palestine—History—1917–1948. 8. Gordon, Aaron David, 1856–1922. I. Title. II. Series.
DS149.N49813 2011
320.5409569409'041—dc22 2011003314

5 4 3 2 1

We must raise up a generation that has no interests and no habits. Iron bars pure and simple. Supple—but iron. Metal from which all that is required for the national machine can be forged. A wheel is lacking?—I am a wheel. A nail, screw, a flywheel?—Take me! Must the soil be dug? —I am a digger. Is there a need to shoot, to be a soldier?—I am a soldier . . . . I have no face, no psychology, no emotions, I don't even have a name: I—the pure concept of service, prepared for anything, I am not tied to anything; I know only one imperative: to build!

—Yosef Trumpeldor, 1916

Contents

Preface

I conducted the research for this book and wrote most of it during the second Palestinian intifada, which began late in the year 2000. It was without a doubt one of the low points in relations between Jews and their neighbors, the Palestinians, in this tract of the Promised Land. F-16 fighter planes bombed densely populated civilian areas, and suicide bombers blew themselves up in crowded city streets. All distinctions between victims were completely blotted out—men, women, old people, children, babies. Terror on both sides.

Over the years, we—both Jews and Palestinians—have learned that the conflict between us is caused by politics, economics, ideology, religion, and history: waves of Jewish immigration to Palestine, the declaration of the establishment of the State of Israel, the expulsion of the Palestinians and the Nakba, the exploitation of cheap Arab labor by Jews, Zionism versus Arabism, and Judaism versus Islam. In myth, the conflict harks back to Abraham's banishment of Hagar from his home. Over the years, writers, historians, and other intellectuals have offered explanations that combine these factors in one way or another.

As an Israeli historian who has been directly involved in this bloody conflict—I served as a soldier in the territories during the first intifada, principally in the Gaza Strip—and as an Israeli citizen who has lived through the second intifada, I find it difficult to accept that these factors are exhaustive, either alone or in combination. I have no doubt that they are all valid, important, and worthy of study. Each would be a necessary component of any endeavor to explain and understand the conflict.

However, the genesis of this book lies in an intuition that, in order to explain aerial bombing missions and exploding buses, we must look beyond politics, economics, ideology, history, and religion. There is something else here that has not yet been addressed by the scholarly literature. I call that something "desire." By this I mean the desire of each party to the conflict for this land, desire that, in clashing, leads both parties to disaster. This book is devoted to the historical manifestations of Jewish desire for the Land of Israel—the territory that the Arabs and the rest of the world called Palestine but that for the Jews was simply "the Land."

In the second intifada, we, Jews and Palestinians, reverted to primal warfare:

rocks, knives, vendettas, an eye for an eye, blood and soil, dismembered bodies. Israelis called it "the situation." The term expressed the enormity of their helplessness. The endless cycle of bloodletting we Israeli Jews experienced during the second intifada produced an acute sense of an end that never ends. A kind of frozen time. Twenty killed in a bus bombing in Jerusalem, nine in a targeted killing in Gaza, thirteen Israeli Arabs shot dead by police, three Palestinians killed in Nablus in another targeted killing, over and over again. Anyone with dark skin and a coat was seen as a potential suicide bomber, every unidentified object as a ticking time bomb. The distinction between home and battlefield melted away. The entire country was the front line. It felt as if politics, economics, ideology, and especially history, in the sense of time that moves and changes, had all come to an end.

The second intifada brought the clash between the two desires for this land to an explosive point. The two could not exist side by side, simply because they are desires for the same place—the Land of Israel/Palestine. This war of desires recalls the words of Virgil in his *Georgics*: "Not all soil can absorb everything." The soil of the Land of Israel has apparently absorbed all it can.

In this book I seek to go back to the constitutive moment of Zionist desire for the Land of Israel, to the moment when it received concrete form and content. In the standard account, Zionism began in the 1880s with the first wave of Jewish immigration motivated by modern nationalist consciousness, the First Aliya (literally, "ascent"; figuratively, wave of immigration). But, in my analysis, the first manifestation of real intention to return to the Land appears only at the beginning of the twentieth century, at the time of the Second Aliya. Many of the Jews who arrived in this wave of immigration were socialist-Zionist immigrants imbued with pioneering ideals: Jewish labor and settlement in the Land. Since that time, the Jewish community in Israel has changed politically, economically, socially, ideologically, and in many other ways. But the existential Zionist experience of being-in-the-Land-of-Israel retains its central place in Israeli experience. The pioneers, as I will show, were the first to equate the concept of being itself with the physical condition of being in Israel. Being-in-the-Land-of-Israel was, for them, not merely being situated in a specific place. Being-in-the-Land-of-Israel was, for them, *to be*.

This book is devoted to a portrayal of pioneering Zionist desire for the Land of Israel, not Palestinian-Arab desire. Like most Jews in Israel, I do not speak Arabic. As I will show, not knowing Arabic is itself a component of the Zionist desire for the Land of Israel, which seeks, and is able, to know the Land only via the Hebrew language. It may well be that a description of Palestinian desire for this land can be produced only by a Palestinian.

Acknowledgments

Writing a book is always a collective endeavor. I would like to thank all my friends and colleagues who participated in writing *this* book by reading either some or all of the manuscript and commenting on it: Yehonatan Alshech, Gabriela Avigur-Rotem, Matan Boord, José Brunner, Nitza Drori-Peremen, Amir Eshel, Shlomo Fischer, Michael Gluzman, Sharon Gordon, Igal Halfin, Hanan Hever, Yotam Hotam, Adriana Kemp, Shay Lavie, Yulia Lerner, Ron Margolin, Ofer Nur, Adi Ophir, Amnon Raz-Krakotzkin, Tammy Razi, Eran Rolnik, Ahmad Saʿdi, Assaf Sagiv, Arieh Saposnik, Eli Shaltiel, Michal Shapira, Naʿama Sheffi, Yehouda Shenhav, Eugene Sheppard, Hamutal Tsamir, Ayelet Triest, and Yossi Yonah.

Haim Watzman translated the book from Hebrew to English, Stephanie Golden edited the English translation, and Jason Warshof copyedited it—together they made the book better than my original.

Special thanks to Sylvia Fuks Fried from Brandeis University Press and Phyllis Deutsch from the University Press of New England for believing in this book and making me take the necessary steps to make it better.

The greatest debt I owe to my teacher Shulamit Volkov for paving the road for me.

This book was published with the generous support of the Lucius N. Littauer Foundation and the Israel Science Foundation.

Land and Desire in Early Zionism

1 Pioneers and Pioneerism

This book articulates the Zionist act of aliya and settlement in the Land of Israel by focusing on the experiences of the *halutzim*, or pioneers, the paradigmatic Zionists. In opposition to almost all Zionist historiography, it presents the pioneers' most central experience—the existential reality of being-in-the-Land-of-Israel and their basic *desire* for the Land—without reducing this desire, as most historians do, to a political, economic, romantic, or psychological phenomenon.

In the May 1925 issue of the Kibbutz Ein Harod newsletter, *MeBifnim*, a member wrote that a distinction should be made between two types of *halutziyyut*, or pioneerism, in the building of the Land of Israel. The first was the *halutziyyut* of conquest, which did not know what goal it sought, and the principal impulse of which was to blaze a trail, move forward, get out into the world. The second was the *halutziyyut* of construction, which burned no bridges and did not proceed blindly, but rather unwound like an unbroken string marking out a road.[1] This kibbutznik was describing here, in brief, the constitutive aspects of pioneer desire as I present it in this book. This desire carries with it an ecstatic, boundary-blurring impetus, alongside an impetus that establishes discipline and creates boundaries. These two impetuses act simultaneously. So, for example, when I discuss the sweat flowing off the pioneer's body onto the soil of the Land, I will show that this both blurs the boundaries between him and the Land (the pioneer who moistens the soil and senses himself as part of it) and creates boundaries (the pioneer moistens the Land, thus making it "Jewish," constituting a boundary between Jewish land and Arab land).

Desire, I claim and intend to prove historically, knows no boundaries yet, in this lack of knowledge, actually establishes them. This book describes the impetus of blurring boundaries as it finds expression in the pioneer-ecstatic relation to the Land of Israel—to its soil, to its inanimate objects, its plants, and its wildlife, to its landscapes and other spaces. Then it shows how, simultaneously, this same boundless ecstatic desire is channeled toward the Land, constituting its borders in the form of wells, paths, roads, settlements, and other such visible realities.

I do not intend to *explain* the pioneer desire for the Land of Israel. Attempts to explain the causes and sources of this phenomenon, as well as its purpose, miss the mark. Instead of explaining, I seek to *describe.* To do so, I simply chart pioneer desire.[2] As the many quotes from the pioneers themselves included here demonstrate, pioneer language, the multiplicity of pioneer texts, and their unrestrained expressiveness themselves constitute part of the pioneer desire for the Land of Israel.

The pioneers expressed this desire in descriptions of their experience of being-in-the-Land as an ecstatic, almost mystical sense of actually merging their flesh with its soil, flora, and fauna, of achieving a symbiosis with it, as though the boundaries between themselves and the Land had dissolved. Yosef Weitz, one of the first settlers at Um Juni, on the shore of Lake Kinneret (the Sea of Galilee), wrote that he had not really understood the mystery of the Zionist need to possess the soil until he made the ascent—*aliya*, the Hebrew word for immigration to the Holy Land—to the Land of Israel and dug his first trench in Rehovot: "Then, when the scent of the soil rose to my nostrils, I sensed something new that had perhaps been hidden away in some secret place under the threshold of consciousness, awakening and spreading through all my bones and sinews. And the deeper I dug, the sensation of the soil became more profound and spread through me, and the feeling overcame me that I [must] embrace the land, merge into it, suck from it the essence of life. The spirit of the generations blew within me from the depths of the soil and I felt, really felt, the powerful connection between me and the soil of Israel."[3]

These expressions of desire could be explicitly erotic. At midnight, on a visit to Ben Shemen Farm, the author Y. H. Brenner was walking to the home of his friend, the farm's manager, Yitzhak Elazari-Volcani. As a compatriot who accompanied Brenner later recounted, they walked along a path that ascended to the farmyard. At some point Brenner began speaking of the Land of Israel. They reached a broad field on the hillside that had been freshly and deeply plowed; large brown clods of earth jutted boldly out from the ground under the light of a full moon. The Herzl forest was to be planted there. Brenner halted. Silence prevailed. No one said a word. Suddenly he fell to his knees on the plowed field, embracing an armful of clods, kissing them, and crying out: "Land of Israel, will you be ours?! Land of Israel, will you be ours?!"[4] Another *halutz* wrote that on one of his trips through the Galilee he found, in a cleft in a boulder, a cyclamen blossom. The flower's petals were still closed, deep in their dream of blooming. "I bent over the boulder, kissed the edge of its red mouth, the red, red mouth of the flower," he wrote.[5]

Yet this pioneer desire for the Land has been almost completely omitted from the historiography. Most historians analyze immigration to and settlement in Palestine as a political, socioeconomic, ideological, or cultural process. The few historians who do take up the issue of desire all see it not on its own terms but as a form of expression, as a manifestation of subjective, internal reality, or in a Freudian sense, as an enactment of oedipal patterns.

This book, in contrast, takes desire as a primal, irreducible condition, a state of being that precedes need or purpose or any action such as farming, construction, or road building. For the pioneers, being-in-the-Land *was* this primal state. I have drawn this concept from the pioneers' own expressions of their feelings and experiences of being-in-the-Land. I take these expressions at face value, not as sublimations of or metaphors for some other feeling or need. This approach to the pioneers' desire for the Land allows us to see the pioneer-Zionist act not only as political, economic, ideological, historical, or religious but first and foremost as existential.

A historical narrative is the product of the period in which the historian writes it, emerging from the historian's identity, political outlook, and worldview. Thus, I focus here on the desire of the *halutzim* for the Land of Israel—not the desires of others, such as the local Arabs—presenting their history from a classic pioneer-Zionist point of view.

The Halutzim

From the beginning of the Second Aliya in 1903–1904 through the end of the Third Aliya in 1923, a new breed of immigrants arrived in Palestine. In Hebrew they were called *halutzim*—pioneers (I will use the Hebrew and English terms interchangeably). A modern Hebrew dictionary defines *halutz* as "the part of the army that precedes the major force, the vanguard," and as "the first of a conquest, an enterprise, paving the way for those who come after."[6] According to this definition, the individuals or groups who were the first to engage in any activity in the Land of Israel can be called pioneers.

But when we seek to discuss pioneerism (I will use the Hebrew term *halutziyyut* from here on) in the framework of Zionist activity, we cannot disregard the way the Zionists viewed themselves. In this respect, *halutziyyut* is a phenomenon with clear form and content. *Halutz*, the dictionary tells us, is also "a name given in the prestate period to a young man who immigrated to the Land of Israel in order to fulfill his Zionist aspiration to engage in manual labor and to participate in [the Land's] construction."[7] According to this definition, to be a pioneer one must live in a certain period, be of a certain age, have certain intentions, and perform a certain kind of work. Those who were the first to perform deeds of any sort in the Land of Israel were, then, pioneers in the simple meaning of the word. They were the vanguard. But they were not *halutzim* in the classic Zionist sense.

The word *halutz*, when it appears in the Bible in the story of Joshua's siege of Jericho (Joshua 6:6–9), is rendered in English as "armed men" or "picked troops." The first Zionists who used the term knew not only this context but also the request that the tribes of Gad and Reuben make in the books of Numbers and Deuteronomy. These tribes have settled to the east of the Jordan River and ask to be exempted from the invasion of Canaan. After an exchange with Moses, they relent. Moses tells them that they may retain their land east of the Jordan on condition that they participate, along with the other tribes, in the conquest of the Promised Land (Numbers 20:20–22). Here, too, the translation of the word *halutz* is "armed man" or "vanguard." The biblical word thus means the warrior in the vanguard of his people. But rather than being an individual soldier, he is a part of a unit, a collective, which leads its people by divine command.

The terms *halutz* and *halutziyyut* first appeared in their Zionist sense at the beginning of the Third Aliya in about 1919. They were applied to the Second Aliya only retroactively. David Ben-Gurion wrote that, while it was in progress, the Second Aliya was not linked with pioneering simply because the term *halutz* had not yet been applied to it. At the time, Ben-Gurion and his cohort were referred to simply as *tze'irim*, young people. The term *halutz* first appeared in its Zionist sense at a convention of Tze'iri Tzion, an early labor-Zionist youth movement, in Vienna at the end of 1913. One of the resolutions adopted there was to promote "the training of pioneers for the Land of Israel." Four years later, the federation of socialist Zionist youth movements and organizations founded by the national hero Yosef Trumpeldor called itself HeHalutz, "The Pioneer." At the time, the term was chosen as a direct translation of the word "vanguard."

We first find a systematic exposition of the term *halutziyyut* in two foundation documents dating from this period. The first, a letter penned in Palestine by socialist leader Berl Katznelson and sent at the end of World War I to Jewish youth groups in the Diaspora, bears the title "To the HeHalutz Movement."[8] Katznelson used a slightly different but also linguistically correct form, *halitzut*, which shows that the term had not yet come into common usage.[9] He defined pioneerism as a "life project" and a "personal vision." It signified restraint and self-control—a pioneer achieved mastery of his world. According to Katznelson, the pioneer Zionist movement stood apart from other contemporary movements in that it focused not on its leadership or its program but rather on the lives and labor of its adherents. The second document that serves as a milestone in the definition of *halutziyyut* was an essay Trumpeldor wrote in 1918, titled "The Pioneer, His Nature and Destiny." This piece echoed Katznelson's major points.[10]

According to Katznelson and Trumpeldor, the *halutz* is defined by the seminal nature of his actions. He does in his life what the nation will do in the future. The pioneer is a soldier, and as such his role is to conquer—but not in the violent sense. Rather, he conquers—that is, lays claim to and takes possession of—the land by working it. His mission is to farm, to homestead, to labor in construction and agricultural industry. The pioneer is a worker himself, not an exploiter of others. In both documents, the *halutz* is part of a collective and a socialist. Katznelson and Trumpeldor sought to turn the pioneer movement into a mass movement. However, they both intimate that political and class criteria determine who is a *halutz* and who is not. The process of pioneer training, in their view, thus includes an element of selection. Not every young Jew has the ability to settle in the Land of Israel.

Over time, the secular incarnations of many religious concepts would permeate the pioneer ethos. Katznelson, as noted, already identified *halutziyyut* not just as an idea or doctrine but as a "personal vision." In the 1920s, additional attributes were ascribed to the pioneer. One was *hagshama*, best translated as "realization" but connoting here the implementation of one's Zionist and personal ideals. Other characteristics were leadership and educational and political activism. The term "conquest" as understood by Zionists first indicated conquering the land by working it with one's own hands, but during the 1920s it took on the additional connotations of guarding and defending the land. Since the *halutz* was to be proficient in military as well as farming skills, he had to be strong, resilient, and prepared for self-sacrifice in the service of his nation, especially through acts of heroism.

In the mid-1930s, the pioneer ethos began to undergo a fundamental change. The *halutz* came to be perceived also as a warrior defending his nation and land. As such, he had not only to defend but also to attack, kill, and be prepared to be killed. His knowledge of the land and his ability to navigate it now served not only the goal of developing it but also of fighting for it. This "new *halutz*" became the man of the elite fighting force of prestatehood Palestine known as the Palmach. But he belongs to the "generation of the sons," which lies outside the framework of this book.[11]

The first *halutzim* were mostly single men and women in their twenties or thirties. They came to Palestine principally from Russia and Poland during the Second and Third Aliyot, motivated in large part by Zionist ideology; many had belonged to youth movements such as HeHalutz and HaShomer HaTzaʿir. They lacked any defined occupation, and had no formal or professional training. Most were socialists by persuasion. The *halutzim* immigrated to Palestine with the express intention of becoming manual laborers. This choice is significant. The labor movement the pioneers established in Palestine was fundamentally different from those in many other countries in that it did not grow out of a tradition of labor or, alternatively and classically, the migration of agricultural laborers from the countryside to work in factories in cities. In other words, in Palestine no process presaged the creation of a proletariat. The *halutzim* who came to the Land of Israel chose their destination from among other, ostensibly more attractive, options available to them, in particular immigration to the New World. They chose not only to settle in Palestine but also to remain there despite the difficulties they faced. The fact that the difficulty of life in and on the Land led many to leave in the end only underlines the determination of those who stayed. After arriving in Palestine, Ben-Gurion concluded that only two types of workers could remain in a land where life was unbearably harsh: those with the capacity to endure such a life—that is, strong young people accustomed to hard labor—and those with an "enormous will."[12]

In Palestine, *halutzim* of the Second and Third Aliyot engaged in various types of manual labor, including farming, construction, and roadwork. They established settlements that were for the most part communal in one way or another. These included the collective (Sejera, 1907), the national farm (Kinneret, 1908), the *moshav poʿalim* (Ein Ganim, 1908), the *kevutza* (Degania, 1910), the *ko'operatzia* (Merhavia, 1911), the *moshav ovdim* (Nahalal, 1921), and the kibbutz (Ein Harod, 1921). (These types of settlements varied regarding the extent of collectivization, size, and ideological origin.) The *halutzim* endured periods of widespread unemployment, hunger, and severe illness. At times, however, their privation and asceticism were deliberate, incurred in order to avoid dependence on others and to remain true to an antibourgeois ideology.[13]

Despite being a minority among the Jewish immigrants to Palestine during the Second and Third Aliyot, the *halutzim* played a decisive role in consolidating Jewish-Zionist settlement in the Land. In this context, the Israeli historian Yosef Gorny has distinguished between "formative aliyot" and "consolidating aliyot." In his view, the first three waves of immigration, from 1882 to 1923, were formative aliyot. While they were quantitatively small, they established standards for the nature and ideology of the Zionist settlement enterprise that later developed into the State of Israel. They were followed by three consolidating aliyot, in the years 1924–1951. While these waves were massive in comparison with their predecessors, Gorny argues, their principal effect was to consolidate what had been set in motion and achieved by the earlier immigrants. They also differed from the first three waves in that most of these latter immigrants came to Palestine because they had no alternative.[14]

In recent years, certain historians have sought to tarnish the pioneer aliyot by claiming that the characterization "pioneering" is no more than an image or, some say, a myth. One of the major arguments these scholars present to support their claim is statistical. The number of immigrants who could be defined as *halutzim*, in their view, is tiny compared to the total number of Jewish immigrants to Palestine during these years. In his study of the Second Aliya, the historian Gur Alroey argues that the pioneer laborers numbered no more than one to two thousand, or 4.5 percent, among the total of 30,000 to 35,000 Jewish immigrants during this period.[15] In a parallel study of the Third Aliya, the historians Baruch Ben-Avram and Henry Near found that no more than 40 percent of the immigrants fit the three defining characteristics of the *halutz:* young, affiliated with a pioneer youth movement, and engaged in manual labor for the purposes of Zionist *hagshama.* In most years of this period, such arrivals numbered about 30 percent. Between 1919 and 1922, some 26,000 Jews immigrated to Palestine, but only 8,000 were pioneers.[16] If we add up the figures from the two studies, we find that in the Second and Third Aliyot, some 9,500 *halutzim* arrived in Palestine, among a total of some 58,500 immigrants—only 16 percent.

Like Gorny, I maintain that, while the *halutzim* indeed constituted a minority of immigrants in their time—Berl Katznelson himself referred to them as "the distillate of the distillate"[17]—in *qualitative* terms these people set the tone for the Jewish community in Palestine and thus for the future state of Israel. Their organizations, political movements, and settlements exemplified the Zionist ethos: Hebrew land, Hebrew labor, Hebrew defense, Hebrew language, and more. As I will show, the pioneers were the first to shape the way Israel and Zionism are experienced in space, in the human body, and through language: they were the first to know the land, the new Jewish body, and the Hebrew language. I maintain that the encounter with the Land of Israel, as it was experienced until the 1960s and 1970s—that is, until the decline of the pioneer ethos and the transition from Zionism to capitalism, or from Zionism to post-Zionism—was largely the work of the *halutzim.*[18] To a great extent, the *halutz* period was the constitutive moment of Zionism in the Land of Israel.

When we Israeli Jews of today gaze at the Land of Israel, we see it largely through the eyes of the *halutzim.* When we feel it with our bodies and souls, we sense it largely through their sensibilities. We are tied to the land and have difficulty giving it up because they were attached to it. The Land of Israel time by which we live is to a great extent the mythic time the pioneers defined by their actions. When we speak Hebrew, we speak their language. When we love the land, we love it largely through their love. And when we are willing to lay down our lives for it, we are prepared to die the "beautiful death" for which they, too, were prepared.

The Second Aliya

The great majority of historians agree that the Second Aliya ended in 1914 with the outbreak of World War I. But they disagree about when it began. Some put the starting point at the end of 1904 with the arrival of the first *halutzim*. Though, as noted, these *halutzim* were a minority among the Jews who immigrated during this period, the Second Aliya has become identified with them. Other historians propose that the Second Aliya began in 1903. They point out that the catalyst for this wave of immigration was the Kishinev pogrom of April 1903. This bloody event stunned Jewish communities in Europe for its brutality but even more so because of the helplessness of the Jewish victims. In this view, the Second Aliya was a pragmatic response to the severity of the attack and to the stinging humiliation felt by many Jews as a result. Many of the pioneers who arrived during this period had been involved, prior to their immigration, in Jewish self-defense organizations.

Another significant event that motivated Jews to move to the Land of Israel was the Uganda controversy during the Sixth Zionist Congress in Basel in August 1903, a crisis that nearly fractured the Zionist movement. The territorialist faction proposed that the Jews accept an alternative location as a temporary or permanent solution to the Jewish problem, whereas those who rejected any alternative and advocated settlement in the Land of Israel sought to establish facts on the ground there, so as to demonstrate that the Land was the only solution to the Jews' tribulations. The death of Theodor Herzl a year later, in July 1904, also induced many young people who had seen him as a father figure to immigrate to the Land. They believed that in immigrating and settling in the Land, they were fulfilling Herzl's legacy.

Aliya to the Land was also, during this period, a recourse for Jews disappointed by the abortive Russian revolution of 1905—not only because it had failed to live up to their high expectations but also because they were being accused of rebellion against the tsar. Their shattered hopes for the equality promised by the revolution prompted many to set out for the Land of Israel in an effort to realize the same ideals on new soil. About two months after the failure of the revolution, Yosef Vitkin, a teacher from Kfar Tavor who had arrived during the First Aliya, beckoned the Jews of Russia to come to the Land of Israel and bring new blood into its Jewish community, which had, he said, degenerated in the years following the arrival of the first wave of Zionist settlers.

During the Second Aliya, the Jewish population of Palestine grew from about 50,000 to 80–85,000. In 1914, the Jews made up approximately 12 percent of the territory's population of about 700,000. One-third of that growth was the result of natural increase, while the rest came from immigration. Most Second Aliya immigrants belonged to two groups that were very different from the *halutzim*. The largest group consisted of middle-class people of modest means who settled principally in the Jewish *moshavot*—farming villages, such as Rishon LeTzion,

Petah Tikva, and Zichron Ya'akov, that had been established over the previous quarter-century by the immigrants of the First Aliya. Socioeconomically, this group resembled the First Aliya immigrants. The second group, pious and urban, came from the same background as the Jews of the Old Yishuv, the Jewish community of Palestine prior to the First Aliya. These immigrants settled largely in the four large Jewish cities, principally Jerusalem. Another small group of immigrants during this period arrived from Yemen, a source of immigrants to the Land beginning during the First Aliya. They arrived in two principal surges, one in 1907 and one in 1912, and numbered about two thousand. Some mixed with members of the Old Yishuv and some worked as laborers in the Jewish farming communities.

While the *halutzim* were indeed a minority among immigrants of the Second Aliya, the role they played in shaping the Jewish community was decisive. The aliya's major figures set the tone for the entire Yishuv, and most of the State of Israel's top leadership positions were occupied, in its early years, by these same people: David Ben-Gurion, Yitzhak Ben-Zvi, Moshe Sharett, Levi Eshkol, Zalman Shazar, and Berl Katznelson.

The pioneers of the Second Aliya would not have achieved what they did without the support of the Zionist Organization, founded in 1897 at the First Zionist Congress in Basel at Herzl's initiative. Its goal was to settle Jews in the Land of Israel with the consent and support of the great powers, in particular the Ottoman Empire, which then controlled Palestine. The Zionist Organization developed the financial means needed to purchase land and fund settlement. In 1903, the Zionist Organization founded the Anglo-Palestine Bank in Jaffa. It also established the Jewish National Fund (JNF; known in Hebrew as the Keren Kayemet LeYisrael) to purchase land that would permanently remain the property of the Jewish people and be leased out to settlers. From 1905 to 1907, the JNF made its first purchases, at Ben Shemen, Hulda, and Hittin. The Palestine Office was founded in 1907 in Jaffa to serve as the Zionist Organization's agent and executive arm, and Dr. Arthur Ruppin was appointed to head it. Hachsharat HaYishuv (the Palestine Land Development Company, established by the Zionist Organization) served as an agent for the purchase of land with private capital.

The Second Aliya's pioneers envisioned and founded new types of settlements unknown to previous Jewish immigrants, including collectives that maintained communal societies and economies. The first such community was founded in 1907 by a group of laborers from the Jewish Colonization Association farm at Sejera, which trained young Jews to live and work as laborers. It was the only farm in the Land at that time in which all the workers and guards were Jewish, and it lasted for about a year before it was dismantled.

Another type of settlement was the national farm, where Jewish agricultural laborers received training. The first national farm, Kinneret, was founded in 1908 on the southern shore of Lake Kinneret by the Palestine Office of the Zionist Organization, on land owned by the JNF that had formerly belonged to the Arab village of Delaika. The establishment of the farm marked the beginning of the Zionist Organization's settlement enterprise in the Land. Its first residents were eight men and one woman. But after a dispute between the workers and the farm's manager over salaries, work quality, and the hiring of Arab laborers, the Jewish laborers left the farm for Hadera, a *moshava*—one of the farming villages established by the immigrants of the First Aliya—on the coastal plain, where they established a commune. In 1910, its members returned to the southern shore of Lake Kinneret and founded the first *kevutza*—a small, independent agricultural commune—which they called Degania. In 1913, the Kinneret national farm was handed over to a group of thirteen men and three women laborers who, along with several others, founded the Kinneret *kevutza*. Other national farms were founded at Hulda and Ben Shemen, both in the center of the Land.

In 1907, the JNF purchased the lands of the Arab village Um Juni, adjacent to the Kinneret national farm. Shortly afterward, the lands were leased by the Hachsharat HaYishuv and the Palestine Office. About a year later, the Palestine Office handed over some of the land, for a year, to a *kevutza* of six men and one woman. At the end of that year the Office permitted the members of the Hadera commune to settle on and farm the Um Juni land. Each settler received a fixed monthly stipend from the Office. Half the annual profits were to be paid to the settlers directly, while all losses would be absorbed by the Office. The Degania communal farmers advocated agricultural labor as the proper way of life and believed they could demonstrate that a farm could be run on Jewish labor alone, without the need for Arab workmen. They were led by Yosef Bussel. The *kevutza* was a settlement partnership based on communal ownership of property, self-sufficiency in labor, equality, and collectivization of production, consumption, and education. The flagship type of Second Aliya settlement, it was by definition small and intimate, based principally on farming. In contrast, most communes established by Third Aliya pioneers were larger kibbutzim, influenced explicitly by Marxism and the October Revolution in Russia. They sought more than just the establishment of ideal societies for themselves—they advocated nationwide collectivization of all labor and production.

The *ko'operatzia*, the first example of which was Merhavia, was inspired explicitly by the ideas of the German economist and sociologist Franz Oppenheimer. Merhavia was the first Jewish settlement in the Jezreel Valley, at the lower boundary of the Galilee. Its land, which had previously belonged to the Arab village of Fula, was purchased by Yehoshua Hankin and transferred to Hachsharat HaYishuv and the JNF. At the end of 1910, a group of HaShomer self-defense organization members arrived to prepare the land for settlement. A short time later the *ko'operatzia* was founded.

Oppenheimer laid out a number of management principles to which the Merhavia members remained faithful. The *ko'operatzia* was not a collectivist settlement in the same sense as Degania. The members worked together to prepare the land for cultivation, but they and their families farmed individual plots and social life was not communal. Supplies were purchased jointly. The settlers decided together what types of crops to grow, to be marketed cooperatively, with individual farmers receiving the profits from their crops. At first, the settlers worked under the supervision of an agronomist, who taught them their craft. Later, after the settlement became profitable, they became administratively independent. The *ko'operatzia* was disbanded in 1918, principally as a result of social and economic problems, and in 1922 it was reestablished as a moshav, with similar operating principles. In 1929, the site became the home of Kibbutz Merhavia, founded by HaShomer HaTzaʿir.

Another innovative settlement created by the Second Aliya *halutzim* was the *moshav poʿalim*, which sought to combine urban and agricultural labor. All families received small kitchen gardens of more or less the same size, which they tended in addition to the adults' work in the city. The *moshav poʿalim* differed from the *moshav ovdim* in that it did not advocate settlement of national lands and collectivism. The first *moshav poʿalim* was founded in 1908 at Ein Ganim, near Petah Tikva. In the end it failed, becoming no more than a passing phenomenon of the Second Aliya. The main reason for its failure was that the kitchen garden was too small to support a family. In 1937, Ein Ganim became a neighborhood of the city of Petah Tikva.

The Second Aliya pioneers also founded the self-defense organization ("guard" organization in Hebrew) Bar Giora in 1907. Bar Giora originated in Jaffa, established by seven members of the Poʿalei Tzion party, among them Yitzhak Ben-Zvi, Alexander Zeid, and Yisrael Shohat, the last of whom served as chief of his Jewish defense organization in Russia. Bar Giora was small and elitist. Its initial members settled in Sejera, where their success led them to accept responsibility for guarding Mes'ha and other Jewish settlements in the Lower Galilee. In 1909, an assembly at Sejera decided to expand the organization's mission, and to change its name to HaShomer. In its new incarnation, the organization also pursued an agenda of settling the Land, developing methods based on learning local conditions and the customs of the local population, the Arabs in particular. It quickly broadened its ranks and deployed throughout the Land, defending Jewish settlements in the south as well. At its height HaShomer had about three hundred members. Some founded settlements of their own—Tel Adashim in 1913, Kfar Giladi in 1916, and Tel Hai in 1918. In 1920, HaShomer was disbanded because of a dispute between two factions: one that sought to make it a broader and more popular force and a second that insisted it remain elitist. Its members were quickly absorbed into a new self-defense organization, the Haganah.

Politically and organizationally, most Second Aliya *halutzim* belonged to one of two parties: the Marxist Poʿalei Tzion or the socialist-nationalist HaPoʿel HaTzaʿir. Both were founded in the Land of Israel in 1905, although the former had political roots in Russia dating to the end of the previous century. Poʿalei Tzion's members viewed themselves, at least in the party's early years, as a part of the world socialist revolution. Its first leader was Yitzhak Ben-Zvi, and most of its activity involved establishing labor unions and staging strikes. In seeking to found a socialist society in the Land of Israel, party members saw the establishment of independent settlements as the principal way of reinforcing the position of Jewish workers. In its early years, Poʿalei Tzion also advocated the use of Yiddish as the Jewish language of culture and creativity. But relatively quickly, Yiddish was abandoned and the party supported the use of Hebrew as the language of the Zionist revival, just as it abandoned its doctrine of international class warfare.

HaPoʿel HaTzaʿir vehemently rejected the principle of class struggle, although it aspired to found an egalitarian Jewish society. It also viewed the allocation of national capital as the correct and proper way to strengthen the working class in the Land of Israel, and from the start advocated the use of Hebrew. The party was founded by Shlomo Tzemach and Eliezer Shohat, with the purpose of "conquering" Hebrew labor. In 1908, it declared that its goal was "an economically and culturally healthy Jewish majority." Members of the party took part in self-defense activity, although they had reservations about HaShomer, which—as mentioned—had been founded by members of Poʿalei Tzion.

The Third Aliya

Palestine's borders were closed during World War I, and transport difficulties made immigration almost impossible. Furthermore, the Ottoman regime expelled Jews who were foreign nationals, and the war and the collapse of the economy caused the death rate to climb among those who remained. Toward the end of the war, in November 1917, the British foreign secretary, Lord Balfour, issued the declaration that granted British recognition to the right of the Jews to settle in Palestine, their ancestral land. After the war, the declaration was incorporated into the League of Nations decision to hand Britain the Mandate for Palestine, thus granting formal international recognition to Jewish rights in the Land.

The Balfour Declaration was a central factor in the decision of many Zionists to move to the Land of Israel as soon as conditions allowed. Another prod was the sense of elation many Jewish youth felt in the wake of the Bolshevik revolution. They believed they could realize their dream of an egalitarian, just society in the Land of Israel, especially since the Bolshevik regime had not lived up to their expectations. Like their predecessors of the Second Aliya, they were also motivated by the pogroms experienced by Jews in Europe, mainly the anti-Jewish riots that erupted in Ukraine during the civil war that followed the revolution. Another, if indirect, influence was the struggle for self-determination by European national groups, culminating in the establishment of new, independent countries such as Poland and Czechoslovakia. These countries served as exemplars of the vision of a Jewish nation-state.

The Third Aliya began in 1919, shortly after the war ended. Its starting point is generally considered to be the arrival of the *Roslan*, a ship bearing Zionist immigrants, in December 1919. The Aliya ended in 1923 when the Land plunged into a severe economic crisis. By this point, the Jewish population in Palestine had recovered its prewar numbers. Given the growth in the population and the lack of income sources, the Yishuv was unable to take in more immigrants. The promulgation by the British of the White Paper on Palestine, which limited Jewish immigration, also made it difficult to maintain, and certainly develop, the Jewish community in the Land of Israel.

As in the Second Aliya, most of the Jews who arrived in this wave settled in existing communities, such as Tel Aviv. Still, thirty-one new Jewish settlements were founded from 1920 to 1923; most were communes of one type or another. The Third Aliya was typified by several forms of settlement. The kibbutz, first called a "large *kevutza*," simply expanded the principles of that earlier form. It grew out of the thinking of Shlomo Lavi of Kevutzat Kinneret, who advocated establishment of a new cooperative system that combined the principles of collectivism with respect for the life of the individual and the nuclear family. Kibbutzim were established for the most part on land purchased by the JNF and placed at the disposal of the settlers. Their economy was based on the labor of the members, eschewing hired workers, and on a range of agricultural work. The kibbutz was meant to be a self-sufficient system not dependent on the urban economy. Full equality was the rule in property, finances, education, and culture. The first kibbutz was founded in 1921 at Ein Harod, in the Jezreel Valley. Unlike the intimate *kevutza*, where members were chosen carefully and the community segregated itself from the surrounding world, the kibbutz was an open, nonisolationist society that saw itself playing an important role in molding Jewish life in the Land of Israel, by working the soil and by absorbing immigrants.

Another type of Third Aliya settlement was the *moshav ovdim*; its founding spirit was Eliezer Yaffe of HaPoʿel HaTzaʿir. Yaffe aspired to meld the principles of collective and private settlement, so as to serve social, national, and collective needs, and respect the initiative of the independent farmer. The basic principles of the *moshav ovdim* were settlement on national land, individual labor and initiative, mutual aid among the members, joint purchase of necessities and joint marketing of crops, as well as common public services. The nuclear family stood at the center of its social structure. In this, the *moshav ovdim* resembled the *ko'operatzia* of the Second Aliya. Like the kibbutz, the moshav was built on national land, but in contrast each family leased its land from the national organization that owned it. Self-sufficient labor was pursued in the framework of the family. No farmhands were hired, and any member who did hire outside help risked being expelled. The profits from each farm accrued to the family that farmed it. The first *moshav ovdim* was founded in 1921 in Nahalal in the Jezreel Valley by agricultural laborers from the Second Aliya, members of HaPoʿel HaTzaʿir, some of whom had been among the founders of Degania.

Among the arrivals during the Third Aliya were the first members of the HaShomer HaTzaʿir youth movement. The movement's inspiration came from a variety of sources, among them central European Jewish nationalism, the German youth movement, the Scout association, and the philosophies of Martin Buber and Siegfried Bernfeld. HaShomer HaTzaʿir rejected Jewish life in the exile (the Jewish Diaspora, called *galut* in Hebrew) and the existing social order. These were to be replaced by an independent youth culture, devotion to labor Zionist ideals, zealous dedication to the Hebrew language, and a synthesis of Jewish nationalism and socialism. About seven hundred members, most from Galicia, arrived in the Land of Israel during the Third Aliya. The movement's first *kevutza* was founded in 1920 at Bitanya Ilit in the Lower Galilee. Its first kibbutz, Beit Alfa, at the eastern end of the Jezreel Valley, was founded in 1922.

In the summer of 1920, members of the HeHalutz youth movement founded the Yosef Trumpeldor Labor Battalion, which went about paving the road from Tiberias to Tzemach, on the southern end of Lake Kinneret. The Labor Battalion aspired to establish a commune that would include all Jewish laborers in the Land of Israel. In its early days, it paved roads, including those leading from Haifa to Jadda (present-day Ramat Yishai, southeast of Haifa) and from Afula to Nazareth. It also engaged in construction, road-grading, laying of railroad tracks, stone quarrying, swamp draining, and hauling. Battalion members lived in tent camps and went to work as labor details they called companies. They took upon themselves the task of rebuilding the ruins of Kfar Giladi at the northern tip of the Galilean panhandle and the settlement of Beer Sheva in the southern Negev Desert, as well as laying train tracks from Rosh HaAyin to Petah Tikva. Their wages were paid into a common pool from which their needs were provided.

Roadwork became the touchstone of a unique culture of equality, social justice, common purpose, brotherhood, joy in living a productive life, and modest needs. The Battalion's ideology drew on that of the Second Aliya *kevutza*, on Russian-Tolstoyan notions of anarchic and self-sufficient communal existence, and on early romantic communism in the Soviet Union. In 1921, some of its members settled at Ein Harod and, a short time later, at Tel Yosef. The two settlements were soon united. The Battalion, which operated for six years, had some seven hundred members at its peak. In 1922, a dispute broke out at the kibbutz and in July 1923 it split into two camps: right wing and communist. In the end, the latter wing of the Battalion membership rejected Zionism, and some of its members moved to the Soviet Union. In August 1927, the three Battalion companies at Tel Yosef, Kfar Giladi, and Ramat Rachel united to form HaKibbutz HaMe'uhad, known in English as the United Kibbutz Movement.

The Histadrut (General Organization of the Hebrew Workers of the Land of Israel) was established in 1920, uniting most of the Land's Jewish wage laborers and a large portion of its self-employed residents. Its founders sought to mitigate the division between the Ahdut HaAvodah (formed by a merger between HaPoʿel HaTzaʿir and the "Independents" led by Berl Katznelson) and Poʿalei Tzion parties, each of which maintained its own health service, labor bureau, agricultural organizations, and trade unions. As laid out in its charters of 1920 and 1923, the Histadrut's goals included creation of craft unions in all labor sectors, establishment of farms and factories in the cities and rural areas, and establishment of credit associations and settlement funds. It also worked as a contractor taking on and carrying out projects, acted to increase labor productivity, organized purchasing and supply cooperatives to raise the economic level of the working public, sought to defend the rights of laborers and improve labor conditions on private farms, and instilled a devotion to the Hebrew language in its members. The Histadrut founded cultural, educational, and training institutions, promoted immigration and the absorption of new immigrants, established ties with Jewish and international labor organizations overseas, and founded mutual aid organizations such as a health fund and a life insurance fund. It thus quickly became the most important political, economic, and social force in the Yishuv.

Ahdut HaAvodah, formed early in 1919, united in a single party some 80 percent of the Land's Jewish workers. Its ideology was socialist and nationalist—it sought the establishment of a Jewish national society in the Land of Israel. Until the creation of the Histadrut a year later, Ahdut HaAvodah operated in the economic, social, political, and settlement fields. After transferring responsibility for these areas to the Histadrut, it remained active in politics and education. HaPoʿel HaTzaʿir remained independent until, in 1930, it merged with Ahdut HaAvodah to form Mapai, the Workers Party of the Land of Israel, of which Israel's Labor Party is a direct descendant.

Many of the Yishuv's central institutions were established during the Third Aliya years. Among these Kupat Holim Klalit, the General Health Fund, was created in 1920 from the unification of the health funds of HaPoʿel HaTzaʿir and Ahdut HaAvodah. Solel Boneh, a company that first engaged in road construction, then in building construction, was founded in 1921. Bank HaPoalim, the Workers' Bank, was established in 1921 and served as the Histadrut's central banking institution.

The Haganah, the Yishuv's underground military force, was founded in 1920, in the wake of Arab attacks on Jewish settlements in the Galilee and Jerusalem. Ahdut HaAvodah had voted at its convention that summer to establish a self-defense organization. The Haganah would function throughout the Mandate period, until it was dismantled in 1948, when the Israel Defense Forces were founded. Unlike HaShomer, which viewed itself as relatively closed and was not subordinate to any political organization, the Haganah's ranks were open. It functioned under the aegis of the labor movement, which provided most of its human and material resources. Its guiding principle was that Jewish arms and fighters should be under exclusively Jewish control. As a result, the Haganah always viewed itself as an illegal underground organization.

Desire for the Land before the Halutzim

Jews have desired the Land of Israel ever since the destruction of the First Temple in the sixth century B.C.E. This desire found expression in different forms: philosophy and scholarship, prayers, fantasies, messianism, art, and pilgrimage.[19] But Jewish desire for the Land prior to Zionism was of a different stripe. This difference goes beyond the Zionists' actual consummation of their desire. Nor does it derive only from the modern nationalist character of Zionist desire, as opposed to traditional religious desire for the Holy Land. More than anything else, the difference emerges from the status and position of the Land of Israel within the framework of that desire.

The Jews of the exile distinguished between the concrete geographic Israel and the spiritual one, a practice that enabled them to decouple the physical land from their vision of redemption. The exilic Jewish bond with the land was not formulated in terms of ownership. This was why the Zionist bond of ownership raised concern among many halachic authorities. The concepts "Land of Israel" and

"Zion" did not express, for the Diaspora Jew, a concrete aspiration to "ascend" to the land and settle in it. Rather, the Land defined the frame of reference for location in space and time. For example, the calendar of the Jew living anywhere in the exile followed the seasons of the Land of Israel.[20]

By contrast, pioneer desire for the Land of Israel was a desire for the real, for a concrete land. Anthropologist Zali Gurevitch and sociologist Gideon Aran note that, prior to pioneer immigration, only in extremely rare instances did a Jew really leave his "land and homeland" in the Diaspora with the intention of reaching the Holy Land. Even when Jews arrived during the course of history, their arrival was more symbolic than real because they viewed themselves as coming not to the physical land but to the Land promised by God. The *halutzim*, in contrast, came to the Land of Israel not to intensify and continue the spirituality of the exile but rather to shatter the holy vessels of traditional spirituality and change their lives utterly. The pioneer revolution was a discovery and revelation of the physical, material Land of Israel. The *halutzim* turned the Land from a magical object, a symbol, a precept of the Torah, into a living actuality. The Zionist revolution was an attempt to redefine the meaning of "being in place" in Jewish consciousness.[21] Pioneer Zionism, as the Judaic scholar Hagai Dagan has put it, was an expression of the seemingly obvious—that one cannot live within an image or symbol.[22]

Berl Katznelson wrote that the stories of the Land of Israel told to him by his father when he was a boy made clear to him once and for all that the Land was not the next world or a mystical concept, but rather that "there is a Land of Israel in our time."[23] When Berl heard from his father of the descendants of a saint who still lived in the Land, he burst into tears. He asked himself why, if the saint's descendants could be there, he could not be there also. This story changed his world entirely, beginning his connection with the real Land of Israel. Five months after arriving in Palestine, David Ben-Gurion wrote to his friend Shmuel Fuchs that Zionism was no longer an ideal for the future but "an actual present reality."[24]

As for the Jews who settled in the Land before the appearance of Zionism, they did not desire the land in a concrete way as did the *halutzim*. For example, the Hasidim who settled there in the eighteenth and nineteenth centuries came primarily because of the Land's sanctity, God's proximity to its inhabitants, and the opportunity it offered for observance of all the Torah's precepts.[25] In general, these pre-Zionist settlers had no real interest in the Land's soil, its natural environment, its landscapes, its sights. Above all, they sought the Land's God.

The pre-Zionist Jewish community in Palestine—the Old Yishuv—did not naturalize itself. These Jews lived as "exiles in the Land," as historian Israel Bartal has termed them. Jews from different countries who settled in the Land almost never mixed with each other. They preserved their languages and customs in the original forms of their Diaspora communities. These settlers kept to their cities, looked upon outsiders with fear, and depended on the protection of locals or the European consulates. Even when these settlers emerged from the walls of their cities, they did so only to make the walls encircle a larger area.[26]

Bartal writes that three parameters characterized the exile in the Land in the pre-Zionist period. First, the Old Yishuv, rather than being an independent entity, functioned as a set of "auxiliaries" of their respective Diaspora communities. Second, its way of life was virtually the same as in Diaspora communities. Third, the exile in the Land constituted a real state of being. The settlers lived in "exile" among the Arabs, vulnerable and dependent on the protection of the Arab majority society. They did not fight this "exile" in the ways that characterized the pioneer Zionist struggle. Bartal concludes that there is good reason for skepticism regarding the existence of a single, common history of the Jews in the Land of Israel before Zionism. The Zionist bond between the people and the land was not part of the experience of the Old Yishuv.[27]

Bartal suggests that we can use these same parameters to understand the pioneer experience. By "ascending" to and settling in the Land of Israel, the *halutzim* sought to negate the exile, its way of life, and its existential presence. In this regard, the pioneer act was revolutionary. It brought about a fundamental transformation.

Recall that I identify the pioneer period as that of the Second and Third Aliyot. Why do I not include the First Aliya? After all, most of the immigrants in all three of these waves were Zionists. What then distinguishes the First Aliya immigrants from the later pioneers? This distinction will emerge more clearly in later chapters, but in general it lies in their attitude toward the Land itself, the Jewish body, and the Hebrew language. While the desire of the *halutzim* Hebraicized the soil, the Jewish body (through labor), and their own speech,[28] settlers of the First Aliya did not bond with the land by working it with their own hands. For the most part they employed local workers, mostly Arabs, to perform agricultural labor and to serve as guards. They viewed the land as "business," and they had no interest in creating a new Jewish body or establishing Hebrew as a native language. For them, the Land of Israel was not Mother Earth.

Many religious Jews came to the Holy Land in order to be buried there. Gur Alroey found that 13 percent of the immigrants who set out from the port of Odessa to Palestine in the years 1905–1913—that is, during the Second Aliya—did so specifically for this reason.[29] The *halutzim*, in contrast, set out for the Land of Israel in order to build it and be built by it and, as we will see, to be "reborn" there.[30] A pioneer who arrived in 1907 wrote shortly afterward that in coming, he was not doing God's will, since he did not believe in God. Rather, he was simply doing what was morally right and in practice absolutely necessary.[31] In a letter from the early 1920s, Berl Katznelson described a period of severe unemployment as one of the low points of the pioneer period. Yet he remained optimistic because "there is a father in heaven, or the Land of Israel—mother."[32] The pioneer desire for the Land belonged to the era after God's death. It was desire for the Promised Land in the absence of He who promised it.

Historiography of the Halutzim

Pioneer immigration and settlement in Palestine during the Second and Third Aliyot—in other words, the process of bonding with the Land of Israel—has been examined by historians from many points of view. Their studies can be divided into two principal groups: the material and the ideological-cultural. The first category sees the process by which the *halutzim* established their connection to the land as principally political or socioeconomic. These studies include analyses focusing on the various pioneering-political organizations (workers' associations, political parties); Zionist organizations in and outside Palestine that played a role in the pioneer enterprise (the JNF, the Zionist Organization, the Palestine Office); along with pioneer socioeconomic structures (the collective, national farm, *kevutza, ko'operatzia*) and their links to other socioeconomic structures (old and new Jewish *moshavot*, cities).

Material historiography addresses principally political or socioeconomic conflicts among the different actors involved in the process of immigration and settlement. Examples include the rivalries between the different labor parties (Po'alei Tzion versus HaPo'el HaTza'ir) and between these two parties and others (religious, bourgeois). These studies also examine socioeconomic conflicts among the pioneers ("conquest of the Land" versus "conquest of labor," communal versus individual settlement, men versus women, youth versus old-timers) and between the pioneer interest and the socioeconomic interests of other groups present in the Land of Israel (settlers of the First Aliya, Sephardi Jews, Arabs). The success or failure of a group's connection to the land is perceived in materialist historiography as a consequence of its ability to implement a political or socioeconomic agenda.

Note that methodologically, no significant difference exists between a study that examines, for example, the immigration and settlement of *halutzim* belonging to the Po'alei Tzion party or the HaShomer HaTza'ir youth movement from a liberal economic point of view and another that takes a Marxist point of view.

Both amount to descriptions and explanations of the political and socioeconomic mechanisms in the process of immigration and settlement.[33]

Materialist historiography also includes studies that examine these same phenomena from a geophysical point of view. By looking at factors such as climate, geographical and topographical conditions, location, and the symbolism of settlement sites, such studies track the process by which the pioneers gained a foothold in the land. They generally answer questions like: Where did the *halutzim* settle? Why in that specific location? What challenges did they face?[34] Also in this category are studies that examine pioneer settlement from an environmental and ecological standpoint.[35]

As their name suggests, ideological-cultural studies view the process by which the *halutzim* became attached to the land as primarily ideological. They include studies addressing various pioneer ideologies and utopias (Zionist, nationalist, socialist, social-nationalist, masculine), the pioneers' struggles amongst themselves, and their common confrontation with other ideologies (autonomist, territorialist, Bundist, bourgeois liberal, feminist). In this category we also find studies of the new culture established by the *halutzim*, a culture that redefined the pioneers' concept of identity, language, the body (the "new Hebrew man"), and self-images (Zionist, national, socialist, masculine, feminine). For these studies, the success or failure of the process of pioneer attachment to the land is determined by the implementation of the idea, the extent of realization of the planned utopia, and the establishment of a new culture. Here, too, no significant methodological difference exists between a study that examines, say, pioneer ideology as a socialist ideology and another that examines it as a masculine ideology. Both focus on the existence of a specific ideology and culture among the pioneers and how these were manifested in reality.[36]

The ideological-cultural category also includes points of view that identify the pioneer connection to the Land of Israel as the actualization of historical or religious bonds. This work focuses on the natural (with or without quotation marks) ties between Jews and the Land of Israel. In this case, the pioneers' attachment to the land is seen as the fulfillment of ancestral Jewish longing, receiving concrete expression in historically unprecedented proportions in the form of the Zionist movement. Historians who take this approach generally identify Zionism as a "secular national religion."[37]

Little, if any, historiography falls exclusively into any one of these methodological categories. Works that present *halutziyyut* from a purely ideological point of view will always include political and economic factors to one extent or another. Some studies deliberately integrate different approaches—for example, ideological and social analyses of the pioneer enterprise based on the assumption that the utopia for which the pioneers strove could not be realized, given practical constraints and external circumstances.[38]

Historiographical debates over the pioneer-Zionist enterprise divide the field in other ways as well. Take, for example, the central debate between intentionalist historians, who view pioneer immigration and settlement as the product of conscious intent, and functionalists, who reject all conscious and unconscious pioneer intent and instead suggest impersonal processes and dynamics that led, in one way or another, to the actualization of *halutziyyut*. Such a debate surrounds the question of the emergence of the *kevutza* during the Second Aliya. The intentionalist historian Henry Near maintains that the establishment of the *kevutza* was a direct result of the ideological and personal contacts among its founders before their immigration to Palestine. According to Near, the future settlers of Degania drew the idea of the *kevutza* from a section on collectivism in the manifesto of HaTehiyya, a movement to which they belonged that originated in Pinsk. In contrast, the functionalist historian Baruch Ben-Avram maintains that this lifestyle, based on sharing in all areas of life, crystallized only in Palestine, in the context of the social reality faced by the agricultural laborers from the Second Aliya, especially those at Degania. The *kevutza*, according to Ben-Avram, was not born out of conscious intention but rather as an authentic innovation spurred by life circumstances.[39]

Other historiographical debates about the Zionist movement as a whole and its pioneer sector in particular touch on questions such as: Was Zionism a national revival movement or a colonial movement? Was it a nationalist movement that should be understood in the context of modern nineteenth-century European nationalism, and if so, was it a Western political nationalism or an Oriental cultural-ethnic nationalism? Nationalist or hypernationalist (i.e., chauvinistic)? A socialist, nationalist, or social-nationalist movement? Conservative or revolutionary? A pragmatic secular movement, a messianic religious movement, or some combination of both? Was the pioneer Zionist movement unique among nationalist, socialist, and social-nationalist movements? Is there a unique Jewish, Zionist, pioneer path in modern history?[40]

As it happens, a reading of the historical documents from the period confirms *all* these different analyses of the pioneer enterprise. The *halutzim* themselves explained their process of bonding with the land in political, economic, ideological, and historical-religious terms. None of these factors emerges as dominant; indeed, each is insufficient in itself. Only by integrating all these points of view can we develop an adequate description and explanation of the process of immigration to and settlement in the Land of Israel.

Yet even this integration would still be inadequate, because one factor has been omitted almost completely from Zionist historiography—the pioneers' *desire* for the Land of Israel. The pioneers themselves explained, described, and justified their enterprise in various political, economic, ideological, and historical-religious terms, given that the political views of Poʿalei Tzion differed from those of HaPoʿel HaTzaʿir, that the economic principle on which the *kevutza* was based differed from the one that grounded the *moshav ovdim*, and that A. D. Gordon's worldview was different from David Ben-Gurion's. But the one recurring motif is *desire* for the Land of Israel. The world and experience of the *halutz* are saturated with articulations of attraction, craving, pining, and love for the Land. While the political, economic, ideological, and historical-religious fields have, over time, been problematized in historiographical discussion of the pioneer phenomenon, in the case of desire this process has been minimal.

Approaches to Pioneer Desire

The few historians who do address the ecstatic-symbiotic pioneer experience use one of three basic paradigms to understand and describe it. All, however, treat it reductively instead of taking it on its own terms.

The first paradigm, *nominalist*, assumes that testimonies by the *halutzim* about such experiences are simply forms of expression, modes of speaking that should not be taken literally by scholars since they do not describe actual events. The second paradigm, *subjectivist-psychological*, assumes that the experiences are real, but personal and internal. As such, they can tell us nothing about the geographical, social, and ideological realities in which the *halutzim* acted. The third paradigm, *psychoanalytic*, presumes that the ecstatic experiences reported by the *halutzim* are reenactments or projections of situations from their early lives. All three paradigms evade real confrontation with pioneer testimonies, because each takes the *halutzim*'s words as an expression of something else—language in the nominalist case; internal reality in the subjectivist-psychological case; and oedipal relationships for the psychoanalytics.

The nominalist paradigm sees *halutzim* testimonies as no more than images, metaphors, allegories, and so on. When *halutzim* wrote, for example, about being children who wished to return to the bosom of Mother Earth, "bosom," "Mother Earth," "sons," and similar terms are viewed simply as forms of speech with no connection to the pioneers' actual feelings and experiences, nor to how they lived and functioned in their world.

We might say that the nominalist paradigm assumes that language is really just "noise" that must somehow be filtered out in order to arrive at true descriptions, explanations, and understandings of historical reality. The better historians are at neutralizing this noise, the better will be the history they write. Correspondingly, the more seriously and literally they take language, the further they will stray from the truth.

Broad areas of scholarship take language as their subject. Literary studies, by definition, address "the textuality of the text"—that is, its construction from linguistic elements. The critic Gershon Shaked, for example, uses this approach in his work on pioneer literature. Among other things, he examines the experiences of aliya, settlement, and labor as depicted in these writings.[41] But as fruitful an approach as this may be, it has its problems. In focusing on the textuality of the text—images, metaphors, allegories—the literary scholar does not address the historical reality behind the texts. Shaked admits as much when he argues that if Hebrew literature were taken as an accurate account of the times in which it was written, one would find that decisive events in the history of the world, the Jewish people, and the Yishuv never occurred.[42]

Studies of pioneer literature, then, are not historical studies, and are distinct from research on the history of the texts themselves. This latter type of inquiry points to connections between the texts and events, describing and explaining the historical background against which a given text was produced. It seeks to answer questions such as: Who wrote it? When? What was the author's overt or covert, conscious or unconscious intention? These studies also examine the text's history and reception. Who read it? When was it read? What did readers understand from their reading?[43] But such studies also maintain a rigorous distinction between language or text and reality. They, too, conceive of pioneer testimonies as linguistic expressions with only a tenuous link to historical reality and the world in which they were produced.

Another group of historical studies focusing on the language of the *halutzim* does consider pioneer testimonies to contain content about the pioneers' historical experience. These works fall into two major categories. The first type examines the pioneers' language as a device of representation. Some, for instance, might account for representations of male and female pioneers in political and social discourse from the pioneer period through the present day. They examine the representations of pioneer language in history books, art, and the writings of the *halutzim* themselves. Other studies might address the various incarnations of the term *halutziyyut*—from being a reverent term of obligation during the pioneer period and the first two decades of the State of Israel, for example, to acquiring negative connotations in the 1960s and 1970s, when Israeli society moved into a capitalist and, perhaps, post-Zionist phase.[44] Still, these historical studies are not fundamentally different from literary inquiries, since they consider pioneer testimonies and language to be distinct from the extratextual historical reality.

The second category of historical studies on language focuses on the history of pioneer language itself. One example is the work of Henry Near, who has looked at the terminology used in defining communal bodies during the early Aliyot, terms like *kevutza*, kibbutz, commune, collective, and *havura* (another form of commune or collective). According to Near, tracking the complex, long-term semantic evolution of these terms can cast light on historical and ideological trends.[45] Historian Aviva Ufaz looks at the world of symbols appearing in the collective diary *Kehilateinu (Our Community)*, written by the HaShomer HaTzaʿir settlers of Beitania.[46] Ufaz's research method is fundamentally exegetical. Taking pioneer language seriously, she argues that the world of symbols in the anthology seems at first sight to be eclectic and lacking in any order or logic. But a more careful look uncovers unity and ties to contemporary history, society, psychology, and esthetics. Ufaz seeks to decipher what she calls the pioneers' "secret language" and to establish its links with other phenomena. She concludes that the symbols "soil," "sky," "sun," "fire," "stone," and "mountains," or "eros," "woman," "man," and "childhood," play both romantic-religious and metaphysical-mythological roles in the anthology. These dual roles support the pioneer aspiration to cloak the secular in sanctity and symbolism. It is impossible, she says, to detach the pioneer "symbolization of reality" from traditions and from both older and contemporary social and artistic currents—the turbulent spirit of the early twentieth century, the influence of messianic religious movements, of Symbolism and Expressionism, of the catastrophe of World War I and the vacuum of values and beliefs created by the war.

Undoubtedly, studies like Near's and, in particular, Ufaz's bring us closer to a more empathetic conception of pioneer language. Significantly, they do not decouple the language from the reality behind it. They show this language to be immersed in the history and the world of the *halutzim*. Language here creates what Anthony Smith calls "poetic spaces."[47] Nevertheless, Near, Ufaz, and others like them still perceive language as having an ontological status different from the other components of the same historical reality. Thus Ufaz, for example, sees pioneer language as a collection of symbols, which are ostensibly less "real" than events. Pioneer language responds to the events, stems from them, and acts on them in return. But in and of itself, the language remains symbolic.

By making this nominalist assumption that language is merely language, historical scholarship overlooks its most important and perhaps its richest source material—language itself. In later chapters, I will demonstrate that pioneer desire, as manifested in pioneer language, was in every sense a praxis, just as was working the soil, paving roads, and sculpting the body. Beyond this, pioneer language—its images, metaphors, and the myths it created through speech—itself played a decisive role in the pioneer desire for the Land of Israel. Just as the *halutzim* created the Land of Israel by working the soil and paving roads, they also created the Land's images, metaphors, and myths.

The subjectivist-psychological paradigm does not reduce pioneer testimonies to linguistic phenomena but rather accepts them and treats them with considerable empathy. In this view, *halutzim* who wrote, for example, about their desire to return to the bosom of Mother Earth were indeed children seeking to return to their earth-mother. Their statements expressed real emotions, feelings, and experiences. We find the subjectivist-psychological paradigm in studies that describe the pioneers' inner world and its roots. Their experiences are understood as deriving from the social and cultural movements to which the *halutzim* belonged or that influenced them either directly or indirectly. Thus, their ecstatic relationship with the Land's open spaces and natural elements appears as an aspiration to return to nature. This inclination may arise from Russian romanticism and Tolstoyan ideas that influenced many *halutzim* of the Second and Third Aliyot. Similarly influential were youth movements in the pioneers' countries of origin, most notably the German Wandervogel. Most historians who take the subjectivist-psychological approach discern the roots of the ecstatic pioneer experience in the romanticism of the contemporary central and Eastern European nationalist movements. Sociologically and psychologically, they surmise that the pioneers' youth amplified the sense of *Sturm und Drang* in their world.

Other historians identify the pioneer experience as primarily religious in character. The sociologist Oz Almog, for example, states that, starting in the first decade of the twentieth century—with the establishment of the city of Tel Aviv on April 11, 1909, the founding of the HaShomer organization in Mes'ha the following day, and the founding of Degania, the "mother of the *kevutzot*," on October 28, 1910—the Zionist movement became a "secular religion" combining belief in a Marxist utopia, ideas from Tolstoy and the Narodniks (Russian populists), Jewish messianism, and European nationalism. Almog depicts the pioneer experience as an "ecstatic spiritual" one.[48] Other historians point to Jewish sources, for example Hasidic ones, to explain the ecstatic bent of the *halutzim*.[49]

Another explanation locates the source of pioneer ecstasy in the dramatic change, both conscious and unconscious, that the new immigrants underwent when they were severed from their former world, their parental homes, tradition, and the exile, and entered the new, young, radical world of the Land of Israel. One historian to take this approach is Yael Weiler, who links the aliya of members of HaShomer HaTzaʿir to such experiences. Weiler sees a connection between the "physical" aliya to the Land of Israel and the "spiritual" aliya that was expressed in "a unique mental-spiritual worldview," whose language and pan-religious expression were drawn from Greek and Roman mythology, from the doctrines of the Buddha and Lao-Tse, from Christianity and Judaism alike, and from the theoretical language of Nietzsche and Freud. She argues that inherent in their aliya to the Land of Israel and settlement activity was a wish for a profound and all-encompassing spiritual and emotional experience. A prominent characteristic of this experience was the search for the wondrous, the sublime, and the enthralling in the world surrounding them. They were primed to be open to these experiences and moved by them. This great openness was part of the conscious and unconscious process of creating a new identity and a new culture.[50] Weiler sees in these young people an ecstatic, boundary-shattering religiosity, melded together from unconventional and daring mystical experiences, principally of the Land of Israel, and an aspiration for self-sacrifice and self-negation.[51]

Zeev Sternhell is one of the only historians who takes the Zionist-pioneer-ecstatic experience seriously. In his history of Zionist and pioneer social-nationalism, he identifies in this experience an expression of a new nationalism born of the central and Eastern European nationalisms of the nineteenth century. Unlike Western European liberal nationalism, which was based on political, legal, and civil concepts of citizenship, social nationalism was an organic nationalism of "blood and soil," based on cultural, historical, and even biological ideas of what made an individual part of the body politic. This organic nationalism subverted the foundations of liberalism's intellectual, moral, and political principles. More than anything else, such nationalism, of which Zionism was the Jewish instance, symbolized the collapse of the cosmopolitan Enlightenment age and its ethos. The new nationalism appeared principally in the territories of the multinational empires of central and Eastern Europe, and it evinced the desire for revival of repressed nations that had been denied more than just independence. In many cases, these nations' cultural identities had also been suppressed. The spiritual father of these nationalisms was Johann Herder. The Jewish version's spiritual father, according to Sternhell, was A. D. Gordon:

> As it began to be implemented in the Land, Zionism developed the classic features of organic nationalism. The experience of contact with the soil, the desire to strike roots in it, and the need to lay a foundation for the legitimization of a return to the Land led to a blossoming of the romantic, historical, and irrational aspects of nationalism. The cult of ancient history, from the conquest of Canaan to the rebellion against Rome, and the "sanctification" of places where Joshua Bin-Nun or the kings of Israel had fought were not very different from similar phenomena in the Czech, Polish, or German national movements of the nineteenth and twentieth centuries. The founders'

> love of the Land and its landscapes, enthusiasm for its vegetation, and sense of the soil's holiness had a truly mystical quality, which was paralleled in Europe.[52]

Despite the great empathy displayed by historians like Weiler and, in particular, Sternhell for the pioneer experience, they (and historians of their ilk)—like the nominalists—still do not completely understand and accept the *halutzim*'s desire for the Land of Israel; they, too, treat it reductively, as an expression of something else. Their working assumption is that the inner, emotional, subjective world of the *halutzim* was distinct from the ostensibly external, material, objective world. They perceive the pioneers' sense that they were the returning sons of Mother Earth as real and true, but only in the pioneers' inner world. The soil of the Land of Israel in and of itself, they would argue, was not *really* Mother Earth, even to the *halutzim*. Furthermore, most writers who take this view also see the internal, emotional, subjective world of the *halutzim* as secondary to their external, political, economic, and social world. To these commentators, therefore, the texts in which the *halutzim* depict their inner world are untrustworthy. Sternhell expresses this point clearly. He interprets the organic nationalism of blood and soil as a kind of superstructure imposed on a foundation consisting of the tangible Zionist-pioneer economic interest. Sternhell certainly would seem able to empathize with the pioneers' sense of themselves as sons returning to the bosom of Mother Earth as an expression of romantic social-nationalism. Yet, at the same time, he would argue that this experience produced socioeconomic structures from which, for example, anyone not perceived as a son of Mother Earth—the Arabs, in this case—would be excluded. He thus sees the return of the *halutzim* to their Mother Earth as real only in a subjectivist-psychological sense, as no more than an expression of a social-nationalist political, economic, and social worldview. He cannot accept pioneer desire on its own terms.

I maintain that it is irrelevant whether the texts of the *halutzim* are subjective or objective, reliable or unreliable, just as I would not use these criteria to categorize working the land or paving a road. In the end, no meaningful distinction can be made between subjective and objective farming. The large quantity of testimonies left to us by the *halutzim* is, in my view, a pioneer praxis in and of itself, one that should be analyzed according to ontological, not epistemological, criteria. The distinction between subjective inner reality and ostensibly objective external reality is both extremely problematic and fundamentally moot. It is difficult, perhaps impossible, for us to distinguish between these two realities, and even more so to locate the boundary between them. Even if we could distinguish between so-called subjective and objective realities in some way, we have no appropriate criteria for determining which reality is more relevant for historical research. For example, psycho-historians will view the experience of returning to the bosom of Mother Earth as a much more "real" experience than any experience supposedly located in the outside world.

As noted, the third basic paradigm historians use to understand the ecstatic-symbiotic pioneer experience, the psychoanalytic, is the only one to make both the modes of desire and the materials from which desire is crafted central to its analysis. Thus, the next chapter explores this paradigm in detail.

2 Desire and Rebirth

Psychoanalytic interpretations of history are speculative in the extreme, as well as more complex than I can present here. Nevertheless, I will examine the various psychoanalytic approaches to the ecstatic-symbiotic pioneer experience at some length because almost every historiographic explanation and description of pioneer Zionism is based—intentionally or unintentionally—on the oedipal mechanism. My critique of psychoanalytic-oedipal explanations applies equally to these other historiographic narratives of the Zionist-pioneer enterprise.

Oedipal Desire

In the psychoanalytic view, the pioneers' desire for the Land of Israel was a reenactment of patterns shaped in their early lives. By this logic, when the *halutzim* experienced themselves as children returning to the bosom of their Mother Earth, they were in effect reenacting in the Land, or projecting onto it, their oedipal relations with their parents.

Certain elements of the pioneer psyche in which a longing was expressed for the Land reproduced, in the psychoanalytic view, the process of psychosexual development as formulated by Freud. Freudian theory provides a way of describing, explaining, and understanding the attraction to Mother Earth and the praxes of amalgamation, assimilation, and suckling that characterized the pioneers' world. The *halutzim* spoke of suckling from the breast of Mother Earth, like a child in the oral stage—a stage at which the child still does not distinguish between "inside" and "outside," between its own body and that of its mother.

Similarly, other elements of the pioneer psyche in which a longing was expressed for the Land of Israel reproduced the anal stage. At this stage, the child derives pleasure principally from its bodily substances, until it undergoes toilet training. The pioneer world was indeed permeated by fluids of all kinds, including bodily fluids. In human life and society, however, progress requires a certain dryness. Culture is based on concealing, or at least channeling, fluids such as sweat, blood, and tears. The pioneer world was, in contrast, saturated with these fluids, and contact with them was often a source of pleasure for the *halutzim*. Accordingly, the pioneers' oral repertoire was augmented by anal-stage praxes such as wetting, absorbing, and adhering. For example, *halutzim* enjoyed sweating and rejoiced in being privileged to "water" the soil with their perspiration—but no less did the soil rejoice to receive their sweat. They slaked the soil's thirst with their perspiration.[1]

Normal psychosexual development concludes, according to Freud, with the genital stage, which appears after the resolution of the oedipal conflict. At this stage, the (male) child redirects his desire from his mother to other objects, and finally to members of the opposite sex and to "culture." The *halutzim* evinced attraction to the opposite sex and to the "culture" that they called the Land of Israel, but significant traces remained of desire for the mother, Mother Earth. The Land as a whole, and its soil in particular, was female: virgin, beloved, and, especially, maternal. No evident sanction prevented enacting this desire in the pioneer world, which included no father figure to forbid the *halutzim* to consummate their desire for this female entity.

An examination of the objects of pioneer desire seems to support the psychoanalytic paradigm. The *halutzim* yearned for the Land of Israel and for nearly every element in it—its soil, its inanimate objects, its plants, its animals, its sights, its landscapes, its natural surroundings, and its open spaces. "From within a burgeoning appetite for life, I opened my arms wide to the broad, open spaces," Tzipora Zeid wrote when she reached Sejera, "because a desire welled up within me to embrace and kiss those fields, to return them love as their reward."[2] But what about desire for the opposite sex? Pioneer testimonies reveal that such expressions were rare. How, then, does this absence affect the psychoanalytic paradigm?

The absence of expressions of desire for the opposite sex does not prove that the *halutzim* had no romantic, erotic, and sexual relationships. Of course, they did. And expressions of such desire appear in pioneer texts. But these expressions are far more puritanical than the pioneers' unbridled effusions about the Land. The historian Amos Elon claims that pioneer depictions of sex, especially those written by members of the Second Aliya, read like "annals of monastic orders." Even though most of the *halutzim* were young men and women in their twenties, and even though they appeared to live freely, displaying contempt for tradition and bourgeois mores, with men and women sometimes sharing rooms, there is barely a trace of sexual life in their writings; the descriptions that do exist sound prudish, lacking in any erotic or sexual imagery. On occasion, the reader encounters a confession like "I blushed deeply" or "I was tense," or descriptions of girls and women with beautiful long hair that aroused male desire. But despite the almost complete freedom with which they lived, relations between pioneer men and women were extremely restrained. Women wrote about men as "brothers" or "friends." Men wrote about women as "mothers," "sisters," or "friends." Instead of romantic or erotic love between the sexes, we find "brotherly love."[3] Platonic friendships, involving melancholy exchanges of prose and poetry, were quite common.[4]

These patterns associated with love were typical of relations between men and women in the various kinds of collective settlements. Hayuta Bussel of Degania wrote about the meaning of "love" in the *kevutza*. True love, she asserted, must encompass all of humanity and not be limited to love "dependent on an object." Therefore, the members of the collective did not think in terms of love relations between young people. They found an original way of formulating their relationships: "We do not love one another, young man or young woman, but instead [love] *the* young man and *the* young woman, using the definite article, who are united by the single national, human idea of bringing hearts close to each other."[5] Esther Sturman of Merhavia wrote that every comrade knew how to overcome desire and give up when seeing that a woman did not return his love. Beyond this (and this next comment is fascinating in the psychoanalytic context), "we always knew how to keep within limits so that we should not be consumed by the flames. . . . Before his [the comrade's] eyes were the images of the fathers and mothers of the Bible. In this light he also saw the women in the environment."[6]

Perhaps the *halutzim* did not want to write about romantic, erotic, and sexual relationships, or perhaps they were unable, for any number of reasons, to write about their intimate relations. After all, this was the (finest) hour of the Zionist-pioneer project, to which they harnessed all their energies. Nevertheless, the absence of references to such relationships between men and women is remarkable given that their writing does not lack expressions of desire. On the contrary, it is steeped in such language. Yet this desire is directed at the Land of Israel.

I thus see little point in conjecturing that the *halutzim* repressed their sexual desire or that they were Puritans. The oral- and anal-stage aspects of their desire for the Land of Israel, for Mother Earth, in conjunction with the almost complete absence of declarations of desire between men and women, can testify either to the reconstruction of a previous pattern of relations or to the projection of this past pattern onto present realities and relationships. If we recall that pioneer men and women had made a radical transition from an old to a new world, their desire can be interpreted as the reaction in physical, mental, and psychological terms of people in the process of settling in a new, unknown land in pursuit of the transcendent goal of recreating the Land of Israel.

Like the nominalist and subjectivist-psychological paradigms, the psychoanalytic one is, in the final analysis, reductive. It presupposes a concept of a "normal," "normative" life, circumscribed by clear, solid, boundaries of body and mind. Normality, according to Freud, is the result of successfully traversing the oedipal stage—that is, of severing the bidirectional flow or diffusion between child and mother.[7] The psychoanalytic assumption is that if the *halutzim* did not live such a life, they can be diagnosed as either reconstructing or projecting primal relationships into their present lives, and therefore their statements can be dismissed as abnormal.

According to Freud's well-known theory of culture, after passing through the oedipal stage, the (male) child rejects his inclination to sleep with his mother, identifies with his father, and turns toward the external world to find alternatives to the forbidden tie to the mother. The child develops his economy of pleasure via sublimation, which is no more than the internalization of the father's law after the father's "murder." Some of the child's desire is directed at the world and creates what Freud calls "culture." A man cannot sleep with his mother, so he becomes a social, cultural creature. The desire for incest is repressed into the unconscious, but continues to influence every act. Thus, one accepted interpretation of the pioneer's romantic and erotic relation to the Land is that since he could not sleep with his mother because his father forbade it, he moved to the Land of Israel. The historian David Biale writes: "In the Zionist case, the tension between sexual liberation and asceticism channeled erotic energies into the tasks of nation building. . . . The eroticization of labor was closely bound up with images of the land of Israel as a lover, a kind of materialistic transformation of the old allegory of love between God and Israel."[8] Ofer Nur, also a historian, makes this point more explicit in his study of HaShomer HaTzaʿir. Unlike Freud, who sought only to interpret the sexuality in his patients' dreams, according to Nur, members of this movement who studied and were influenced by Freud sought consciously to harness sexuality to the settlement enterprise in order to create a new society and a new Hebrew man.[9] Lesley Hazelton, a writer and student of psychology, goes even further, arguing that real "incest" occurred between the *halutzim* and the Land of Israel. The young *halutzim* who rebelled against their biological parents, she maintains, searched for a new form of son-mother relation: "Zion played Jocasta to the male pioneers' Oedipus."[10] Hazelton's reference specifically to *male* pioneers, together with the earlier quote by Tzipora Zeid, signals another problematic aspect of the psychoanalytic model: that it does not take into account the experience of the female pioneers, who expressed feelings toward the Land that were similar to those of men but were unlikely to be the consequence of suppressed desire for the mother.

A number of historical studies are based on psychoanalytic insights. Jay Gonen, a psychohistorian, writes that for centuries, the promise of renewed possession of the motherland kept alive Jewish hopes of returning to it. The Zionists, sons of Zion, were inflamed by a sacred fervor to "inseminate" Zion. This, according to Gonen, explains the pioneer-Zionist obsession with making the desert bloom. But the first Zionist settlers depicted their return to Zion not only in terms of "returning home" or "rebuilding" but also as a return to the "womb" of history or to Zion, their "bride." They established a libidinal relationship to the land, he maintains. "Mother Zion" was impregnated by the sons who mounted her, who returned to her, who came to her aid. She, in turn, granted them the "new life" they yearned for. This produced the experience of "Zionist rebirth." The *halutzim* gave oblique and concentrated expression to these urges when they sang, "We came to the land to build and be built." In psychoanalytic terms, the song really means: "We came to the land of our mother to sire and to be reborn."[11]

We also find psychoanalytic explanations of individual pioneers. In his biography of A. D. Gordon, Eliezer Schweid argues that the experience of the mother and of maternal warmth was central to the progress of Gordon's life and to his intellectual development. Gordon had a particularly strong emotional relationship with his mother, in part because four of his older brothers had died in childhood. Gordon was the spoiled and beloved chosen son, fussed and worried over by his parents. Schweid links the motherly love Gordon experienced to the centrality of the experience of the maternal in his writings. Gordon frequently cites maternal love as the primal human experience and as solid proof of the natural tendency of life to enrich and improve. Schweid maintains that Gordon's relationship to Zionism was that of a son to his mother, not of a son to the authority of a father and teacher.[12] It goes without saying that, in Gordon's philosophy, the Land of Israel is experienced as maternal and feminine.

Avner Falk, another psychohistorian, offers a similar examination of a *halutz* whose complete desire for the Land of Israel was, Falk says, a reconstruction of his relationship with his mother. Since this *halutz* could not properly mourn and separate from his mother at her death when he was eleven years old, he was overcome with vast anger at her for having abandoned him forever, as well as profound sadness at his loss. Denying these emotions, he preserved in his heart the image of an ideal mother and unconsciously searched for a new and benevolent mother, seeking to experience a rebirth. The legendary Land of Israel of which he had heard so much from his grandfather, father, and brothers became etched in his consciousness as a perfect mother, the ideal replacement for his biological mother. Writes Falk: "The Land of Israel was now an unconscious symbol of the great, benevolent mother, the perfect, ideal mother. The motherland was the mother from which we were born."[13] The name of this boy was David Ben-Gurion.

Thus, the oedipal model of the son's rebellion against the father leading to the creation of culture constitutes the background to depictions of the pioneer enterprise as:

- A rebellion by children against their biological mothers and fathers, whom they replace with a Mother Earth and a Fatherland (the psychological and psychoanalytic theses).
- A rebellion by a younger generation against tradition, which it replaces with *halutziyyut* pioneer enterprise (the intergenerational conflict and modernization theses).
- A rebellion by a younger generation against Judaism, which it replaces with secularism (the secularization thesis).
- A rebellion of a younger generation against life in the exile and its replacement by life in the Land of Israel (the negation of the exile thesis).
- A rebellion by sons against the feminine life and body of the exile, which they replace with masculine lives and bodies in the Land of Israel (the gender thesis).[14]
- A rebellion by a younger generation against the past and its replacement by the future (the progress thesis).
- A rebellion by a younger generation against myth and its replacement with history (the thesis of the return to history or of normalization).
- A rebellion against the mother tongue, Yiddish, and its replacement by the father tongue, Hebrew (the sociolinguistic theory).[15]

To dismantle this entire "oedipal complex" of Zionist historiography, I first use the work of the psychoanalyst Melanie Klein, who both carried on Freud's work and rebelled against him, and second the work of the philosopher Gilles Deleuze and the psychiatrist Felix Guattari. Breaking free of the oedipal model enables us to understand the essential, primal nature of the pioneers' desire and liberates us from precisely what pioneer desire itself sought to shed—the weight of the past. In their desire for the Land of Israel, the *halutzim* longed to be born again.

Anti-Oedipal Desire

We begin with Melanie Klein. Many psychoanalytic theories understand the processes of normalization and maturation as outcomes of patriarchal intervention that reach completion with the banishment of the mother. Klein argues, in contrast, that the superego comes into being even before the appearance of the father—that is, during the period when the child's relation to the breast is the decisive variable that will determine its future emotional and sexual life.[16] If, for

Freud, the superego is constituted by feelings of guilt at the murder of the father, in Klein's model the mother plays this role. The child develops a feeling of love toward the mother, who gives her breast, but also a hatred for her for withholding her breast. The child's relationships with the mother and the milk that wells up from her are the decisive factors determining relationships with the objects encountered over the course of a life. The child redirects love from the mother's breast to other objects out of intense fear of developing too great a dependence on the breast or of its disappearance. As with Freud, this abandonment is the act that constitutes culture.

Klein's version of the superego is not, then, based on stable and solid boundaries like Freud's. Rather, it relies on boundaries that are more fluid, in both senses of the word. Milk is the primordial fluid that connects the child to the mother and also separates them. This symbiotic relationship between child and mother will characterize the texture of relationships with other objects the person encounters over the years. So, for example, the child may redirect its love for the mother to the motherland. Klein offers this particularly relevant example. "We speak of our own country as the 'motherland,'" she writes, "because in the unconscious mind our country may come to stand for our mother, and then it can be loved with feelings which borrow their nature from the relation to her."[17] The child, who lives in symbiotic relationship with the mother's breast and body, functions, in practice, as an investigator of the mother's body. The investigation grows out of the child's possessiveness and even an aggressive sexual desire, but also out of curiosity and love. From these forces will come, in the future, the adult motivation to explore new countries, for example. The new land compensates for the loss of the biological mother. "In the explorer's unconscious mind," writes Klein, "a new territory stands for a new mother, one that will replace the loss of the real mother. He is seeking the 'promised land'—the 'land flowing with milk and honey.'"[18] I can only wonder whether Klein was aware that she was writing about the Land of Israel.

In effect, Klein rehabilitates the *halutzim* for precisely their tendencies that are apt to be perceived as reconstruction or projection of childhood relations, or even regression to those relations. She allows us to see the pioneers' ecstatic-symbiotic experience as a normal relationship. Indeed, if the relationship with the maternal breast is the basis of relationships with other objects, then the entire experience of rebirth, which we will soon examine, as well as oral and anal praxes cease to be pathological symptoms. The *halutzim* returning to Mother Earth did not need to sublimate anything. Their relationship with the Land of Israel did not have symbolic meaning: it was a normal, normative relationship. They experienced desire for the Land of Israel, for Mother Earth, through true flows of water, sweat, blood, tears, labor, and more. In a similar way, we can see the pioneer relationship with the Land as an expression of the archetypical relationship with the Great Mother.[19] This context allows us to understand the pioneer experience in the Land of Israel as an experience of mythic time manifesting itself in history.[20]

Avraham Shlonsky, the classic poet of the Third Aliya, portrayed this relationship between the *halutzim* and the Great Mother (and her breast in particular) in many of his poems. Reading him in sequence reveals a process of radicalization in relationship to the breast, identified first with distinct objects in the world, and later with the world as a whole.

Klein thus softens the rigid oedipal structure imposed on desire by Freud. She shows that we do not need the Oedipus complex to understand the mechanism of desire, which in itself is much more fluid, and that the desire for Mother Earth, and the praxes and symbiotic experiences associated with it, should not be treated reductively as an expression of something else. Nevertheless, she still accepts Freud's basic assumptions—in particular, the necessary presence of the sanction-imposing parent. What the father does at the oedipal stage, according to Freud, is what Klein attributes to the mother at the oral stage. Likewise, she accepts the Freudian principle that the pattern structuring the psyche and future behavior is established in early childhood as a consequence of a given model of child-parent relations. Like Freud, she makes the superego the master of the individual, acting from within. In both Freudian and Kleinian readings, then, the *halutzim*'s desire for the Land of Israel is ultimately no more than a reconstruction or projection of child-parent relations onto the Land of Israel.

Deleuze and Guattari take Klein's work a step farther away from Freud, arguing against imposing any structure at all on desire. In their book *Anti-Oedipus*, they attack the idea of the oedipal structure of the ego, and in particular the concept of the unconscious as proposed by Freud and developed by his successors.[21] They present the unconscious as desire that seeks to break out of the "territory" set aside for it, in order to achieve maximum pleasure. But they oppose identifying the creative power of the unconscious with the concept of an ego that derives from the threefold oedipal stage (Freud) or the dual stage of the child-mother relationship (Klein). Adopting Marxist language, Deleuze and Guattari describe the unconscious as a means of production—indeed a factory. This factory knows how to do just one thing—produce! It does not know names or people, including the names of mothers and fathers. It does not know where it came from (e.g., the breast) or where it is going (e.g., toward the construction of culture). The unconscious has no memory (e.g., of what its parents did to it in childhood). Any goal

The following poems were composed by the *halutz* Avraham Shlonsky.

And I set out
But with no provisions for the road—

I said:
I am at home under the vault of the entire sky
And, rushing among human homes, for they are many
Here I gather up stars like the grain of the fields
There I will suckle from a sun as round as a breast
And it is good, and I will bleat like a lamb-man:
"To life!"[22]
—"Rushing," 1927

Here is my Land—the body of a wild ass. . . .
Flog, flog, summer sun, the coarse body of my Land,
We will milk dew-cream from night-breasts on its upturned earth![23]
—"Here," 1927

You rhymed: our heart is a palace, a temple, an inner sanctum
Line it with cushions and costly objects
And I will not be shamed were my heart a barn, a stable, a pen
And if every beast were to drop its offal on me
Because every heart is dear to me, with its beasts and its droppings.
Come hither, sheep! Be fruitful and multiply with me!
I will imbibe milk from ample teats
And from all warm dung will I fertilize my fields.[24]
—"Produce," 1927

Here, I have fallen on my face
And I will suckle your teats
With parched, thirsty lips
With myriad mouths of brothers and sisters
And with its tongue the wind will lick me
Like the cow licks her newborn calf
As the calf itself suckles
The teats of the cow.
Your milk will flow now
And my bones will be slaked by primeval sustenance

With the myriad nettles who will flourish here
Like me![25]
—"Soil," 1927

Like a train of nursing camels with humps to the sky
God made the Gilboa mountains kneel
And the fields of Jezreel like tender calves
Fastened on to their breasts.

Flow, flow river milk, overflow your banks
And the land—(Ho, black filly, to the mount!)—
Will stretch out her neck, her nostrils flare, she'll snort
For she has scented water.

Water! Water!
O, the holy milk from your breasts, Lord!

But here the teats, too, have filled with milk
The teats of man!
And my flesh—a flowing breast will raise from the soil.

Ho, plowed fields of Jezreel!
Suckle! To the last drop!

Come, camel calves! Horses! Man! God!
And I will suckle you—
Because for you are the nipples of my breasts.[26]
—"Jezreel," 1927

of this unconscious productive power is irrelevant; its purpose does not matter. What matters is that it acts and produces all the time.

What is the mechanism of this unconscious activity? Deleuze and Guattari say that the unconscious (i.e., desire) flows from one part of its object to another and achieves satisfaction when different parts connect to other objects, disconnect, and reconnect in a new system of relations. In suckling, for example, the breast produces milk and enables it to flow. The suckling mouth halts or cuts off this flow when its hunger is satisfied and a new flow is created—for example, the child's move into play. The unconscious is a universal producer of infinite and anarchic flow halted by a distribution that creates a new flow.

In contrast to the oedipal rules Freud imposed on this anarchic flow, Deleuze and Guattari assume that no need exists for a special psychological mechanism—

an Oedipus complex or breast complex or any other complex—in order to cause the child's desire to turn upon the world. There is no reason why the child should crave to copulate with the mother rather than with Mother Earth or any other object. The child's desire for the mother derives, they maintain, from the concrete social conditions characterizing the place where the child lives. A child who lives in a monogamous culture that grants the object "mother" precedence over all other objects will crave her. In such a culture, parents will also see to it that their child does not desire something outside the family. Incest, then, is not an expression of the child's primal, biological, "natural" desire but rather one arbitrary form of social code imposed on desire. Deleuze and Guattari reverse Freud's formulation: a child who is forbidden to have the world will crave only the mother.

The oedipal, breast, or any other paradigm is simply imposed on desire as part of a mechanism that includes the primal desire to copulate with the mother and the primal sanction by the father forbidding the actualization of this desire. It is this mechanism that creates, a posteriori, the child's feeling of guilt. The law commands, "You may not marry your mother and you may not murder your father," and we, subject to this discipline, say to ourselves: "Aha, if that's what the law forbids, that must be what we want." The unconscious is then constructed out of desire for the forbidden. This, say Deleuze and Guattari, is Freud's unconscious—desire that wants that which it is forbidden to desire and that represses itself just for this reason. Whereas Freud turned the unconscious into the enforcer defining social authority, for Delueze and Guattari, the unconscious, being simply energy that craves to be free, is a means of production with the potential to break free of social authority.

What Deleuze and Guattari do is purge desire of its essence and meaning. For them, desire knows only to crave, to produce. It is pure energy, a fluidity that knows no origins (i.e., derives from no needs) or destinations (i.e., makes no demands) and is not essentially connected to any particular body. And this is how I understand the desire of the *halutzim* for the Land of Israel. It is true that, whereas Deleuze and Guattari see this energy as a machine and discuss it as a means of production, I am talking about an ecstatic state of being. But fundamentally these amount to the same thing. As we will see, when *halutzim* desire the Land of Israel through their sweat (the sweat, the liquid that materializes the ecstatic mode, waters the soil), they are actually merging with the Land and making it "Hebrew"—or, in Deleuze and Guattari's terms, producing the Land as a Hebrew land.

In my view, the correct way to depict pioneer desire is precisely as an anarchic flow, devoid of reason or purpose, neither a biological need nor a social demand nor an act of will. Note too that while, as mentioned, the failure to take pioneer women's experience of desire into account undermines the psychoanalytic historians' argument, this problem disappears once we reject the oedipal construct and define desire as a primal, existential condition. In the following sections and chapters, then, I propose simply to let the desire of the *halutzim* tell us about itself. In the final analysis, the *halutzim* themselves refuse to accept, exclusively, the oedipal generation of their desire; they testify to other genealogies. Instead of imposing an oedipal paradigm on their desire, I will allow myself to be swept up by its current.

Desire versus "Need" and "Demand"

The distinction between the *halutzim*'s desire and a simple need or demand for the Land is significant.[27] Needs are biological—that is, their objects (e.g., food) are the resources necessary for life. Demands are social, aimed at realizing definite goals. Ideology is an expression of demand. There can be no doubt that needs and demands played central roles in the pioneer act of aliya and settlement in the Land of Israel. The Land certainly served to meet pioneer needs (e.g., economic ones) and was a place where demands (e.g., ideological ones) could be realized.

Desire, however, is not motivated by deficiencies or aspirations but by what Lacan, following Hegel, defines as the desire for the desire of the other.[28] If your desire for the Land means that it also desires you, you become one with the Land. In other words, when the *halutzim* experienced themselves as part of the Land and vice versa, their relation to it constituted a kind of desire. By contrast, defining the *halutzim*'s relationship to the Land as "need" means that they are somewhat removed from the Land, not a part of it; the same is true of "demand."

To sum up, a historical analysis that places pioneer needs at its center describes the deficiencies for which the Land of Israel will provide. An analysis that centers on pioneer demands describes the goals that the pioneers will achieve through the Land. Here, however, I treat the *halutzim*'s desire for the Land as a desire for the Land's desire for them.

Desire, then, only desires. It does not need anything and does not demand anything. Obviously, the *halutzim* needed and demanded the Land of Israel, which provided for their needs and enabled them to realize their political, economic, and other demands. But all these needs and demands could be satisfied by many other lands—the United States, for example, or Uganda. Indeed, most Jews immigrated to places that undoubtedly met their needs and realized their demands better than did the Land of Israel.

What was the Land of Israel to the *halutzim*? asked Zionist leader Yosef Aharonovich. Did they choose it because it was a good land, the one most fitting for them to settle in? No, he maintained. It could well be that it was a good land and fitting for settlement. But one could find better lands to fill this role. The Land of Israel, Aharonovich asserted, was the Jewish people's historic land, the Land to which Jews had been tied by thousands of cords for generation after generation. Therefore, the quality of the Land could not be a consideration or a precondition for Jewish settlement there; it could only be an ex post facto condition.[29] Aharonovich thus gave priority to the desire for the Land above any need for which it could provide and any demand it could ostensibly satisfy: "Just as a father does not love his son because he is intelligent, but rather, on the contrary, tries to discover intelligence within him because he loves him, because he is his son, so we do not seek practical, special reasons for the tie between us and our historic Land."[30]

We cannot understand why *halutzim* desired the Land of Israel, which was perhaps the most difficult option they could choose, by examining needs and demands. We can understand their desire and their choice only in terms of desire—and in particular, their desire for the Land's desire of them. In truth, the *halutzim* chose the Land of Israel because it chose them.

Let us listen to the Land of Israel's desire for the *halutzim*. Pioneers came on aliya because it "awaited" them and even "wept" when they were slow in arriving.[31] Before making his "ascent," Yedidya Shoham wrote in his diary that the Land was calling out to him and his comrades: "'Come! Come!' The Land pleads and you are sitting on your hands outside. 'Come! Come!' These words have rung in my ears incessantly this past month, without ceasing."[32]

After the *halutzim*'s aliya, the Land desired that they build, create, and redeem it. The body-of-the-Land-without-organs desired the desire that would articulate it and create its organs. Ruhama Farm sat on the peak of a high hill. A pioneer who worked there gazed at the landscape around him, which bore the forlorn imprint of neglect and ruin. "When you look at it and see the desolation," he wrote, "it seems as if the terrain is in mourning, waiting for her redeemer, and that until her sons and builders return she will remain abandoned and bear the shameful name of *Jamama*, which in Hebrew means 'wasteland.'"[33] A. Ben-Barak, who went with his comrades to the northern end of the Jezreel Valley to survey the territory for possible settlement, identified the boundary of the tribe of Zevulun and many other settlements bearing their original biblical names. All these sites, he wrote, had been linked to "the sinews of our souls" from the time he and his friends were boys in *heder*, the traditional Jewish elementary school. These places were not imaginary—they were a living reality. "Real places, and they rejoice at our arrival as if whispering, 'the children have returned to their country.'"[34] David Ben-Gurion claimed that the Arabs were not capable of redeeming the Land of

Israel. Their labor was outdated and primitive; it depleted and impoverished the soil, providing only the barest sustenance to its owners. The Land was waiting for a cultured, diligent people, well-endowed both materially and spiritually, a people armed with the weapons of science and modern technology. The Land of Israel awaited this nation "which will come to inhabit it, and which will exploit its natural wealth and the unique qualities of its soil and climate; that will water its dry land, make its desolate mountains fertile, improve and enrich its depleted soil, forest its sands, and the parched Land will become a Garden of Eden."[35]

From the moment that Jewish hoes and picks disappeared from the Land, it went to waste, maintained the socialist leader Haim Arlosoroff. During the centuries of Jewish exile, no other people had been able to awaken the Land's soul from its slumber. The Land "shouts to us bitterly: 'Come back, come back, far-flung children!'"[36] The Ben Shemen tract lay barren, waiting "with longing for its true owners to come and extract from it all the good concealed within it, that nature granted it so generously."[37] And when *halutzim* did not requite it or were unable to desire it, the Land cried out to them: "You are alien to me." This is what Yaʿakov Berkowitz of Degania heard it say when he learned that his comrades had ceased living off their own labor and had sought outside support from the Palestine Office.[38]

The *halutzim* worked the Land because everywhere they trod it called out, "Work me! Dig into the belly of my soil and find everything, find things that you did not imagine, merely work me. . . . The Land of Israel pleads, work me! Come, my children, work me, and your labor will bear fruit."[39] The *halutzim* plowed the soil because it "craved the plow."[40] They furrowed the soil because it called out in its silent tongue, "Plow me, furrow me, sow me with the seeds of life!"[41] They sowed the Land and cared for each sprout that emerged because each sprout asked: "Give your heart to me, take me!"[42] Ben-Zion Israeli went to Haifa but returned to Kinneret as quickly as he could. In a letter to a friend he explained, "My beloved onion and my garlic, my wheat, my tomatoes cry out to me from the earth: 'water us, hoe us, our lord—our friend!'"[43] The soil, one *halutz* wrote, "pulls and draws me to it with a prodigious force, and I am filled with a potent urge to cast myself upon its bosom, its stone bosom, and to lie there forever, to lie and rest, to rest . . . to press my head to the hard, gray breast, to press it with all my might until it ceases to pound and to crash."[44]

Just as the *halutzim* desired to saturate the soil with water, sweat, and blood, so the Land was "thirsty," seeking to slake that thirst with these fluids. In one of his letters, Shimon Kushnir of Petah Tikva described a trip through the desolate southern Arava plain. He passed through large areas bare of vegetation, where his feet sank into black, flaky soil that "called to me to water and revive it."[45] Likewise, the Land desired the perspiration of the *halutzim*. From this desire, the bleak Jordan Valley prayed with a still, small voice out of the gullies in the hills: "O Lord, how long? Where is the man who will bring the omens of redemption with him, who will come and water us with his sweat and blood, where is the man who, in his strength and spirit, will raise us up from the depths and pour out his spirit on us?"[46]

The Land soaked in the blood of fallen pioneers also called out to the living *halutzim*.[47] "Rise up, comrades, for the construction of the Upper Galilee," cried Gad Avigdorov of HaShomer after the battle of Tel Hai. "The blood of our friends on the mountain boils and calls on us to rise up and rebuild with all our energy."[48] "The blood of our brothers still boils in their graves and cries out to us," the editors of *HaAhdut* declared after the murder of several *halutzim*, "and here we are digging new graves, and here we have fresh victims."[49] "Will he rest peacefully in this dust?" remonstrated Shmuel Dayan in his eulogy for the murdered Moshe Barsky of Degania. "But dust is not pleasant to rest in! And it is only with the blood of his murderers that we can silence the voice of his young blood, which is crying out to us from the earth."[50]

The Genealogy of Desire: Pioneer Rebirth

The *halutzim* were not just children of their biological parents. Expressing their desire for the Land of Israel, they discovered and proclaimed other genealogies. As we have seen, they were also the children of the Land, of Mother Earth. In addition, they had a father—the Land of the Fathers, the soil of the forefathers.[51] The Land of Israel, therefore, was simultaneously the Land of the Fathers and the Land of the Sons. Since it was the Land of the Fathers, the *halutzim* were sons returning to till it.[52] Eliezer Yaffe, the ideologist of the *moshav ovdim*, claimed that no land was as suitable for the Jews as the Land of Israel, because one could not choose one's land, just as one could not choose one's mother and father.[53]

But the *halutzim* were not simply sons returning to the Land of Israel, Mother Earth, and the Land of the Fathers. In the Land, they were reborn.[54] Before embarking for Palestine, Tzvi Shatz, father of the intimate *kevutza* type of settlement,

> This my land exults, this it avows: "All sons-without-names
> All tempest-tossed sailors
> To you I'll be mother
> A shelter to sons-without-homes."[55]
> —Menachem Zalman Valfovsky, "A Song to Sons-Without-Names," 1929

wrote to Yosef Trumpeldor that the two of them might yet meet there. But he added that even if such a meeting were to occur, Trumpeldor would not see him—because the man writing the letter would no longer exist. "I will be reborn," he explained. "I will become someone else in the Land of Israel. For that purpose, too, do I go there."[56] As one about to be born again in a new world, Shatz assumed the role of father and gave himself a new name—Tzvi (Deer), in place of Grisha/Gregory. "Greetings, Osia [Trumpeldor]! Here, from here Grisha writes to you, the one with the passport in the name of Gregory . . . but in the Land of Israel a mountain-dweller, a Communist, Tzvi will write to you. Perhaps you will not recognize him."[57]

Tehiya Lieberson testified that following her aliya to the Land of Israel she began to celebrate her birthday on the first day of Hanukkah. That was not really the date of her birth, but rather the day she first went out into the field in her new land. She did so in Petah Tikva, the "mother of the *moshavot*," when she picked up a hoe and began to do labor. It was the beginning of 1905, the third day after her arrival. On that day, she declared, a nineteen-year-old girl, a native of Dvinsk, Latvia, was privileged to fulfill her greatest dream: to tread on the soil of her homeland and till it with her own hands. "No other day," Lieberson wrote, "is more fitting to serve as my birthday, and from which to count the years of my mortal life."[58] In the same spirit, the pioneer Rachel Yanait wrote that the reckoning of her days in the Land was tantamount to the reckoning of the days of her life.[59]

Shoshana Bogen recounted in her diary an experience of rebirth as she worked in an orange grove in Petah Tikva. She had a vision that inspired her to live without compromises, because to compromise, she believed, was in fact to lose life, to die. At that point she felt herself coming into the world anew, being reborn from within the earth, and she gave herself a new name: "Shoshana [literally, "rose"]—you were born with two names: the first Shoshana, the second Haya ["alive"]. You ostensibly lived for twenty years as Shoshana, but you in fact bore death within your body. Because the flower withered at birth, and the body bore it. After my twenty years of great experience, I give you the second name—Haya. To live."[60] The writer Shmuel Yosef Agnon, who came to Palestine in the Second Aliya, also claimed an alternative genealogy. Because the emperor Titus destroyed Jerusalem and exiled the Jews, Agnon wrote, he was born in one of the cities of the exile but always regarded himself as one who "was born in Jerusalem."[61]

The claim that the pioneer experience of rebirth is but a linguistic trope, a poetic expression, a literary metaphor, a subjective experience, a symbolic reenactment of biological birth, or some similar phenomenon[62] stamps the *halutzim* with precisely the tags from which they sought to liberate themselves: mother, father, tradition, Judaism, the exile, femininity, the past, myth, mother tongue. But, in reality, the pioneer experience of rebirth had no meaning beyond itself. It was not a manifestation of something else. Rebirth was a genealogical option, one of many, that pioneer desire adopted in its desire for the Land of Israel. Mother Earth and the Land of the Fathers must also be seen as biological parents in the deep sense of the word—parents who give life, parents in every way. The *halutz* was truly reborn in the Land of Israel.

In addition to identifying as the "children of the motherland" and the "children of the Jewish nation,"[63] the pioneers were born of the sea. "It again seems to me that I was born on the shores of this [Mediterranean] sea," wrote Rabbi Binyamin (the pen name of Yehoshua Radler-Feldman), "nay, this sea vomited me up, and I myself am a piece of flotsam."[64] The *halutz* was also the son of the soil. "I am of whole spirit and strong body," wrote one, "I am simple and natural, for whole and strong, simple and natural is the soil that bore me. And I, too, will give her such sons, young, strong, stalwart, brave, high-spirited, and singing."[65] Eliyahu Rappaport of Beitania pleaded with his father in a letter to leave him alone: "I will bury you tomorrow in the bosom of my new world. You will not be mine any longer, because I saw life not because of you—from its womb I emerged, from the bosom of the bride, the woman, and not from the womb of any other mother."[66] The "bride" he refers to was the Nuris lands on which his *kevutza* had settled.[67]

The *halutz* was also born of the boulders and mountains of the Land of Israel.[68] After his arrival, Tzvi Nadav, a leader of HaShomer, thought about his parents' home, but shoved aside the memory of the people dear to him. Instead, he sought to give himself over entirely to the new natural life of the Land of Israel. He did not respond to letters sent to him and fashioned a legend about having been born of a rock, in a cave. He would tell this story to people who asked who his parents were. He said to himself that if a rock had borne him, he would be more at ease. In time, he indeed felt that a rock had given birth to him and that the mountains had adopted him as their son.[69]

Pioneer rebirth in the Land of Israel served as the most radical manifestation of the "negation of the exile" phenomenon.[70] Here, negation meant not just shaking free of the exile but a retroactive annulment of its very existence. Y. Reznichenko, a member of the Labor Battalion, wrote that devotion to the ideal of renewal led necessarily to negation of the exile in the most extreme way: not only in the Zionist and social sense but also in a personal sense. This entailed a desire to totally cast off the old and uproot all that remained of the past, he wrote. The *halutz* had to "be reborn here [in the Land]."[71] In this sense, the Zionist return to history was nothing less than the creation of a new history ex nihilo. Reznichenko argued further that the position of the *halutzim* was unique because they had severed the cord that connected them to the past. They were beginning "from a primeval point." Neither their labor nor their lives was a continuation of what had been before. "We began from the beginning, after casting off the past in the days in which we moved to the Land of Israel," wrote Reznichenko. "We came empty, like a tender babe."[72]

As noted in the case of Tzvi Shatz, for the *halutzim* rebirth in the Land meant adopting the "father" role and giving themselves new Hebrew names. Ernst Polack concluded the first letter he wrote to his parents after arriving in Palestine with a declaration that he had changed his name to Natan Ikar (Nathan the Farmer), asking that henceforth they write to him only under this name.[73] In this way the *halutzim* subverted the oedipal genealogy imposed on them by their biological parents by altering their names.

Tehiya Lieberson was born in 1886 and again in 1905, when she "ascended" to the Land, as she put it. From that point forward she refused to bear her given name, Haina. In consultation with her comrades, she replaced the letter *nun* in that name with a *tav* and then rearranged the letters to spell "Tehiya," meaning "rebirth." She bore this name as if it had been hers from infancy. "In fact," she wrote, "that's the way it really was, because from the beginning of my aliya to the Land, from the day I took up a hoe to work with, it was as if I had been born again, and I reckon from that day the years of my real life. Whatever came before I cast behind me as if it never was, and I really live and exist from that day forward."[74]

The pioneers' desire for new names, Amos Elon writes, expressed their powerful desire to be united, in body and name, with the landscape of their renewed homeland—its rivers and mountains, its trees and brambles. They sought a covenant with nature and searched for roots.[75] So Eliyahu Binder became Eliyahu Ben-Horin (Freeman), Simha Alter Gutman became Simha Ben-Zion (Son of Zion), Rachel Goldin became Rachel Yanait (from Alexander Yanai, a Hasmonean

> If you ask me today what my name will be tomorrow, I swear that I don't know how to answer. If, for example, the sun rises tomorrow . . . I will be honored to report to you tomorrow under the name Mr. Shimshi [Sunny], or Ben-Shemesh [Son of the Sun], or Harsi [derived from another biblical term for the sun]. If I cross the Jordan [*Yarden* in Hebrew], for example, . . . I would not be able to avoid calling myself Yardeni on that day. . . .
>
> Today I am drawn after the vineyards . . . so I am called Karmi [of the vineyards]; and tomorrow I will be entirely enchanted by the music of the spring streams in the Galilean mountains, and my name will be Galili.[76]
>
> —David Shimonovitz, *Son of My Land: From the Notebook of a Wanderer*, 1909–1919

king), David Green became David Ben-Gurion (Son of Gurion), Ze'ev Duner became Ze'ev Ivry (Hebrew), Meir Wald became Meir Ya'ari (of the forest), Shmuel Varshovsky became Shmuel Yavniel (after a *moshava* near Tiberias), Aryeh Yaffe became Aryeh Galili (of the Galilee), Shlomo Levkowitz became Shlomo Lavi (Lion), Yitzhak Landberg became Yitzhak Sadeh (Field), Menachem Moshkovitz became Menachem Ben-Shahar (Son of the Dawn), Baruch Feinbrun became Baruch HaSharoni (of the Sharon), Yehuda Friedlander became Yehuda HaRo'eh (the Shepherd), Ben-Zion Chernomursky became Ben-Zion Yisraeli (Israeli), Shmuel Kashpitzky became Shmuel Polani (of Poland) and, later, Shmuel Yehuda'i (of Judea), Tzipora Reiver became Tzipora Karmelit (of Mount Carmel), Yitzhak Shimshlevitz became Yitzhak Ben-Zvi (Son of Deer), David Shimonovitz became David Shimoni (Son of Simon), Yitzhak Shpak became Yitzhak Ben-Yisrael (son of Israel), Yitzhak Levi Shkolnik became Levi Eshkol (Grape Cluster), and Leah (whose original family name is not known) became Leah Yisraelit (Israeli).[77] With these rebirths and name changes, the *halutzim* became part of the Land: part of its geography (Galili—Galilean), part of its landscape (Sadeh—field), part of its mythology (Yanait—after Alexander Yanai, the Hasmonean monarch), and part of its family (Ben-Yisrael—son of Israel).

Not just the *halutzim* but the entire Jewish people were reborn in the Land. A. D. Gordon argued that Zionist-pioneer settlement was an act of creation unparalleled in human history, involving the revival of a "half-dead" nation that had been uprooted and scattered to the four winds.[78] In the same spirit, David Ben-Gurion called the Zionist project a "national resurrection."[79]

Martin Buber and the Regeneration of the National Body

One of the few thinkers to discern the revolutionary nature of the pioneer enterprise was Martin Buber.[80] "Regeneration," or the renewal of life, he wrote, manifested itself in two principal areas in general: psychology and biology. Psychological renewal is generally the result of a religious experience that overwhelms a person's entire being. After reaching a particular point on a meandering road, by virtue of this complete internal revolution a person can begin again. Coming into the world for a second time, the individual feels he or she is the product of a new birth. Biological regeneration, in contrast, is expressed in organic changes. It takes place when tissue degenerates and is replaced with healthy tissue, or when an organ that has ceased to function regains its vitality. Alternatively, the old organs may have been destroyed, with new ones growing to carry out the role of their predecessors, of which nothing remains. Regeneration in the biological sense is thus the reverse of degeneration.[81]

In the particular renewal of the Jewish people's life through the Zionist-pioneer enterprise, Buber perceived a unique quality that was immune to psychological or biological conceptualization. He argued that the renewal of this national life testified to more than a decisive change in the consciousness, aspiration, and position of the nation, or part of it. Rather, he said, the nation's very essence was transformed into something different from what it had been at the beginning of the regenerative process.

The Jews had been in a pathological state in the exile, Buber maintained. They had degenerated, had deviated from their "genus," or inherent original quality. The degenerative process had penetrated deeply into the Jewish national organism and even taken hold of the national mind. To counteract this disintegration, more than the soul required healing. "The most renewable parts of the people"[82] had to be introduced into fundamentally different conditions that could regenerate the Jews' organic selves—conditions appropriate to the nation's unique nature. The ideal situation would be new living conditions that exactly reproduced those in which the collective had originally developed. Buber believed that such conditions were present in the Land of Israel, noting that "the complete regeneration of a community is beginning to take place before our very eyes—a regeneration in which not merely a national awareness and a people's will achieve new vitality, but also the objective existence of the people is rejuvenated through the growth of new cellular tissue, new structures, new limbs."[83] This was precisely what had taken place among the vanguard that settled in the Land.

"The most renewable parts of the people," in Buber's view, were the *halutzim*. The Hebrew pioneers, unlike those of other national movements, were not performing a onetime historical act, nor were they reacting to a given historical circumstance through an act formulated programmatically or ideologically. They offered a positive response to the question of life itself, a response expressed in the language of living. The *halutzim*, who personified the regenerative type in the Jewish nation, were pioneers not only in developing and farming the Land. They were pioneers of a new life. In sum, this *halutziyyut* was not responding to any specific need, nor was it directed at achieving a specific goal. Rather, it was the "*halutziyyut* of life."[84]

In other words, Buber did not see the pioneer act in terms of a dialectic of renewal, degeneration, and further renewal, whether psychological or biological. To him, the act overcame dialectics. The creation of the *halutz* was a self-creation.

Having been born again on the soil of the Land of Israel, the *halutzim* felt a potent, amplified sense of life beating within them and in the world around them. The pioneer philosophy was actualized in the space of the Land, which was not only an idea or a particular reality, nor did it simply supply pioneers' life needs and allow them to achieve their aspirations: it *was* "life."[85] According to Yosef Aharonovich, the Hebrew nation's renaissance was first and foremost an aspiration for a change in life values. Life in the exile had been fundamentally rotten. The *halutzim* sought to leave that life not for any specific, individual purpose but rather for the purpose of "*life itself* [all emphases in the original unless otherwise noted]."[86] David Horowitz of HaShomer HaTzaʿir wrote that he and his comrades had long sought "the totality of life," until they finally found it in "heroic Zionism" and not in "intelligent Zionism." For them, Zionism was not a political movement but rather "an act of devotion for all of life."[87] A few months after arriving in the Land, Horowitz wrote: "We left Lvov with the happy feeling that we were sailing on the true waves of life, that we wished to give and take much from life, to scoop up full handfuls, and that we wanted to prostrate ourselves before the gods of youth and devour them, that we approached life with the eternal demand of 'all or nothing.' We longed for power, for tension, for the surge of life overflowing its banks, for freedom and intoxicating beauty."[88] When he discussed his heady desire to actualize his Zionism by moving to the Land, Haim Arlosoroff confessed to a friend that many thought him "mad." But, he said, the move had to happen. The Jews demanded to live, he said, and they would: "I demand, therefore I am."[89]

3 Dissolving Boundaries

The Land of Israel is soil that the *halutzim* crave. Their desire is channeled first of all through labor, working the land. All *halutzim* who immigrate to Palestine cultivate the land. Some do so for a few days before turning to other Zionist activities. Others make labor on the land the labor of their lives. In either case, contact with the soil through working the land is a practice that constitutes the pioneer desire for the Land of Israel. It is the basis of the pioneer experience of being-in-the-Land-of-Israel.

Through labor, the *halutzim* "unite" and "merge" with the land, are "assimilated" and "soaked up" by it.[1] Only working the land, wrote HaPoʿel HaTzaʿir cofounder Eliezer Shohat, can allow for the weaving of those threads that enable true, inner connection with it. Shohat distinguished between two types of connection—mechanical-external and organic-internal. Working the land enables the latter type, he maintained. And such a connection creates the same profound esthetic and spiritual relationship that an artist has with a picture he has painted—as opposed to the legal, superficial, possessive relationship experienced by the person who purchases land.[2]

Um Juni settler Yosef Weitz wrote to a friend in the exile that he, living outside the Land, could not truly grasp the meaning of "feeling the earth under one's feet" to which Zionism aspired, including the need to possess and cultivate Jewish soil in the Land of Israel. The only person who could "feel the need, live it, touch it in all its actuality is one who has embraced the soil in his hands, dug it, who has thrust his plow into it, who has rooted his tree in it and grown his grain and produce in it."[3]

A. D. Gordon took an even more radical position, identifying pioneer labor on the soil of the Land of Israel as part of nature's work itself. In effect, Gordon negated the customary relationship between the laborer and his environment and replaced it with a state of diffusion between them. Through labor, on the land in particular, the *halutz* amalgamates himself with nature and becomes part of it. Gordon asserted that while at labor, however arduous and prosaic it may be—"laden with the profane," in his words—an ineffable moment always arrives when the laborer senses his entire being interwoven with the work of nature, a moment when he begins to penetrate nature, to become rooted in it, and to grow and live within nature itself, partaking in nature's work of creation. "At such moments," Gordon wrote, "the human heart is seized by a kind of eternal elation, divine purity. The furthest depths penetrate him. And it seems that here he sends roots down into the earth in which he digs, that he, too, like all that grows around him, is nourished by the sun's rays, by the sustenance of the sky; that he, too, lives a common life with the tiniest blade of grass, with every flower and every tree, living intensely within the depths of nature, rising up from it and growing above into the spaces of the great world."[4]

The *halutzim* worked the land in a variety of ways, with their bare hands and using tools—plow, hoe, mechanized equipment. Of all types of labor, they perceived plowing as the fullest realization of their bond with their land. Many testified that plowing drew them out of the concrete and prosaic reality of hard labor, which was often difficult and cruel, into an ecstasy in which they sensed the almost metaphysical Gordonian bond between themselves and the Land.[5] In his diary, David Gilad, a member of Degania, admits that plowing entirely transported him in such a way. All parts of his life entered into harmony with one another. His life and his labor became a realization of utopia. "The material body ascends to a spiritual height. This is the eternal plowman. His plow clangs among shadows and spirits, and he, the eternal, passes from field to field, from boundary to boundary," Gilad wrote.[6]

Pioneer desire for the Land of Israel also becomes actualized by direct physical contact.[7] The *halutzim* "grip" the land with their fingernails and "plant" their feet in it.[8] At the end of a day's labor, Yehudit Edelman of Ein Harod had difficulty leaving the land, her land, so she lay down on it. "You prostrate yourself on the land that breathes with quiet weariness," she wrote, "before sinking into night rest, listening to the rustle around you."[9] A man treading on the clods of the furrow he has tilled, claimed Eliyahu Karmieli of Degania, feels almost at one with these clods. It is a primeval sensation that cannot be expressed in words, a sense of "warmth and bliss, shelter and sanctuary." Sometimes the man is drawn to the field even at night, tramping over the hard clods, taking them up in his palm. He "lies between the furrows in order to feel the land, his land."[10]

The practice of walking, working, and patrolling barefoot intensifies the pioneer's bond with the land.[11] Rachel Yanait testified that every touch of her bare foot on the soil delighted her, and awakened latent chords in her body and soul. She maintained that all new immigrants should walk the land's length and breadth in order to soak in its essence and spirit, to give themselves over to the sun and wind and cling to the soil. After all, she wondered, a person lives only once in this world, so why not permit oneself this wonderful, unmediated contact with nature—which is, after all, the real reason to live?[12]

Ein Harod, 1920. Central Zionist Archives, Jerusalem

Intimacy with the Land

The pioneers were not satisfied with working the land and touching it. They longed to know it in other ways as well. Standing on the soil of Kibbutz Kiryat Anavim, Yitzhak Pelah hungered to know how the seed buried deep down felt.[13] As mentioned in earlier chapters, the *halutzim* also expressed their special relationship with the land erotically. Beyond lying on the land, they sometimes kissed and embraced it. Some kissed it when they reached the coast en route from their former homelands, others during trips through the Land, and others while at work.[14]

The Zionist narrative of many *halutzim* is a story of falling in love romantically, even sexually, with the Land of Israel. Eliyahu Rappaport of Beitania recounted his pre-aliya life as a chronicle of falling in love with girls who always disappointed his masculine desire. He decided to go to the Land of Israel. Boarding a ship sailing for Jaffa, he was "full of wounds." In the Land, working the soil, in direct contact with it, he was able to "purge" himself of sexual desire and learn what true love is. It was the love formulated by Spinoza, according to whom "there is but one love—between object and object, between man and man, between husband and wife; there is but one love—God's love for his creation, within and from which he has divided himself among all things."[15]

The *halutzim*, thus, love and are in love with the Land of Israel and its soil. In the pioneers' writings, the Land is always female: virgin, beloved, Mother Earth.[16] Male *halutzim* seek to pierce that virginity and cause their beloved to fall in love with and even wed them.[17] Like many others, David Ben-Gurion described his first years in the Land as a "honeymoon."[18] In one of his early letters, the future prime minister called the Land a beautiful "widow" who ignites flames of love in his spirit and in his blood.[19] Others said that they courted the Land, or called it their "betrothed."[20] Berl Katznelson described Lake Kinneret as an "enchanting bride."[21] Eliyahu Rappaport wrote the following of the land where the Beitania *kevutza* settled: "Nuris land! Is that not the name of a bride? . . . As a groom who delivers himself and all the echelons of future generations into his bride's womb, so we will deliver ourselves into the mother-belly of the betrothed soil."[22] Rappaport identified himself and his comrades not only as the husband(s) of the soil but as the grooms of the entire world. Here again, unmediated physical, erotic contact with the land opened Rappaport to desire for the world as a whole: "And my bed—bed of loneliness, room, house, city, land, world—hah, world! Attend, hear, world! I love you with all my heart, with all my soul, and with all my might, and by force of this law of love I hereby betroth you—you will be a husband to my bride forever and ever."[23] Mordechai Snir of Kibbutz Geva condemned those who left the Land because such an act amounted to abandoning their pregnant wives as soon as the men heard their groans and cries.[24]

As we have seen, the soil was also Mother Earth to the *halutzim*.[25] "It is now a year since I came here," one pioneer woman wrote in her diary. "I have been feeling the ground under my feet. . . . My love for Eretz Israel is what I imagine the love of a daughter for her mother to be."[26] The *halutzim* found comfort and healing in their Mother Earth. Yitzhak Shweiger wrote a letter to his brother in the exile about his yearning for a mother figure: "Sometimes I have an attack of a potent spiritual craving to steal out to a pit, to lie down and nestle my head in the plundered bosom of the earth as in the lap of a kindhearted, comforting mother."[27] For Rachel Bluwstein—who became Rachel the Poet, the lyric voice of the Second Aliya—the Zionist revolution was a revolution in the life of the Jew in which she no longer rose in the morning to pursue teaching or bookkeeping, but rather to go out to the field, to the garden, "for the purifying, renewing, exhilarating touch of Mother Earth."[28]

Like a human mother, the soil of the Land had breasts from which her children sought to suckle. Eliezer Yaffe, the ideologist of the *moshav ovdim*, said that the proper relationship between man and his land, and between the land and its possessors-husbands (the Hebrew word *ba'al* means "husband," "master," and "possessor" as well as soil that is watered solely by rain, without irrigation), was the same as the relationship between the child who seeks to suckle from his mother's breast and the mother who, in turn, seeks to nurse him. Even more than the man wants to suckle, the land wants to nurse him. Wrote Yaffe, "The greatest sin on this earth is that man does not cling to the bosom of Mother Earth in order to drink the bounty that will turn bitter if she has no one to suckle."[29] "When I see a man working the soil in his field," Yaffe confessed, "I see the image of an infant grasping his sleeping mother's breast, trying to attach his lips to her nipple."[30] In the same way, Yitzhak Pelah of Kiryat Anavim described the relationship between the commune and the mountain on which its members settle. Before the settlement, the mountain is a mountain of death. Now it lies "like a huge breast, on which thousands of nipples will grant vigor to the new settlement."[31] It is not surprising, then, that all those who do not treat properly this feminine Land are viewed as no more than "pimps."[32]

The *halutzim* also seek passionately to ingest or swallow up the Land. They repeatedly speak of the "hunger" and "thirst" for it that had developed over the long years of exile and separation from it.[33] These feelings heighten once they are physically present on the Land. Yosef Weitz wrote of remaining alone in the field, with one more plot to plow for the winter crop. Thus he portrayed working in a broad field in the beautiful open space of the Jordan Valley. "In such a situation," Weitz wrote, "you are sometimes overcome by an intense wish to swallow up the entire plain before you all at once, to turn it over and over and conquer it, and you spur yourself and your animals on to the point of fatigue and exhaustion."[34] *Halutzim* made a practice of tasting the soil.[35]

Water

The pioneers' ecstasy toward the Land was based in part on the various liquids that allowed them, and particularly their bodies, to diffuse into the soil. First was water, a crucial fluid, since it was a scarce resource and the climate was hot and, in some areas, arid. The *halutzim* had come to Palestine from cold and rainy places. In the Land of Israel, they encountered for the first time a dry, hot, desert environment. It is hardly surprising, then, that water was a central motif in pioneer-Zionist imagination and semiology.[36] But it also played a role in actualizing the pioneer desire for the Land. A. D. Gordon described the new world revealed to him as he crossed the Mediterranean Sea to the Land of Israel: "The open sea had a huge, profound, sudden effect on me. The open sea awakened joy in me, of a kind that I had never before felt, in its infinite expanse and—and it is impossible not to say this—in its divine purity. . . . It spoke with me of things intuitive, of the infinite, of endless love for all creatures, of man, of God."[37]

Thus, drinking the Land's water satisfied more than simple physiological need. When Rachel Bluwstein drank from Lake Kinneret, she sensed a necessary and direct connection between herself and the place. "What bliss it is to sink onto the gravel," she wrote, "and drink endlessly, like a beast of the forest. To dip one's burning face into the water, to inhale and draw in spirit. And again to quench one's thirst until all strength is gone. They say that these waters have special powers: one who drinks them, even once, will always return to them. Is not that the reason that all children [of Israel] in foreign lands long for the quiet shores of the Kinneret, since their forefathers slaked their thirst here?"[38] When he roamed, Tzvi Nadav, a leader of HaShomer, drank not only out of thirst but also because of the pure joy of his encounter with the Land's springs.[39] No wonder, then, that for the pioneers, the water of Israel tasted like "potent wine."[40]

The *halutzim* also swam in the waters of the Land. Bathing, for Tzvi Shatz, father of the *kevutza* settlement type, roused primal feelings and urges to which he was unaccustomed. Immersing himself in water returned him to a direct relationship with the natural world. As a soldier in the Jewish Legion, for example, he came to the springs near Jericho, with one in particular capturing his heart: "This jubilant spring, joyful and fertile, awakens desire in me, desire to be jubilant, wild, to impregnate women, many women! Such were the wild men, the sons of nature, strong as nature, whose strength we have inherited."[41] And when he came to a river, these feelings returned with equal strength: "The stars shone, the water caressed me, and I felt that I was content in 'the bosom of nature as I united with it!'"[42] Only after bathing in the river did he understand that in the Land of Israel alone could he be at one with nature."[43]

The author Meir Wilkansky maintained that swimming in Lake Kinneret was an obligatory purifying process that marked the transition from the exile to the new land. He and his friends bathed at the point where the Jordan River flowed out from the lake. According to Wilkansky, this was a true religious act. Before they immersed themselves, they had felt they were not actually inhabitants of the Land. But the water washed away all the "contamination and filth" that had adhered to them and their forefathers in the exile.[44] One laborer at the Kinneret farm wrote that when he gazed out of his east-facing window, a spectacular, exhilarating sight stretched before him. This was the lake, in all its magnificence, in a profusion of magical colors, "and it looked as if you, together with all those in the house with you, are actually immersed in the sea."[45]

The *halutzim* sank water wells, an act that went beyond the mechanics of digging. They saw removing earth as another way to become intimate with and to penetrate the Land.[46] As Meir Yaʿari put it, "We will dig a well; we will dig a deep, deep well. We will open the bosom of the great mother—the earth. The mother will bare her breast, and from all her arteries water will rise into the well."[47] And when Rachel Yanait arrived at Beʿer Yaʿakov (the Well of Jacob) on a trip through the Land, she prostrated herself on one of its broad edge stones. The water level was far down, but visible. Inside, the well was dark and cool. The upper courses of stone were new, but the stones farther down were ancient. She lay on the well's edge for a long time. "In its waters," she later wrote, "I searched out the riddle of my people, the memory of Jacob our forefather, the dawn of our nation's childhood."[48]

The pioneers felt that the Land of Israel's thirst was their thirst, its suffering their suffering.[49] Moshe Hallenberg of Beitania came to the northern settlement of Poria, where the land was dry from drought. "I felt the land's thirst with my whole being," he testified. "I pitied it as one pities a living creature that is close to you."[50] At times, the *halutzim* treated water as if it were alive. On his way to Mesʾha, Tzvi Nadav came upon a spring that asked him to prevent its waters from being wasted. Instead of just seeping back into the earth, Nadav wrote, the spring wanted its water to be used to irrigate a small vegetable garden and a few trees. It wanted little children to play at its edge, to slake their thirst, to bathe joyfully in its water. It longed for bands of stalwart, high-spirited young men, like Nadav and his comrades, to stride past it each day.[51] Michael Oved, a member of Kevutzat Sharon, noted that when he came to Degania, he would stop first to sit by the Jordan River for a short while, listening to its gurgle. He seemed to hear many sublime voices in the river's whispers.[52] Dialogues between the *halutzim* and the Land of Israel's sources of water were a recurring motif in their prose and poetry.[53]

Blood, Sweat, and Tears

Like water, bodily fluids such as sweat and blood played a decisive role in the pioneers' process of connecting with the Land and its soil. For the *halutzim*, intense perspiration was a new physical experience; they had not known it in the lands where they were born. Like hard physical labor, the Land's heat and humidity was a new experience for most. But, as with other such phenomena, the *halutzim* elevated this experience beyond the level of the physiological.

One of the pioneers' main reasons for making aliya to the Land of Israel was to moisten its soil with their sweat.[54] Like water, perspiration "quenched" the soil's thirst and actualized the diffusion of *halutz* and Land into each other.[55] Like water, sweat was a token of this bond. "And as my seed proliferates in her bosom and the sweat of my brow drenches her stiff neck," one *halutz* wrote, "my soul is bonded to her forever."[56] But watering the soil with sweat amounted to more than a linking of consciousness, spirit, and body; this action turned the soil into the pioneer's soil. In the words of Ben-Shemni, "As long as the soil has not been drenched with our sweat, it will not belong to us!"[57]

Haim Arlosoroff identified sweat as a key component of the "glue" that held the farmer fast to his land. In his view, a person's willingness to bond to the land through manual labor fittingly entitled him to occupy it. This adhesion was formed, said Arlosoroff, by laborers willing to knead their sweat into the dust of the earth.[58] One reason Ben-Gurion migrated from Judea (the *halutzim*'s name for the area of Jewish settlement on the coastal plain, extending south and north of Jaffa) to the Galilee was that he wished to engage in agricultural labor at the estate of a Jewish farmer. While the estate was not a wealthy one, it was "drenched" with the sweat of his brow.[59] And whereas the *halutz* enjoyed sweating, the soil rejoiced equally to receive his sweat.

Blood was another fluid through which the body of the *halutz* laborer or guard diffused into the body of the Land. The laborer's blood "watered" and fertilized the soil.[60] Like sweat, blood transformed the soil from just dirt into the soil of the *halutz*: "Just as the body must have blood, as must an entire nation, so must the soil. . . . Had we not watered the Land with our blood, we would not be standing on it today. . . . We shed our blood and live here."[61]

Indeed the dissolving of the *halutz* into the land sometimes involved the confluence of sweat and blood—the sweat of the workers and the blood of the armed men. When Menachem Portugali and his friends in HaShomer marched to the Sharona lands to found their movement's first settlement, they passed the place where their comrade Yehezkel Nisanov had been murdered. They halted to pay their respects. One of them declared: "Now we must mix our sweat with the blood of our friend."[62]

Tears too played a role, though a less central one, in pioneer desire.[63] Shmuel Dayan, a member of Degania and later of Nahalal, described the suffering of a young woman of the *kevutza*, which grew out of her difficult and traumatic transition from her parents' home to the Land of Israel. At a particularly painful moment, the woman allowed herself to break into tears. "Before the eyes of the ripened ears of grain and the stars—here, in freedom," Dayan wrote, "in revelation and alone with herself in nature . . . the stalks in the field also soaked up the beads of sorrow and suffering of a disheartened soul, which rolled into the living depths of a new world."[64]

Nature, Open Space, and Sublimity

The *halutzim* also directed their desire toward the space of the Land of Israel and all its elements, animate and inanimate. They felt close to rocks, to archaeological remains, to ruins, and to gravestones.[65] One *halutz* who encountered grave markers as he walked the Land saw them as signs of ancient settlements, memorials to heroes. As he recorded, "I kissed the silent gravestones, my relatives . . . they embed me as an inhabitant of the land . . . these fine sinews of feeling will tie me even more strongly to the soil of these beautiful graves. Blood cries out from the earth . . . I must remain here! . . . It is a covenant of blood."[66]

The *halutzim* felt an affinity for the Land's plants that amounted to love, even to the profound bond between parent and child.[67] Tzvia, a member of Kevutzat HaSharon, described a night at Nahalal when suddenly a warm wind buffeted her face. She inhaled the sharp but pleasant scent of crocuses, which intoxicated her. The breeze was like the breath, the souls of the plants, which remained awake as she did. The fragrance was "like the greeting of brothers, so close and beloved of the soul it was."[68] For Yosef Aharonovich, caring for plants was like caring for infants. "You jump from one to the other," he wrote, "cutting that which has been designated for cutting, propping up that which needs support, bandaging and wrapping in rubber [*sic*] every wound, so that [the plant] will not get chilled. Like a nurse to the young infant, you care for all these."[69]

On one of his treks, Absalom Feinberg, one of the founders of the Nili espionage network, came across two trees with "open" wounds that had been inflicted by a logger. He felt absolute empathy for the gashed trees, as if he had found a friend sprawled on the ground with a knife protruding from his neck, or discovered his mother wounded. "This ax, which has blemished and stripped our land for so many generations, has it not made a direct and painful wound in my heart?" he asked. "Old ethical proverbs came to mind, about the revenge a man must take against those who abuse his mother. I imagined that my feet put down roots here and that they hurt and ache. I was never able to see a picture of the crucified [Jesus], with nails driven through his bleeding palms, without feeling weakness in my own hands. Such is the weakness I felt a short while ago, in my arms and my thighs."[70]

Alongside their affinity for its plants, the pioneers felt very close to the Land's fauna. Rachel Bluwstein argued that the return to the Land of Israel not only reconstituted the pioneers' relationship to its soil but also created a wonderful new bond with its animals. This relationship involved a "blood tie" between man and animal and a potent sense that all living things belonged to one "cosmic family."[71] The intimacy with animals was expressed in different ways. Pioneers spoke with animals as they fed them, and embraced and kissed them. They saw their domestic animals as part of their extended family.[72] When a mare she cared for birthed a colt, Tova Portugali, a member of Kibbutz Kfar Giladi, viewed him as an "eldest son" in her family.[73] A member of Kibbutz Ayelet HaShahar described the

Hulda, 1920. Central Zionist Archives, Jerusalem

horror she felt when chicks died in the yard. "Each chick that dies," she lamented, "blackens the spirit and you walk bereaved as if a member of your family had died."[74] This close relationship with animals inspired an aversion to eating their flesh—many *halutzim* were vegetarians.[75]

Members of HaShomer, the first pioneer paramilitary organization, were renowned for their love of horses. They adorned their horses with all kinds of ornaments, gave them names (Yehezkel Henkin called his mare "Tzipora"), hugged and kissed them. They wrote paeans to and about them.[76] Tzipora Zeid, for example, described a noble, beautiful mare with a light coat and brown spots on her slender, supple frame: "May you be the first of my desires, which I dream of at night and I think of in the fiercest heat of the day."[77] Alexander Zeid, her husband, let his mares and their colts feed in his room, off his own plate.[78] Another HaShomer member, Meir Spector, explained the pioneers' profound love of horses by reference to shared fate of Jews and their horses in the fight for the Land of Israel. It was no wonder, he wrote, that the Hebrew youth who stood on and tilled his soil, while also coming to know and love the animals and beasts of the field, developed a devoted love for his graceful, intelligent mare: "Because she extricates her rider from all misfortune and saves him from death, and you hold fast to her in the darkest night, lower your head and with your hand stroke her neck, and she, too, feels the peril that lies in wait, pricks up her ears, listens, softly whinnies—sees, understands, and feels all that happens—trust her!"[79]

Gazing on the Land of Israel's landscapes, amid its open spaces, the *halutzim* experienced a sublimity they could barely contain or express. Their encounter with the Land produced powerful feelings of "turbulence," "intoxication," and "dreaminess."[80] "At times you raise your eyes to the wide spaces visible among the trees," Yosef Aharonovich wrote, "and look at the majesty of eternity around you . . . you negate yourself before the infinite."[81] Michael Oved wrote in a letter to a friend that in the Land of Israel, man has a broad base from which to delve deeper into God's creation. When you stand in a sea of grain and its waves caress you and the full ears touch you, you feel yourself "a brother of the entire universe, a plant among the plants."[82] A. D. Gordon experienced the Land's open spaces as if he were a "son" clasped and enfolded in his mother's arms. The Land's natural environment, he wrote, is a "loving and compassionate mother," with a silent sorrow in her glance. "You feel yourself embraced in the tender arms of a wise, prodigious mother, who gazes at you as at a beloved son who was raised in slavery and who has now returned to her home, without upbringing, of low culture, and in her full, wise heart she understands you well, but you have not been taught to understand her."[83]

To the *halutzim*, the landscapes, nature, and open spaces of their new home were not just beautiful; they were exemplars of beauty. Many viewed the Land as a picture and listened to its sounds as a musical composition. Both visual and auditory experiences of the Land were intensely emotional.[84] "A day of work such as I had today opens all the depths of life," Rachel Katznelson said of her first days working in the Land. "At a late hour, after hard labor, Michelangelo revealed to me what I had never seen in him before."[85] "We rowed in a boat on the calm waters of the Jordan," a member of Degania wrote. "The moon was out. We sat, enchanted, still before the sight around us . . . to become one with the beauty that imbues this place."[86]

Like their relationship to the soil, the pioneers' bond with nature and open spaces included erotic elements. They opened themselves up to the Land and yearned to assimilate into it. There are moments, one *halutz* wrote, when it seems as if "I embrace the entire world, I kiss it all. And within that embrace I approach God, like a child I climb onto his lap. I hide my head in his chest, press myself against his heart, close my eyes, surrender my heart to silence."[87] When Absalom Feinberg gazed at Mount Hermon, the snows of which melted from the love of the great sun, he yearned to become part of nature. "And an urge awakened in me to race [the burbling streams]," he wrote, "to unite with them, to be melting snow, bounding water, golden rays of sun, grasses trembling from the passion of love."[88]

The *halutzim* saw their romantic, erotic, and sexual relations permeating the landscape.[89] The waves on the Mediterranean "engage in battle and fight and then

"The Prayer of Light" illustration for a HaShomer HaTzaʿir pamphlet, undated. Hugo Höppener (Fidus)

return to embrace and kiss each other, cheering and laughing."[90] Lake Kinneret and the moon "woo each other."[91] The flowers thirstily drink "the moon's kisses, pale and trembling."[92] Standing on the peak of Mount Carmel, David Kahana of Beitania glanced at the horizon and saw that the vault of the sky and the mirror of the sea "had coupled and become one: a wedding of heaven and sea. They adhered to each other with a fervent embrace, like two blue lovers; a gentle breeze blew, setting in motion waves of air, which touched the waves of the sea, kissed them lightly, and shied away."[93]

These sublime experiences were not only passive. The *halutzim* took measures to produce and amplify them. The most important such action, as we have seen, was labor. But trips and hikes the length and breadth of the Land also actualized desire for the Land by deepening the pioneers' knowledge of it.[94] Berl Katznelson wrote to his brothers who remained in the exile that the feeling of a trip in the Land could not be described because words were merely words. His brothers would be able to understand him only if they came to Palestine and saw with their own eyes the Land that he saw.[95] "I have no way of describing such a picture," wrote a *halutz* of Telha to his brother about one of his hikes along the Litani River. "The natural majesty of the deep abyss between the terrible mountains where the Litani is situated amazed us so much that we stood with open mouths, not knowing what to say."[96]

Surging song and ecstatic dancing of the hora also fused the *halutzim* with the Land.[97] The pioneers sang on their way to work, as they worked, on their way home, as they hiked, and while on patrol. The echoes of their singing enhanced their sense of oneness with the landscape. "In every song that broke out of our hearts then, out of hidden sorrow," wrote Yosef Aharonovich, "we immediately heard the echo of the mountains answering us, as if saying: return, return to nature, because there, and only there, will you find healing for your wretched soul and your shattered body."[98] Here is a description of the founding of Kevutzat Beitania: "We broke out in song, and it cut through the stillness of the moonlight-strewn spring night. 'Here, what is more good and pleasant than brothers sitting together'—the sound climbed and rushed up to the mountaintops, penetrated the fissures in the stones, disturbing their rest, the slumber of many generations. . . . Mount Carmel responded to the singing of the dancers 'together.' . . . What our lips could not express, our feet, bounding to the rhythm and stamping on the soil of the homeland, spoke."[99]

All the *halutzim*'s senses took part in this merging with the Land. Their eyes "held fast to" and "caressed" it. They longed to "feast" their eyes on its sights. Their gaze was "enslaved" by the landscape and sought to "absorb" and "penetrate" it.[100] The pioneer gaze at the Land of Israel was not simply a "look"; in it the viewer was transformed into part of the landscape and the landscape into part of the viewer. Ben-Gurion and his friends walked for three hours among mountains, valleys, citrus groves, vineyards, and almond and olive orchards, and the sights around them, he wrote, "swallowed up our senses" to the point that they did not feel the heat of the blazing sun over their heads or the weariness of their feet.[101] When A. Ben-Barak first arrived in the valley where he and his comrades were to found Nahalal, he surveyed it with his eyes, taking in the beautiful, promising, fertile, neglected landscape, with its abundant breezes, dangerous and threatening climate, pleasing appearance, and many green marshes. "It has all become so precious to me, as if I were glued to the place," he reflected. "How can I detach myself from it?"[102] And the Land returned the pioneers' gaze. David Gilad sat looking out over the Jordan River and wrote in his diary: "The mountains gaze at you from on high. They will follow you with their gaze even when you are borne to your grave through the grove and the vineyard, along the banks of the Jordan."[103]

The *halutzim* also "inhale" and "soak up" the Land of Israel via the "perfumed" and "intoxicating" air.[104] In one of his first letters to his father after his arrival, Ben-Gurion described his journey from Jaffa to Petah Tikva: "The air was wonderful, full of good aromas like the air of Eden, clear and transparent like pure glass."[105] Perfumed, pure, transparent air was a motif in Ben-Gurion's experience of the Land, at least during his first period there.[106] Yosef Fried described the air's effect on him as he rode his donkey to the winery at Rishon LeTzion. On his right he saw magnificent citrus groves, on his left gardens and vineyards. It was all beautiful, and the sun above blazed and warmed him. "You inhale clean, free air, and your mind broadens and exults," he wrote in a letter. "You feel yourself light, young, free, juvenile."[107] Even the aromas of hay and manure were pleasant.[108] Hearing, too, was a means of becoming one with the Land. The whistling wind and the sounds made by the herds "envelop" the *halutzim* and "penetrate" them.[109]

Rachel Bluwstein referred to the *halutzim*'s yearning for nature and the Land's open terrain as the "passion for space."[110] Above all, the pioneers perceived the Land of Israel as an open space that allowed this passion to be consummated. In this it was the opposite of the closed space of the exile. The Land had a wondrous beauty, one pioneer wrote in her diary, with huge open spaces. The mountains and boulders "call for liberty. I feel free, capable of anything."[111] The space hypnotized the *halutzim*.[112] In an early letter to his family, Haim Arlosoroff described the Land of Israel as magical. Everyone who breathed its air and lifted his gaze to its skies was compelled to return to it. He conjectured further of some mysterious force inherent in the Orient as a whole that amplified the Land's hypnotic effect. "A person must be here, to see everything concretely and to sense what the meaning of the Land of Israel is, and only then will he be drawn into the enchanted circle . . . ," he wrote in a letter. "If only you could be captured by it!"[113]

One expression of the pioneer longing for open spaces, especially during the Second Aliya, was that many *halutzim* left Judea for the Galilee. Immediately after arriving in Palestine, they felt hemmed in and as if degenerating in the Jewish farming villages of Judea. Meir Wilkansky claimed that he and his peers had not come to the Land of Israel to open stores or work as accountants. They wanted to stand on its soil and be absorbed into its open spaces, to breathe the clean air and feel the spirit of freedom so sorely lacking during centuries of exile.[114] The Galilee, with its wide open spaces, was the real Land of Israel, some believed.[115] Working alone in an orange grove, Yosef Weitz felt "a hunger of the soul and a longing for open spaces." He dreamed then of the Galilee and understood that he could no longer remain in Judea: "The horizon was too small for me. . . . I yearned for open spaces and resolved to ascend to the Galilee, where I would work in open fields and find what I lacked here, in Judea."[116] In the Galilee, the *halutzim* were establishing their own new kinds of settlements (as discussed in earlier chapters)—the collective, the national farm, the *kevutza*, the *ko'operatzia*, the *moshav ovdim*, the kibbutz. They gave the first *ko'operatzia* the name Merhavia (literally, "God's space").[117] "I want to take a full breath of air, seek the beauty before which I will stand stunned and happy," wrote Shimon Wolf of Beitania, "and I will feel within me my hot, stormy blood, bursting through my arteries and crying out to the endless reaches—to God's open spaces (*Merhavia*)."[118]

Only when he had become part of his natural surroundings did Tzvi Nadav understand how primeval man felt in sensing a life spirit in every element of nature. That was how he now experienced the land, water, and vegetation around him. Hundreds of times he picked up a handful of earth, crumbled it, and smelled it. He quickly came to treat the land as a living, breathing organism that absorbed the sun's rays and changed over time. Like primeval man, he felt a vital spirit everywhere in nature; each spring had its own spirit, as did each eucalyptus tree and raspberry bush. In the rustle of the eucalyptuses swaying in the breeze or the soft gurgle of a spring, he heard secrets welling up from the deep strata of rocks from which the water sprang.[119]

Hills and Mountains

Hills and especially mountains attracted the pioneers' gaze, impressing and enchanting them.[120] Every time Yaʿakov Zerubavel, a member of Poʿalei Tzion, went to the Galilee and saw Mount Tabor, he was overcome with a sense of joy, a feeling of celebration. "I crave to rush up to it," he wrote, "to scale it, to exult on its meadows and roar with delight. I sit up in my wagon and cry out: 'Greetings, my Tabor, how are you?' It seems to me that he knows me, rejoices that I have returned to the Galilee."[121] Tzvi Nadav liked to sit for hours facing the mountains of the Galilee and gaze on them like a lover looking into his beloved's eyes, without ever seeing them enough. No words could express all this beauty, he said, and certainly not its internal, hidden beauty, which penetrates the soul and makes a man feel happy, whole, part of the mountains that have attracted him so powerfully.[122] Pesya Abramson, who lived and worked in Petah Tikva, longed for the Galilee, in part because she wanted to "listen to the mountains."[123]

The *halutzim* ascended hilltops and mountain peaks to experience exceptional happiness, elation, even revelation.[124] But the most important effect of such vantage points was that they offered a panoramic view of the Land. In a letter to his father written from Sejera, Ben-Gurion described one of the wonderful hot, clear days on which the light imbues all, capturing the eye and focusing its gaze on great distances. Ben-Gurion ascended a high hill, and a sublime, majestic, infinite view met his eyes: "Here, at my feet, were intensely green fields, flowering valleys carpeted with young grain, and blue mountains—and before me, to the north (two days' journey away), juts a huge mountain, the elder of the Land of Israel's mountains, covered with sparkling, blinding snow—it's Mount Hermon, on which lies timeless snow! . . . And this land of wonders is the Land of Israel!"[125]

Spending time on mountaintops had other beneficial effects.[126] In a letter, A. D. Gordon wrote of the painful mental state he was in when he arrived in the Galilee. From his description, we can conjecture that he was referring to some sort of depression. But the Galilee, he said, welcomes visitors warmly and generously, calling on them to open their souls completely and promising to fill them. Gordon responded to this call. He went out to commune with nature and his spirits revived. As he wrote, "That pandemonium in my soul, the constant and the new, all that so burdened my heart, turned at once into vitality—vitality that swept through me and sought an outlet. . . . When a person's heart overflows its banks . . . it seems to him that the soul in his heart can embrace the entire world."[127] As Gordon stood on a high Galilean mountain, he felt that the territory of the Land became part of the territory of his soul:

> Here is nature—it is so alive, so it seems to me, in my soul, and I am unable to portray it. And perhaps the one is connected to the other.
>
> Now I sit, as I write these words, on the peak of a tall mountain, on a spur of rock. My eyes take in a huge distance, and my soul encompasses much, much more. Around me are mountains and hills, valleys and gullies . . . the green of grains and of grasses, the black of plowed fields, the dark brown of boulders and promontories . . . the view is great and wonderful. . . . And the skies above, and this soft silence, all of it, all of it—are they not all within my soul? . . . Are they not manifestations of the soul of our nation?[128]

The blurring of the boundaries between Gordon and his surroundings resulted from breaking through not just geographic borders but also the barriers around his internal mental space. Just as the geographical space manifested itself in the great flow within his soul, so his soul broke through and became part of the Land's geography:

> And if you please, my brother, take the most accurate record of the look of this place in nature—our dearly beloved Bible. And I will record in it a few points, and you will see that all I have to do is touch one of those points—and I have touched one of the finest and most hidden cords in your body. Here, to my right, at not such a great distance—Mount Tabor, handsome and prominent among mountains, a head higher than all its brothers, with a round face and a straight, soft outline, a sort of hero and "gem" of the family. . . . And all that is around me, far and near, all this great family of mountains and hills . . . all these, even if we do not know the names of them all, do they not speak within our souls as forgotten feelings or lost thoughts, great, great ones, that have trouble coming forth into the world?[129]

Mes'ha, view from Mount Tabor, 1922. Central Zionist Archives, Jerusalem

Heavenly Bodies

Having observed the Land of Israel from mountaintops through the eyes of the *halutzim*, we now lift our gaze to the sky. Unaccustomed to the intensity of the sun's light and heat, newly arrived pioneers mentioned it often. In itself, as Yosef Aharonovich maintained, the Zionist enterprise was in part a protest against the sunless, gloomy life of the exile.[130] The *halutzim* were moved again and again by the Israeli sunrise, its powerful light, its "grace," its "glow," its "magic." The sun, like many other elements of the landscape, "caressed" and "intoxicated" them.[131] S. Ben-Zvi wrote that the high, cavernous, clear sky made him feel he was seeing the sky for the first time.[132]

The *halutzim* also conceived of tilling the soil as liberating the earth and the plants that grew on it from the darkness of centuries of neglect. They saw themselves as the first since the exile to expose the soil to the sun's precious light.[133]

And they marveled at the sunsets.[134] In a letter to his father, David Ben-Gurion described one of the first sunsets he experienced in Petah Tikva:

> The sun sets—and a wondrous sight, glorious, appears in the sea's sky . . . a sight that only the skies of the Land of Israel display! The most vulgar man, lacking all poetic and esthetic sensibility, could not but stand, astounded and dumbfounded, at the

Lake Kinneret, 1920. Central Zionist Archives, Jerusalem

sight of the setting sun, especially on rainy days. An array of clouds, like a string of mountains and hills, enveloped in mist and blue, its edges burning with purple and rose fire. . . . The sun's disk, blood-red, descends and settles into the sea, which glitters with golden rays, and the sky turns, changing colors, and, magically, blue, white fire, intense red, purple fuse and alternate; the sun dives into the sea and the sky turns even more red and blazes and burns as if igniting the clouds with its fire, bursting into flames of splendor and blood. Little by little [the clouds] fade out, their radiance pales and lightens, the sky's fire goes out, and an intense shade of blue-green covers the sea's rim. Darkness spreads over the blue heavens and the stars burst forth one after the other.[135]

When the *halutzim* lifted their eyes to the night sky, they were moved and intoxicated by the light of the moon and the stars.[136] Here is a typical depiction of a moonrise, in this case at Lake Kinneret:

Like an unhurried, unhurried [*sic*] acrobatic act, the moon emerges and rises in the guise of a red ball of fire, the red of passion. . . . And as if wondering at herself, at her very appearance, she delays an instant, surveying with a guarded glance the free landscape, as if unsure over which side she should start to roam first. . . . And here burst out of her bonds a few golden filaments from her hungering heart, falling and intermingling on the clear, cool surface of the sea, intermingled and stretched as they quivered and trembled, breaking and disintegrating into slivers, into sparkles, and reassembling and stringing into pearl beads. And the beads, multiplying, interlock and interweave, by length and breadth, into a golden trail.[137]

In his diary, Tahki, a member of Kibbutz Bet of HaShomer HaTzaʿir, described the nights when the members of his commune gathered on the threshing-floor to sing "How Beautiful the Nights in Canaan": "Sometimes I consider the beautiful moon casting its light on us, on our camp, and I think about the important role of the moon in the life of our commune. What would we do without it?"[138] The nights at Kinneret were "like an ongoing *redemption*," the writer Rabbi Binyamin, a founder of the settlement, wrote. The moon and myriad shining stars cast gentleness and pleasantness over all and "lift the human spirit."[139] Shmuel Dayan wrote that only late in the evening, when his farmwork was over, was he able to look up to see the sky sown with stars, reminding him of the world and all it contained: "A dark blue sky, and always deep, full of secrets, for a moment I listen to the beating of my heart, and want to rebel against all the barriers and limits, all ideologies and principles—I want to live a life in which there is freedom from everything."[140]

On her first night in the Land, in Petah Tikva, Tehiya Lieberson felt an intense desire to encompass the entire firmament. A broad sky stretched above her, an end-of-month sky strewn with large, twinkling stars. "I had an urge . . . to pick one of them, a heavy golden star, and sink into it my young teeth, the healthy, strong teeth of a nineteen-year old," she wrote.[141] "I went out to the road," wrote Yosef Heller of Beitania, "I sat on a stone and it seemed to me that I had found my soul's love. The night was a real night of silver, the stars winked at me and laughed and I understood their speech: they viewed me as an old friend and called me over to them. And I felt that my soul was rising, being borne to the heights, approaching the sky and the stars, and what delight of love ran through all my limbs."[142]

The *halutzim* lying on their land and gazing up at the skies serve as a paradigm of the pioneer desire to become one with the landscape of the Land of Israel. Through both direct contact with the soil and this panoramic gaze, they arrive at the moment when they feel themselves, with their entire beings and in a most concrete way, an integral, organic part of the Land of Israel.[143] "I walked to one of the sand dunes," Ami Asaf wrote in a letter from Mikve Yisrael. "I lay down on the pleasant, delightful sand and watched the splendor of the sunset and listened to the stillness. Light and shadows filled my heart."[144] In a later letter, he wrote, "I lay beside my tent on a summer night, and a moon was imbued with a kind of complete joy, a sort of endless happiness . . . I wanted such moments to last forever, that they never end."[145]

It was at this precise point of the gaze directed skyward that A. D. Gordon located the human fusion with nature, the pure existential moment in which all barriers fall between individuals and their own being and between the human and the world. In his magnum opus, *Man and Nature*, he wrote: "And on that day you rose up and gazed around you, Son of Man, and you lifted up your eyes, and you saw the Land and the entire universe contained within it, and you saw heaven and all its hosts, with all the worlds within them unending and unknowable, and they all, all, are close to your soul, and they all welcome it. Then you will achieve eternity in the moment."[146]

Mythic Time

The same ecstatic, boundary-blurring that *halutzim* experienced in relation to their environment also occurred with respect to time. The Land's past was, to a large extent, a past that still lived. Alongside the present in which the *halutzim* lived and acted, the past, particularly the biblical past, continued as a presence. This past manifested itself not only as association or memory, but also as concrete experience.

As Zionist leader Yitzhak Tabenkin noted, the Bible connected the pioneers to the Land and enabled them to recognize and grasp it through the associations between places it mentioned and those the *halutzim* encountered as they lived, worked, and walked around the Land. The Bible, he wrote, was a kind of "birth certificate" that helped remove the barrier between the pioneers and their land and helped them feel they were in "the homeland."[147] When Ya'akov Meir arrived in the Galilee, he saw the same sight his forefathers had seen thousands of years before, when they had come to build the homeland of the Hebrew nation. The landscape, he wrote, was "like a Bible open before you."[148] During his trips around the Land, Yitzhak Ben-Zvi held his Bible open before him as if to breathe life into every artifact and ruin. "We thirstily inhaled the fragrance of the homeland," wrote his traveling companion Rachel Yanait, "the primal fragrance of our land."[149] When David Ben-Gurion came to Kinneret, he gazed at the Gilead Mountains on the east side of the Jordan River and saw in their gullies and folds the time "that had interred within them eternal secrets and primeval memories." Over them "hovers the spirit of the hero of old, Yiftach the Gileadite."[150]

Thus, the pioneers' biographical time was interwoven with biblical time.[151] When the *halutzim* saw places in the Land for the first time, they frequently identified them by ancient biblical events. Rachel Yanait came to Ekron, in the biblical land of the Philistines, and recalled the hero Samson who there took his revenge on these enemies of Israel. In these fields, he released foxes after tying torches to their tails. "An ancient scent envelops us," she wrote.[152] When Zalman Lifschitz of Havat Migdal sank with his horse into mud near Mount Tabor, he suddenly comprehended the victory won by the prophetess Deborah and her general Barak over Sisera and his iron chariots. Sisera and his men had been compelled to abandon their chariots, which sank into the mud.[153] The pioneer world of the first three decades of the twentieth century was filled with mythical biblical heroes—Moses, Saul and Jonathan, Ruth and Boaz, David and Jesse and others.[154] "We truly feel here on our land like their descendants," Yosef Fried wrote in his diary a short time after arriving in Palestine, "who speak their language and till their land and think their thoughts."[155]

Events and figures from other periods in Jewish history also populated the landscape. Around the mountains of Betar the *halutzim* "saw" Bar-Kochba and his fighters, so skilled and strong they could uproot a tree while mounted on a horse.[156] The sight of the mountains and caves around Tiberias sent the *halutzim* back to the time of Josephus Flavius.[157] Wherever they went, they sought to ascertain "which of our forefathers walked here, stepped here, chased here, and fled here?"

Often these "sightings" were more than a simple association or reference to the past. When Yitzhak Ben-Zvi went to the valley of Svinit and climbed the mountain, he envisioned the war between Saul and the Philistines: "To my right, eastward, Michmash (Mahamas) appeared before me, and an entire episode from the dawn of Israeli history came alive before my eyes: 'And Saul chose him three thousand men. . . . And Jonathan smote the garrison of the Philistines that was in Geba. . . .' Entire pages from our people's history awakened from their stagnation and came to life. . . . You are taken despite yourself [from the top of the mountains of Samaria] into ancient times."[158]

The *halutzim* also heard voices from the past. "We strode over the soil that preserves the tracks of Abraham's feet," Rachel Bluwstein wrote at Kinneret. "We have heard the echo of God's ancient words: 'I will magnify your name.' . . . Lake Kinneret is not just a view. It is not only a patch of nature—the fate of a nation has been tied up with its name. Our past gazes at us from within it with thousands of eyes, and with a thousand lips it speaks to the heart."[159] One *halutz* who longed to know the Land decided to abandon his work and travel through the Land: "I want to know my people, the people of Israel! This Land—every stone in it tells me about an ancient people that resided within it. I still hear at times sighs break out of the bosom of the earth, which is longing for its past owners. . . . And I am a scion of that nation, so why should I not know it?"[160]

When Michael Oved reached the Jordan River, he closed his eyes. Song poured over him, he testified. He felt as if he were walking through the crystal palace of the princess of the Jordan. Golden, shining dreams enveloped him. Suddenly, he himself became a hero. Emulating the Children of Israel crossing the Jordan into the Promised Land, he took twelve large stones and placed them at his feet: "[And then] the two and a half tribes that built themselves fortified cities on the eastern bank of the Jordan came to life. . . . Spectacular images flashed by me—and I within them. Here a band of young men, tall and sturdy, came by, children of the east of the Jordan, no, the progeny of Reuven, Gad, and the half-tribe of Menashe. They are the vanguard into the land of Benjamin, setting out to establish the unifying, complete sanctuary of the nation, to build an eternal building. O, entire passages from the Bible rise up alive and pass before my mind's eye."[161] As one immigrant claimed, when the *halutzim* returned to the Land, they indeed returned to the "womb" of history.[162]

S. Levitin, a member of Gdud HaAvodah (the Labor Corps), had a similar experience on his way to a job in the Jezreel Valley. A misty feeling, as he described it, had consumed him from the moment he began to plan his trip. On the actual journey, his senses were overwhelmed: "The impressions I absorb from the places around me also contribute to weaving that magical world, legend and imagination, a world of the past and the future, that has imbued my soul in recent days."[163] Crossing the Jezreel Valley, he sighted from afar the peak of Mount Tabor: "And while the ancient heroes of the Jewish people still have not vanished from your mind's eye, descending from the mountain and pursuing Sisera's army and his iron chariots, swept away by the primal river, the Kishon River—you see before you near Mount Tabor and HaMoreh Hill the tents of the People of Israel's future heroes, fighting a new defensive war and redeeming their land not with sword and shield, but rather with labor and the sweat of their brows."[164] Here Levitin comprehended that feeling he could not name: a sense of the amorphousness that preceded creation. "That formlessness," he wrote, "in which there is no order of time: past and future mingle and within them the transition period, like the raw material of creation, flawed, unordered, with myriad possibilities, alternately instigating concern and hope, important only in relation to the future, runs and blurs the present. A sense of sacred dread and of discernment of the glory and majesty of creation fill the soul, and fear the space of the heart: I am a witness to creation, an eyewitness to the creation of a nation's new life and society."[165]

Levitin was saying that the time of the Land of Israel was mythic time—time that does not pass. The writer Nathan Bistritzky of the Second Aliya distinguished between two kinds of time. One was chronological "clock" time, measured by a mechanical device, while the other was mythic "musical" time—the first was the time of human construction, the second of divine creation. The human place in mythic time, said Bistritzky, is not one of temporal points arranged in a relationship of before and after, but rather a locus where no difference exists among past, present, and future, the place where God calls himself "I am that I am." "[This is like] the drops in a wave on the sea," he explained, "in which each and every drop contains within it, in its story, the entire sea, meaning the story of its existence."[166] The Jews' relationship with the Land of Israel is mythic, unconcerned with the chronological sequence of events, and is experienced simultaneously in past and present. Bistritzky himself had immigrated in 1913, but the Land had been part of him from his childhood. The Land of Israel was for him "a kind of treasure buried deep within my person, a treasure buried before I was born."[167] After coming to Palestine he had only to locate evidence of this mythic link and to prove it.

Zalman Rubashov (later Shazar) experienced mythical time at the Western Wall. Academic historians, he wrote, are apt to misunderstand the consciousness of a nation when they divide its history into separate periods. Their method treats each period as an independent entity, disconnected from the organic body of the nation, which flits between life and death according to its own internal rhythm. This dynamic was even more true of the Jewish people, who had been dispersed over the world in tiny fragments. Facing the Western Wall, however, one could not fail to sense the mythic time of the "secret of eternity that lies in our past." Tears welled up in Rubashov's eyes out of the Jewish history of suffering. These tears are not a response to the Wall itself but rather the "tears of a loving son in the arms of a compassionate mother."[168] Every Jew experiences such eternal time at the Western Wall, Rubashov wrote, as if he lay on his mother's bosom: "And when your feet approach the Western Wall you sense and feel how your soul is woven into the eternal fabric, thousands of years old, how you have touched those threads that run through a long and complex sequence of many lost eras, far in the mists of the past."[169]

Even away from the Western Wall, the *halutzim* felt this mythic time beating within themselves. Yedidya Shoham of HaShomer HaTzaʿir wrote in a letter that when he began to ponder his Jewish identity, he felt a profound link between him and the Jewish people. It was the link to a common idea, three thousand years old, that came into being with Moses, the prophets, Jesus, and the period of exile. This idea was forged and tempered into a great chain that he and his comrades who immigrated to the Land of Israel would join. Thus, the pioneers' actions took place not at a specific moment of chronological time, but rather within eternity: "Yes, our lives—they have a purpose when we join, attach ourselves to this chain, become a link in this great, eternal chain. In this way we create something eternal. If our lives remain outside the chain, they will go by without leaving a trace."[170]

Ben-Zion Israeli of Sejera also felt that time did not progress on a chronological axis, but rather seemed to move in cycles. Each moment in the Land of Israel, he wrote in a letter, was nothing but an expression of an eternal, ongoing present: "As always—my life flows, whether as breaking waves or a soft burble. And my deeds and work each day are testimony. And from the year—a grain of infinite time—I learn: the brilliance of the summer and the life of spring are one. The autumn does not delight me and the clouds of winter do not warm me, [time's] flow is eternal and full of majesty!"[171] A. D. Gordon formulated the concept of mythic time in the clearest possible way when he claimed that in "real life" there is no room for spatial or chronological distinctions. Real life is complete life that contains no separations: "[In life] there is no mechanical division of labor, in life there is no before and after, in life there is no turning back."[172]

The blood of the *halutzim*, central to blurring the boundaries between them and the Land, also brought them into mythic time. The blood flowing in their veins was the same blood that had flowed in the veins of their forefathers. We can paraphrase Gordon by saying that blood, too, had neither before nor after. In one of their communal talks, the members of Beitania grieved over the tears shed in the past and still being shed in the world, tears dissolved in a greater sea of tears. They also lamented the enormous amount of blood that had been shed and lost in a sea of blood. Billions of people, it seemed, left nothing after them. Yisachar Reiss, a member of the commune, commented that life would be meaningless if it were not for the connections maintained between the generations, the "golden chain" that linked fathers and sons, elders and their grandchildren: "We are a link in this chain, and in our veins flows the blood of thousands of years . . . and so to the end of all generations."[173] "The blood of the Maccabees still flows in our veins," declared the writer Moshe Smilansky after the battle of Tel Hai.[174]

Rachel, Mother of Mothers,
who shepherded Laban's sheep—
it is her blood that flows in my blood,
her voice that sings in me.[175]
—Rachel, "Rachel," 1926

4 Articulating the Physical Territory of the Land

On earlier pages, I noted that the first of two simultaneous aspects of pioneer desire is a kind of ecstatic-symbiosis. The second aspect is that which creates boundaries. This impetus constituted the Land of Israel by delineating its territory.

As we saw, Deleuze and Guattari define desire as an anarchic flow that knows no boundaries. But this flow also results in the creation of boundaries. We noted, for example, that the flow of sweat blurred the boundaries between the *halutz* and the Land. The *halutzim* wet the Land and thus became part of it. But by watering the soil with their sweat they transformed it from undifferentiated earth into cultivated soil, and from unowned soil into Jewish soil. Their act marked a boundary between Jewish soil and Arab earth. Deleuze and Guattari make little distinction between "territory" and "body." Territory always has bodily form, and a body is always territorial; territory might better be called a "geo-body."[1] Thus, the boundary-blurring and boundary-creating effects of desire act not only on physical space—here, the Land—but also on the body of the individual *halutz* (see chapter 5) and on pioneer language (see chapter 6).

As Deleuze and Guattari describe the process, the flow of desire through the (undifferentiated) "body-without-organs" actually articulates the body's organs. The body-without-organs is therefore a body that has not yet undergone socialization. It is, in fact, a *no-body*. Because it lacks organs, it does not exist. And it has no organs because it lacks any defining characteristic that would make it a separate, distinct entity and enable differentiated organs to develop. Deleuze and Guattari use the terms "deterritorialization" for the boundary-blurring impetus and "reterritorialization" for the boundary-creating impetus. Thus, the ecstatic-symbiotic aspect of pioneer desire can be described as deterritorialization, and pioneer desire's boundary-creating impetus, which intersects with the ecstatic-symbiotic experience and establishes boundaries, as reterritorialization. As opposed to boundary-blurring, boundary-creating channels and disciplines the flow of desire, in effect fashioning the organs in the body-without-organs.

Nahalal, 1940. Central Zionist Archives, Jerusalem

The mechanism of pioneer desire manifests itself visually in the ground plan of Nahalal, the first *moshav ovdim* (semicooperative farming village), established in 1921. A bird's-eye view of the community shows desire scattering anarchically from the center in all directions, like a drop of water when it falls on a solid surface. This desire, in its anarchic flow, leaves in its wake a village, roads, and cultivated land.

This chapter focuses on the boundary-creating impetus in the physical territory of the Land of Israel.[2] Before addressing the regeneration of the physical territory of the Land, we must take a look at the body-without-organs, the nonexistent space of the exile.

The Space of the Exile

The space of the exile is a space-without-organs, the space where the "eternal," "wandering," *luftmensch*, or airhead, Jew exists. It is a utopian space in the original meaning of the word—a nonexistent place (*ou-topos*) that does not allow the Jew "to be" within it. Just before his aliya to the Land of Israel, Tzvi Nadav described the angst that overcame him in the endless space of the exile. On the eve of the Pesach holiday, in Shavli, Lithuania, Nadav went out into "a street of the Jewish city": "I feel that the earth is being pulled out from under my feet and that I am falling into an abyss, as in a nightmare. . . . I am terrified by the thought of the 'infinite.' And this was not a *thought*, but rather a real *intuition*. . . . I sensed that a chill, an absolute, infinite chill, a cosmic chill, was penetrating my heart. I felt abandoned, alone, isolated, in this cosmos."[3]

The exile is a space of endless, purposeless movement. Yitzhak Ben-Zvi wrote that an existential state of migration and itinerancy sets the Jewish people apart from the existential condition of other nations, which live on and feel connected to their own soil. History teaches that many nations have wandered and continued to wander. But, in general, Ben-Zvi maintained, all the members of such nations pass their lives in the land where their people have settled. This is not the case with the Jews. Migration is not a lone or rare event in the Jewish people's life; it is their permanent state. Since they were exiled from their land, Jews have passed their lives in different countries, each of which has been only a way station in their wandering.[4]

Exile is a space that threatens Jewish existence. It is characterized, for example, by physical harm in the form of pogroms that cause "the earth to be pulled out from under the Jewish people's feet."[5] To the *halutzim*, the exile was a space without stable ground on which to stand, where Jews were at risk of falling into the cracks. Oceanic metaphors also prevailed. "Our life in the exile is a stormy sea," wrote one *halutz*, "a thundering, unending torrent of clashing and falling waves, of waves assaulting and exploding on boulders and again assaulting, over and over again."[6] David Ben-Gurion claimed that the Jews were mummified, sunk up to their necks in "the swamps of the exile."[7] "I feel myself in exile as if I were sinking in a mire," confessed Eliezer Yaffe. "I must make one last move: to live or to die but not to suffocate."[8] Yehuda Gothelf of HaShomer HaTzaʿir said the Jew in the exile is like a man on the edge of a yawning abyss that seeks to swallow up its victims. The exile is the primordial chaos. "Shards of tablets, shreds of hearts, crumbs scattering and dividing, sinking in the depths, choking from loneliness and sinking into the abyss," he wrote.[9] The assimilation that occurred in the exile was also like a menacing tidal wave. If, in earlier times, assimilation had been a "creek" whose waters swept up only a few, now it was "a swift river, carrying off all it encounters on its path."[10]

The exile space was also inundated with currents and surges of blood; it was "engorged" with Jewish blood. The Jews of the exile were submerged in "rivers of blood," "blood baths," and "blood deluges."[11] When gentile nations fought against one another, both victors and losers assuaged their anger by drawing Jewish blood. In the entire contemptible exile, the Jew had no place he could walk securely.[12] It was terribly sad and shocking to see people drowning in their own spilt blood, lamented Eliezer Yaffe in contemplating the exilic life of these "non-people with no-land."[13]

Yosef Aharonovich feared the exile and exilic existence and hated the peoples of Europe, principally because of the huge amounts of Jewish blood they had spilled, the blood of millions of Jewish victims of all eras and in all lands. The Jews, and the individual Jew, were, as a result, a "non-people and no-body."[14] During World War I, David Ben-Gurion called attention to a tidal wave of blood that threatened to drown Jewish existence everywhere. More than any other catastrophe, he maintained, this war had amplified the Jewish problem and cast it in the starkest, bitterest, most tragic light. The Zionist solution was meant to halt this threatening surge. "This huge, piercing, plummeting disaster of a depleted, disconnected, helpless nation, without a hold on life, without a place of its own on earth, without any resting point," Ben-Gurion wrote, "is now revealed in all its awful nakedness. . . . Our catastrophe is that we are being destroyed, hemorrhaging, for no reason, without purpose, without intention."[15] Each day, Berl Katznelson argued, the world wrote the history of the Jews with their blood.[16] The exile's tide of foreign blood, wrote another *halutz*, "breaks through into our hearts and poisons our blood."[17]

A 1904 public appeal written by a group of young Jews living in Palestine combined several such images to describe exilic Jewish existence as lacking in everything of value. The exile was the lack of a land and of a language. It killed national sentiments. The Jews of the exile stood with their feet "in the mouth of a volcano, a burning abyss" that threatened to swallow them up. The Jews were descending into this chasm and drowning in it.[18] Ben-Gurion wrote his father that the exile was as dark as a graveyard.[19] Berl Katznelson called it a desert.[20] Mordechai Shenhavi of HaShomer HaTzaʿir felt in the exile as if he were "hanging in the air between sky and earth."[21] The exile was "hell."[22]

Exile from the Land of Israel threw the Jew not only outside space but also outside time and history. Tzvi Shatz wrote that the Jews in the Land of Israel were awakening as from a bad dream, after thousands of years in the "mire of the exile." They now strode, once again, on the hills and across the broad horizons of their land. At the same time, Shatz believed that even this secure place that granted them soil under their feet was no more than a single moment in their progress through the raging sea of Jewish history. The soil of the Land, Shatz wrote, was a respite between one storm and the next. No one could guarantee that the Jews would not again descend into exile and destitution: "Here rise and fall the waves of war and revolution, rise and fall the breaking waves, bloom and wilt wondrous moments of individual life, raising the soul to divine purity and, in an instant, sending it down to the nethermost hell."[23]

The fact that Jewish history was drenched in Jewish blood proved, said Yitzhak Elazari-Volcani, that with regard to time and Jewish history, "there is no chronological sequence in the chronicles of our blood."[24] In his view, the year 1648 (most likely referring to riots in Poland led by Bohdan Khmelnytsky) could be interchanged with the date for the anti-Jewish riots of 1919, and the "bloody chapters" of modern Jewish history recorded by the historian Heinrich Graetz could be read as an account of ancient times. No historian would be able to discern that such an account would be mixing up incidents and dates. It would only be necessary to replace words like "machine gun" with "sword" and "spear."[25] The exile arrested the "wheels of history," as Eliezer Riger of HaShomer HaTzaʿir put it.[26]

Heading into exile, then, the Jewish nation was transformed from an entity positioned in concrete place and time into an "eternal people," an amorphous entity that exists in every space and every time, outside geography and outside history.[27] Zionism "reterritorialized" the Jews, once again making them "the people of the Land" (the Hebrew term, *Am HaAretz*, also connotes "simple people," workaday people as opposed to intellectuals). Zionism is the "territorial turn" in Jewish history that returned the Jew to space (the Land of Israel) and time (history).[28]

> The space of the homeland restored to me the space of the world![29]
> —David Shimonovitz, *Son of My Land: From the Notebook of a Wanderer*, 1909–1919

The Space of the Homeland

The Land of Israel is the "shore that calls over the stormy sea," as Haim Arlosoroff put it.[30] Berl Katznelson saw the Land as his "final shore."[31] In a historical irony, the name "territorialism" was given to the idea of resolving the Jewish problem by evacuating all the Jews to a place other than the Land of Israel (such as Uganda).[32] Yitzhak Ben-Zvi argued in this context that only the "Zionism of Zion" was worthy of being called territorialism. Zionism in the Land of Israel was *the* territorialism; any other "territorialism" was abstract and distant from reality. The Zionist aspiration was simply to establish Jewish identity on a territorial basis in the only land where such territorial existence had ever been realized.[33] Ben-Zvi translated the concept of territorialism into Hebrew as "*hitʾartzut*," the literal translation of which might be "becoming the land." To be a territorialist was thus to become part of the Land.[34] While the Zionists defined themselves territorially by the term "Zion," after World War I Jewish settlers in Palestine began calling themselves "Eretz Israelis" (*Eretz-Yisraelim*) rather than "Jews."[35] Returning to the Land after years of exile, they became part of it.

A land-without-organs: Judean Desert, 1918. Central Zionist Archives, Jerusalem

Where the exilic-space-without-organs was quicksand, currents and tidal waves of blood, an abyss yawning amid an earthquake and threatening to swallow up the Jews, the Land of Israel was stable and safe, the place where the *halutzim* found earth under their feet. Yet at the same time, the Land was a body-without-organs that had to be articulated by pioneer desire, which would enable its organs to appear.

The *halutzim* saw the Land as a tabula rasa. It was "hollow," "ruined," "bare," "dead," "abandoned," "naked," "stripped," "downfallen," "wild," "withered," "bald," "empty," "desolate," "virgin."[36] Its climate and geographical conditions made it a "land of desert and desolation."[37] The Land was also a body-without-organs because it was for them a "new world," unfamiliar, menacing, terra incognita.[38] To them, the Land of Israel was a "land without a people" that awaited, yearned for, desired the "people without a land."[39]

The Land's intimidating human environment, with its threats of constant, concrete danger, was another reason that the *halutzim* perceived it as a continuation of the exilic-space-without-organs.[40] HaShomer member Yitzhak Hoz described an attack on Merhavia in May–June 1914, instigated by the killing of the nephew of a local Arab sheikh: "The mob streamed up the hill with gunfire and shrieks. . . . The assailants were already very close . . . our nerves were taut. One thought pursued another with lightning speed, the bullets of the assailants whistled over our heads, and our eyes pressed into the darkness and made out a swaying black mass spitting fire and charging toward us."[41]

Other aspects of the exile also persisted in the Land of Israel, leading the pioneer community to see itself as "sinking in its swamp, degenerating further and further."[42] To the *halutzim*, Jaffa, the first city encountered by most *halutzim* when they arrived; the old *moshavot*, with their dependence on Arab labor; and the old Jewish community supported by charity from abroad all represented the extension of exilic space into the Land.[43] Some *halutzim* felt that even now, in the Land, they were still "always hanging in the air."[44] They continued to feel "foreign" and "alien" in their own land.[45] Many *halutzim* continued to wander, in this case around the Land. Arab labor was a "swamp" or "sea" threatening to drown them.[46] A member of Kibbutz Kiryat Anavim wrote that daily life was nothing "but a simple swamp, a pool of water collected from a flowing river in some deserted corner. A pool without depth, covered in scum, with papyrus reeds growing around it. Quiet and silence always prevail there."[47]

The *halutzim* also perceived the substantial emigration from Palestine (especially in the Second Aliya) of those for whom the difficulties proved too great as part of exilic existence. It was, Rachel Yanait lamented, as if heaven had decreed that the question of migration would always remain—even in the Land of Israel, "in the place in which we want to break free of exilic life."[48]

These preoccupations explain why the *halutzim* did not and could not perceive themselves as conquering the Land in the common sense of economic, colonial, violent conquest. A Land-without-organs could not be conquered because nothing yet existed to conquer. "The *halutz* came to settle a desolate land," wrote Labor Battalion member Y. Reznichenko. "Everything is being done from the beginning, there is not yet anything to destroy and there is no one to fight against."[49]

They did describe themselves as conquerors, but in a very different sense. They saw all their acts as "construction," "creation," and "redemption."[50] This explained the meaning of terms like "conquest of the soil," "conquest of labor," "conquest of defense," and "conquest of the self." David Ben-Gurion asserted that a people does not receive a land. A people conquers a land. But to him conquest was an act of creation. "We will conquer the Land," he wrote, "by our *building* of it."[51] In contrast with the violent military or economic conquest that typified the history of other lands in other circumstances, Yosef Aharonovich described the conquest of the Land of Israel as "a truly moral conquest," as a result of which human beings lived and created cultural values. These values, he maintained, could be created only by the farmer with his plow and hoe, the smith and his anvil, the teacher and his school. In other words, the values were produced by those millions of people who sowed with tears and sweat the seeds of their cultural life.[52] The Land of Israel could be conquered again and forever, Franz Oppenheimer wrote, "not [with] the sword, but [with] the plough and the hoe!"[53]

Pioneer conquest in all its forms was the classic expression of the boundary-creating aspect of pioneer desire for the Land. Conquest meant the redemption of the body-of-the-Land-without-organs through creating its organs. In their desire for the Land the *halutzim* created the object of that desire.

With this notion of conquest in mind, we can understand the pioneer declaration: "We will be the first!"[54] The *halutzim* desired primacy. When Rabbi Binyamin reached Kinneret, he was disappointed to find that his comrades had preceded him by ten days. He was jealous "since on arriving I found everything 'ready and waiting' for me . . . but they found nothing when they arrived, no-thing in the strongest sense of the word."[55] Mordechai Hadash, who was planning to go to Kinneret, felt that he was fulfilling the dream of creating a new settlement, because "there was a kind of craving, an almost physical desire, for primal life, for the hard beginning, the feeling of conquest, the plow piercing virgin soil."[56] The novelist Yehuda Ya'ari expressed regret that "only once in his life can a person arrive in the Land of Israel for the first time."[57]

The boundary-articulating impetus also created a map of the Land. A new settler at Kfar Uria described the view from the roof of a house: "To the west, the buildings of Hulda can be seen in the distance. To the east—the ridges of Judea; and there, behind those hills, on the Jerusalem side, Har Tuv is concealed. But more than this, one's eyes are drawn northward, to another vanishing point that will fill in the third apex of the new triangle—to *Tel Gezer*."[58] His gaze created a Zionist geography.

Still another effect of pioneer desire was to constitute the Land of Israel as a place to which one "ascends" (the literal meaning of aliya) and from which one "descends" (*yerida*, denoting emigration from the Land). These terms did not come into use until after World War I, in the period between the Second and Third Aliyot. Before then, Jews did not "ascend" to the Land—they "migrated" or "immigrated." People who emigrated from the Land did not "descend"—they simply "left" or "departed." The term "Second Aliya" was not applied to that wave of immigration until the beginning of the Third Aliya. Those who participated in the Second Aliya identified themselves as belonging to the "youth movement" or to the "workers' [wave of] immigration."

The value judgments inherent in the terms aliya and *yerida* hardly need explication, but their topographic implication should be stressed. The Land of Israel is located at a higher position than the rest of the world. After World War I, the relatively indifferent attitude to the "leavers" and "departers" vanished. Now such individuals were called "absconders," "deserters," "refugees," "irresolute weaklings," "slackers," "gypsies," "eternal wanderers," and other epithets. "Descent" from the Land of Israel became an act of "irresponsibility," "disobedience," "weakness," "frailty," "moral failure," "a stab in the heart" of the settlement and political enterprise.[59] In 1908, Yitzhak Ben-Zvi and his wife, Rachel, spoke with an Arab carpenter who told them he wanted to immigrate to America. "Their heart is for immigration," Rachel later wrote in her memoirs, "*our* heart is for aliya."[60]

Pioneer desire thus transformed an Arab Land-without-organs into the Jewish Land of Israel. Some three years after the Arab village of Fula became the Hebrew Merhavia, one settler wrote: "Whoever still remembers the Arab huts . . . would not recognize Merhavia now. The Arab village has been almost completely eliminated; on the beautiful hill next to it now rise the buildings of the cooperative moshav . . . the soil that the hand of culture had not yet touched has also shed its old appearance and taken on a new one, and is now cultivated in the best possible way."[61]

Present Absentees

How did the local population, and the Arabs specifically, fit into the pioneers' Land-without-organs? How can an empty Land have an existing population?

I admit that neither the question "Where is the local population located in pioneer desire for the Land of Israel?" nor the answer—"Nowhere!"—is legitimate in the framework I have set forth for this discussion. This value-laden question assumes that pioneer desire *ought* to have contained a certain element or, to put it another way, should have been something that it was not. Making any accusatory or apologetic assumption about pioneer desire takes us back to precisely those approaches that I seek to avoid. Nevertheless, I pose the question because I believe that the disregard for the local population—Arab, for the most part—that characterized pioneer desire for the Land of Israel is too important morally to ignore.

True love, the historian Amos Elon has written, is always blind,[62] and the pioneers' desire for the Land of Israel indeed blinded them. They "were seen but did not see," to use an expression coined (in a different context) by Noah Naftulsky of Kinneret.[63] For them, in their state of boundary-blurring symbiosis with the Land, there could be no place for a foreign element. The totality of this experience left no living space for the Other, neither in consciousness nor in territory. Consequently, pioneer desire could not recognize any alternative desire for the Land.

When the *halutzim* settled on the soil and desired to penetrate it, when the pioneer eye sated itself on its landscapes, when the *halutzim* constituted the connection between themselves and their land with currents of blood, no room remained for the Other. When Others appeared, they were generally experienced as an interference, literally an ecological hazard. More than once, the *halutzim* described attacks by the local population, usually Arab, on Hebrew settlements in the same breath as public health dangers like malaria.[64]

Likewise, the *halutzim* often described local inhabitants as blots on the environment. One *halutz* noted his regret that Arab workers were still employed in the old *moshavot*. To his chagrin, he found Arab laborers even at the new farms, which were supposed to be built purely by Jewish labor. Immediately after remarking on these phenomena, he described the beauty of the new farm at Ramat Delaika, which sat on a hilltop overlooking a large area that encompassed Sejera, Bayyit Gan, Yavniel, Menahemiyya, Um Juni, and Kinneret. "The cultivated fields of the Jews astound the eye," he reflected.[65] The natural landscape of the Land of Israel, he claimed further, had a unique Jewish identity. As such, only Hebrew labor could maintain and act within it. The local Arabs were a foreign element in this Jewish ecology: "Healthy air, wide and rich Jewish nature. Will *Jewish building* also happen here?"[66]

"And you gaze on the black tents pitched in this wasteland, and encounter the crafty gaze of the black Bedouin . . . and a sense of sadness overcomes you," wrote another *halutz*. He stressed the desolation of the place: "You see at this moment the great valley mourning the sparkle of splendor and the majesty of glory that has been denied it for generations. And you have a great desire to unite with these hills and to pour their prayer down into the heart of the turbulent Jordan, to intensify its anger at the lost man [Jew] whose steps were late in coming, who has not yet arrived to ascertain its huge spirit and to bestow something of its splendor on this wasteland."[67]

Michael Oved wrote that his *kevutza* had settled in "Arab buildings" at the foot of Mount Carmel, across from the Zichron Yaʿakov train station. On the right was a vast citrus orchard, grape arbors, and eucalyptus groves. Ahead and to the left were well-tended, impressive fields. On the horizon was the sea, sparkling blue under the sun and blending with the blue sky into a single, infinite expanse. On moonlit nights, he wrote, when you climb up a pile of moist, fragrant hay to rest a bit from the heat of the day, there is no greater pleasure than listening to the murmur of the waves blending with the whisper of the fields of grain. It was a wonderful harmony, magical music. "And it happens," he continued, "that [the baying of] jackals suddenly rips through the air, and this wonderful music halts for a moment. Or an Arab plods by on his ass, and suddenly he warbles and pours out his heart in melancholy fragments. . . . But then he, too, passes and the music resumes as it was before."[68]

Many other *halutzim* had reactions similar to those of Oved. Generally they thought, meditated, and envisioned one Land, and upon arriving at one of its ports—usually Jaffa—they encountered a different Land, typified by the Arab porters of Jaffa who carried them to the shore.[69] Shlomo Kinnarti arrived in Jaffa on August 10, 1920, with twenty-seven companions from Kevutzat Vilna, all scions of Zionist youth movements and members of HeHalutz. When their feet touched the paving stones of Jaffa, they raised the blue-and-white HeHalutz flag and sang the Zionist anthem, "HaTikva." Kinnarti's eyes shone with tears of joy. "We searched out a tract of land [whose potential] we could actualize and unshackle," he wrote, "but all around us were only filthy cobblestones, discarded watermelon rinds, and masses of Arab dock laborers and officials."[70]

Obviously the *halutzim* were aware of the local Arab population. Despite the newcomers' conception of the Land of Israel as empty, the native population was present in their world—but at the same time, absent. Indeed, from the pioneer perspective, the emptiness of the Land, its status as a Land-without-organs, was magnified by the Arab presence within it. In the *halutzim*'s eyes, the local Arabs not only had failed to build, create, and redeem the Land but were incapable of doing so—because they lacked desire. Thus the Arabs had not conquered the Land of Israel and could not conquer it in the pioneer sense of the word, largely owing to character traits such as laziness and primitiveness, expressed in a lack of technological capability.[71] This was the "Arab labor" so maligned by the Jews. "They [the Arabs] never cleared their fields of stones and never improved them, never plowed with expensive, heavy European plows. . . ," wrote Melech Zagorodsky, an agronomist who served as an envoy and consultant for the Land of Israel Office (the Zionist movement's executive arm in Palestine). "In truth, he actually does not plow; instead he scratches or scrapes the surface of his soil with his plowshare."[72]

David Ben-Gurion was well aware that the great majority of the Land's population was Arab. Yet this fact, as far as he was concerned, was irrelevant to the kind of relationship different populations had with the Land. "*The Land of Israel*," he wrote in April 1915, "*is now a desolate and half-ruined land—and the small Arab element is incapable of reviving it and rebuilding its ruins*."[73] Ben-Gurion derived from this narrative the moral and human basis for the Jewish Yishuv's aspirations and labor in the Land of Israel. The Jews, after all, had proven and continued to prove with their own hands that they were competent to fill the noble role of "original Jewish national creation," which was at the same time a "*human cultural enterprise of great value*, a civilizing enterprise."[74] The Jews brought sophisticated work tools and practices into the Land, enriched it with new farming settlements, improved the climate and made it healthier, improved sanitary conditions in its cities, created advanced farms, built exemplary urban neighborhoods, paved roads, established

An Arab plowing the field. Unidentified location, 1913. Central Zionist Archives, Jerusalem

modern educational institutions, enhanced the Land's value and increased its income, raised wages, and crafted new forms of social life.[75]

For these reasons the presence of a local population consisting principally of Arabs only amplified the *halutzim*'s conception of the Land of Israel as a Land-without-organs. The Arab presence even amounted to a necessary condition for conceiving of the Land in this way: it was a Land-without-organs because the Arab population lacked all desire to create organs. The local Arabs lived an arbitrary, purposeless existence. Their very presence on the Land served only to make their "absence" more palpable,[76] and actually intensified pioneer desire.

Recall that the pioneers experienced the Land of Israel as female, a virgin whose virginity the pioneers pierced, a lover whom they sought to marry, the Mother Earth to whose womb they sought to return. Their desire did not allow them to see that the Land had other lovers, husbands, and sons who desired it no less than they did.

As a virgin, the Land *expected* to be penetrated; the Arabs were impotent. As a bride, the Land demanded love; the Arabs did not love it, even neglected it. As Mother Earth, the Land demanded to be respected and cared for; the Arabs were not attuned to its requirements. The *halutzim*'s desire acted on the body-without-organs because the Arab who made a pretense of penetrating, loving, respecting,

As the sun emerged from behind the mountains we pierced the soil with our plowshares. . . . Yes, there is something great about cutting through the ground with a plow! But there is something seventy-seven times greater about cutting through virgin land that no plow had touched for thousands of years! We felt that we were gathering in this soil's ancient shame, that we were betrothing with this plow the fields of the valley. . . .

The shepherds gathered on the mountains around us and gazed in wonder and astonishment and admiration, clapped their hands and cheered us from above: "*Sah bedanqum!*" ("Health to your bodies!"). They watched and jeered us as we drained the swamp. They did not believe that it was possible to remove the divine curse imposed on it from days beyond their memory.[77]

—Yehuda Ya'ari, *As a Glowing Light*, 1937

and caring for it was only pretending. In the pioneers' view, their desire would eventually result in Arab revival in the Land of Israel. According to Ben-Gurion, Zionism's goals were in no way opposed to Arab goals. Jewish settlement in the Land of Israel was not aimed at destroying the Arab community. On the contrary, only Zionist action could "save [the Arab community] from its economic straits, raise it up from its social degradation, and extricate it from its bodily and moral degeneration. *Our revival in the Land of Israel will be accomplished through the revival of the Land of Israel—in other words, the revival of the Arabs who dwell in it.*"[78] Some *halutzim* believed that the Arab fellahs were the descendants of the ancient Hebrews who had remained in the Land after the exile, afterward converting to Islam.[79] Pioneer desire for the Land of Israel thus even "knew how" to Judaize the non-Jews.

"A Hidden Question": *Arab Desire for the Land*

As shown by the pioneers' relationship to existing Arab residents, their desire for the Land of Israel blinded them to other desires for it. As chapter 2 noted, the pioneers' desire for the Land was identical to the Land's desire for them. Thus, no "space" remained for other desires. Not surprisingly, the few Jewish settlers who did discern other non-Jewish and mostly Arab desires for the Land were not *halutzim*.

"Among the difficult questions linked to the idea of the rebirth of our people on its soil, there is one question as weighty as all the others together: *the question of our treatment of the Arabs*. The reestablishment of our national hope depends on the correct answer to this question, which has not been *forgotten*, but has rather been entirely *hidden* from the Zionists, and there is virtually no reference to it, in its true form, in our movement's literature."[80] This is how the educator Yitzhak Epstein (1863–1943) began his article "A Hidden Question," first presented as a lecture to the Seventh Zionist Congress, convened in Basel in 1905.[81] As a member of the First Aliya, Epstein could perhaps see the "Arab question" more clearly than those of subsequent immigration waves. His was one of the first Zionist voices to note the collision between the two desires for the Land of Israel. Epstein pointed out that more than half a million Arabs lived in the Land of Israel, as opposed to about 80,000 Jews. The Jews had indeed bought tracts in the Land completely legally. Yet, Epstein wondered, what were the fellahs who tilled this soil supposed to do after their fields passed into Hebrew hands? The fellah was a settled inhabitant, and in some cases his forefathers had been tenants on the same land. Even when the fellahs received monetary compensation for leaving their land, they had nevertheless been evicted. They lost their source of sustenance and had nowhere else to go. Even if the Jewish colony provided the fellah with work, he could not depend on this work in the long term. He could never see his employment as a wage laborer as a fair exchange for the land taken from him. He could never accept these new circumstances, in which strangers employed him on his own land.

Epstein maintained that a conflict between the Arabs and the new Jewish settlers was inescapable. While no Arab movement yet existed in the national and political sense, such a movement was not needed because the Arab nation, unlike the Jewish nation, was strong and numerous. It did not need to be reborn because it had never stopped living. Moreover, the Arabs were stronger and healthier than all the European nations. Epstein called on the Zionist settlers not to take Arab rights lightly: "We must not provoke a sleeping lion! We must not trust the ashes that cover the coals; a single spark will escape and there will be a conflagration that cannot be quenched."[82]

Beyond diagnosing the socioeconomic injustice inflicted and apt to be inflicted on the Arab fellahs, Epstein noted the Arabs' physical presence on the soil of the Land of Israel and stressed their profound connection to that soil. The Arab did not only subsist on the land—he clung to it. "In our beloved Land there is an entire nation," Epstein wrote, "that has held fast to it for hundreds of years and has no intention of leaving it."[83] This hold on the Land was a direct product of that nation's love for it. "While we feel love in all its potency for the Land of our Fathers," continued Epstein, "we forget that the people living in it now has a feeling heart and a loving soul. The Arab, like all human beings, is tied by strong cords to his homeland. And the lower the level of a man's development and the more narrow his outlook, the stronger will be the connection that links him to his land and territory and the harder it will be for him to part from his village and his field."[84]

The Arab fellah is tied to his soil by virtue of the labor he and his forebears have invested in it. He is also tied to it by the graves of his ancestors. He kisses its stones and its earth. Arab desire for the Land is also channeled through bodily fluids. "If there are any farmers who water their fields with their perspiration and their vital fluids," Epstein wrote, "they are the Arabs."[85]

Of course Epstein also acknowledged the Jewish people's desire for the Land of Israel and their right to "renew their blood" on its soil.[86] They had the right to reconquer, through their knowledge and sweat, what their forefathers had conquered by the sword and spear, and to redeem the Land from "drought, desolation, and neglect."[87] But he believed that this conquest should be undertaken intelligently. The Jews should not buy land on which Arab fellahs lived, even if the owners offered it for sale. Only take "*what others have not secured, hold fast to all places that others have not taken hold of, find in it everything that others have not found,*"[88] he asserted. In any case, the Zionists should check carefully to see who lived on the Land, who worked it, what rights its inhabitants and tillers possessed, and who would be hurt by the transfer of ownership. When buying inhabited, cultivated land, it was absolutely wrong—and should be absolutely forbidden—to evict the fellahs who worked it. Instead of exploiting their labor, the Jews should teach them modern scientific agricultural techniques. Then these *fellahs* would hold the Jews in high esteem, and some would agree or even ask to sell their land. In the end, Epstein believed in a common Jewish and Arab fate on the same land, based on common blood.

Unlike the later pioneer view, which would seek to channel Jewish blood exclusively into the soil of the Land, Epstein concluded, "to our delight, this [Arab] nation occupies such a huge area of the globe that it can let us, an ancient nation so closely related to it by blood, language, and the inclinations of the soul, take hold, in the Land of our Fathers, of all that part of it which it has not yet taken hold of."[89]

Voices like Epstein's, raised on behalf of the Arabs' connection with the Land, were extremely rare. Certainly the *halutzim* did not perceive the local Arab population as desiring the Land of Israel in the same way they themselves did. Although they did not say so directly, they saw the Arabs' relation to the Land as one of need, or at best demand. The Land of Israel did not belong to non-Jews because only Jews desired it, which is to say—because the Land desired the Jews. Here, in the collision between the desire of the *halutzim* for the Land and the needs or demands of the Arabs, the seeds of conflict between the two peoples were sown. Zionist-pioneer desire was simply unable to tolerate anyone who merely "needed" or "demanded" the Land, and certainly not anyone who made a pretense of "desiring" it.[90]

Pioneer desire for the Land articulated its body-without-organs vertically and horizontally, both penetrating and building on it. Pioneer desire left tracks through the land—furrows, canals, dirt paths, roads, drained swamps, trenches, excavations, wells, and more. It turned the "earth" into "soil," the "space" into "place," the "land" into the "Land of Israel."[91]

Pioneer desire was channeled in the Land of Israel principally through the classic pioneer praxis: labor. The *halutzim* did not think of labor only instrumentally, as resulting from a need or as a means of achieving a given goal. Labor had an ontological dimension in that it created organs in the body of the Land-without-organs. For example, Yosef Aharonovich wrote that a people that lacked a broad "backbone" of laborers close to nature and the raw materials of creation would, in the end, degenerate in body and spirit. Such a people had no right to exist, even when they could successfully maintain their material existence. Labor was a condition for the "existence" of such existence. "If there is labor here, there is revival here," Aharonovich concluded. "And if there is no labor here, there is nothing here."[92]

"All our pain, all the awful protests and sighs held back in our throats since we could not give them full vent, out of fear of the enemy [in the exile]," wrote several young people from Palestine in a public appeal published on the eve of the Second Aliya, "must now be poured out in a huge and unnatural [*sic*] national labor to save and revive us!"[93] Thus David Kahana of Beitania described how, on the "old giant," Mount Carmel, "[the *halutzim*] disperse over your frozen body, operating on your dried wounds with sharp scalpels, striking and digging. . . . They dig out your kidneys [in Jewish tradition, this organ is the seat of the moral faculty]—stones—exhuming them one by one, shattering them and paving a road to redemption."[94]

Plowing, as noted earlier, was one type of work through which pioneer desire was channeled. The *halutzim* generally identified themselves as the first to labor on the surface of the body-of-the-Land-without-organs. "We are now the first to have thrust [into the ground] here a plow that will proceed to conquer this entire valley," wrote a *halutz* who farmed the soil of Um Juni.[95] This drive for primacy magnified desire for the Land. Yehudit E-N (probably Edelman), who worked near Karkur, said her desire to furrow the earth grew out of the depression she felt at seeing the body-of-the-Land-without-organs. Not only did the *halutzim* yearn to plow the land; the land and all nature yearned for them. "The horrible nakedness is very upsetting," she wrote. "All around, the entire landscape that the eye takes in—is naked of trees. . . . You want to grab a weeder feverishly, cut through the

I will now know my border. The line of the furrow has been extended.
Go and trample the myriad stumbling stones! . . . .

Ascend and dig in the blade! Arise and turn over the clod!
The flesh of the wretched soil is bared to the sun . . .
Ha, my Lord, when, with the fingers of your hand,
Will you appear to crumble the soil's wounds?[96]
—Levi Ben-Amitai, "With the Furrow," 1934

earth, prepare it and plant it and cover it with green. The sun would certainly also rejoice if it had something to nurture, on which to pour its heat."[97] The furrows plowed by the *halutzim* sealed the connection between themselves and the soil. "Today I made a covenant with our soil," wrote Yaʿakov Pat of the moshav Ein Hai to his parents. "For the first time, I plowed the soil of the Land of Israel. There is no happiness like mine."[98] The furrow opened by the pioneer's plow was also viewed as a boundary that in the end would determine the borders of the Land.[99]

Once furrowed, the earth manifested itself not just as soil but as Jewish soil. Shmuel Dayan described this phenomenon in a letter to his son, Moshe. He and his comrades had begun to conquer the fields of Nahalal little by little, not by war, he stressed, but by plowing. Their furrows established the boundary between themselves and the Arabs of the village, and in this way the land would remain in their hands, Jewish hands. "If all the Jews and their children did this all over the country," Dayan concluded, "it would return to be ours. Securely and forever."[100] Pioneer plowing was always "conquest plowing," in the *halutzim*'s terms, because through it they conquered both the soil and labor itself. And as we will see in the next chapter, they also conquered their own bodies.

Paving roads also had a horizontally constructive effect on the body-of-the-Land-without-organs. "There was always something intoxicating for me about a white road extending into the distance, with trees or mountains around it," Rachel Katznelson remarked.[101]

Other types of labor penetrated the body-of-the-Land-without-organs—for example, stone quarrying.[102] A member of the Labor Battalion from Migdal described this process:

> The Kinneret sends its quiet waters into distant spaces. Giant mountains cast themselves around it like loyal brothers guarding their delicate and innocent sister. The waters of the lake give off softness and warmth, the mountains lofty simplicity. An infinitely deep blue sky stretches over them like a temple's majestic dome. And a hush of sacred awe pervades all. The blue, bright lake waters are silent, the mountains

To you, road, giant's son, to you I sing

We have sent out your white back like an arrow
Through greening fields,
Through the hills—to the valley!—

Now declare across the Land
And a well-watered meadow will lie under you;
And imagine: Did you know that we paved you—
Proud youth—

And we—
Here we will stand before you, wondrous stones,
And we will marvel:
How were we able to overcome you?
And in you we found our very selves.

Freedom we desired—
And you we paved;
The bold command
That shows the way and on ways decrees—

Justice we sought—
And you we created:
Strong and sure
Scornful of byways—

And for love we left our souls
And an image of you we traced.
We quarried stones for you
From the womb of a boulder-cliff—[103]
—Tzvi Lederer, "To the Road," 1922

stand quietly as if deep in thought, dreaming of the transparent blue sky overhead. Sit here and relax, old wanderer, wash your dust-covered feet in the lake's living waters, sit and say not a word. Here your weary soul can rest, you can unite and meld with the majesty of creation, lose yourself in the concealing waves of stillness that reign all around. . . .

And in shaking off your sleep . . . rise up and approach the mountain and here there is something that will make your soul marvel. Listen to the pounding sound of hundreds of picks and hammers, and see blocks of stone rising in the air and rolling

The paving of the road to Ein Harod, 1921. Central Zionist Archives, Jerusalem

> down, sparks flying, the mountain trembling, trembling here and there from the detonation of dynamite. And from within this great roar and clamor a great and vigorous singing like the breath of spring will reach your ear—this is the song of the smiths beating life from death, and this is their song, the song of war.[104]

Planting trees was another form of labor that penetrated the earth.[105] It made the *halutzim* feel they were establishing a connection with the place.[106] As they set plants in the soil, the *halutzim* saw themselves being planted in it as well.[107] "With the planting of each seedling," testified Hasia Drori of the *moshav ovdim* Kfar Yehezkel, "I felt as if I were also planting myself."[108] "You see yourself as one of the trees in the garden, intrinsically one of them," Shmuel Dayan wrote, "joined to this soil forever."[109] Saplings also defined borders.[110]

The body-of-the-Land-without-organs was a flaccid body, but the pioneers' desire turned it into a strong, muscular body. Yitzhak Pelah described how the creation of Kiryat Anavim, a kibbutz built on a mountainside, awoke the mountain to new life: "The ancient mountain shook off the dust of generations and suddenly stood erect at full height after a destruction-slumber of two thousand years."[111] In quarries, *halutzim* dynamited bedrock and revealed the body-of-the-Land in its full glory: "A liberating blow. The stone bared a cool chest. Yellowish spots are scattered over it like freckles, hairy roots grant masculinity to this stony torso."[112]

The body-of-the-Land-without-organs was a naked body, its earth, boulders, and mountains as bare as on the day they were born.[113] The *halutzim*'s desire clothed this body and covered its private parts. "Our land has dozens of mountains and hills, higher and more lofty than these [the mountains near our settlement], which still stand bald and bare," wrote A. Shapira of Kibbutz Mishmar HaEmek, "and there is no one to cover their nakedness and to remove their shame. . . . And now every naked hill and every bare mountain stands yearning and awaiting the redeemer who will come and repair them. . . . And here the hand of the guard of the Land has begun to cover the nakedness of this mountain [belonging to the Mishmar HaEmek settlers], which has become their inheritance."[114] Yisrael Haderi of Mishmar HaEmek described the pioneer foothold in similar terms: "The tree-planting season is approaching. . . . In a month's time the surface of one of the desolate and bare mountains of the Land of Israel will put on a new, fine garment."[115]

The body-of-the-Land-without-organs was an aging, deteriorating body.[116] Plowing revealed its original "face" once again.[117] Planting trees also renewed its youth and restored "its former visage."[118] The body-of-the-Land-without-organs was a sick body. Draining swamps "healed" it.[119]

Finally, once labor was done, celebration through dance offered another way for the pioneers to sanctify the soil. The members of Ein Harod, for example, did

Unidentified location, 1920. Central Zionist Archives, Jerusalem

this in their new settlement by dancing the hora at the end of their first day of work.[120]

The Conquest of Defense

The *halutzim* saw defense as a praxis complementary to labor. Without conquest of defense, they maintained, there could be no conquest of labor and therefore no conquest of the Land. Menachem Portugali asserted that it was pointless to conquer labor if defense was not also conquered. He warned his comrades, the laborers of Petah Tikva, that if they left guarding the fields to non-Jews, the laborers of the Second Aliya would be expelled from the Land along with the veteran Jewish settlers. The *halutzim* had to raise up a healthy, strong generation, because they had come to an untamed land where justice was in the hands that held the rifle and that had physical strength.[121]

Yitzhak Ben-Zvi also noted the fundamental link between labor and defense. When the Jewish people lived in its own land, the Land itself would serve as a foundation for developing the Jews' physical and other capabilities. Only a person who cultivates his land could really be capable of defending it. The natural devotion of the farmer to his land, "the mother of all living," his allegiance to his homeland, and his heroism were what made thousands and thousands of Jews willing to be killed and not surrender, to die with honor instead of delivering their land to their enemy with their own hands and facilitating their own exile. This was Ben-Zvi's explanation of why the Jewish people, after not bearing arms for centuries, nonetheless held impressive military talents. In just a few years, this nation had produced a great army under the leadership of the Maccabees, which not only liberated its homeland from a foreign yoke but also served as an example for all the peoples around it. These ancient Jews had forced even great empires to take them seriously and seek their support and friendship. After the destruction of the Second Temple, the link between the people and their land had faded, and the soil was slowly appropriated from under the feet of the Jewish people, who were dispersed over the entire world.[122]

"When you walk through the vineyards of Rehovot," wrote a visitor to the *moshava* in the period before defense of Jewish settlements was performed by Jews, "you can easily see the evidence of lawlessness and neglect."[123] The landscape was abandoned, derelict, a space-without-organs, open to incursions by strangers who uprooted saplings and trees and stole property. Sometimes, the same Arab laborers who worked for Jewish farmers and planted their seedlings during the day robbed them at night.[124]

Pioneer self-defense thus created a Hebrew ecology—that is, a purely Jewish space.[125] The contracts between the *moshavot* and the Jewish defense organizations granted the Hebrew guards the right to evict any Arab from the territory of a *moshava*.[126] In Hadera, where Arabs often stole from the granary, HaShomer men blocked the main road, forcing the Arabs to use a different route that skirted the silo.[127] In Rehovot, the Hebrew guards removed the tents of the Bedouins who had previously served as guards. They also instituted a regime of ringing a bell each evening, after which time Arabs could not be present in the *moshava*. Arabs who lived in the barns had to lock themselves in. Most of the roads that led from the Jewish settlement to the nearby Arab villages and to Ramla were blocked.[128] When the *halutzim* sought to prohibit Arabs from setting foot in Jewish settlements under their protection, they meant that literally—they wanted no Arab foot to tread there.[129] The Hebrew ecology reached its apogee when the *halutzim* abandoned the old *moshavot* in favor of new collective settlements where labor, defense, and language were exclusively Hebrew.

By conquering defense, Jews were able, for the first time since the beginning of the exile, to die a "beautiful death."[130] The death of Jews in the exile was a useless death, a death with no alternative. For a Jew to die in a pogrom was meaningless. But in dying on the soil of the Land, the *halutzim* did not die, because a "beautiful death" replaced mortal life with immortality. And through their deaths they bestowed life: they bequeathed the Land of Israel. The pioneers' blood seeped into the ground and constituted it as Jewish soil. Their blood watered, sanctified, fertilized the ground. Even after death, their legacies continued to pulse among living *halutzim*. Their lives were recorded forever in the history of the renaissance and redemption of the Land of Israel, through the trees and forests planted in their names, the memorials established to commemorate them, and a historiography that glorified their lives and acts. In 1921, an assembly of collective farm and road workers at Kinneret resolved to plant a grove of ten thousand trees in memory of the fallen defenders of the Upper Galilee.[131] "The eucalyptuses of Hadera were planted on our graves," wrote Ben-Eliav, "and they feed and flourish on the marrow of the laborers' bones."[132] *Halutzim* who committed suicide, who according to Jewish religious law were to be buried outside the cemetery wall, were interred by the *halutzim* alongside comrades who had died of disease or who had been murdered. They were considered to have died a "beautiful death" and were accorded the same respect as those who had fallen in battle.[133]

Berl Katznelson claimed that the exile did not allow a Jew to die honorably—only a "scoundrel's death" was possible there.[134] The exile meant "contemptible life and ongoing death." But in the Land of Israel, death was "death with honor."[135] A woman who had survived the Ukrainian pogroms asserted upon her arrival in Palestine on the deck of the *Roslan* that if no Land of Israel existed, Russia's Jews would be unable to simply die, since pogroms were occurring everywhere and the fate suffered in a pogrom was worse than death.[136] Yitzhak Ben-Zvi wrote that dying for the Land was "a spring of life"—a metaphor traditionally applied to the Torah.[137] Not surprisingly, when Ben-Zvi, then a soldier in the Jewish Legion, learned that the Galilee had been captured by the British, he was overjoyed by the liberation, but his enthusiasm was dampened by bitterness over not having taken part in the conquest himself.[138]

The "beautiful death" of the *halutz* found its purest expression in Yosef Trumpeldor's legendary last words after being mortally wounded in defending Tel Hai: "It is good to die for our land!" Trumpeldor's cry, whether apocryphal or not, whether he used precisely those words or not, reverberated through the pioneer world and beyond.[139] He had earlier spoken himself of the "beautiful death." "A day will come," he wrote in his diary before his aliya to the Land of Israel, "when I, weary and fatigued from hard labor, will happily and joyfully survey my fields, I in my own Land. And no one will say: 'Get out of here, scum—you are a stranger in this land.' And if some person says this, I will defend my fields, my rights, with force and by the sword. . . . And if I fall in battle, I will be happy, knowing what I die for."[140] On his way to Palestine, Trumpeldor imagined his ship sinking in an enemy submarine attack. "If such a thing were to happen to me," he declared, "I want to die a beautiful death, in joy, as befits a Jew dying for the Land of Israel."[141] He feared that in his final moments, his heart would grow faint and that he would die in a cowardly and unseemly way, "not as a lion, but like a hatchling. If that were to happen—shame on me, son of the free Jewish people! I do not want such a disgraceful death."[142]

It was clear to the pioneers of Tel Hai under Trumpeldor's leadership that they would not abandon their settlement—they would defend it. In winter 1920, before the attack, Trumpeldor wrote in his diary that everyone at Tel Hai knew that the local Arabs were armed with rifles and on their way to the settlement. An assault by these "crazed" Arabs was unavoidable, and the question of whether to retreat to Metulla was in the air. But no one dared even mention such a possibility. A hastily called assembly decided "to remain where we are no matter what."[143] "Members of a new generation, a generation of free natives of the Land of Israel, stand on the border and are prepared to give their lives to guard this border," Trumpeldor wrote in his diary.[144] When the defenders of Tel Hai realized that no other settlers would come to their aid, they issued a manifesto to the young people of the Land: "We will resist the enemy surrounding us to the last man; we will not budge from here until our final breaths."[145]

Eliezer Lubrani, a member of the paramilitary organization Magen, eulogized the fallen defenders of Tel Hai: "'Please make us proud and courageous. . . .' Your

A "beautiful death": unveiling the Roaring Lion Memorial, in memory of the heroes of Tel Hai (at the foot of the statue, in glasses is Yitzhak Ben-Zvi); Tel Hai, February 22, 1934. Central Zionist Archives, Jerusalem. Sculpture by Avraham Melinkov; photograph by Tzvi Oron.

glorious and heroic death has given us grounds for hope that our people will return to a new life, like that hero of alien lore who, on touching his land—his mother—was rejuvenated."[146]

Study of the Land

The body-of-the-Land-without-organs was unfamiliar and in reality unknown. So another way that the *halutzim* created its organs was by coming to know it through study, research, trips, and hikes. Melech Zagorodsky, the agronomist who served with the Land of Israel Office, asserted that the Land had been studied and researched even in ancient times, by the Greeks and Romans. They and those who followed them described it with the same precision as early twentieth-century scholars. But none of these latter scholars had pursued research for its own sake. Most of the studies sponsored by the research societies and associations active in Palestine were not aimed at gaining knowledge of the Land. Instead, they were designed to garner support for a particular theory—for example, proving the truth of Christian claims. While many fine scholars had studied the Land of Israel, including its flora and fauna, Zagorodsky claimed, the Land still awaited its "redeemers." And these could come only from among the Jews. They would explore the Land of Israel and discover "its secrets with great fondness, with the love of a child for its mother. Only our children born and immersed in the Land can study it in every detail, with scientific precision, without rushing and without preconceptions."[147] David Ben-Gurion and Yitzhak Ben-Zvi asserted that Jewish settlers should acquire intimate and thorough familiarity with the Land, which was still "virgin territory" for the Jews. The Jews could redeem it only if Jewish scholars reclaimed as their own—that is, redeemed—the study of the Land.[148]

The *halutzim* thirsted for knowledge of the Land.[149] As suggested earlier, one way they slaked this thirst was by traveling and hiking its length and breadth.[150] Ze᾽ev Vilnay, born in the pioneer era, formulated the categorical imperative of the pioneer traveler and hiker: "You will come to know the Land through the sweat of your feet."[151] Ben-Gurion wrote his father that he and his comrades lived like their forefathers of three thousand years ago, because they walked much more than they rode.[152] "Thus we learned to know and love the Land," wrote Moshe David Glicksman. "When you tread the roads alone on foot, you have the leisure to look at everything and to absorb the beauty of this great and wide land."[153] Yitzhak Ben-Zvi wrote of the first time he ascended to Jerusalem by foot. The trek took eighteen hours. He felt profound spiritual satisfaction from his first encounter with the wild natural surroundings of his homeland. His soul was stirred. Absolutely no comparison could be made between riding and walking: "You descend and ascend each hill, feel each inch with the soles of your feet, look at each tree, tarry as you wish by every spring, cave, or holy tomb. It can hardly be surprising that the impressions of the countryside of the Land of Israel, etched in my heart in those days, never fade and are imprinted in my memory as alive and as fresh as when they were first experienced, when I first strode the length and breadth of the Land."[154]

Some traveled the Land to see it, others to study it. Noah Naftulsky went on botanical expeditions, sometimes accompanied by Berl Katznelson and Rachel Bluwstein. He collected plants and flowers, dried them, and classified each by species and genus. On his trips, he would explain to his companions the plants' patterns of growth and means of reproduction.[155] For Yitzhak Ben-Zvi, expeditions provided an opportunity to study the Land's past through its artifacts. He described, for example, his search for the remains of the stones on which Jacob laid his head the night after he fled from his brother, Esau, and the traces of the altar he built when fleeing from his father-in-law, Laban, as well as the ruins of the great altar built by Yerav῾am, the first king of the biblical northern kingdom of Israel. When Ben-Zvi failed to find these sites, he expressed the hope that future excavators would dismantle the cairns, dig down into the tells, and uncover the mysteries beneath them.[156] Rachel Yanait described the moment when she and Ben-Zvi found potsherds bearing names in ancient Hebrew script at the ruins of Sebastia: "For more than 2,500 years they lay silent, deep in the earth, hidden from the rays of the sun, and now they are redeemed and testify like a thousand witnesses to the magnificent Jewish life of old."[157]

Some *halutzim* left signs of their presence on their trips and hikes. Carving their names into the surface of the Land-without-organs, they signed, both actually and figuratively, the connection between themselves and the Land. Tehiya Lieberson visited the Horns of Hittin with some friends. Climbing the ruins of Arbel, the ancient fortress from the days of the Second Temple, they entered the structure's vast halls, where they found archaeological artifacts. They inscribed their names on the wall "for eternal memory."[158] When Rachel Yanait and Yitzhak Ben-Zvi wandered through the territory of the ancient Israelite tribe of Benjamin, they encountered an acquaintance, Kalman Marmor, who was busy writing his name on every jutting stone on each wall of a ruin. With pencil ready, Yanait wrote, he observed this "precept" immediately each time he found a stone.[159]

The *halutzim*'s experience was also marked by formal study, an endeavor tied to the boundary-creating impetus of pioneer desire. Ben-Gurion studied law. Knowledge of Ottoman law, in particular that relating to landownership, he reasoned, would make it easier to conquer the Land.[160] Shlomo Tzemach studied agronomy and developed a number of innovations.[161] His fellow HaPoʿel HaTzaʿir founder, Eliezer Shohat, studied botany and zoology.[162] Members of the Labor Battalion studied plant physiology, political economy, geography, and other subjects. They also studied geology in the quarries where they worked.[163] At one of the first pioneer exhibitions, held in 1912 at Kinneret, displays included grains, types of vegetables and fodder, homegrown farm animals, and fowl.[164] Sejera put on an exhibition of stones, plants, and animals from the local area. A special section was devoted to historical artifacts.[165]

Water, Sweat, and Blood as Boundary Creators

We have seen the role played by water, sweat, and blood in the boundary-blurring aspect of pioneer desire. These fluids also had a boundary-creating effect.

By channeling the water of the Land into the earth, the *halutzim* turned it into soil. A *halutz* who worked at Jamama said that the Negev region had been neglected and deserted for centuries. Nature was sovereign and did as it wished without encountering any opposition or restraint from the nomadic inhabitants. "The rains beat down brutally on the hills and split them, and the earth filled with valleys and puddles," wrote the Jamama settler.[166] He and his comrades decided to channel the water so as to enable soil to emerge from the earth, soil that would support Jewish settlement and the establishment of a farm on the site: "The puddles that can be repaired are repaired, and those that cannot are subject to treatment to prevent the water from again destroying the earth. All the labor is performed by Jewish hands."[167]

When Tzvi Nadav settled in the Galilee, rains flooded the earth and swept away the soil. Only the construction of drainage canals enabled the settlers to prepare farmland. At Metulla, Nadav saw how water could destroy farmland in an instant. But then, he recorded, "with a single stroke of a hoe I opened a canal. The water broke through and flowed fiercely down the steep slope. . . . It is an art to open canals so that the current shows the lay of the land, and to let the soil absorb the water little by little."[168] Only when the flow was channeled could the soil soak up the water so that cultivation was possible. When the canal works were complete, Nadav saw fertile, well-watered soil transformed into a sunlit cornfield.[169] On such soil the *halutzim* could for the first time stand "on their two feet." And from such soil they could "suckle their strength."[170]

The most prominent aspect of articulating the body of the Land by controlling its water involved the draining of malarial swamps. "O, give us days and we will dry them up," declared Ben-Eliav of the Labor Battalion, who took part in draining swamps in the Kinneret area. "Raise up the depths—and we will close them up!"[171]

As we saw, channeling sweat into the Land also articulated organs in the body-of-the-Land-without-organs. Here we find the source of the pioneer obsession with labor performed by Jews rather than Arabs. This conquest of labor ensured that Jewish sweat exclusively would be channeled into the Land. The *halutzim* feared the moistening of the soil of the Land by gentile—especially Arab—perspiration. According to Shmuel Dayan, building the Land would be hopeless if it was done not with Jewish strength but with the strength "and sweat of strangers."[172] A Metulla pioneer wrote that the Arabs who served as virtual tenant farmers in his settlement, while the Jews farmed only in name, "watered [the Land] with their perspiration" and therefore had an "irrevocable spiritual connection" to it.[173]

The belief in watering the soil with only Jewish sweat also underlies the meaning of communal pioneer settlement. According to Franz Oppenheimer, the existence of a collective Hebrew body was a necessary condition for channeling Jewish sweat exclusively into the soil of the Land of Israel. A new home could be found for the wandering Jew in just one way: "Only where the soil is manured with the sweat of the [Jewish] peasant will the land become nationalized. And

Digging a manhole, Kfar Hasidim, 1925. Central Zionist Archives, Jerusalem. Photograph by Shmuel Yosef Schweig.

only where the cooperative association owns the land which it cultivates is there a guarantee that it is not Arab sweat that manures and wins the land."[174]

Wherever they saw work—worst of all, working the land—being accomplished by non-Jews, especially Arabs, *halutzim* responded with a range of feelings, from insult and shame, to anger, depression, and fear, to alarm, pain, and anxiety.[175] Yitzhak Elazari-Volcani claimed that the Hebrew cannot find rest in the shade of trees planted by strangers, or slake his thirst with the water of wells sunk by other hands.[176] For Eliezer Shohat, non-Jewish labor produced a fear of death. "When we enter a Hebrew *moshava*," he wrote, "and begin to inhale the air of a Hebrew village, see the green trees and the crop-covered fields, and our hearts fill with endless pride and happiness at the sight of our national property, then it is sufficient for us to learn that it was not Jews who accomplished this, that it was all done by the hands of others, for our joy to be ruined. A bitter sense of disappointment and insult fills our hearts. Is this not our memento mori?"[177] Therefore, Shohat continued, the only way to create the Land of Israel was by actualizing pioneer desire exclusively. And that could happen only through unmediated contact by the *halutzim* with everything in the Land. "Yes," he wrote, "all that will be created in the Land must be created with our hands—every tree, every plant, every house, every fence. All in which man becomes a partner of nature. . . . And we must water our soil only with our sweat. Only with our hands must we revitalize its soil."[178] Anything the *halutzim* did not create with their own hands would be alien. It would engender an emptiness in their hearts, bitter offense, the same feeling that a barren mother has toward a child she has adopted: "She cannot forget that she did not bear him. So, despite all her love for him, he is a stranger to her always."[179]

Jewish labor and sweat signaled purity. Sending a crate of oranges to his brothers and sisters overseas, Berl Katznelson included a letter saying that these were "kosher" fruits—that is, they had been picked in a Hebrew orchard tended by Hebrew laborers.[180] Others referred to the work of non-Jews in the Land of Israel—for example, the planting of trees—as a sacrilege, or an impurity. Trees planted by Arab laborers were considered "abominations."[181] Non-Jewish labor was a "sin," even "the mother of all sins."[182] For this reason, *halutzim* actually uprooted trees planted by non-Jews.[183] One of the most notable such incidents occurred in Ben Shemen in May 1908, where the agronomist Moshe Berman had been appointed by the Keren Kayemet LeYisrael to direct the planting of the Herzl Forest. Berman wanted to economize and employed Arab laborers, who could be paid less than Jewish ones. The Jewish workers of Petah Tikva, who were unemployed at the time, protested. They walked to Jaffa, where they were joined by other laborers, and then proceeded to Ben Shemen. The protestors uprooted trees that had been planted by Arabs, whereupon shocked Jewish workers at Ben Shemen who saw the uprooted trees forced their comrades to replant them. Before complying with this demand, the protestors uprooted all the saplings—so that no tree planted by an Arab would be left—and replanted them the next day, ensuring that Jewish hands were responsible. Word of the action quickly spread. On the following Saturday, large groups of workers from Jaffa, Petah Tikva, Rehovot, and Rishon LeTzion streamed to the site to congratulate the uprooters. They celebrated the deed with song and dance.[184]

The conquest of labor, or the sanctification of Jewish sweat, was the most important contribution made by the *halutzim* of the Second and Third Aliyot to the Zionist enterprise. The term "conquest of labor" was apparently coined by Shlomo Tzemach of the Second Aliya.[185] Members of the First Aliya, who proclaimed the principle of conquest of the Land, considered labor simply a means for achieving this goal and therefore saw nothing wrong with employing natives, including Arabs. The desire among members of the First Aliya for the Land of Israel, if it can indeed be called "desire," was thus channeled through the labor and sweat (and blood) of others. In contrast, the *halutzim* of the Second and Third Aliyot assumed that the ground of the Land of Israel would become soil, their

The uprooters of the saplings in the Herzl Forest. Ben Shemen, 1908.

soil, only when it was infused with their desire through their labor, their sweat, and their blood.[186]

The motto of the Bar Giora and HaShomer paramilitary defense organizations, "Judea fell in blood and fire and in blood and fire Judea will rise," clearly expressed the role of blood in the two aspects of pioneer desire: boundary-blurring and boundary-creating.[187] The same blood that had inundated and destroyed the Land of Israel and created the body-of-the-Land-without-organs would be channeled to recreate and reestablish the Land of Israel. According to Yisrael Shohat of Poʿalei Tzion, the men of HaShomer understood that victory could not be achieved without blood and sacrifice. This was an iron law.[188] It meant: "Have no hesitation about expending blood [of HaShomer] when it can be used to buy freedom."[189]

In response to a violent clash between members of the Poʿalei Tzion party and Arab youths in Jaffa in 1908, Turkish soldiers raided the Spector Hotel, shooting indiscriminately and wounding more than a dozen young Jewish workers. Yitzhak Ben-Zvi noted that the Jews had always anticipated that a confrontation with the Turkish regime was inevitable, and never deluded themselves that becoming empowered would be a calm, placid process. Therefore, links had to be created among elements of the Yishuv so that the Jewish people's problems could be resolved "not by paper rights but by blood and iron."[190] Calling himself a native of

Arab laborers, both men and women, working under the watchful eye of a Jewish foreman. Unidentified location, 1910. Central Zionist Archives, Jerusalem

the Land, Ben-Zvi declared that, after a hiatus of hundreds of years, Canaan had again tasted "the warm blood of its children."[191] Nationalism demanded blood like a mother sacrificing her son.[192]

Like sweat, this blood channeled into the soil sealed the link between the *halutz* and the Land. National aspirations could not be realized, said Yehoshua Thon, unless some gave their lives; no national hope had ever been realized without a seal of blood. "Our hope has already been sealed in blood, warm blood, young blood," he wrote.[193] Pioneer blood sealed a relationship of right to and ownership of the soil.[194] Yosef Saltzman was murdered in an ambush on his way back to Kinneret at the end of a day of plowing. His friends decided not to bury him near the settlement but rather at the place he was killed, where the soil had been "slaked" by his blood. "With his spilt blood, we have reestablished our covenant with Kinneret," they declared.[195]

Pioneer blood sanctified the soil. "The soil of Sejera has again been watered with youthful blood, the blood of its defenders . . . ," proclaimed a death notice for the murdered Yaʿakov Feldman. "The place is sacred!"[196] Yaʿakov Zerubavel felt trepidation over the very idea, the shame and disgrace, of "a foreign foot treading on land watered with the blood of Jews fallen while on guard duty. . . . In your blood, live!"[197] Indeed the *halutzim* may have longed to water the Land with their blood even more than with their sweat. "We want to die and wet it with our

Delivering the flag of HaShomer to the Jewish Legion during the volunteer period (standing third from left is Rachel Yanait). Emblazoned on the center of the flag: "HaShomer." The lettering above it reads "In blood and fire Judea fell," and the lettering below reads "In blood and fire Judea will rise." Unidentified location, undated.

blood," declared Yosef Nahmani, chief of the Lower Galilee Defense Committee. "And every inch of the soil of our land will call us and we are prepared to lay down our lives for it."[198] "Masses of Hebrews will settle on the Land, cultivate it, water it with their blood and the best of their vital fluids," cried Yaʿakov Zerubavel. "This is the essence of redemption."[199] Here, said Zerubavel, lay the fundamental difference between Jewish blood spilt in the exile and Jewish blood spilt on the soil of the Land. Quantitatively, more Jewish blood had been shed in the exile, while in the Land of Israel it had only begun to flow. But the way blood was spilt in the Land differed—here it was shed alongside the sweat of the workers. Jewish blood "kissed" the soil of the Land of Israel that the workers had furrowed, slaking its thirst.[200]

The *halutzim* comprehended more powerfully the blood tie between themselves and the soil after the death of their comrades, in particular after murders committed by the native population.[201] The brother of Sarah Chizik, who was killed in the attack on Tel Hai, wrote in a letter to his family that his sister would be remembered as a hero. They should neither mourn her death nor accuse anyone of causing it, he wrote, because they lived in the twentieth century, when "only with the blood of our brothers and sisters can we take possession of the Land."[202] In the name of the Association of Workers of the Galilee, Shmuel Dayan described what blood meant for the *halutz* following the murders of Moshe Barsky at Degania, Yosef Saltzman at Kinneret, and Yaʿakov Feldman at Sejera:

> Soil of our homeland, are you still thirsty for our blood? Have you not been slaked by the blood of our fathers from the day they placed it in our hands? . . .
>
> Our land does not remember us, because we have forgotten it. The blood of our fathers has long since congealed and scabbed. The blood and sweat of gentiles has washed the fields of Israel. . . . The memory in prayers and the outpourings in books, from that time until the previous generation, do nothing to redeem the soil. . . . The soil is parched, the soil is thirsty for the blood and sweat of its children! . . .
>
> We will soften it with blood and sweat, we will wet it with the dew of our youth and renew its youth, and it will remember us. We will renew that which flows with milk and honey—that which breeds giants—and heroes will rise among us and we will be redeemed.[203]

In their death, with their blood, the murdered *halutzim* secured the lives of their pioneer comrades and the life of the pioneer enterprise. A short time after Yaʿakov Feldman's murder, his friend Yaʿakov Meir arrived at Sejera and saw the silent jet of blood spurting from Feldman's right eye, a stream that slowed drop by drop. A large puddle formed around the body, the blood was diluted with rain, and Feldman lay silent and tranquil. His comrades dug a pit on the spot where he had fallen and planted a pine tree there. "Here," they promised him, "in the place where your blood was spilled, a tree of life will grow!"[204]

As a fluid that flowed through and then from the individual pioneer body, spilt blood sealed the spatial connection between the *halutz* and the soil of the Land. As a fluid that flowed through the body of the Jewish people (see chapter 5), blood sealed the historical and genealogical connection between people and Land. Shimon Kushnir has argued that spilt pioneer blood was nothing less than a "transfusion of Jewish blood" offered by the *halutz* to the soil.[205] In a letter to his friend Tzvi Shatz, Trumpeldor expounded on his desire for the Land of Israel. On the one hand, he could not help feeling bitter about every Jew who came to Israel, because such a person had abandoned his homeland, Russia. Trumpeldor confessed that he still loved Russia because "my blood was shed on it."[206] But the concept of a free life for his people, the Jewish people, in the Land of Israel was immeasurably dearer to him, "because the blood of Jews courses through my veins."[207] Blood could be spilled anywhere. But Jewish blood should fall only on the soil of the Land.

Just as communal settlements allowed the soil to receive exclusively Jewish

The mass grave of the fallen defenders of Tel Hai. Kfar Giladi, 1920. Central Zionist Archives, Jerusalem

perspiration, these settlements also allowed the soil to receive only Jewish blood. Yitzhak Elazari-Volcani said that the Jewish religion was a racial religion because it had been founded on national creativity and had protected itself from foreign influences over many generations. But the racial purity of the Jewish religion did not necessarily require Jews to continue to "live a purely religious life." This was because nationalism was also racial. And race was always determined by blood. "And pure blood," argued Elazari-Volcani, "depends on the nation living a common life and on the extent to which it maintains its distinctiveness."[208] Therefore, Zionist-Jewish settlement was the best way of preserving the race—that is, Jewish blood. Elazari-Volcani saw blood as a "vital substance" that persists through the generations. The blood of the forefathers always flows in the veins of their descendants, and the blood of the descendants fuses into that of their own children. But it ceases to be a "vital substance" in a "foreign organism"—meaning, of course, the Jew in the exile. The Jews sought to achieve full expression of themselves, both in body and in spirit. This could happen only in their homeland, the Land of their forefathers—"A Land where we can rest our tired heads in the bosom of its soil, where our thoughts will find their expression."[209]

At the same time that they exalted the spilling of pioneer blood, the *halutzim* feared bloodshed resulting from Arab revenge and blood feuds.[210] From Sejera, David Ben-Gurion wrote to his father about a fight in Jaffa between a young Jew and a young Arab. Usually such incidents ended in a good beating for both parties. But this particular fight was more serious because the Arab wielded a pole against the Jew and, in response, the Jew drew a knife and stabbed his assailant to death. Ben-Gurion feared the vendetta that the Arabs, "like all primitives," would feel honor-bound to pursue.[211] He conceived of such blood feuds in their broadest sense, and saw them as a very real threat to the Jewish people's existence in the Land of Israel. The blood feud, he wrote, "applies not only to the murderer himself, but also to his family, his tribe, and his entire nation."[212] The members of HaShomer learned to defend their settlements without killing their attackers, so as to avert vendettas that could well endanger the entire Yishuv. In practice, HaShomer guards avoided inflicting any physical harm on Arab attackers unless they entered the settlements themselves.[213]

Fears of vendettas also derived from Arab threats to drown the entire Yishuv in the pioneers' blood. While the *halutzim* perceived the spilling of their blood on the soil of the Land as an imperative, they also feared the physical destruction of the Yishuv. "Our comrades fall . . . ," wrote one pioneer, "and the scent of their blood wafts over the Lower Galilee and spreads to every corner of the Yishuv."[214] "Two Jewish spots in the heart of a raging sea of insurgents," was how Yosef Trumpeldor described Tel Hai and Kfar Giladi on the eve of the Arab attack. "A sea that threatens to swallow them up in an instant."[215]

The conquest of Hebrew defense, or the sanctification of Jewish blood, was the second important contribution—after the conquest of labor—that the *halutzim* of the Second and Third Aliyot made to the Zionist enterprise. Yet even as this conquest of self-defense was meant to rectify the balance of blood in favor of the Jews, to ensure that the Land would be Jewish and Hebrew, the *halutzim* also felt they could not tolerate Jewish blood being spilt "like water" on the soil of the Land of Israel.[216]

Some *halutzim* reasoned that menacing threats from Arabs should be met not with Jewish blood but with Jewish sweat. One of the severest attacks on Merhavia, in May and June of 1911, caused great trepidation among the settlers, one of whom concluded that blood was not the right response to blood. "Maybe all these bloodlettings have actually come," he declared, "to teach the builders of our settlement that the foundation of all construction is work and the foundation of national construction is the labor and sweat of the members of that nation!"[217]

Sweat or blood? The debate between the advocates of each ran through the pioneer period and found expression in the two central values of the conquest of labor and the conquest of self-defense. Supporters of the former advocated conquering the Land with perspiration. The latter's backers, while recognizing the importance of sweat, held that it was not sufficient and that blood, too, was necessary.[218] The conflict between these camps reached a climax during World War I, when the *halutzim* had to choose whether to join the war effort, and if so on which

Tel Hai, 1920. Central Zionist Archives, Jerusalem

side. During this fierce dispute, Eliezer Yaffe maintained that the Jews must not be swept off their feet by the awful idea of purchasing rights to land not based on who cultivated it but on "the spillers of human blood upon it."[219] The moment the Jewish people based their demand for rights to the Land on wars and bloodshed rather than on labor and peace, they would for all intents and purposes be acknowledging that might makes right, and that justice lies with the most violent acts. Such an acknowledgment would doom Zionism to failure. Yaffe attacked those who advocated participation in the war on the grounds that the Jews must do their part "with blood spilt for the conquest of the Land, lest the Land be conquered for us by the blood of others [i.e., British soldiers]."[220] He argued that the Land of Israel would be acquired through the sweat of its laborers, not their blood. A nation rises and is built only by its sons who plow its soil and who do not abandon their work even in wartime. Yaffe was prepared to accept the first half of the HaShomer motto. Judea had indeed fallen in blood and fire. But he rejected the second half and maintained: "Only and solely with the shovel and the plow will it rise again."[221]

On October 18, 1918, following the British army's conquest of the Galilee, the Association of Workers of the Galilee convened to discuss whether its members should volunteer for the Jewish Legion, a British unit composed of Zionist Jews, many of whom lived in Palestine. Those who supported joining the British war effort argued that even if the British liberated the Land, the Jews would not be the rightful inheritors if they did not shed their own blood for it. The Jewish people could not be saved with gifts, only through their own strength, maintained Shmuel Apter. The Jews, he said, could not purchase their right to the Land through labor, because no one would recognize that title. He supported the liberation of the Land with Jewish—rather than, say, Indian or Australian—blood.[222] "Emblazoned on our flag is 'in blood and fire Judea will rise,' and that is the motto we work by always," declared Yisachar Sitkov, a member of HaShomer, during the same debate. He also argued that the Land should not be conquered by foreigners, only by Jews. If Jews could not redeem the Land with their labor, they should at least be capable of spilling their blood for it.[223] Yosef Elkin declared that, as a native of Degania, whose inhabitants had faced and overcome so many troubles, he might be expected to believe that the Land should not be purchased with blood. But Elkin supported enlistment in the Jewish Legion precisely because of the blood equation. The Jews must pay their debt to the British forces who had spilled blood for them, and they could only do so by now spilling their own blood.[224] Another participant argued that the blood shed by Jews on all fronts of the World War had in essence been for naught, because it was shed by Jews but not the Jewish people. If the Jews did not want to give their blood in vain, they must channel it into the soil of the Land of Israel. Only by participating in the war could they sanctify the Land with their blood and, more important, reveal the "life-will" that beat within the Hebrew nation.[225]

One of the few *halutzim* who objected to redeeming the Land with blood was A. D. Gordon, the zealot of Jewish labor and sweat. The "primitive truth" that a people gained its right to its land through bloodshed was widely believed, he said, but it was in fact a gross falsehood. Were it possible to win a country with blood, then the *conquered* nation would receive it, because it had spilt more blood. A land, Gordon insisted, was not purchased with blood but by living in it. The Land of Israel also belonged to its Arab residents, who cultivated its soil, and the Jews would gain title to it by settling and working it. "Because the Land is mine, said the Lord—it only belongs to those who work it," Gordon maintained.[226]

Some *halutzim* advocated both courses of action. They argued that the Land of Israel could be built only with pioneer sweat *and* blood.[227] In the manifesto "Our Program," Menachem Ussishkin declared that before the Land of Israel could come into the possession of the Jewish people de jure, it must become theirs de facto. The Jewish people had to be loyal and devoted to their land, and their soul intimately tied to its soul. The Jews had to "saturate the soil with their blood and the sweat of their labors."[228] Rabbi Binyamin agreed that the Land had to be watered with both fluids: "The dunam [a thousand square meters] is all we speak of, we dream of it each day. The existence of this piece of land requires one more condition: that, respectfully asking its indulgence, it be worked with our own limbs and watered with drops of our sweat, our tears, and our blood—there must be an inner spiritual link between the Land and man."[229]

In 1916, David Ben-Gurion and Alexander Heshin had written that "the sweat of those working the fields and the blood of those killed on guard mix together in the bloodstream of new Jewish life."[230] The men and women of Tel Hai held fast to their place and did not leave it because the fields, homes, and mountains were "saturated with the sweat" and "soaked with the blood" of their comrades.[231] One advocate of volunteering for the Jewish Legion stated that each fluid played a designated role in the process of establishing ties with the Land: "Sweat—this is the evolutionary process; blood—this is the revolutionary process. What sweat cannot do for generations will be done by the blood spilt for years."[232] In the end, the Association of Workers of the Galilee decided that both those who volunteered for the Jewish Legion and those who remained to labor on the Land could be considered loyal to the ideal of creating a free and working Jewish settlement in the Land of Israel.

Difficulty and Despair: Back to Oedipus

We saw that the Land of Israel, especially its soil, was usually experienced as female—virgin, beloved, Mother Earth, submissive and yielding or motherly and welcoming. But the boundary-creating aspect of pioneer desire reveals the Land as hard and treacherous, refusing to submit, respond, receive.

In contrast with the soft, passive attitude that characterizes the boundary-blurring aspect of pioneer desire, boundary-creation is active and determined. The articulation of organs involves a struggle between the *halutzim* and the Land—its soil, its landscapes, its spaces, and its local population. The process is difficult, painful, violent. The body-without-organs does not easily surrender to the articulation of its limbs.

Shimon Wolf of Beitania described to his friends a day when he felt a huge desire to work. Suddenly, hidden powers revealed themselves, a flame flared under the earth, and a great upwelling burst out of him. On that day he shattered rocks in an entirely different way. He dealt them blows and penetrated the heart of each stone: "The stone could not defend itself, it could not withstand me, so it took its revenge on me, spraying chips in my face, scoring my bare chest."[233]

While the ecstatic-symbiotic experience unites the *halutz* with the Land, the articulation of the body-of-the-Land-without-organs entails a dialectical relation between the *halutz* and the Land. This latter process placed the pioneers between the Land's beauty and its ugliness, between its inherently good and bad qualities, between life and death. Articulation was ultimately a surgical act. Deleuze and Guattari (discussed in chapter 2) argue that the body-without-organs is self-sufficient and needs no organs. Organs are the body's enemy because the process of creating organs requires their being torn out of the body. They grant the "organness" of the body an intense experience of life but are also the source of all its suffering. In chapter 5, we will see how truly painful this articulation process was for the individual body-without-organs of each *halutz*.

Not surprisingly, the articulation process was accompanied by doubts, difficulties, despair, and failures. "Light and shadow alternate within it," Berl Katznelson said about the Land of Israel in a letter.[234] He wrote his brother Yisrael, who lived in the exile, that the Land was no paradise, and that he would face many difficulties and obstacles were he to decide on aliya. "There is no escaping agonies, illnesses, and heartsickness in any place," he maintained.[235] Articulating the Land confronted the pioneers with the melancholy associated with action and the small details of life—existential melancholy.[236] A member of the Labor Battalion described the difficult emotions that overcame him precisely as he was actualizing his desire for the Land: "There are times when my muscles stretch and my strength tenses as my soul immerses itself in a life of creativity and labor, and at such times in the intoxication of this creation I celebrate my joy, the joy of our victory here. Yes. But: I do hurt. . . . Because I create—and there is no creation without sorrow and without pain . . . the sorrow of creation, an awful sorrow, a sorrow on the edge of madness and divine joy, the joy of victory, the victory of existence over nothingness—this is our great destiny."[237]

Many *halutzim* overcame the harshness and betrayal with which, it was sometimes felt, the Land of Israel responded to their arrival. But quite a few left the Land. During the Second Aliya, about 40 percent of those who came on aliya ended up as *yordim*—descenders, those who abandoned the Land. During the Third Aliya, about 24 percent left.[238] Those who left—who did not perceive the Land as Mother Earth—"returned" to the same "oedipal" genealogy from which they had so wanted to break free. Many *halutzim* who "descended" back to their countries of origin returned to the homes of their parents, to religious tradition, to Judaism, to the exile.

Some *halutzim* killed themselves.[239] Gur Alroey has tallied fifty-nine suicides in the years 1910–1923.[240] In the summer of 1916, Yoske Michaeli shot himself at Degania. His friend Haya Kastelanitz explained the act by saying that suicide was part of the course of nature in the Land of Israel. The same currents that awakened the ecstatic-symbiotic experience in the *halutzim* also bore a few of them into oblivion. "The life force impelled us to die," Kastelanitz wrote. "Do not the Jordan's living waters, in their massive flow, seek the Dead Sea? . . . The current was too strong, and life was like a small toy in its hands."[241] "And at times the power to live is depleted, and death is still far off," wrote Mordechai Snir. "And at times a huge wave rolls by and in the veins the magical blood of youth flows and eradicates the senses, and why? And from time to time a member of the band goes missing, and leaves the world . . . we are in mid-sea, surrounded by waves upon waves. A wave lifts up, and a wave brings down."[242] Many of the *halutzim* who put an end to their lives drowned themselves in one of the Land's bodies of water—the Mediterranean Sea, Lake Kinneret, the Jordan River.[243]

In contrast with the *halutzim* who articulated the Land-without-organs into soil on which they could stand, those who committed suicide could not find their footing. Eulogizing Rachel Meizel, who drowned herself at the Jaffa beach, Yosef Aharonovich related that "she was suddenly uprooted from the earth and she found no other earth to stand on. . . . Loneliness and hunger, hunger for life in all its senses, hunger for work that did not find her, hunger for ideals—loneliness and hunger, these two, followed her to her eternal repose."[244] In contrast with pioneers who articulated the Land and gave expression to its beauty, the suicides felt too strongly its bitter ugliness. "May all those close to me forgive me," Rachel Meizel apologized in the note she left behind. "One should make no step without God. Life is beautiful from a distance, but I lost the distance; up close life is coarse and not beautiful; I am going on my way. I am at peace and feel good. Farewell. Rachel."[245] Those who committed suicide did so because they were unsuccessful at articulating either their bodies or the Land. In a eulogy for Mordechai Vachsberg of Merhavia, one of his friends explained that the dead man had sought a revolution in his private life that was beyond his physical capabilities: "Once his body weakened . . . he saw no possibility of living in the company of the strong, and he chose death. He did not have the strength to live and girded up all his strength to die a romantic death, and he deposited his final sigh at the insult of life in the depths of the Jordan."[246] As opposed to the *halutzim* who through the articulation process were born again, the suicides were unable to be reborn. "I so much wanted to find here a man who could penetrate my soul," wrote a pioneer woman of Migdal, "who could touch my pains and with his expertise operate on me. After such surgery I would feel as if I were born again. . . . My comrade Moshe has recently died. He shot himself. I frequently think of suicide."[247]

Yosef Fried was a *halutz* who ascended to the Land and then descended a short time later. He confessed in his diary from his time there that those who remained desired the Land and were not motivated by concrete needs or demands. Nothing else could explain their decision to stay. Their desire was unconditional.[248] Fried describes a process of disillusionment with Mother Earth and the Land of the

Fathers. In a letter to his wife a year after his aliya, quoted in his diary, he wrote that the year was decisive in his biography because his aliya had enabled him, for the first time, to deviate from the road paved by his ancestors, from the way of his brothers and sisters who would not budge from within the boundaries imposed by their forebears. Unlike them, he had replaced his forefathers with the *land* of his fathers. But he quickly sobered up. All his dreams and hopes melted away. He began to ask himself why he had come to the Land. He had expected no Arabs or old people who wither and grow weak. Suddenly he saw the blackest of shadows.[249]

In the end, Fried left the Land because he was unable to connect with Mother Earth. Neither did she respond to him. She turned out to be a bad mother who was unresponsive to her son and did not provide him with the sustenance he needed. "I came to her to bring about an utter change in my life values," he wrote, "for me and for my children after me; to return to Mother Earth, to cultivate her and to revive her so that she could revive me. . . . I thought that here, only in the Land, my Land, could I realize my idea. And then came the riots, and these deeds gave me a slap in the face."[250] Fried accused his exilic forebears of having "seen to it" that he lacked physical strength. He still felt great fondness for the Land of Israel, its language, and its people. But fondness was not enough. He needed strength as well. He needed desire.

In a letter of Fried's to a female friend shortly before leaving, we can discern remnants of his ecstatic-symbiotic relationship with the Land. He wrote that he could see his feelings mirrored in the Land's natural surroundings. "The rains do not end," Fried wrote. "They poured and poured all night, my window was open, and my pencils, books, and paper all got soaked from the rain that seeped through the window onto my desk. . . . It looks as if the skies of the Land of Israel are crying over its departing children, and neither can the sea cease its fury."[251] Fried,

Soil!
I but listened to the wine-song in your veins—
But it came not to my lips . . .
Why did your wine not numb me
So I could not rise from kneeling at your side?
Why have you not bared your breast to my mouth,
When, like a tender puppy, blind
My head groped among your clods,
And with a whimper of thirst I searched for it?[252]
—Yitzhak Lamdan, "Bridge," 1924

despite his aspiration to be reborn in the Land of Israel, went back to his old "oedipal" genealogy. He returned to his mother and father: "Yes, there were times when I aspired to destroy, mercilessly to destroy the entire old structure, to uproot all that my parents and my previous surroundings had planted in me, and now how have I changed!!"[253]

It is true that the pioneers who remained also saw Mother Earth betray them at times. The *halutzim* sought to suckle on Mother Earth, but she did not always respond by providing for their needs. At plowing time, Shmuel Dayan wrote, the large, heavy clods of earth turned over, exposing dead soil to wind, sun, and life. But the soil was very poor and pale in color. It was overgrown with brush and full of stalks of wild grain and onions that had been planted but failed to grow. The shoots froze in place. "The land was fatigued, like a weak mother with shriveled breasts that have no power to suckle the fruit of her womb."[254]

Nevertheless, the *halutzim* who remained were able to see past such barren periods. In a letter from Nahalal, Eliezer Shohat reported to his wife on the end of the threshing season, saying that Mother Earth had been miserly this time. He apologized for not yet being able to support her, but said he was still happy for the little given them because "it was given to us by our Mother Earth."[255]

5 Articulating the Pioneer Body

Pioneer desire for the Land of Israel articulated the bodies-without-organs of the individual *halutzim* as well as the body of the Land-without-organs. For the *halutzim*, their exilic "old Jewish bodies" were bodies-without-organs that could not hold fast to a place. The exilic Jew was a nomad, rootless, a *luftmensch*—an air-head, or "airy-Jew" (*yehudi avriri*), as Berl Katznelson put it. Because the exilic Jewish body was not part of a territory, it lacked solid existence. Others attributed the same quality to the body of the entire Jewish people, who were an "air-people" (*am avir*).[1]

The Body of the Jew in the Exile

The body of the exilic Jew was a body-without-organs not only because it lacked a place in the world but also because it was dysfunctional. Through centuries of exile, since Jews had been separated from their land, their ability to work and produce had atrophied. Over the generations, wrote Mordechai Kushnir, the Jewish body had lost its feel for physical labor, the capacity to enjoy the sensation of its muscles flexing, the secret of rhythmic labor. An inclination to seek out an easy life, in which the Jew ate bread produced by other hands, had been passed down from father to son. The result was that the senses of most Jews lacked vitality, and they no longer had the ability to enjoy physical exertion. "Our fingers are degenerate," wrote Mordechai Snir, "and down to our toes, we are lacking in all the repetitive movements innate in the muscles, instilled in them over long generations. Our natural senses, the conduits of abundance that suckle from primal sources, have become blocked. We have come to the Land and to labor by seven routes, the inheritance of our forefathers is in our hands—great desires. And our fathers have bequeathed us a shortness of grasp."[2] The body of the exilic Jew suffered from "internal impotence," due both to inexperience with labor and to difficult, constraining external conditions.[3]

To Yosef Trumpeldor, the exilic-body-without-organs was an ugly, contaminated object; in men, it was concealed under "high stiff collars" and in women under "expensive dresses." Exilic Jews sought to keep up an appearance of purity and wholesomeness. But it was all counterfeit, abject, and disgusting, manifesting humiliation, stupidity, and hideousness. No matter what direction it took, the life of this body disintegrated.[4] The exile stripped the Jew of his inner freedom and his naturalness. At best, he imitated others, negating himself. But in general, he lived without imitating anyone. Life in the exile made the Jew "high-strung, sickly, odd, conflicted, querulous, and contemptible."[5] His body was incomplete, sick, "a caricature of a person normal and healthy in body and in spirit."[6]

In a letter to a friend, Berl Katznelson wrote of his desire to ascend to the Land and to steel his body for labor. The friend replied that this could be accomplished only in a very limited way. The Jews could set out on a new road, but they could not leave behind all their former attributes. The Jewish aspiration to be someone else would not turn out well because "we are cripples, failures. Life, or we ourselves—it amounts to the same thing, after all—has maimed us by making us intellectuals."[7] A. D. Gordon described the exilic body as "mummified," persisting only thanks to being embalmed in the past. Even after the Jews emerged from the ghetto, they had not undergone the necessary internal awakening "because a wind from outside broke through the mummified body and into it. The mummified body began to awaken, but also to disintegrate."[8] Gordon is apparently saying that the internal awakening—that is, becoming a new Hebrew body with organs—had never occurred because of assimilation and also pogroms.

The exilic-body-without-organs was a parasite that lived at the expense of other bodies.[9] Its organs were ineffectual; it needed the organs of another body to survive. The *halutzim* fought this parasitism with their own bodies, believing that every human being had to work and produce, especially in the Land of Israel.[10] This explains the pioneer perception of *olim*, new immigrants to the Land (in Hebrew *olim* also means "ascenders"), as "human material," a raw substance that had to be refashioned and reshaped before settling in the Land.[11]

The condition of the exilic-body-without-organs was also the result of physical injury. The history of the Jews in exile was a *Leidengeschichte*, a history of the suffering Jewish body.[12] The exilic-body-without-organs was a wounded body, even a cadaver. Even when not actually injured, it was flaccid, passive, weak, defenseless, and powerless.[13]

Many *halutzim* of the Second and Third Aliyot had personally experienced or witnessed the pogroms that ravaged their people at the end of the nineteenth century. During the Kishinev pogrom of 1903, some fifty Jews were murdered and some five hundred wounded, a hundred critically. Most of the wounded had suffered blows to their heads and faces from clubs, sticks, and poles. Women and girls were beaten and raped. In one case, attackers tore the tongue from the mouth of a two-year-old child while he was still alive. Meir Weisman, blind in one

Body-without-organs I: yeshiva student, Jerusalem, 1914. Central Zionist Archives, Jerusalem

eye since boyhood, pleaded for his life and offered his assailants sixty rubles. After taking his money, the leader of the gang destroyed Weisman's small store and gouged out his seeing eye. "You'll never again look at a Christian boy," the gang leader admonished his victim.[14] During the pogrom, rioters hammered nails into the heads of Jewish victims. They mutilated bodies, stuffed feathers into gaping abdomens, and cut off women's breasts. Some two thousand pogroms took place in the Ukraine during the years 1917–1921, during which tens of thousands of Jews were killed—estimates ranged from 70,000 to 140,000. A similar number were injured.[15] The pogroms made the Jewish body into a body-without-organs—a no-body in the literal sense.

Berl Katznelson witnessed a pogrom in Smila when he was seventeen.[16] Yedidya Shoham witnessed the Lvov riots of 1918. "Plunderers on Zolkovska Street," he wrote in his diary. "The Jewish city is in flames and living people, or burnt bodies, are buried under the demolished houses."[17] A few days later he wrote: "More than a thousand victims were murdered brutally, women raped, men—bayonet wounds and bullet holes in their bodies, piles of burnt bodies, people were trapped in blazing houses and doomed to die in the flames."[18] A. D. Gordon's son was murdered in one of the Ukrainian pogroms of 1920–1921.[19]

The exilic-Jewish-body-without-organs was the body of the so-called eternal Jew. The Jew's eternity, wrote Yaʿakov Zerubavel, was a consequence both of end-

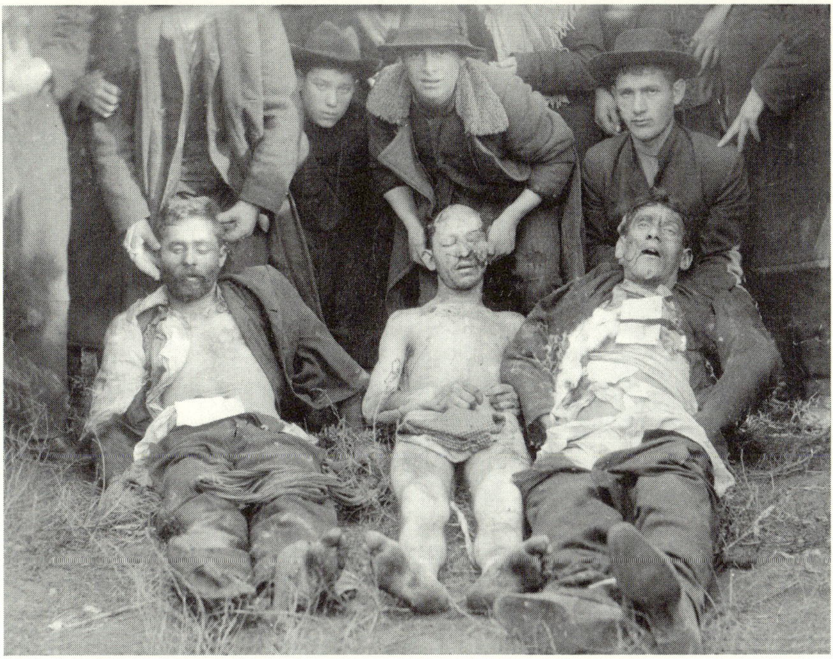

Jewish bodies-without-organs II: Jews murdered in pogroms. Unidentified location, 1903. Central Zionist Archives, Jerusalem

less wandering—of "existing" within an exilic-space-without-borders—and of physical vulnerability and injury. The eternal Jew wandered through an endless, infinite world of death, fear, and anxiety, of silences and desperate screams and cries. The eternal Jew lived in a nightmare world constructed out of the bodies of dead Jews. "Under and around the crosses the entire square is carpeted with the crumpled bodies of the dead, men and women, old people and infants. . . ," wrote Zerubavel. "An old Jew ran, his arms crooked before him. His hair was wild and sparse, his eyes terrified and gaping. The Jew runs through the world, but with every step and stride he trips over huge wooden crosses and his feet stumble over countless corpses. And he falls, falls, gets up, and falls again."[20]

For many Second Aliya *halutzim*, the experience of the Jew as a body-without-organs was shaped by Hayim Nahman Bialik's poem "City of the Killings" ("BaIr HaHarega"), written in the aftermath of the Kishinev pogrom.[21] Soon after the pogrom ended, Bialik, a member of a commission chaired by the historian Simon Dubnov, began to collect and document testimonies. Dubnov assigned Bialik to interview hospitalized victims, especially those with serious injuries, to photograph sites and people, to document instances of organized and improvised self-defense, and to record cases of rape. After reading Bialik's poem, Haim Arlosoroff described the Jewish people as a degenerate people whose powers were atrophied, whose life was always on the line, a nation that "had been divided and separated and hacked into several thousand scraps and pieces and pieces of pieces of pieces, piled up to the sky." After the pogrom, the Jews faced the most basic of questions: "To be or not to be."[22] The Kishinev pogrom seems to have been the first such event to be documented with photographs.[23] Undoubtedly, the visual impact of these photographs only served to amplify the presence of the exilic-body-without-organs in the world of the *halutzim*.

> The case of a disemboweled chest filled with feathers,
> The case of nostrils and nine-inch nails and skulls and hammers,
> The case of slaughtered human beings hung up from beams like fish,
> And the case of a baby found by the side of his stabbed mother
> Still dozing with her cold nipple in his sucking mouth.[24]
> —Hayim Nahman Bialik, "City of the Killings," 1904

Rachel Katznelson related that she dreamed frequently as a child. Dreams of flying gave her a feeling of sublime joy. But there were also dreams of horror in which she wanted to scream but could not. She tried to speak but was struck dumb. She strained to open her eyes, which remained closed, and to move limbs that turned out not to exist. She desperately fled from something that chased her but could not elude it. She maintained that these childhood fears could not be explained without reference to the centrality of fear in her life, lived in constant apprehension of a pogrom, which could come at any moment. She was aware of all the likely fates for a girl in a pogrom, which she thought would certainly be worse than those for a boy. She was often frightened by gentiles she encountered when alone in a field, the woods, or on a mountain. Even in adolescence she was unable to overcome that childhood terror. Most of these fears were connected to her body and to the sense of *schmutz*, its filthiness and pollution.[25] Prior to her aliya, Katznelson wrote in her diary: "And I seem to feel as if my body withers without joy, without substance."[26] After coming to Kinneret, she wrote: "Before the Land of Israel, I felt like a cripple, like a person without hands."[27]

The exilic-Jewish-body-without-organs was shaped by harsh living conditions as well as injury. Before making aliya, Baruch Zuckerman, a member of Kibbutz Gvat, visited an orphanage in Pinsk that held seventy-five children. Most of their parents had been killed during the World War; some had died of hunger. He described one seven-year-old girl who looked no older than two: "All her limbs were horribly deformed. The thickness of her legs was no more than that of the finger of an adult. There is no trace of a muscle, the bones are wasted, and she does not know how to speak. The eyes—a pair of large, black eyes, the eyes of a Jewish girl, and her tiny face looks smaller than her eyes."[28] Elsewhere in the city, Zuckerman encountered ravaged families. Apartments the size of a single bedroom housed anywhere from four to nine people, who all lay on beds or the ground. All—men, women, old people, children—were stark naked. "You encounter emaciated, pinched faces with eyes flashing with hunger," he wrote, "or you see a hand or other body part swollen and covered with bruises and pus-filled wounds."[29]

Pinsker, Nordau, and the Jewish Body

The *halutzim* were not the first to diagnose the "Jewish problem" as one of the body. This observation appeared initially in the antisemitic European political and scientific discourse, in which the Jewish body (especially that of the *Ostjude*, or Eastern European Jew) was described as weak, deformed, and degenerate.[30] The body-without-organs was also the subject of a broader argument in which it was asserted that a life form deficient in some trait would be compensated by nature in some other way, in the end making the ostensibly deficient creature superior to other organisms. The compensation for human beings overall, who lacked attributes such as great strength, horns, sharp teeth, hooves, and thick hair, was greater brainpower. Some "spiritual" Jewish leaders extended this notion to explain the difference between the Jews and other peoples. In their view, nature had granted the Jews better brains and deeper souls than others as compensation for their physical weakness. While the gentiles were endowed with large territories, abundant natural resources, and huge stores of arms, the Jews possessed intellectual and spiritual power. This claim that the spirit was superior to the body belongs to a longstanding Jewish tradition considered by the *halutzim*, and Zionists in general, to be merely an attempt to justify the state of Jews outside their land.[31]

Accordingly, Eliezer Riger attacked the argument suggesting superior Jewish spirituality and the Jews who subscribed to it, basing his critique on the prophetic call to toughen the body's organs: "Arise and thresh, O daughter of Zion; for I will make your horn iron, and I will make your hooves brass; and you will beat in pieces many peoples."[32] He focused on the most important organ for working the land: the hand. The fist was superior to any act of culture produced by the spirit. It was primal—it made the spirit concrete and was thus superior to it.[33]

Voiced in many quarters, the notion of the degenerated Jewish body became one of the sources of Zionism. In Zionist discourse, it appears in particular in the writings of two of the movement's seminal thinkers, Yehuda Leib Pinsker (1821–1891) and Max Nordau (1849–1923).[34] Both physicians by training, they characterized the condition of their people with unusual precision. Pinsker and Nordau identified three causes of the physical degeneration of the Jewish people, which brought spiritual and mental degeneration in their wake: the severing of the Jew from his land, the Jew's preference for the intellect over the body, and physical injury to his body.

Pinsker maintained that the principal physical problem arose from the substandard living conditions of the Jews in the Diaspora. They lived mostly in big cities in highly crowded conditions. This dangerous congestion was the source of all ills, including antisemitism and the degeneration of the body. Most of all, though, the Jewish body suffered because it had been cut off from its homeland, from its soil, and from a life of physical labor. While other peoples who lived on their own soil worked the land while also engaging in commerce, the exilic Jew engaged primarily in small trade and minor crafts, in "shopkeeping," as Pinsker put it. This was why other nations remained productive in other areas, such as science and the arts, and enjoyed normal physical and spiritual development.

Once the Jews were forced out of agricultural labor, Pinsker argued, over the course of their subsequent history they lost their instinct for such work. The resulting lack of physical activity was extremely detrimental to their physical development. The only solution, said Pinsker, was to return to the soil. "Up until now we have been the intermediaries in the commerce between one person and another," he concluded. "Now we are returning to nature, our mother, who gratefully welcomes the hands that till her and who makes no distinction between human beings except in the matter of diligence. As we once knew how to move from the plow to the scale, so let us now boldly grasp the plow."[35]

Nordau's diagnosis was more comprehensive and detailed than Pinsker's. The goal of emancipation, he maintained, was to liberate the Jew from the ghetto. But while emancipation tore the Jew out of his old world, it did not really enable him to find a place in the new world opening before him. As the desire to assimilate among the gentiles grew, the Jews had begun to internalize the antisemites' view of them and to adopt the external characteristics, including the body image, of the Other. However, while alienated from his old body, the Jew could never fully adopt the new one. The liberated Jew had become a person without roots, lacking security even in his immediate surroundings. He had no choice but to exhaust his strength in an effort to conceal his true self. This was the source of the new Jewish "neuroticism": "His best powers are exhausted in the suppression, or at least in the difficult concealment, of his own real character. For he fears that this character might be recognized as Jewish, and he has never the satisfaction of showing himself as he is in all his thoughts and sentiments. He becomes an inner cripple, and externally inauthentic, and thereby always ridiculous and hateful to all higher feeling men, as is everything that is inauthentic."[36] Even the proudest Jews, according to Nordau, accepted as fact that the Jew was "physically clumsy, pitifully awkward, lamentably feeble, that he is all thumbs, is constantly falling over his own feet, prefers to stand crooked and lopsided rather than straight, and so on. This is what the antisemites say, and we repeat it after them."[37]

Thus, Nordau asserted, the Jewish-body-without-organs came into being both because of the tension between the Jew's actual body and the ideal body he was unable to fully adopt and because of his body's physical degeneration owing to substandard living conditions. It was time, he added, to create a new kind of Jew, a "muscular Jew." For too long others had occupied themselves with "killing our flesh"—witness the hundreds of thousands of Jewish martyrs of the Middle Ages. But "killing the flesh" referred also to the neglect of the body in the ghettoes. The Aristotelian elements—light, air, water, and earth—were allotted to the Jews in only tiny amounts: "In the confines of the Street of the Jews, our poor limbs forgot to move joyfully, in the gloom of their sunless houses our eyes became accustomed to blinking timidly, in the fear of constant persecution the power of our voices turned into a frightened whisper, which would only rise to a powerful rejoicing when our martyrs at the stake cried out their dying prayers in the face of their executioners."[38]

Now, when the living space assigned to the Jews in Europe was no longer restricted and they could live their lives in full, Nordau called for a renewal of the link to ancient Jewish tradition: "Let us once again become deep-chested, strapping men with bold eyes."[39] This call for the creation of a muscular Judaism was undoubtedly a challenge to the longstanding ethos that valued the intellect and spirit over the body. The Zionist act was explicitly meant to renew and heal the Jewish body. Nordau's call was an important source of inspiration for the *halutzim* of the Second and Third Aliyot in the enterprise of fashioning their pioneer bodies.[40]

The Exilic Body in the Land

This enterprise of refashioning the pioneer body was accomplished only with great effort. Even after their aliya, the *halutzim* experienced their bodies as bodies-without-organs. Their desire to till the soil of the Land intensified this sense of lacking organs. Most *halutzim*, especially those of the Second Aliya, ended their first day of labor with a sense of utter impotence, feeling that their bodies had betrayed them. Everything hurt—arms, back, feet, muscles. They could not stand up straight after a day of work. Every step required superhuman effort. They were exhausted, their hands were scratched, bruised, covered with festering sores.

Some even passed out from the effort of hard labor. They felt ashamed and degraded not just by their failure but also because the established Jewish farmers in the *moshavot* forced them to engage in labor contests with Arab workers and inspected the muscles of *halutzim* at the "slave market" where day laborers lined up to seek work. No wonder, then, that the "first day" was a constitutive experience in the world of the *halutzim*.[41]

The pioneer-body-without-organs also lacked proficiency in work beyond tilling the land and in the use of tools. Hasia Drori of Kfar Yehezkel, for example, wrote of the agonies she endured in learning to milk cows. Many weeks passed before she could grasp the cow's teats properly. Her fingers, unaccustomed to such work, hurt for a long time, and the pain spread into the muscles of her arms and back.[42]

A. D. Gordon's diagnosis was that "We have no hands, and we do not even feel that we lack hands."[43] Before his aliya and during the first stages of his introduction to manual labor in the Land, Berl Katznelson referred to his "hands of clay."[44] In short, many *halutzim* experienced their bodies as alien. They felt they had no control over their limbs. In a letter to his father from Petah Tikva, David Ben-Gurion described how his body broke down as he worked. Having never engaged in physical labor, he was suddenly required to dig trenches, plow untilled land, and lug manure. "Sweat pours off you, your hands fill with calluses and cuts, and all your limbs feel as if they are falling to pieces," he wrote.[45] Shlomo Tzemach offered a similar account of his initial experience: "I had never done any manual labor, and my fingers were unpracticed and inept. . . . I was ashamed of how my exhausted hands did not do as I told them."[46]

At the conclusion of his initial days of work in the Land, Um Juni resident Yosef Weitz felt that his hands and feet no longer obeyed him. He envied the fellow workers who had already adjusted and gazed longingly at those who walked with a spring in their step as if they had not spent the entire day with the hoe. As he worked, his soul was borne down by an "iron weight"; "every step is hard, hard."[47] Real laborers and non-Jewish farmers did not experience this type of strain. They were steady at their work. Unlike the "neurotic" Jewish body, the body of the gentile laborer was quiet and stable and accommodated to the job at hand. Weitz recalled a non-Jew he had once seen while taking a walk on a noble's estate in the exile. The man had stood on the banks of a brook, fishing from morning to night, with great ease. "And we, scions of an impetuous nation," he wrote, "wondered at this patience, this ease, free of all concern and burden and thought and contemplation." In recalling this non-Jew, he was hugely envious. He had worked as a farmer for two years and still had not acquired this steadiness, this ability to focus on a single task, this easy, effortless concentration. "Restlessness rules me," he wrote.[48]

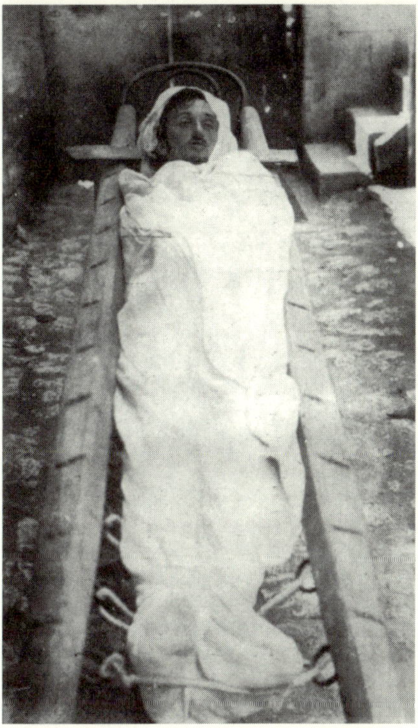

The Jewish-body-without-organs III: the corpse of Avraham Yosef Berl, killed while guarding at Sejera. Unidentified location, June 2, 1910.

The pioneer-body-without-organs, facing a physical threat from the surrounding mostly Arab population, was also impotent—*walad mit*, doomed to die, as the Arabs said.[49] *Halutzim* were sometimes murdered and their bodies mutilated. On his way to the moshava Menahemiyya, Moshe Barsky was attacked and murdered by Arabs. His body, when found, had three bullet holes in it; his assailants had smashed in his face with clubs.[50] On July 23, 1912, David Saharov, a Hebrew guard, was slain in Rishon LeTzion. His murderers beheaded him.[51] During the grape harvest, Meir Hazanovitz, one of the first Hebrew guards, set out for a vineyard. He encountered five Arabs whom he knew well. They accompanied him to his tent and while he prepared coffee they struck him from behind, stabbed him, cut off his head, and fled with it.[52] Avraham Hartzfeld described the pogrom at Tel Hai: "The blood, feathers, and pieces of household implements were all mixed up with raw human flesh."[53]

Creating the Individual Body-with-Organs

The desire that articulated the organs of the *halutzim*'s own bodies resulted in the most important physical transformation in modern Jewish history. The boundary-

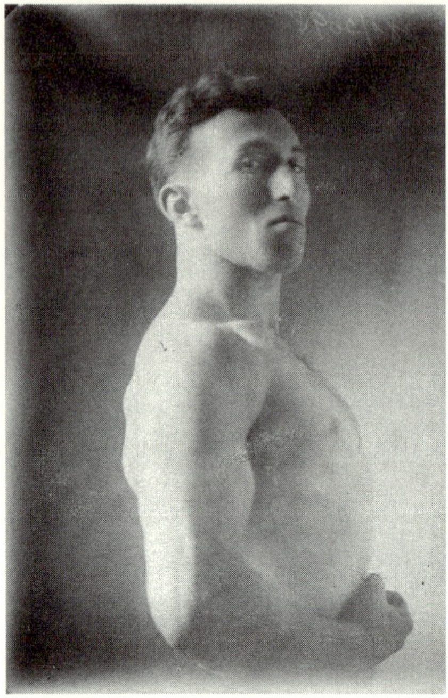

Jewish-body-with-organs; the guard Leibel Goldvag, born in Kishinev, who made aliya in 1904 with the "Kishinev orphans" (Yaʿari-Poleskin 1922, 88–90). Unidentified location, undated. The Pinhas Lavon Institute for Labour Movement Research, Tel Aviv. Photograph by Avraham Soskin.

creating aspect of pioneer desire for the Land of Israel turned the "old Jew" into a "new Jew," into a Hebrew, a *halutz*,[54] a "new man" returning "to the 'image of God' in which he was created."[55] In giving expression to their limbs, the *halutzim* also reconstituted their egos. But this new ego was constructed on the material foundation of the body. It was a true "body-ego." As we will see, the pioneer was present in the Land of Israel principally as a body. The classic pioneer values of self-confidence, honor, and self-respect, and the *halutzim*'s very sense of existence, all derived from this experience of a new body. Furthermore, the body-ego of the *halutzim* contained more than the physical body; it also included those parts of the Land's territory on which the pioneer targeted his desire.

Articulating the Body through Labor

The *halutzim* began to create and fashion their bodies' organs even before their aliya. They worked on themselves at pioneer training farms (*hachsharot*), in youth movements, and in other settings.[56] Before his aliya, Berl Katznelson prepared himself for physical labor by working as a metalworker and blacksmith.[57] Yedidya Shoham joined a pioneer training farm before he came to the Land of Israel. He described his eleven days of hard labor there as a "revolution" in his life.[58] "Oh! In the field I feel like a human being," he wrote in his diary. "In the near future I will ascend to the Land of Israel and labor on the land."[59] The members of HaShomer HaTzaʿir prepared their bodies through physical education, hikes, and camping. According to David Horowitz, the movement exploited young people's inborn fondness for mobility, games, and hikes, which it used to motivate them and toughen their bodies. Beyond stirring national pride and offering an outlet for youthful energy, these pursuits served to counter the inferiority complex that afflicted many young Jews. Polish youth engaged in sports and exercise but did not allow Jews into their clubs. In turn, these young Jews learned to play games, build up their bodies, and spend time outdoors.[60]

But the *halutzim* focused most intensively on their exilic-bodies-without-organs once they arrived in the Land of Israel, where they had ascended "to build and be built."[61] In the Land, they exchanged the life of the spirit, unemployment and idleness, the life of "shopkeepers and speculators," as Ben-Gurion put it, for a life of labor and creation—in the field, on the roads, in the quarries, in workshops, and in factories.[62] There they turned from "shopkeepers and mere intellectuals" into real farmers.[63] After ascending to the Land, Berl Katznelson maintained, the criteria for measuring a person's value changed. In the exile, the difference between a good or bad Zionist was one of ideology. But in the Land of Israel, a person's value was measured by his ability to work.[64]

When Shlomo Tzemach arrived in the Land, a veteran pioneer asked why he had decided to come. Tzemach answered that he was a Zionist who had ascended from a land where the regime did not allow a person to live according to his own values. He had come to the Land of Israel for *svoboda*, freedom. The veteran mocked him and his delusion that he would find freedom in the Land, saying that the source of freedom was within himself, because a person must first be able to hold up physically. In other words, freedom began with the body. Influenced by this exchange, Tzemach set out to seek physical labor. Despite the many difficulties he encountered, he learned to use his willpower to overcome his body's pain and began to accept the pain with love. In the end, he was able to labor routinely, without even thinking about it, and discovered within his body strength he had never known existed.[65]

The pioneers' organs were shaped first through the labor that "swept away" the *halutzim*, "filled" their lives, "conquered," "intoxicated," and "engulfed" them.[66] Yedidya Shoham wrote in his diary that the battle between his muscles and the demands of labor filled his entire being in the Land of Israel.[67] "I require physical labor," wrote Menachem Portugali. "My body demands it."[68] The *halutzim* subscribed to a "religion of labor."[69] Labor was part of their identity. Shoshana Bogen wrote in her diary that labor and only labor produced in her "intoxication," "self-oblivion," and "creative powers." The rest period after an illness or a bout of fatigue was always unbearable. She had no interest in inactivity, and relaxation offered no rest. "We would flee back to work in order to find ourselves," wrote Hannah Katznelson.[70] As one *halutz* testified, the pioneers worked from dawn until dusk because they sought absolution for the sins of entire generations that had not labored and had lived as parasites.[71] No wonder that, for many, labor was an act of purification[72] as well as a source of healing. "We fell ill because of labor (I do not say 'we sinned' because it was not our fault that we reached this state)," A. D. Gordon declared, "and with labor we will heal."[73]

The pioneer body itself can be seen as the most concrete expression of the pioneer experience of being reborn in the Land of Israel.[74] When *halutzim* sang "Labor is our life,"[75] they did not mean only that labor filled their lives. They meant that it really was indistinguishable from their lives. Eliezer Yaffe, the founder of the *moshav ovdim*, explained that the *halutzim* had to conquer labor not only on behalf of the Hebrew nation but also as a basic precondition for conquering the body. In his view, the time had come for the *halutzim* to work for themselves; otherwise, "we will never grow arms."[76] Berl Katznelson confessed in a letter that, in boyhood, he was actually praised for his "hands of clay"—for being too clumsy for any act requiring dexterity and strength. This was considered a superior trait, a sign of spirituality, and was attributed to rabbis. He devoted all his years in the Land, he wrote, to the "repair" of his hands, to reviving them and making them instruments of creation, accustomed to labor and action. Nevertheless, despite the self-change he had enacted by laboring on the Land, he was still disadvantaged by his earlier education, which tried to make him "not a healthy workingman but a thinking instrument." He had been weakened by childhood illnesses and by the fact that, in physical terms, he had been born a "shattered vessel."[77]

The old-Jewish-body-without-organs was soft; the new pioneer body was tough. Through labor, the hands of the *halutzim* became, wrote one pioneer, "as hard and as large as those of the gentiles."[78] "Our muscles must be like iron," wrote Yisachar Reiss, "and our will—like steel."[79]

The most important organs in the pioneer body were the arms and hands. As Hashomer HaTzaʿir leader Meir Yaʿari said, Zionism aspired to raise a tough, strong generation that did not let its imagination lead it astray. Jewish youth should prepare themselves for a life of labor and abjure their role in the exile in favor of their mission in the Land of the Fathers: to make uncultivated, rocky, sandy, desert land fertile. Only the "arms of heroes," not poets, could perform such labor, affirmed Yaʿari. "Not pens, paper, and ink, not odes and hymns, not confessions and the outpourings of the soul, but saws, axes, hoes, and principally—hands! Give us hands!"[80] The *halutzim* saw no point in a life that did not derive from "the labor of their hands."[81] A critical component of their desire was unmediated

Look at my chest
And look at my arms!
My muscles are made
of stone, iron, and adamant.[82]
—Yosef Haftman, "Quarry," 1925

contact between their hands and the Land. Over and over they stressed their desire to conquer the Land of Israel and its soil, to conquer labor and self-defense, with their own hands.[83] According to A. D. Gordon, such a conquest was the only path to national rebirth.[84] "All we ask in the Land of Israel," he wrote, "is to do with our very hands all those things that make life, to perform with our very hands all those labors, crafts, and acts."[85] In her first years in the Land, Tehiya Lieberson testified, she had nothing but her hands, which knew how to grasp a hoe and to work.[86]

The *halutzim* took pleasure in the new existential experience of the rebirth of their organs and the currents that coursed through their bodies. They exulted in the flow of their sweat. "When I walked behind Tanhum [Tanpilov?], hoeing the first cypress-lined avenue," testified a member of Degania, "and the calluses on my hand burst and sweat blinded me—*I was happy*."[87] They reveled in the sense of their blood flowing. Golda Meyerson of Merhavia wrote that after a day of labor, a person is tired, exhausted. But it is a pleasant exhaustion: "Your body warms up, your blood flows through your veins like a brook, and you feel that you have created something in your day of work."[88] A woman at Degania was given her first opportunity to harvest a field with a scythe. "I felt my heart pounding within me," she recounted, "and blood flowing."[89] The body's fatigue after a day's labor was likened by one *halutz* to "sparkling wine."[90]

Labor disciplined the organs to work together naturally. Berl Katznelson meant precisely this when he spoke of "manual skill"—the literal translation of his Hebrew idiom, *tevunat kapayyim*, is "wisdom of the hands."[91] He wrote to his sister trying to persuade her to accept any form of labor, to accustom herself to it, to know it. Labor, he said, was a precondition for the body's proper functioning. It was essential for the vitality of the body, soul, and organs. It ensured that one's eyes would not go blind, one's hands not grow clumsy, one's brain not doze, one's body not become "a lump of wax." It was particularly essential in the Land of Israel, where one lived a life of labor on the soil, in a place where "speech is [not] the most important thing, but rather heroism and capability, the capability of understanding a thing. 'Wisdom of the hands' is what the ancient Hebrews called it."[92] In a later letter, Katznelson described his difficult journey as a laborer in the Land. For him labor required mobilizing body, spirit, consciousness, and soul: "Not only have my hands not worked as they should, but my brain has not grasped the work. My eye has not seen it and I have not understood what is around me. I lack 'wisdom of the hands.'"[93]

As the pioneers' bodies were shaped through their organs, their senses awakened. As we saw, defective senses were characteristic of the exilic-body-without-organs, and the Land the *halutzim* encountered upon arrival also lacked organs. A land-without-organs cannot be perceived because there is nothing to perceive. As one pioneer noted, when it came to the Land's plant life, most of the new settlers "had eyes that did not see."[94] In channeling their desire into the Land, the *halutzim* constituted themselves as bodies capable of perceiving the Land, while simultaneously creating the Land as an object of their senses. Yitzhak Pelah of Kiryat Anavim testified that in working outdoors and building the Land, the pioneer eye learned to see.[95] Tzvi Nadav noted that, day by day, his eyes were learning to distinguish wheat from barley while the crops were still sprouting.[96] Berl Katznelson wrote that the more that "the potion of labor makes its way slowly into my bones," so "the eye begins to see."[97] As the eye learned to make distinctions, Tzvi Nadav wrote, the sense of smell developed. "I learned to recognize plants at a distance by their fragrance. I never before knew that fava beans, for example, emit such a wonderful aroma."[98] The same was true of the ear: "My sense of hearing is developing. How inadequate the hearing of city people seems now to me!"[99]

Shoshana Bluwstein's experience at the Kinneret women's farm demonstrates "conquest of the self," the process of disciplining the body into an organic whole possessing a "wisdom" of its own. *Sehel avodah*, "the common sense of work," demanded not only the hands but also the head—in fact, the entire person—she wrote. The flow of work dictated not only the movement of the body's organs but also the smallest details. It determined even the way a worker tied her kerchief, because if the kerchief was not tied properly, she would have to pause in her task to tighten it. That would interrupt the flow of work. Only a disciplined body could be swept away into the current:

> Then, of their own volition, the fingers persist with a living movement, rapid and unbroken, and then you breathe deeply. There is fulfillment in the labor. You live in it. And even more so—in life! So you must instruct your feet, your hands, your entire body in labor. Because you are "the subject." The heart needs also to sanctify itself in purity in anticipation of the day. If you are angry, or bad thoughts plague you and you have not slept well, your work immediately suffers. The life that depends on you, on your hands, which you must create and develop, is ruined and wasted. To work badly—that, of course, is a sin. You won't even be able to do mechanical work

properly. And then the returning wave doesn't bring satisfaction and relief, but rather the opposite. You are affected by the countercurrent, which bears you down, down.[100]

The "wisdom of the hands" and the "common sense of work" can be seen as the therapy *halutziyyut* offered for the neurotic state of the exilic Jew. The *halutzim* explicitly viewed labor as therapy for the dark moods that oppressed them during their process of aliya and settlement in the Land.[101] "Hard physical labor," Mordechai Snir wrote, "drives away, for a moment, inner gnawing that corrodes like rust, and heals the heart. The pieces come back together."[102] In a letter, Yosef Aharonovich described the soothing effect of farming: "And we worked. Oh, how hard and how pleasant, how exhausting and how calming was work for our angry nerves."[103]

Pioneer labor molded the disharmonious, ugly exilic-body-without-organs so that it developed both external and inner beauty.[104] The *halutzim* repeatedly stressed this effect on their bodies and on their entire beings. "The goal is to be beautiful," Yedidya Shoham wrote in his diary, "to deepen relationships, in order to progress, in order to work. *To work?* Yes! To work on creating my human form."[105] The *halutzim* worked beautifully and became beautiful as the body entered into the rhythm of the labor.[106] "[The body] is wonderful as it stands erect," Meir Wilkansky wrote, "beautiful as it works, in its work itself."[107]

Beyond their physical reality, the organs of the *halutz* body were tools that became part of the pioneer's ego-body. Tools were not simply instrumental objects separate from the pioneer. At work, tools became part of the pioneer body and the pioneer being.[108]

The hoe (as well as the mattock and similar tools) was a central implement of pioneer praxis.[109] A. D. Gordon asserted that the hoe was "sacred."[110] During a trip through the Land, the historian Yosef Klausner met Gordon at Migdal and asked what he was doing there. Gordon responded that he, too, was touring the Land: "You tour with a carriage and I tour with a hoe."[111] According to Berl Katznelson, the hoe operated not just on a physical level but on a metaphysical-mystical one. "Raising the hoe . . . ," he said, "makes a mark on all the *sefirot* (the ten divine "enumerations" or emanations of Jewish mysticism), including those termed the most sublime."[112] Meir Wilkansky went so far as to call pioneer ideology as a whole "hoeism."[113]

A woman at Degania wrote that her greatest cause for agony was that, as a woman, she was always compelled to work at home. "And I dreamed of a hoe," she lamented, "of a field and of a young seedling."[114] Yaʿakov Shmueli, a *halutz* who was injured at work, desired with all his being to return to his hoe: "In the corner of the shadowy room glittered cold iron, like an encouraging gaze, fortifying and bracing me. On my humble bed of boards my exhausted body agonized at night, and in my dreams—heaps of clods of earth, black clumps shining in the sunlight."[115]

More than simply an object to "grasp" and "work" with, the hoe was a "toy" with which the *halutzim* "played" on the soil.[116] In a world where labor was considered a kind of "poetry,"[117] it is hardly surprising that the hoe was also a musical instrument.[118] Rachel Bluwstein called the hoe "my harp."[119] "Oh, to be healthy, whole in all your limbs, and to work, to work," wrote her sister, Shoshana Bluwstein, describing her feelings as she hoed, "'to play yourself,' your life. Is that not the meaning of labor? The hoe is a musical instrument. Its players—the workers."[120] The *halutzim* also used the hoe to "draw" on the soil.[121] "The hoe and the hoer," maintained S. D. Yaffe of Kinneret, "are a single soul."[122]

The hoe marked class distinctions among the *halutzim*. Higher status accrued to expert hoers who were able to "play" their tool like a musical instrument. These were the pioneers whom the old-time First Aliya owners of citrus orchards gladly employed. Lesser in status were workers who were not proficient and had to stand in the daily lineup and fight for a day's work.[123] The more furrows a laborer could dig with his hoe in a day, the greater glory and honor he won. In the Land of Israel, Berl Katznelson wrote, everyone knew how many furrows each *halutz* could dig in a single day.[124] In Petah Tikva, a team of the seven best laborers was referred to as the "hoemen."[125] Meir Rotenberg of Rehovot, secretary of the Judean Workers' Council, was considered the "king of the hoe."[126]

Through direct contact with the hoe, *halutzim* felt close to the soil. Shortly after arriving in the Land of Israel, Yosef Weitz described for his parents the hoeing that amplified his awareness of his limbs and his sense of connection with the soil: "I admire the pangs of labor and the anguish I suffered in conquering it in recent days in every bone and every sinew of my body. . . . Only after digging for two days did I begin to feel invisible threads intertwining, intertwining between my soul and the Land and from it back to my soul, tying me to it forever."[127]

I am a Levite, and have made myself a *harp* on which I will train my fingers, a shiny harp of pure silver—and you, too [the Land of Israel, the bride] have seen it in my hand—yes, it is *the* hoe that I bear on my shoulder before sunrise! . . .

Sincere, sincere are my words: my hoe is my harp! . . .

And see, each man with his harp, each man with his hoe, and each with his heart's desire, we have set out, to our devastated Land we have come. . . .[128]
—Simcha Ben-Zion, "The Levites," 1919

Tanhum Tanpilov of Degania claimed that, while working in an almond grove, he approached a tree and sensed that the better he hoed around it the better would be the almonds the tree produced.[129]

The place of the hoe among the pioneer laborers of Judea was held by the plow in the Galilee, where the different climate and soil required different agricultural techniques. As discussed earlier, many *halutzim* abandoned the *moshavot* of Judea for the Galilee; one reason was that they found plowing qualitatively different from hoeing.[130] David Ben-Gurion claimed that hoeing was mechanical and monotonous work. "A scent of the factory wafted from the endless banging of the mattocks," he wrote.[131] "I was overcome by a desire to plow," admitted Tzvi Nadav, "to grasp the handle of a plow. From the time I left the *moshavot* of Judea, plowing was my dream."[132] The *halutzim* who plowed the soil of the Galilee felt that the plow allowed them to become real farmers, to connect to the soil. In plowing the Galilee, a new soul was created, Yosef Weitz wrote, and the *halutz* was betrothed to the Land for eternity.[133]

Learning to plow, Tzvi Nadav discovered, involved more than simple technique. A good plowman plows with his eye, with his feelings, intuitively. "How happy I am!" he wrote, describing his first day of work. "I, too, have gotten a feel for the plow."[134] "I approached the plow reverently," Haim Rosenfeld of Kibbutz Geva wrote. "I took it in my hands and told the oxen to move. They moved and I plowed one furrow after another, feeling I was in seventh heaven. That is how I became tied to my work with my heart and my soul. I left everything and began a new life, as if up to that point I had not lived at all."[135] At times the relationship between *halutz* and plow took on a tinge of eroticism. Shmuel Dayan described the feelings among his comrades when they gathered around the plows before work commenced: "Craving and envy welled up as we fondled and pressed against the plows. Each person grasped one of them and yearned to make a furrow, a first furrow in our new soil."[136] One of the principles of HaShomer was that in an Arab attack the members would not abandon their plows alive.[137]

The hoe and the plow were the central tools in the pioneer world, but others played a role as well. The first tool Shulamit Hayyut held in the Land of Israel was a hammer, with which she shattered stones into gravel. She kept it in her bed under her pillow: "I caress it as if it were a dear gift. A rough hammer, rounded on both sides. The handle is worn, black. It was sacred for me, my first tool in the Land!"[138] Like the hoe, the hammer had a poetic quality.[139] Eliyahu Rappaport, who worked in a quarry, conceived of his work with hammer and chisel in mythic terms. One of his comrades sat on a boulder and held the chisel between his legs with both hands while another worker hit it with a sledgehammer. "Here are thousands of burnt offerings, thousands of martyrs' deaths, thousands of kind-

Making gravel. The Afula-Nazareth road, 1920. Central Zionist Archives, Jerusalem

nesses, and tens of thousands of acts of cruelty," Rappaport wrote. "Here, every time the hammer is hoisted, stands Abraham prepared and willing to offer up his son to God. But each time the hammer deals a shrieking blow to the chisel and death falls on the boulder's head, God redeems Abraham and his seed. And in the end the hammer rests."[140]

Articulating the Body through Defense

Like labor, pioneer self-defense articulated the Jewish-body-without-organs. Members of the Bar Giora and HaShomer self-defense groups shaped and toughened their bodies with exercise, horseback riding, wrestling, weightlifting, survival training, military exercises, and self-defense activities.[141] So did members of the Jewish Legion. Two weeks after beginning his training in the Jewish Legion, Yitzhak Ben-Zvi felt he was a soldier in the full sense of the word, who knew how to drill and to perform tasks previously unknown to him. Exercises, maneuvers, discipline, and living in a tent made him feel capable of carrying out any mission without difficulty.[142] "It is not just mechanical work," Ben-Zvi wrote in a letter. "Mental powers must cooperate with the body's work. . . . The body adapts and grows stronger, and I feel healthier."[143] David Ben-Gurion, who served with Ben-

Zvi, had a similar reaction. For the first time in his life, he experienced military discipline, which hardened and trained his body.[144]

The pioneer body was also improved by struggles with adversaries, as a result of which it displayed "eternal tokens," as Meir Spector of HaShomer referred to the scars he bore with great pride.[145] While Aryeh Shahar of Tel Adashim plowed a tract with a friend, Arab neighbors took a shortcut through his field. The Arabs outnumbered them and did not heed Shahar's calls to get out of the field. A fight broke out, and the Arabs prevailed. Shahar was proud of the blows he received.[146]

Like work tools, weapons became part of the pioneer body and served to channel desire for the Land.[147] The desire to take up tools was replicated in taking up arms.[148] In the pioneer view, weapons themselves complemented tools. The ideal *halutz* was expected to grasp the plow in one hand and a rifle in the other.[149] The rifle became part of pioneer guards' image and made them stand out more prominently in the landscape. Tzipora Zeid went out to patrol the area around Ruhama each evening, mounted on a horse, with a Browning rifle hanging from her belt. Her partner, Tzvi Hirshfeld, wore a bandolier across his chest "to inspire fear." Rumors spread among the Arabs about Zeid's Browning, which was said to sever heads without making a noise.[150] The rifle was indeed a critical component of the pioneer "society of dignity."[151] David Ben-Gurion, at Sejera, thought that in such a wild place a rifle per person was as vital as food and clothing—sometimes even more so.[152] Calling on his nephew Binyamin to ascend to the Land, Ben-Gurion promised, "Here the two of us will climb Mount Hermon and I will let you gallop on an Arabian horse and give you a Martin [rifle] and you will be a Hebrew hero."[153] Before his aliya, in 1904, David Yisraeli spoke with Menachem Ussishkin. When they parted, Ussishkin placed a pistol in Yisraeli's pocket.[154]

The guards took pride in their rifles and spent considerable time talking about them, as well as preening and showing off with them, both to each other and when they entered hostile territory.[155] They regarded the rifle as the guard's "best friend."[156] Ben-Gurion described the tremendous excitement that he and his comrades felt when they received their first rifles at Sejera. They had waited impatiently for days and spoke of nothing else. When the wagon piled with gear arrived, they were ecstatic. Even though the arms were inferior shotguns from local Arabs, to the *halutzim* they were "absolute perfection." "We played with the rifles like little children and didn't put them down even for a minute," Ben-Gurion wrote. "The next day we set out for work unwillingly—we had to be separated from our rifles for an entire day! As soon as we got home . . . we rushed over to our rifles, and again they did not leave our hands until we fell asleep. We ate, walked, showered, read, and talked with the rifles in our hands or over our shoulders."[157]

Pioneer guards treated their guns, like their tools, as sacred objects. They compared the experience of being handed their first gun with that of receiving their first set of tefillin—prayer phylacteries—from their fathers.[158] Cleaning their rifles was a "sacred service," meaning that no one else could come near while the cleaning was in progress.[159] "One evening I was guarding at Yavniel," wrote M. Lvovsky, who was on duty together with Yehuda Zariz, " . . . and I saw Yehuda approaching me. I ran toward him . . . but he turned to me and said: 'Let me first kiss the Jewish rifle.' And when I handed over the rifle to him, he kissed it ardently, trembling at its holiness."[160] The *halutzim* even used rifles as the poles of wedding canopies when their comrades were married.[161]

The close, organic relationship between the guard and his weapon is typified by the pioneer precept that a guard was forbidden to give up his rifle without a struggle, even at the price of death. Many death announcements from the period state explicitly that the victim did not abandon his gun until his last breath. This was true of Yaʿakov Feldman, whose murder while on duty at Sejera was discussed earlier. "The young guard valiantly defended himself and, despite the wounds inflicted by his attackers, did not let his gun out of his hand."[162] Haya Kroll cared for a comrade who was wounded when he was attacked in a field. The assailants had jumped on him from behind and beat him over the head. Just as he was about to draw his gun, he received another blow that broke his arm. The assailants stole his rifle and he lost much blood. Lying on the ground, his eyes closed, he suddenly opened them wide and shrieked wildly: "They have taken my rifle from my hands and I am still alive?!"[163] The rifle was another limb, a constitutive part of the pioneer's ego-body. "The heavier my rifle hangs on me and the more its sling cuts into my body," explained Moshe Greenwald, "the harder it is for me to leave it and the harsher is the feeling when it is not on me."[164]

Horses were another component of the ego-body. "I felt her warm, supple, muscular body between my feet. . . ," wrote Tzvi Nadav, describing a ride on his mare. "I could not, and maybe I did not really want to, halt her, because the pleasure was so great! Why does a man get such joy from speed? Perhaps it is an ancient inheritance, and my forefathers were creatures with wings? We were like a single, lithe body, full of life."[165] The horse, like the gun, made the body of the new Jew stand erect. This upright stance derived not only from upright posture but from the impressive deterrent effect that horse and rider had on everyone around them.[166] The Jewish horseback rider learned to sit fearlessly on his horse,

> I remember but one thing: I and my rifle are a single body, a single soul, a single automatic fire-and-thunder breathing machine.[167]
> —Simcha Ben-Zion, "On Guard (from the Recent Past)," undated

The finger of guard Moshe Segalowitz did not leave the trigger even when Arabs shot him in the face (Yaʿari-Poleskin 1922, 145). Merhavia, June 20, 1918.

Meir Spector wrote, because this stance in itself imposed order on his wild surroundings.[168] Menachem Portugali imagined the appearance of a new Jewish generation. He dreamed of having twelve sons: "All of us mounted on horses—everyone around will tremble with fear."[169]

Shining in the sun's rays, my gun
Radiates security around me.
No fear or dread around me,
My horse, and my rifle in my hand.[170]
—Mordechai Yigal, "Trip through the Jordan Valley," 1957

The Test of Suffering

Articulating the individual body-without-organs was as arduous, painful, and traumatic a process as articulating the body-of-the-Land-without-organs. But the *halutzim* did not necessarily see this pain and suffering in a negative light. They often perceived it as worthy and normative, a vital element in establishing their connection to the Land.[171] "We longed for the sacrifice, for the affliction, for the prisoner's irons with which we would supremely sanctify our homeland," Rachel Bluwstein wrote.[172]

Guard. Kibbutz Ein Harod, 1925. Central Zionist Archives, Jerusalem

The ability to face the test of suffering divided the real *halutzim* from those who failed. In a discussion of the Arab question, A. D. Gordon argued that the Land of Israel would belong to those who could endure the most suffering in working it.[173] The Land differed from all other countries because the agonies that the *halutzim* suffered here were not for naught; they were channeled into the Land and did not go to waste. "Here, in the Land of Israel," wrote Gordon, "suffering will be the bitterest, the most poisonous, the most banal, but it always has a reason and a purpose. Here we suffer no blow that gets lost in the primeval formless void, there is no pain that drains into empty space."[174] The pioneer's only solace, Gordon continued, lay in the awareness that he felt his pain utterly. The *halutz* was like "a woman who was barren for many years, despite all her prayers to God, and suddenly feels that she is about to give birth. Every pain she feels makes her happy and her only concern is that perhaps the pain is not reliable, that it is perhaps just a pain and not also a *sign*. In the exile we did not feel *such* pains. They are the pains of creation."[175] Shulamit Ron-Polani dreamed of reaching Degania, but she decided that she would not go until calluses appeared on her hands.[176] She would not be worthy of Degania until then. For the *halutzim*, where there was pain, there was the Land of Israel.

We find the same attitude toward pain and suffering when the *halutzim* write of the "pioneer disease"—malaria.[177] For many, contracting malaria was a normal and even necessary part of the process of steeling their bodies and strengthening their tie to the Land. Often they displayed no fear of the potentially fatal disease, even when they risked infecting themselves and their families. Nor did they always see it as a reason to rest. The ability to continue working while the disease raged in their bodies proved for them their profound connection with the Land.[178] "More than one of us afterward shivered with fever on his humble bed," Rachel Bluwstein recalled, "but not one of us ever stopped thanking fate. We worked with our souls soaring."[179]

Having malaria was an "emblem of naturalization in the Land."[180] When Baruch Ben-Yehuda of Degania was infected, he declared: "I have thus become a citizen of the Yishuv and I have the Galilee's identity card: malaria! I am proud of this achievement."[181] "I have malaria. I have finally been privileged to be malarial," wrote Hannah Katznelson. "I have been hallowed! Now I am a real worker. I lie on my bed on the floor, my fever rises, and I feel—so good! Malaria! In the eyes of Berl [Katznelson]—love. And the guests . . . they look at me—and I read in their eyes: she, too, his sister, has been hallowed. Malaria."[182] According to Ben-Gurion, the few who did not come down with the disease were a bit ashamed before their friends. How could one ascend to the Land of Israel and not get a taste of Israeli malaria?[183] It was no wonder, then, that malaria was often not perceived as a disease at all. "In fact, 'malaria is not a disease,'" Ben-Gurion wrote to his father. "Did not the patriarch Jacob suffer from intense heat in the day and cold at night for his beloved? . . . If for the love of a girl—then all the more so for the Land of Israel!"[184]

Two *halutzim* became mythical figures in their lifetimes: A. D. Gordon and Yosef Trumpeldor.[185] They personified the physical transformation from the old Jewish body to the new Hebrew body, from the exilic-body-without-organs to the pioneer-body-with-organs. Gordon, who ascended to the Land when he was forty-eight, was an old man in comparison with the young *halutzim*, most of whom were in their teens or twenties. Trumpeldor was an amputee—he had lost an arm while fighting in the Russo-Japanese War. Thus, his and Gordon's physical and mythical presence in the pioneer world were heightened precisely because their bodies exemplified the passage from what they had come from—physical degeneration, physical injury—to what they aspired to attain: physical rebirth.

Trumpeldor's "invisible arm" was actually ever-present; it became a concrete expression of the pioneer desire to articulate the body-without-organs and thus manifest organs within it. The *halutzim* were astounded by Trumpeldor's capacity for labor and his insistence on working no less than others, despite his handicap. Their wonder was magnified by the fact that the arm was such an essential organ. Some claimed that Trumpeldor with his single arm worked better than a good

A. D. Gordon in the vegetable garden. Degania, undated. The Pinhas Lavon Institute for Labour Movement Research, Tel Aviv

worker with two.[186] In a letter to his father, written shortly after the limb was amputated, Trumpeldor himself claimed that his single right hand would soon attract the envy of men with two.[187]

Perhaps because of his handicap, Yosef Trumpeldor personified the Hebrew pioneer as a "desire machine," to use Deleuze and Guattari's phrase. Such a machine has no essential qualities and is subject to only one imperative: production. Desire for the Land of Israel turns the body-without-organs of the *halutz* into anything—which is to say, into everything—in the service of the "national machine." Here the pioneer body manifests itself in all its splendor, a body that out of its desire creates both the organs of the Land and its own organs. In the summer of 1916, Trumpeldor had a conversation with Ze'ev Jabotinsky, who asked him whether *halutzim* were by definition workers. Trumpeldor answered in the words I have used as the epigraph to this book:

> No, it is a much broader concept. Of course, we also need workers, but that is not the meaning of the word *halutz*. We need people who are prepared for "everything," for everything that the Land of Israel requires. A "worker" has his proletarian interests. Soldiers have their esprit de corps; the doctor, engineer, and all the rest have their habits, if we can call them that. We must raise up a generation that has no interests and no habits. Iron bars pure and simple. Supple—but iron. Metal from which all that

Yosef Trumpeldor, son of Ze'ev
His tale few could recite;
But his name went out before him,
Like a fire burning bright;

Crowned with hero's laurels,
Wounded, with one hand,
Like a myth appeared here
Among his people in their land. . . .

With that one hand he plowed here,
Held hoe and hacked out weeds,
Refused consideration,
For his injuries;

Roused wonder in his comrades
At everything succeeds
They gazed at him with honor
Admired all his deeds.[188]
—Yisrael Cohen, "To Their Land: The Pioneer Haggadah," 1973

> is required for the national machine can be forged. A wheel is lacking?—I am a wheel. A nail, screw, a flywheel?—Take me! Must the soil be dug? I am a digger. Is there a need to shoot, to be a soldier?—I am a soldier. Policeman? Doctor? Lawyers? Teachers? Drawers of water? Fine, I do it all. I have no face, no psychology, no emotions, I don't even have a name: I—the pure concept of service, prepared for anything, I am not tied to anything; I know only one imperative: to build![189]

Jabotinsky objected that no such people existed. Trumpeldor responded: "There will be!"

The National Body-without-Organs of the Jews in the Exile

The pioneer's ego-body, which included tools and weapons as well as parts of the territory of the Land, itself belonged to a larger body: the body of the Jewish people. Like the individual exilic body, the Jewish national body in the exile existed in a degenerated state.

Pinsker and Nordau diagnosed the condition of the body of the Jewish people, like the body of the individual exilic Jew, as a body-without-organs. Pinsker opened his pamphlet "Auto-Emancipation" by describing the paradox of Jewish

Yosef Trumpeldor (front right). His coat covers the stump of his arm. Migdal, 1913. From the film *The Life of the Jews in Palestine* 1913, directed by Noah Sokolovsky. The Israel Film Archive, The Jerusalem Cinematheque

existence. The people had a fatherland, but also many homelands. The Jews lived everywhere, but none of these places was their real home. Although the world had many Jews, its nations did not recognize the existence of a Jewish nation. Because of these paradoxes, Pinsker argued, the Jews had forgotten the existence of their common homeland and had adopted traits from the foreigners among whom they lived that were not inherent in them as Jews. Not only had they ceased to aspire to independent national existence—they no longer even felt any need for it:

> With the loss of their country, the Jewish people lost their independence and fell into a decay which is not compatible with existence as a whole vital organism. . . . But after the Jewish people had ceased to exist as an actual state, as a political entity, they could nevertheless not submit to total annihilation—they lived on spiritually as a nation. The world saw in this people the uncanny form of one of the dead walking among the living. The ghostlike apparition of a living corpse, of a people without unity or organization, without land or other bonds of unity, no longer alive, and yet walking among the living—this spectral form is without precedent in history. . . .[190]

Thus, the gentiles' fear of the Jew was a response to the Jewish nation's body-without-organs, which existed only as a ghost. Pinsker called this fear "Judeophobia" and defined it as "fear of the Jewish specter" that passed from one generation to the next. He maintained that Judeophobia was a variation of demonopathy—a disease in which the affected patient believes he is controlled by demons. But while demonopathy was restricted to only some nations, Judeophobia could be found in every nation of the world. It was a psychosis, and as such was an inheritable, incurable disease. As a result of this fear, the Jew was subject to physical injury at the hands of the gentiles, and "must endure pain inflicted by the fearful mob that imagines itself endangered."[191]

In other words, the Jewish nation's lack of a body was a metaphysical source of hatred of the Jews. Pinsker went on to discuss the association of the entire Jewish nation with ersatz crimes such as the crucifixion of Jesus, drinking Christian blood, poisoning wells, usurious lending, and exploitation of peasants. Since the nation lacked a real body, there was no way to point at a guilty individual. All were guilty.

At the same time, Pinsker said, the national body of the Jews appeared parasitic. A nation for which every place serves as home, but no place is its own home, will always be perceived as a foreign body by its host, a thing "of distorted countenance and maimed limbs."[192] The body of the Jewish nation, scattered among all the lands of the world, was caught in an existential condition in which it could not continue to live yet was unable to die. A despised Jew, ostracized from his society, can commit suicide. But the Jewish people could not, because what instrument of death could deal such a blow to all the limbs of the Jewish body scattered over the world? "Who would lend his hand to it?" asked Pinsker.[193] The only solution he could conceive was to consolidate the limbs of the Jewish national body into an organic whole by concentrating them in a single place.

Max Nordau too saw the Jewish people as a body-without-organs. He maintained that the central purpose of Zionism was to purchase the Land of Israel for the Jewish people and train them to live there. Exile had turned the Jews into a nation sunk in chaos, manifested physically in its individual members; life in the exile had destroyed the Jewish body. The Jewish nation was a scattered herd of individuals lacking any organic connection among themselves. They had to reestablish such a connection in order to survive. If the Jewish people returned to the Land of Israel as "a loose bunch of individuals with no organic connections," as "human dust" rather than as a "a live, united being," they would always fear the world's realization that they did not deserve a place of their own.[194] Nordau described the Jewish national body-without-organs in terms of the prophet Ezekiel's vision of the valley of the dry bones. The Jews, he wrote, had aspired and still aspired to be incarnated in a physical body, formed through the gathering together of scattered dry bones, one by one, and these bones' taking on flesh and having life breathed into them. But this prophecy would not be granted to the Jews as a gift. They had to purchase it, at full price, through the strength of their hands, the sweat of their brows, and the full depth of their souls.[195]

Both Pinsker and Nordau expected that concentrated settlement in a single place would renew both the body of the individual Jew and the body of the Jewish nation. Nordau, more optimistic than Pinsker, wrote that the future of the Jewish body was ensured despite its current condition, if only because the will to live still beat within it. Nordau maintained that the Jewish people, like every other, would survive for only a finite time. But he did not believe that its end was imminent. The Jewish nation was still vigorous, full of desire to live. Perhaps its members could be eliminated one by one, but it was not yet in danger of dying from the weakness of age or exhaustion of its strength. No nation with a fierce desire for life flowing through its veins would commit suicide.[196]

Ezekiel's vision reverberated through the world of the *halutzim* as well. Many lived in apprehension of the physical degeneration of the dry bones and were pessimistic about the prospects for reviving them.[197] In the United States, before his aliya, Eliezer Yaffe lamented the state of the Jewish national body:

> My blood boils, a fire burns in my heart! I see dry bones before me! Dry bones scattered and dispersed. Far dryer than the bones in the vale seen by the prophet Ezekiel. When Ezekiel pressed his blood on the bones in the vale and swathed them with his flesh and sinews, he at least warmed the dry bones and they revived. But infinitely worse is the state in our valley—the bones are dry, dead, rotting, and scattered. Sprinkle your blood on them and they will warm no more than a stone. Apply to them all your marrow, all the vigor in your body, they will evince no vitality!
>
> Listen, dry bones, to the crumbling! Are you the host that affects to build our nation?! Do you pretend that you can be the soldiers of our renaissance? You are cadavers, you will not come to life!
>
> Awaken yourselves! And then you can wake the others!
>
> Dry bones, hear me![198]

Like Pinsker and Nordau, the *halutzim* believed that the Jewish people had become a national body-without-organs principally because of the exile. According to A. D. Gordon, the Jews had forgotten a living nation's reason to live because life in the exile was not life. The Jewish people had become a parasitic nation without roots in the soil or earth under their feet, apt to be swept away by whatever current flowed in the lives of other nations. Every wind that blew caught and spun them like a driven leaf. "We do not take hold of a place among them as a nation, as a unique national body, as a link or as a limb within humankind," Gordon wrote, "but rather we are parasites on the bodies of other nations."[199] This parasitism was so advanced that although the Jews lived at the expense of other national bodies, they no longer could discern that they were parasites.[200] According to Haim Arlosoroff, a parasite that did not work, such as the exilic Jew, was to the "national organism" what "a putrid cell is for the body of a human being." A parasite does not really live, he maintained; it is dead its entire life because to live

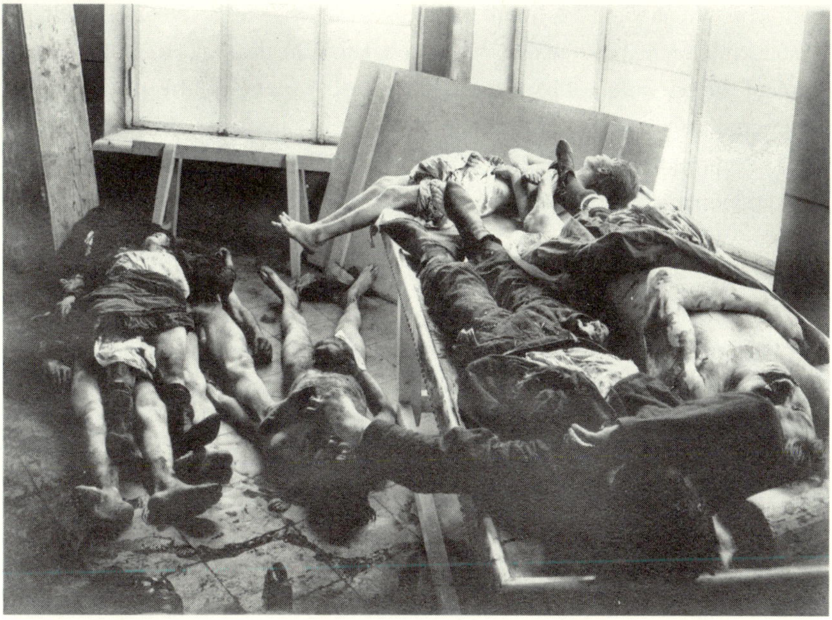

The Jewish national body-without-organs: the bodies of Jews murdered in the Yekaterinoslav (today, Dnepropetrovsk) pogrom, Ukraine, October 21–23, 1905. Central Zionist Archives, Jerusalem

is to create. To create, one must be organically connected to the whole of one's nation, to humanity, to the world. "He [the creative Jew] becomes a cell in the body of the nation, fulfilling his role flawlessly and healthily, for the quivering nerve, the drop of blood in its endless movement, the flexed sinew of the living being."[201] In the exile, the body of the Jewish people did not exist except as a bodiless host for the national will and soul.[202]

The Jewish national body-without-organs was a "torn body," as, for example, in the pogroms unleashed on it.[203] "[It is] like a sick organ in the body of a person, whom every blow hurts more than [it hurts] others," wrote Shmuel Yavnieli, one of the founders of Kevutzat HaHoresh. "Such is Israel in exile."[204] "How long will we creep among the nations, with our wounds and defects sullying every step we take . . . ," Mordechai Snir grieved. "[We] are the withered organs of a wasting national body."[205]

The Jewish national body faced other dangers in the exile. In 1904, on the eve of the Second Aliya, Arthur Ruppin voiced his concern that it would vanish as a result of assimilation. True, the annihilation of the Jewish people was not, he wrote, likely to happen within decades. Nevertheless, over a century, say, this process could swallow up the last of the Jews, and their existence as a "public body" could come to an end.[206] A number of causes might be responsible: a decline in the birthrate to the point where it did not balance the death rate; dispersion as a result of the migration of Jews around the world, especially into large cities; the adoption of the language of the country where they lived; secular higher education; a decline in religious values. The most critical danger, Ruppin believed, had been and remained intermarriage. Quantitatively, this act reduced the number of offspring who would remain part of the Jewish community. Qualitatively, it stained the Jews as a race through the "incursion of gentile blood."[207]

The *halutzim* shared Ruppin's concerns. "The threat of obliteration is not a new facet of our lives," one wrote. "From time to time waves come upon us, detaching many among us from knowledge of their creator and tearing limb after limb from us."[208] In the previous generation, in whom the healthy national sensibility still lived and pulsed, a Jew who had converted could feel intense opposition to his abandonment of his nation's body. "He himself felt that he was an organ torn out of a living creature and that he had brutally torn something living and twitching out of his soul," wrote the same *halutz*. "The convert knows that the living body from which he has been slashed is ill and he feels its pain."[209] But now, when the body of the nation itself had been shattered, the excision of individual organs lost its significance. The Jew who left the fold no longer felt like an amputated organ.[210]

The National Body-without-Organs in the Land

Like the individual pioneer body, the Jewish national body experienced itself as a body-without-organs once it arrived in the Land of Israel. Even there, it was unable to become productive. One *halutz* who came to Petah Tikva tried to conquer labor from the Arabs—that is, to do the manual labor customarily hired out by Jewish farmers to Arabs. He failed, and confessed that he no longer believed in himself. He was plagued by doubt as to whether "you are nothing but a withered limb that has been blown here by chance."[211] The divisions among the Jews themselves intensified this experience. Ben-Gurion, for example, described Yemenite workers who arrived in the *moshavot* but could not fit in with the other Jewish workers. They established their own colonies within the farming villages, remaining both distinct and distant in their public and family lives. As a result, Ashkenazim and Yemenites viewed each other as foreigners. The Yemenites' arrival, Ben-Gurion concluded, had caused "one of the most painful wounds in the body of our nation, a smashing of organs, dissolution and segregation between Ashkenazim, Sephardim, Yemenites, et cetera, and separation into different communities."[212]

The *halutzim*'s desire for the Land included the desire to articulate organs in the Jewish national body-without-organs. A. D. Gordon called this desired body the *am-adam*, the "nation-person."[213] In 1907, Absalom Feinberg pondered the possibility of Bulgarian, Serbian, and Armenian national uprisings against the Turks. He believed that such revolts would inspire the Jews to express themselves as a nation, especially since the Jews were more numerous than those three nations put together. On the other hand, the Jews were much farther from consolidating their national consciousness. Like so many *halutzim*, Feinberg invoked the vision of the dry bones:

> But the "dry bones" of the ancient skeleton must be put together, flesh must be placed on it, muscles must be created, blood must be given, and it must be borne home [to the Land of Israel], where a soul will also be found for it. . . .
>
> And it seems as if the times of which Ezekiel spoke in chapter 37, in the vision of the vale of bones, have actually arrived: "*I will raise you from your graves, O my people, and I will put my spirit into you and you will live!*"
>
> This life-spirit unwinds and thunders in my heart. And I see portents of the nation and it is creeping out of its grave.
>
> Rip the shrouds off my people and they will live! This is the call I wish to shout, to shout again and again! . . .
>
> From a "nation of the dead" we will become a "nation of the living." Living people who can live as human beings and die as heroes.[214]

When Yitzhak Ben-Zvi arrived in the Land in 1904, he heard about archaeological excavations being conducted at Gezer, where human bones had been discovered in a cave. The leader of the excavation team told Ben-Zvi that the bones dated to the Hasmonean period. Ben-Zvi saw him throwing the bones away and asked to take one to remind himself that it was "one of the bones of my ancient forefathers."[215] The archaeologist refused, since the Ottoman government forbade taking findings from an excavation site, even if they were without interest. All the artifacts had to be sent to the central museum in Istanbul. Ben-Zvi saw other items in the excavators' tent, including a sword, an arrow, a bronze ring, a small oil lamp, glass objects, and many other human bones, including a lower jaw with teeth. His companions, who were in a hurry to return to Ramla, pressed him to leave. But he felt he had not examined the findings closely enough. "Melancholy thoughts churned inside me," he wrote. "Lying here in the ground was a former era and scholars were uncovering artifacts and fitting piece to piece and shard to shard, and the ancient period rises up before us as if it lived—will we not succeed in putting together the remnants of the nation, until it rises and becomes a single body, a living people in control of its fate?"[216]

How did the *halutzim* intend to reanimate the Jewish national body-without-organs? First, the pieces of the body had to be assembled by bringing the Jews to the Land of Israel. A. D. Gordon argued that consolidation into a living national body could take place only by concentrating all Jews in one place, on the piece of the globe that they could call their own. This concentration would be "like injecting a drug of life into all the organs of our organism, in all the places in which they are scattered and separated; new strength would enter the organism, to recreate its life in the image and appearance of its living soul."[217] Consolidation into a single place could actualize the vision of reviving the national body: "If we all, all 12 million of us, free ourselves to become a single body, one nation with a single will, with a single strength devoted to a single labor, then we still have hope."[218]

Even if a part of the nation remained in exile, Gordon added, a critical mass could nevertheless reestablish the body of the Jewish people, rooting it deeply in the Land: "Then the scattered parts would not be like parasites on the bodies of others, but would rather be like branches imbibing from their root and spreading beyond the circle of their sustenance. Then we will once more be a link in the chain of nations, an organ in the body of humanity."[219] Making the same diagnosis, Yosef Aharonovich called on the Jews, "indigent in matter and rich in spirit," to return to the Land of their forefathers in order to establish a healthy national center that could unite all "withered organs" and revive the "dry bones."[220] In this endeavor, the Jewish people had no altruistic intentions. They did not seek to offer aid to the poor or to repair this world, only to help themselves: "To straighten our bodies, hunched from their many wanderings and burdens, to fuse together our soul, which has been ripped to shreds."[221] For Haim Arlosoroff, the territory of the Land of Israel was the "heart of the nation-body and the breath of its soul."[222]

Reconstituting the body of the Jewish people required that currents of aliya continue to flow to the Land of Israel and "inject new blood corpuscles into our veins."[223] But this flow must be selective; not every Jewish body was fit to pass through the gates to the Land of Israel. The proletariat was fit to come, because it was perceived as "the blood of the essence of the nation."[224] A member of HaPoʿel HaTzaʿir maintained that "reviving the dry bones" of the Jewish people required that only individuals who were young and healthy in body and mind should come—that is, only those capable of "living and reviving, suckling from the Land and suckling it."[225] Yemenite Jews, he thought, did not meet these criteria.

The survival of the renewed Jewish national body in the Land of Israel required an organic, direct connection to the soil, like "a tree, sprouting and growing from within its seed, not from outside." The seed was the territory of the Land, which attracted "the cells of the nation, scattered among all the lands, to unite into a single living body."[226] Arthur Ruppin saw settlement on the Land as a primary condition for existence of the body of the Jewish nation, because only a Jew who lived off the fruit of his soil and was tied to his place of habitation could be renewed in body and withstand the waves of assimilation that threatened him. This settlement, Ruppin said, was "*the manifestation of the will to live.*"[227] Yosef Aharonovich asserted that the natural current of life deliverable by a single settlement of healthy workers of the Land into the "body of our nation" was of much greater value than a hundred academies of language and literature and other such institutions.[228] According to another view, the *kevutza* was "the first healthy cell in the sick body of humanity."[229]

> We do not require those who leave us without returning. They are objects that have become alien to the nation's body, and it therefore ejects them to preserve its existence. But those who are required will not leave us, and if they leave, they will return. These are the strong, the genuine, the original. . . . All are bearers of the seed, the seed of the future, the hope of generations.[230]
>
> —David Shimonovitz, Son of My Land: From the Notebook of a Wanderer, 1909–1919

6 Pioneer Language

The Conquest of Hebrew

When the Second Aliya pioneers arrived in the Land, they heard almost no Hebrew being spoken in the *moshavot* or in the cities. There, the Jews spoke Russian or "jargon"—that is, Yiddish.[1] For the *halutzim*, reviving the Hebrew language was part of their mission, and they saw its rebirth as one of their accomplishments.[2]

As the Second Aliya began, Shlomo Tzemach knew of only five families in which parents and children spoke Hebrew.[3] According to Yitzhak Ben-Zvi, most Jewish farmers spoke Yiddish at this time. In the Old Yishuv, three major languages were spoken: Yiddish by the Ashkenazim; Spaniolit (Ladino, or Judeo-Spanish) by the Sephardim; and Arabic by the Middle Eastern Jews, for whom the "aristocratic" language had always been French. Most of the well-off Zionists who had come on aliya spoke Russian or German. Given this Babel of languages, Ben-Zvi wrote, it was difficult to find a foothold for Hebrew.[4] In 1914, at the end of the Second Aliya, Yosef Aharonovich wrote that the number of Hebrew speakers had grown but only to a few hundred, while Yiddish remained the vernacular for thousands. He predicted, however, that this would change, because the Yiddish speakers were "devoid of consciousness and ideals," whereas the Hebrew speakers were "militant idealists."[5]

The arriving *halutzim* encountered Hebrew as a spoken language principally in the new Jewish settlements in the Galilee. They marveled at and exulted in the sound of it.[6] Natan Hofshi and his friends were amazed to hear mothers using Hebrew to comfort their children, and even more awed by the children crying in Hebrew.[7] Shulamit Hayyut described an encounter with a group of children speaking Hebrew on their way home from school. She knew there were Hebrew-speaking children in the Land, and the scene was a perfectly ordinary one. Yet she ended up walking with them for a long time. "It was hard for me to believe," she wrote. "Are there really children in the world for whom Hebrew is their mother tongue? And will my own children speak Hebrew some day? Only Hebrew? And they will call me *Ima* [mother]? It sounds like a fantasy."[8]

Hebrew in the Land

The members of the First Aliya who spoke Hebrew used it only rarely, and even then their speech was not effortless. Hebrew was rarely taught in schools; in 1892, only nineteen Hebrew teachers operated in the entire Yishuv, and the language was taught, at best, as a second foreign language. Nevertheless, even during this period, enclaves of Hebrew speakers could be found, generally outside the schools. They consisted mostly of graduates of the Yishuv's schools, Hebrew writers, and adults who had committed themselves to speak Hebrew.

A Total Hebrew Environment

One such committed adult was Eliezer Ben-Yehuda, a prime mover and an embodiment of the Hebrew revival, who created what might be called a "total Hebrew-language environment" around his eldest son, Itamar, born in 1882.[9] (Itamar's original name was Ben-Zion. He changed it after the death of his mother, Devorah, who had told him that they originally wanted to name him "Itamar" but were deterred by a very traditional, conservative society that took exception to this untraditional name.) Ben-Yehuda made his wife vow never to speak to their son in any language other than Hebrew.

A week after Itamar's circumcision ceremony, Ben-Yehuda dismissed the woman who had been the midwife and the baby's first caretaker, because she spoke to the child in Yiddish. Despite the hardship this imposed on Devorah, the parents agreed not to employ another nanny so that the child would not be exposed to languages other than Hebrew. "We feared the walls of our house," Ben-Yehuda wrote, "we feared the air in our room, lest [the boy] hear a foreign language from the maid, and the sound of voices impinge on the boy's ears, foreign sounds blemish his hearing of Hebrew, and the Hebrew words not be absorbed as they should, to their fullest extent, so the child would not speak Hebrew."[10]

At times, Ben-Yehuda demanded that Itamar be put to bed before the arrival of guests who did not know or make a practice of speaking Hebrew. He feared his son making friends with other children, lest they teach him Ashkenazi and Sephardi jargon and he forget his Hebrew. When he was small, his mother sang him a Hebrew lullaby that Ben-Yehuda himself wrote. On one occasion she rocked him in her lap and sang him a Russian song. When Ben-Yehuda heard her, he was so angry that he banged on a small table with enough force to shatter it.

Devorah could not take her son to visit neighbors, except for two or three Hebrew speakers. One neighbor, Shayna-Malka, agreed to not say a word so that she could pick up and cuddle the child. Many predicted that the boy would become a simpleton if he was not spoken to in a "human" language and did not grow up in human company. "A boy in the Land without a language, spoken to only with hand-signals [i.e., by the few people he came in contact with who did not speak Hebrew], will certainly be dumb," they warned.[11] But Ben-Yehuda persisted. He forbade his son to associate with two children who played in the yard his house shared with several others, even prohibiting him from listening to their voices. Itamar was not sent to a preschool; a special one was set up for him alone at home. Until he was three his linguistic development was slow and he did not say a word. Ben-Yehuda declared that even if the experiment failed, he would attempt it again with his younger children, until he achieved his goal. When Itamar asked to keep a dog he found in the street, his father agreed on condition that the boy speak to the dog only in Hebrew.[12]

When Devorah came down with tuberculosis and could not take care of the children, Ben-Yehuda wrote to his mother in Russia and asked her to come. She was seventy years old, but made the trip and took over the household management and care of Devorah and the children. The mother knew no Hebrew other than a few prayers whose meaning she did not understand. Nevertheless, Ben-Yehuda continued to insist that Hebrew be the family's sole language. He forbade his mother to speak Yiddish. In the end, he agreed that she could speak Russian with the children, since he considered Russian less of a danger than Yiddish.[13]

Ben-Yehuda's original plan was to keep Itamar at home until he was seven. But ultimately he gave in and sent the boy to school when he was five.[14] There, Itamar fell in love with French and occasionally "transgressed" by speaking it. Once his father caught him singing the French national anthem in the schoolyard. All the other children fled because they knew that Itamar was forbidden to speak anything but Hebrew. Ben-Yehuda took his son home, brought him into his study, and whipped him. "One, two, three, four," Itamar later recalled his father counting, "one for each verse of the French anthem he had sung, one stroke per verse."[15] Nevertheless, when Itamar was sick, he still sometimes uttered words in other languages.[16]

Like the pioneers, Ben-Yehuda associated the Hebrew revival with the revival of the Land and its soil. He was well aware of the connection between Hebrew, the language of the forefathers, and the Land of Israel, the Land of the Fathers.[17] As fate would have it, the day of Itamar's birth coincided with the purchase of a plot of land where the first Hebrew *moshava*, Rishon LeTzion, would be established. Ben-Yehuda commented:

> Is it not astounding that, among all the events in the world, our revival on the soil, if it is proper to speak that way, and the beginning of our linguistic revival occurred

together, on a single day, almost at the same hour? On the day that the first *moshava* was established on the soil of the fathers by a people who had determined to return to the Land of their Fathers, on that same day a boy was born who was destined to be the first of that nation's children who would again speak the language of the fathers. . . .

[On that day] our national rebirth was founded in its two aspects, the soil and the language, each of which cannot exist without the other.[18]

Hebrew's Great Leap Forward

By 1914, the end of the Second Aliya, about a quarter of the Land's Jewish adults spoke Hebrew as their principal language. This growth resulted from efforts by veteran teachers, along with Second Aliya *halutzim* and their leaders, who were the first to make the conquest of Hebrew a guiding principle in their lives, alongside labor and self-defense. During the Second Aliya the network of schools in which Hebrew was the language of instruction expanded considerably, the quality of the teaching improved, and teachers began teaching what is known as Hebrew in Hebrew, as opposed to from the basis of another language. The *halutzim* were a vanguard in disseminating the language, working in tandem with the teachers. Together, these two groups transformed Hebrew from the language of a few to the language of many. Among the new immigrants who served as Hebrew teachers were Berl Katznelson and Y. H. Brenner.[19] The Second Aliya *halutzim* thus contributed to the revival of the language not just by using it but mainly by creating a society of Hebrew speakers that extended beyond the schools and educated class.[20]

The Second Aliya was thus the period of Hebrew's great leap forward. During this brief time, it was transformed into a vernacular and soon thereafter became a native tongue—that is, the language used by parents to talk to their children. The first Hebrew high school, the Herzliyya Gymnasium in Jaffa, was founded at this time. By 1913, it had five hundred students. In 1906, the Bezalel Academy of the Arts was established, and two years later the Hebrew Academy was founded in Jerusalem. The next year, at the Eighth Zionist Congress in The Hague, the Zionist movement adopted Hebrew as its official language. In 1913, a "language war" erupted over what should be the language of instruction at the Technion in Haifa, whose non-Zionist German Jewish founders insisted on using German; the advocates of Hebrew prevailed. By the eve of World War I, most of the Yishuv's schools had adopted Hebrew.[21]

In the years 1916–1919, 39.9 percent of the Jews living in the Land of Israel spoke Hebrew as their principal language. Among the Ashkenazim, the figure was 45.5 percent. The geographic breakdown among settlements was significant. In the Jewish rural areas, 57.2 percent spoke Hebrew. In the Yishuv overall, among those whose first language was not Hebrew, 36 percent spoke Yiddish, 18 percent Arabic, and 4 percent Ladino.[22] A survey conducted in 1922 among Jewish workers found that some 90 percent of them spoke, read, and wrote in Hebrew.[23] The Hebrew revolution had been completed.

How was the revolution accomplished? The *halutzim* were organized in two principal movements, which served both as political parties and providers of basic services—HaPoʿel HaTzaʿir and Poʿalei Tzion. The former was the first to include in its platform a statement recognizing Hebrew as the national language of the Jewish community in the Land of Israel. Party members worked to establish Hebrew in the Land and also instructed their delegates at the Eighth Zionist Congress and all future congresses to speak only Hebrew.[24] The Marxist (at least in its early years) Poʿalei Tzion was initially committed to Yiddish, which it viewed as the language of the Jewish masses it sought to enlist. Nevertheless, the party's members soon began to voice other points of view on the language question. The first Poʿalei Tzion members to ascend to the Land tended to favor Yiddish largely for pragmatic reasons, mainly the need to communicate with workers who did not know Hebrew. Yiddish, they maintained, was also vital for maintaining the party's links with its parent organization in the exile.[25]

Thus, Poʿalei Tzion conducted many of its public meetings in the Land in Yiddish. At the end of 1907, it began to publish a Yiddish newspaper, *Der Anfang*. Yitzhak Ben-Zvi was a leader of the Yiddishist faction, as opposed to David Ben-Gurion, who resigned his membership in the party's executive committee in part because the newspaper was published in a "foreign" language. Soon, however, the movement decided to publish its newspaper in Hebrew. It was Poʿalei Tzion members who in 1908 founded the Hebrew Academy in Jerusalem, the city's first school to teach entirely in Hebrew. Among the faculty members were Yitzhak Ben-Zvi, who taught Hebrew, Bible, and grammar, and Rachel Yanait, who taught general and Jewish history. In 1910, the movement put out a new newspaper, again in Hebrew, called *HaAhdut*. That year Poʿalei Tzion's sixth congress recognized Hebrew as the Jewish national language. The party committed itself to disseminating Hebrew among the Jews living in the Land, and to lobby for its recognition as an official language. Nevertheless, the party continued to use other languages as well—Yiddish, Ladino, and Arabic—in its public campaigns.[26] The Independents—a group led by Berl Katznelson, who did not belong to either of the other movements—also preferred Hebrew. Katznelson initiated the merger of the Independents and Poʿalei Tzion into Ahdut HaAvodah and made promotion of Hebrew an explicit goal of the new party.[27]

Some *halutzim* already knew Hebrew when they arrived in the Land. Their parents had spoken it, or they had learned it in *heder* (the traditional Eastern European religious school for boys), from private teachers, in clubs, in youth movements, and in pioneer training camps.[28] David Ben-Gurion received his first lessons in the language from his grandfather, who held the three-year-old David on his lap and taught him Hebrew in Hebrew. He pointed to objects and identified them by their Hebrew names, and the boy repeated the words. Ben-Gurion quickly acquired a vocabulary of hundreds of nouns and verbs. Later, the grandfather began to speak with the child exclusively in Hebrew, forcing him to answer in the same language.[29]

Ben-Gurion founded a number of Zionist organizations in Poland, and always one of his central goals was instilling Hebrew as a spoken language. With two close friends, Shmuel Fuchs and Shlomo Tzemach, he founded a group in his birthplace, Plonsk, the purpose of which was to revive and propagate spoken Hebrew. They named the group Ezra after Ezra the Scribe of the Bible, who reinstituted study of the Torah at the time of the Jewish return from the Babylonian exile. Ezra members insisted on speaking Hebrew everywhere—in the *beit midrash* (religious study hall), on the city streets, and in Hasidic synagogues. They considered it their duty to teach Hebrew to uneducated and impoverished Jewish families. Ben-Gurion, Fuchs, and Tzemach would go to religious schools and tell the boys that their parents had agreed to Hebrew-language instruction between the afternoon and evening prayers. Dozens of teenage boys soon gathered around them, including apprentices to carpenters, tailors, and cobblers. In 1904 in Warsaw, Ben-Gurion founded the Herzl movement, which also had instilling Hebrew as a goal. After his aliya, Ben-Gurion founded an organization called Ivria (from the Hebrew word for Hebrew, *ivrit*) at Sejera, which offered evening Hebrew lessons.[30]

Ben-Gurion was obsessive. Even though Hebrew was not his mother tongue, he wrote all his letters in it, except when his correspondent did not know the language. He never stopped talking about the need to learn and use Hebrew in speech, writing, and reading as a precondition for the rebirth of the Jewish people in its land. He taught the language to his friends and associates, including his wife, Paula, whom he goaded endlessly to learn it.[31] In a will he wrote shortly before shipping out with the Jewish Legion during World War I, he stipulated that, in case of his death, his children should be brought to the Land of Israel at the earliest possible opportunity, educated in Hebrew schools, and taught Hebrew before any other language. He commanded his wife to speak only Hebrew to them, which was why she had to learn the language. Later letters show his pride in the linguistic talents of his elder daughter, Geula, and his son, Amos, who ultimately taught their mother Hebrew.[32] In one letter from 1923, he wrote that

Amos had placed his finger on his "tiny" nose and chided his mother: "You must not speak Yiddish, only Hebrew."[33]

But Ben-Gurion and other *halutzim* who arrived in the Land speaking fluent Hebrew were exceptions. Most did not know it at all. When they arrived at the Judean *moshavot*, they spoke to each other in their native tongues, mostly Yiddish and Russian. These were also the languages they used to communicate with their Jewish employers. By the time they learned Hebrew, the *halutzim* had already absorbed Arabic words and idioms. The first pioneer language in the Land of Israel was thus a patois of Yiddish, Russian, Arabic, and Hebrew.[34]

Articulating the Hebrew Body-with-Organs

Just as with the conquests of the Land of Israel and of labor, the conquest of Hebrew was a process of articulating a body-without-organs, in this case the "body" of the language.[35] As before, I begin by describing the language-without-organs upon which pioneer desire operated.

The *halutzim* themselves portrayed Hebrew as a paralyzed language that had been silenced since the Jewish people's exile from their land. While Hebrew continued to be written and read during the exile, it ceased to be commonly spoken. But the *halutzim* considered a language known only through writing a "dead" one.[36] Ben-Gurion, for example, argued that the Jewish people had to be redeemed from what he called "the calamity of muteness."[37] The *halutzim* perceived themselves in large measure in what might be termed the "pre-oedipal" stage preceding the acquisition of language. "We are all infants," grieved Rachel Katznelson, "because we have no language."[38] The language-without-organs on which pioneer desire operated also included the pioneers' mother tongues. The principal one was Yiddish, which they considered a weak, limp language, lacking the power of articulation, as we will see. Another component of the language-without-organs was the Babel of languages spoken by the inhabitants of the Land, including the Jewish settlers themselves.

The *halutzim* thus set themselves to "conquer" Hebrew. The "conquest of Hebrew," according to Shmuel Dayan, was "a labor of self-conquest" with effects similar to those of the conquest of the soil and of labor.[39] Given Hebrew's "muteness" and the multitude of foreign mother tongues, many *halutzim* decided when they arrived in the Land to speak only in Hebrew—even if they had only very limited facility.[40] When Noah Naftulsky debarked at Jaffa, he made two vows: first, that he would never return to the exile, and second, that henceforth no language but Hebrew would leave his lips.[41] Berl Katznelson had never spoken Hebrew before his aliya; he had preferred Yiddish. Prior to his arrival in the Land he felt that speaking Hebrew was not natural. He caused his Hebrew teacher, Y. L. Dobrov, great consternation by replying in Yiddish when Dobrov addressed him in Hebrew. When he arrived in the Land, Katznelson could not even put together a grammatical sentence in Hebrew. And yet the minute he set foot there, he decided to stop speaking any other language. For nearly ten full days he did not speak at all; when he had no choice, he would quote a verse from the Bible that was related in one way or another to the subject at hand, even if it really made no sense in the context.[42] In the same spirit, Yosef Aharonovich asserted that it was better to stammer in Hebrew than to speak fluently in a foreign language.[43]

Knowing how tenuous the position of Hebrew was in the real world, and how much reinforcement it needed in the face of immigrants speaking other languages, Arthur Ruppin saw fit to refrain from speaking German in public. Since his Hebrew was weak, he avoided public appearances. After an intense effort over a long period, he learned to speak some Hebrew, even if badly. He explained that he generally avoided speaking other languages in which he was not fluent but made an exception for Hebrew.[44]

The *halutzim* applied the same attitude to the written language.[45] "I decided that the language of this new notebook will be Hebrew," wrote Alexander Heshin at the beginning of his diary. "Even if I lack many expressions and words, I will not be ashamed, as I used to be, of making mistakes: my writing will be as my speech. I rejoice even in this."[46] While still living in Poland, Yedidya Shoham began his diary in Polish. On January 4, 1919, he decided to write every other day in Hebrew. His first Hebrew sentences were: "I will endeavor to write Hebrew from this day forward and I will see how many mistakes I make. I will correct them each time and in this way I will practice using the language to describe my thoughts and feelings."[47] Later, writing in Hebrew became an inner need for Shoham: "I write in Hebrew. I cannot do otherwise, I simply can't. Nevertheless, I love the Polish language truly. I am tied to it strongly. I reached the logical conclusion that I must continue to write in Polish. But when I sat down to write I was unable to do so. How awful! Which is my language?"[48] And on the day he left for the Land of Israel, he declared this in Hebrew: "Lvov. Seven in the morning. *Today we are setting out for the Land.*"[49] The connection between Hebrew words and the Land of Israel was sealed.

Many *halutzim* responded sharply to people who knew Hebrew but nevertheless addressed them in a foreign language.[50] Some, like Eliezer Ben-Yehuda, replied only in Hebrew. The first Second Aliya *halutz* to adopt this practice was a farm laborer named Alterman, who upon arriving at the *moshava* decided to speak only in Hebrew. He insisted on replying in Hebrew even to an elderly Jewish woman and an Arab who clearly did not know the language. He did not mind being an object of ridicule.[51] Others refused to respond at all to Hebrew-speakers who addressed them in other languages.[52] Shlomo Tzemach was a member of the "Group of Nine," a company of Second Aliya Hebrew-language zealots who made this their rule. Two of them went so far as to not reply to any Jew who addressed them in a foreign language, even if the person did not know Hebrew.[53]

Yael Gordon, daughter of A. D. Gordon, was invited to Merhavia to teach Hebrew to the commune's children. The classroom was in an Arab hut. The children spoke four mother tongues, according to their parents' provenance—Arabic, English, Russian, and Yiddish. None spoke Hebrew. They did not understand one another, much less their teacher. But Gordon adamantly refused to display any comprehension of the four other languages and spoke only Hebrew. She began her instruction during walks through fields and gardens and in conversations with the children. She taught them nouns during their walks, naming objects as the children encountered them.[54]

Some *halutzim* pretended to be deaf and dumb when spoken to in a foreign language.[55] Noah Tamir, a leading campaigner for Hebrew, testified that when he lived in Jerusalem he used Hebrew to ask for goods in stores, even when the storekeeper did not understand Hebrew. If he met with incomprehension, Tamir would point or use other gestures to indicate what he wanted. When a person stopped him in the street to ask directions, he would respond in Hebrew, and if the inquirer did not understand, Tamir would accompany him to his destination, all the while offering explanations in Hebrew—"there," "right," "above," and so on.[56]

When Shlomo Tzemach and his Group of Nine returned to Petah Tikva after a day's work in the orchards, they would encounter the *moshava*'s young men and women strolling through the streets. They would interrupt the young people's conversations and badger them to speak in Hebrew. At first the youths laughed at the Hebrew fanatics, but soon, largely because of the group's determination, the streets became "a demonstrative place, in which Hebrew laughed, loved, and desired, thundered and reconciled each evening in the mouths of all the boys and girls of the *moshava*."[57] Tzemach recalled how even back in his birthplace, Plonsk, he and his friends, including Ben-Gurion, zealously advocated Hebrew in public. In the late afternoon, when the city's "respectable women and pretty girls" went for walks, the Hebrew speakers would saunter down the sidewalks opposite speaking Hebrew loudly. They were not yet fluent in the language but still insisted on using it in public.[58]

Dov Hoz, one of the founders of the Haganah, made a rule stating that if two comrades were speaking to each other in a foreign language, a third person should approach them, call it to their attention, and demand that they speak in

Hebrew.[59] A member of Kibbutz Gan Shmuel used both Hebrew and Yiddish. He would speak first in Hebrew and immediately thereafter translate his words into Yiddish, so as to teach Hebrew to his interlocutor. Another comrade spoke only Hebrew, disregarding whether others understood him or not.[60]

The *halutzim* learned Hebrew in different ways. They picked it up on the street, for example, by listening to Hebrew-speaking children in preschools.[61] Formal instruction was given in the *moshavot*, in some workplaces (such as among the road-paving teams of the Labor Battalion), and to the men and women who served in HaShomer and the Jewish Legion.[62] Communal settlements organized study groups and hired teachers.[63] Berl Katznelson, as secretary of the Judean Farm Workers' Committee, organized Hebrew classes in Ben Shemen, Rehovot, and Petah Tikva. He himself taught Hebrew at Kinneret, together with Rachel Katznelson. Berl urged making Hebrew instruction part of the training received by pioneers prior to aliya.[64] Y. H. Brenner taught Hebrew at Migdal in 1920–1921 to one of the Jewish Legion's companies. He also trained teachers to teach the language to Jewish laborers.[65] Some *halutzim*, in particular those who joined HaShomer, also learned Arabic.[66]

Neta Harpaz, a Second Aliya pioneer, wrote that Yiddish was his mother tongue, in the most profound sense of the word. It had been his language of education since infancy, and the language in which he dreamed and fantasized, through which he discovered the world, and that he used to communicate with the Jewish proletarian masses. He loved Yiddish literature and read it avidly. Above all, he felt it was the only language in which he could express, in speech and writing, the stirrings of his heart. To cast it aside would mean being "doomed to be mute in thought as well, to choke with my own hands my wellspring of energy and strength that enables me to face the challenges of the [Zionist] revolution that is happening to me."[67] Therefore, Harpaz at first could not accept the Zionist-pioneer demand to give up Yiddish for Hebrew. Requiring this was "like tearing me away from the roots of my soul and spirit."[68]

During his early period in the Land, Harpaz remonstrated against those who disparaged Yiddish. He felt that they displayed contempt for the Jewish masses in the exile, as if they were an aloof aristocracy. After all, the Jewish national struggle of most workers was conducted in Yiddish, and to be allowed to speak in Yiddish, the workers' native language, was one of their nationalist demands. Yiddish, he argued, was the language that could call forth great spiritual strength and reach to the source of their love for their own people. He thus could not understand why he was forbidden to speak Yiddish to the workers in the Land of Israel. Harpaz respected Hebrew but still became a leader of the fight against it.

Each time a speaker at a workers' assembly used Yiddish and was heckled by

Hebrew lesson. Unidentified location, about 1910. Central Zionist Archives, Jerusalem

Hebrew zealots, the language war reignited. At one turbulent gathering, Harpaz burst out: "What do you want of me? I have accepted with love all the tribulations of the Land; I have broken myself in switching to hard physical labor in conditions of hunger . . . my malaria does not let up—is all this so little to you that you seek to steal my language, in which I was born and raised and to which I am connected by all the cords of my soul, and to make me mute in this Land?"[69] He walked out of the assembly along with several dozen other workers.

HaPoʿel HaTzaʿir's central committee sent him a letter warning that if he did not stop fighting against Hebrew, he would be expelled. Harpaz did not revise his position until after the dramatic and decisive crusade by most of the Yishuv to make Hebrew the language of instruction at the Technion. By this time, Harpaz no longer saw Hebrew as a "dominating" language being enlisted to banish Yiddish but rather as a language under attack. He now understood the revolutionary nature of the pioneer battle for the Hebrew language as essential to raising up and reviving the Jewish people, which touched on every area of life. Renewing the life of the nation also meant renewing its ways of thinking and reacting, as well as its manner of expression. "Just as physical rooting in the Land requires uprooting the roots of the exile," Harpaz concluded, "so spiritual rooting requires uprooting the atmosphere of the exile. Furthermore, I now realize that this is not a war

Will I too sing to you,
Degania, sister and mother?
I reside, I live here;
My best words—mute labor.

I have adhered to your soil
Like a greening tree in a field.
I have suckled at your breast,
Yours is the fruit, the shade, the song.

Your vale to me is a homeland cradle,
Each silent mount speaks out to me.
I will know no other birthplace,
And foreign is my mother-tongue.[70]
—Levi Ben-Amitai, "To Degania," 1966

against Yiddish, but rather a war for Hebrew, for a language in need of revival and renewal, and of huge spiritual effort and fundamental revolution."[71]

Harpaz's change of heart was caused by his association with a Petah Tikva farmer for whom he had worked for two months. The farmer taught him how to graft and care for fruit trees, and accompanied his practical instruction with explanations about the characteristics of soils and trees. This farmer implanted in Harpaz recognition of "the organic connection between the nation, the language, and the Land" by giving him agricultural examples of this connection. Only then did Harpaz understand that, with respect to language, he needed to be "like an infant who has been reborn."[72]

Hebrew as a Territory

As with their bodies and the Land itself, the *halutzim* perceived the Hebrew language as a territory they had to conquer. Berl Katznelson argued that teaching Hebrew should be termed not "instruction" but "bequest" (*hanhala*, from the word *nahala*, an ancestral plot of land) of the language. He initially used this term at Ahdut HaAvodah's first convention in 1919.[73] About two months later, he wrote that it was vital to treat Hebrew language and culture as an "inheritance" (*nahala*) of the entire nation, not one restricted to a handful of scholars.[74] In other words, Katznelson conceived the dissemination of Hebrew in explicitly territorial terms. It had to be "bequeathed" just like a plot of land, just as the Land as a whole was an inheritance. His use of the word was entirely consistent with construing it in the biblical sense of inheriting the Land (see, for example, Exodus 23:30 and Isaiah 57:13).[75]

Rachel Katznelson described the transition from Yiddish to Hebrew similarly in an article Berl titled "Language Migrations." He had proposed another title with a territorial cast to it—"Language Territories"—but she rejected it.[76] Nevertheless, the perception of the language in terms of territory is evident. If it is indeed a territory to be inherited, the transition from one language to another is tantamount to migration from one place to another, from one land to another. It is thus not surprising that Berl Katznelson called the ideology of the opponents of spoken Hebrew "linguistic Ugandism."[77]

As Katznelson proposed, the connection between the Hebrew language and the territory of the Land of Israel was more than conceptual. Arthur Ruppin argued for the necessary connection between the Jewish people's return to their land and revival and inculcation of Hebrew. Only where a Jew tilled his own soil—that is, in the agricultural settlements—could Hebrew gain a firm position. Ruppin pointed out that the urban economy in the Yishuv was based on interaction with foreigners. In contrast, the agricultural economy was cut off from foreign influence, because it was based on Jewish labor performed by Hebrew speakers. As Hebrew laborers grew in numbers, the language would become a living organism with a future. In any other situation, Ruppin maintained, the language was at risk of turning into an "artificial creature, whose life hangs by a hair."[78]

Beyond the socioeconomic connection between the Hebrew language and the Land of Israel, the *halutzim* realized that a mental link existed between language and territory. According to David Gilad, the Jews, unlike other people, could understand themselves only within their natural space, the Land of Israel, and only in their natural language, Hebrew.[79] Similarly, Mordechai Snir maintained that there was an organic connection between Hebrew and the Land. The language needed a homeland if it wished to live. It could renew itself only in the Land of Israel, in the Land's "atmosphere," and only there return to its "racial connections." "For us, the Hebrew workers in the Land, forged in the furnace of life in the Land and in labor," Snir wrote, "it is the only language in which our innermost thoughts can emerge and in which our lives are contained."[80]

To the *halutzim*, the Land of Israel itself spoke Hebrew. They saw the Land as a living being that could breathe only pure Hebrew air.[81] One *halutz* said that every Hebrew word was an extension of a "material point" in the Land of Israel, "from which it goes out and to which it returns."[82] Once, when Zalman Shazar, Rachel Bluwstein, and some friends walked the Galilean hills, Rachel began to sing to her companions, who were in a wadi below. The echo of her song, Shazar said,

And the mountain is witness, the song affirms
That its brilliance has not been lost,
Since the Shunamite sang
On these hills to her lover—[83]
—Zalman Shazar, poem from his diary, 1912

reverberated with the ancient Spanish-accented Hebrew that imbued the area. He wrote: "It was as if our most distant forebears, the Judean shepherds and Israelite maidens of yore, when they went out to the mountains on days of joy and mourning, secreted the mysteries of their authentic Hebrew melodies in the clefts of those boulders, in the full purity of their brilliance and in their precise intonation, to be preserved there until their day came. And now the day has begun to come. Here Rachel calls out to them from the topmost peak, and they fly to her from the fissures of the rocks, from their hidden recesses, as clean as the day they were buried and as joyous as in the nation's dawn."[84]

The *halutzim* conquered labor to make it *Hebrew* labor and self-defense to make it *Hebrew* self defense. Note that they did not talk about Jewish labor and Jewish self-defense. At the beginning of the Second Aliya, the Jew became a Hebrew; many *halutzim* referred to themselves as Hebrews, not Jews. They were Hebrew workers, Hebrew laborers, part of the Hebrew nation or Hebrew people. They lived and worked on Hebrew settlements in the Land of the Hebrews. They tilled Hebrew soil and desired to be Hebrew men and women. The pioneers' desire for the Land of Israel was thus a desire for a Hebrew Land where the connection between the new entity and the Hebrew language was fundamental and necessary. Pioneer labor and self-defense, pioneer blood, the pioneers themselves and the soil could all only speak Hebrew.

For the *halutzim*, Hebrew was the only language capable of articulating the organs of the body-of-the-Land-without-organs. One reason the Land lacked or-

Yemini strolled among the trees, and had the feeling that he was walking among friends whose speech he heard. It was a language whose idioms he had comprehended from the day he became passionate about his work directly in nature. He was content to know that via the language of the trees that he understood, he was becoming one with a new world, discovering things he had not known and the finest threads interwoven between it and himself, and the craving to feel that the sense of nature and the splendor that would sojourn within him always were slowly taking form.[85]
—Yosef Weitz, "Shining Rays [A Story from the Days of the Second Aliya]," 1958

gans was that it had not yet come into contact with the only language that could articulate it and so manifest it. Just as the Land desired the labor of the *halutzim* to redeem it from its desolation, so it awaited their language. Some even compared the pioneer word to the divine word—the word that creates the world.[86] Other languages, Yiddish in particular, were impotent and inadequate to the task of redeeming the Land. As I have noted, Yiddish was a "soft language," a *mame-loshen* or mother tongue—weak, exilic, adaptable, compromising—that lacked the strength to articulate the body-of-the-Land-without-organs. Unlike Hebrew, which had a historical connection to the territory of the Land of Israel, Yiddish did not belong to this territory. It belonged to no territory, since it was spoken by a parasitic population on territory belonging to other languages.[87]

Hebrew, the language of the fathers, was closely tied to the history and soil of the Land. It was not adaptable, did not compromise. Its weapon of conquest was Hebrew speech, which, claimed Rachel Katznelson, was hugely powerful. "From within every Hebrew word whose true meaning we still hear, our battle for Hebrew is joined by Moses and Jeremiah, prayer and *aggadah*, Rabbi Yehuda Halevi, and Rabbi Nachman Krochmal."[88] Another *halutz* maintained that only in Hebrew could one feel the "historical links that fasten us in a single 'golden chain,' and a living and unique national tradition."[89] Not surprisingly, Katznelson believed that any Jewish minority in the exile that did not speak Hebrew harmed the Hebrew language.[90]

When she and her friends arrived on aliya, Rachel Katznelson wrote, she no longer felt that they were "children" of Yiddish. They no longer marveled at its beauty and at their closeness to it. Even if they continued to speak Yiddish and enjoy its sound, their enjoyment was that of "a person who speaks a language all of whose secrets are visible, but to which there is no connection and no devotion. We are fluent in this language, but it no longer controls us."[91] Even if Yiddish was close to their hearts, it was Hebrew that revealed their ability to rebel, to clash with their surroundings. It was Hebrew, and no other language, that opened the pioneers' eyes to reality, enabling them to break free of illusion and convention and from seeing something where there was nothing while not seeing what was actually there. Although Yiddish was their mother tongue, the language of warmth and love before their aliya, its softness also confused and sedated them.[92]

When Yedidya Shoham was still a young member of HaShomer HaTzaʿir, he was invited to debate in a forum of assimilationist Jews in Lvov. At the event, he attacked the assimilators for depriving Jews of their love for their people, their ideals, their faith, the source of their longing. Instead, he said, they offered Jews merely material rather than spiritual sustenance. As part of this defense of Zionism, he argued that Hebrew was not simply a neutral means of communication but rather the medium through which existence manifested itself. When Jews spoke Hebrew, the things they spoke of came into being:

> Have you ever felt your heart pound at the sound of our beloved language? You must live far away and not hear those sounds for many years, in order to understand what it means to suddenly hear, among the constant din of foreign languages, words that, when heard, make the past appear before our eyes, and the figures of Moses the legislator and David the poet materialize before us, images of those people who gave the world their most exalted ideals. To deny young Jews the sublime sense of pride, to take from them the feeling of homey warmth that they feel when they hear the sound of this language—you call this granting them the ability to live. How miserable you are! Have you ever felt what is contained in the Kol Nidre prayer, in the sound of the shofar? Can that be compared to how we feel when we hear the Polish anthem, "*Jeszcze Polska nie zginęła*" ["Poland is not yet lost"])? Are you capable of understanding what the words "Our hope is not lost" [from the Zionist anthem "HaTikva"] mean to us? Do you hear that? Our hope is not yet lost.[93]

Hebrew was a means of production just like the hoe, the plow, and the hammer. When the language and the Land of Israel intersected, the Hebrew word metamorphosed into the thing that it signified. "Where can you feel the prayer for dew on Pesach more powerfully than the way it is felt here [in the Land of Israel]," the teacher Moshe Kalvari asked rhetorically, "being that it is the most natural concern of the settler? If before, prayers were a kind of distraction and lip service, here they are full of unvoiced intent."[94] Soon after ascending to the Land, Berl Katznelson wrote to his sister, Hannah, that only now had he really understood biblical Hebrew: "Now, as I pass through the Land in the place where things happened—I see visions and signs, and childhood dreams that I never dreamed possible have been revealed before me in waking moments. How can I explain in words what boulders are, eternal boulders and breakers in the sea? Everlasting hills, a narrow path between mountains and a spring gushing on a slope? And mountain air, and the beauty of the valleys? And what 'dawn spread over the mountains' is?"[95]

Tzvi Shatz, who served in the Jewish Legion in southern Palestine, described how the Land's intersection with the Hebrew language was indispensable to his experience of the Land. The gap between words and things disappeared, since in the Land of Israel, Hebrew no longer simply represented things but became the things themselves. Hebrew, said Shatz, actually preceded objects and was a condition of their appearance: "It is interesting that some Hebrew concepts and expressions, which were previously alien to me when I learned the language, have now become utterly clear to me. . . . A 'breeze that restores the soul'—the expression used to be strange to me, but when I was 'soulless' and the breeze came and returned it to me, I said: I want the breeze to return again and again and 'restore my soul.'"[96]

Eliezer Yaffe expressed regret that the new Hebrew worker could not name the objects that abounded in every corner of his garden in his own language, Hebrew. Yaffe believed that the *halutz* should turn the field where he worked into his school and unify his labor, language, life, and Land. This could occur only when Hebrew labor was combined with calling things by their Hebrew names. "Now we want to give clear, correct names to every sight and every concept that enriches our experience. . . ," he explained. "Can we give a specific name (not just 'a tool') to each of our work implements and to each and every part of these implements? And the various vegetables themselves, what are their names [in Hebrew], what is celery and what is artichoke and asparagus, and a 'tooth' [clove] of garlic, is the tooth part of a 'head' of garlic or are these not [properly called] 'tooth' and 'head?'"[97] Y. H. Brenner claimed that Jews lost an entire world by speaking foreign languages. There was no choice but to speak and write Hebrew, he maintained, "because the divine spark within us emerges of its own accord only in this flame, because this glimmer does not take full form except in this language, not in any other language, not even in the syncretic, beloved language, the language of our mothers, that is so familiar to us [apparently Yiddish]."[98]

Like the hoe and plow, Hebrew was a means of penetrating the Land. Z. Feller of Rafah wrote that the lack of Hebrew among many sectors of the Yishuv constituted a spiritual rupture in the life of the Land's Jewish community, detaching these sectors from the essence of the Land. The fact that fruit-growers still used foreign terms—engaging in *tahmir* (hoeing), digging *amal* (irrigation channels), saying that the *tzilinder* (cylinder) of a machine was very hot and the *vint* (screw) was getting stripped—kept them from profoundly understanding their work, because the worker who did not speak Hebrew remained disengaged from his land and its produce. The necessary vital connection could exist only in groups and collectives that used Hebrew to speak about work tools, machines, the field, and labor itself. Hebrew demanded to be the language of Jewish laborers who practiced autonomous labor in the Land. Only under this condition would the language demand that its people sink their historic roots into the soil. When workers demanded that Hebrew be their language, the language would respond by rooting itself within them, just as it rooted itself in the soil. Then the language would penetrate the workers' bodies with each physical movement and permeate their every thought.[99]

From the time that the Hebrews became a nation, Jewish thought could be expressed only in Hebrew, claimed Yitzhak Elazari-Volcani. This was not because

God had spoken Hebrew at Mount Sinai or because the Bible was written in Hebrew. The real reason was that thoughts thought in Hebrew were "the self of our selves, the flesh of our flesh."[100] The ancient Hebrews' view of the world had left its impression on the "slate of the nation's heart," which passed from fathers to sons. Therefore, the Jews' aspiration for wholeness of the soul and the manifestation of the self impelled them to return instinctively to Hebrew, the language that derived from that selfhood. They had to divest themselves of the languages of the exile, which were no more than a jumble of "shreds of selfhood."[101] Elazari-Volcani believed that Hebrew would reconnect the Hebrews to the broken chain of their national existence. When they became disconnected from Hebrew long ago, they lost the balance crucial to natural development and the healthy instincts that, even more than intellect, guided a person. As a result, they ceased to comprehend not only the environment around them but their very selves. Cut off from Hebrew, they no longer knew what was imprinted within them and what they had taken in from "foreign climes."[102]

The *halutzim* thus saw the Hebrew language as the only instrument for articulating entities in the Land of Israel and thereby redeeming these entities from their silence and nullification. Such entities included tools,[103] plants and animals,[104] the natural environment,[105] the names of the *halutzim* themselves (as we have seen), and the names of settlements. The Aramaic/Arabic name Mahalul did not ring true to the pioneers who settled this area in the north of the Land. They insisted on replacing it with a Hebrew name, because they saw their return to the soil as creating a connection between the rich, distant past and the future that this past deserved. After long study and discussion, the settlers chose the biblical name Nahalal, after a city in the territory of the tribe of Zevulun (Joshua 21:35) that included the site of the new Zionist farming village. The site was also called Nahalul (Judges 1:30), which meant a well-watering place where herds grazed. But the settlers chose the biblical version of the name. Deep down, they hoped that reestablishing Jewish settlement on the site and using its ancient name would elicit its ancient character, so that it would provide plentiful water for both beasts and humans.[106] In the same way, Um Juni became Degania (from the Hebrew root *dagan*, meaning "grain," after the five species of grain growing there), Dilb became Kiryat Anavim (literally, the town of grapes), Delaika became Kinneret, Hamra became Kfar Giladi, Telha became Tel Hai, Nuris became Ein Harod, and Ein Kateb became Mitzpeh.[107]

In addition to using language to Hebraicize the Land of Israel, the *halutzim* Hebraicized the measure of time. During the Second Aliya they began to cite dates using the Hebrew calendar rather than the gentile civil one.[108]

The process of conquering Hebrew was fully realized in the cooperative settle-

Naked and mute they [the fields of the Land] lie, but they will receive their garments from our hands, and their language will be ours![109]
—Meir Wilkansky, "My First Day of Work," 1906–1911

ments. The *halutzim* of the Second and Third Aliyot were the first to create settlements where the Hebrew language prevailed, along with Hebrew labor and Hebrew self-defense. These settlements, in which Hebrew was spoken exclusively, provided for a true Hebrew environment and ecology. Languages other than Hebrew were outlawed, even if some settlers spoke them. So, for example, the charter of the *moshav ovdim* demanded "complete dominance of the Hebrew language in the life [of every farm laborer] and in all his private actions."[110] If Jews had settled the Land in large numbers at the end of the nineteenth and beginning of the twentieth centuries, Yiddish would most likely have become the Yishuv's prevailing language; Hebrew would hardly have had a chance. (It is thus ironic that Eliezer Ben-Yehuda, who hailed from that period, was a vocal proponent of mass Jewish immigration.[111]) Shlomo Tzemach argued that the secret behind the pioneers' success in the Land was that they were rejected by the old Yishuv and forced to live as an "alien body" within it. Otherwise, they would have been assimilated, never produced the labor movement, and not been capable of reviving Hebrew.[112]

During the Second and Third Aliyot, the boundaries of the Land of Israel as a Jewish, Hebrew territory were not yet in place. In the absence of territorial borders, Hebrew itself became an important means to define and bound the Land. A letter written by members of the central committee of Poʿalei Tzion in December 1913 stated that, in the framework of political and economic war among nations, language always played a primary role, especially among nations lacking territorial borders. For the Yishuv in the Land of Israel, language was even more important, because the Jews lived among another people more numerous than they. For all these reasons, it was vital that Hebrew be recognized as the Jewish people's greatest national asset, for which they should be willing to give their lives. Therefore, the letter stated, Jewish settlers in the Land sought to unite all elements of the nation on the basis of language—not just to create a national culture but to "bound" the nation externally as well.[113] Hebrew had the power to unite the Jews of the entire world. Geography divided them, but the Hebrew language could bring them together. The limits of the Hebrew language were also the limits of the *halutzim*'s world—that is, the borders of their land. The Hebrew language was the home of their being in the Land of Israel.

The pioneers therefore replaced the exilic written text with a territory, exchanging the Torah, halacha, and their sacred books for the soil of the Land. In the Land, said Shmuel Dayan, the *halutzim* put away the Book of Books "for which we always thirsted, in which we tasted and felt all of life."[114] They instead subjected themselves to another life, tilling the soil. The old Jew had accepted the imperative "and you spoke of [the Torah] day and night"; the *halutz* thought of nothing but his soil day and night.[115] "It was clear that we could not conquer ourselves in any other way," Dayan wrote. If the *halutzim* did not turn away from the sacred books, "we would not become workers of the soil, which demands that we consider only it, labor, the beasts around us, the plants, the tools, improving them, and above all, hard labor for many hours a day, to the point of exhaustion, to the point of physical inability to attend to a book."[116] Zalman Lifschitz ascended to the Land of Israel and practiced speaking Hebrew with a Sephardi accent by reciting chapters of the Bible as he walked behind his plow.[117]

God spoke to the old Jews through scripture, but he began to speak to the Hebrew pioneers through the territory, the soil of the Land. In Degania, settlers felt very close to their new God: "Here they walk in the furrow and He [God] speaks to them from the furrow, from the sprouting, burgeoning field, from the gold of the grain field as evening falls."[118] They exchanged the *shekhina* (divine presence) of the exile for the holy presence of nature. Eliezer Yaffe wrote from Kinneret in a letter to his brother: "When the *shekhina* permeates you, you are focused within yourself, and all the clamor around you that reaches your ears is but a distant echo, like the song of the birds in the forest or the croaking of the frogs in the marsh. Sounds indeed strike the eardrum, but one simply senses the harmony that makes them part of the song of the entire universe—the song that awakens and lifts the soul higher and higher, taking pleasure and dissolving in longing and in pleasure. . . ."[119] The pioneer devotion to the soil, Tzvi Sokolovsky claimed, was not a "cult of" [*pulhan*] the soil but rather a "cut into" [*pilu'ah*] it.[120] Following Aharon Sher's murder by Arabs in the Galilee, the executive committee of Ahdut HaAvodah issued the following statement: "Sher, you were one of the first conquerors. This corner of our land has been conquered with the blood of the loyal Israeli youths. . . . Your name has not been recorded in the 'Golden' Book. We have another book, the book of the soil, in which you have been recorded with eternal honor. Many will be those who ascend in your wake."[121]

The pioneer transition from text to territory was also expressed in the turn from language to action.[122] The *halutzim* acted according to the principle that "in the beginning was the deed."[123] They traded the pen for the shovel, speech and writing for action.[124] They saw themselves as a movement that operated on the principle enunciated by the Children of Israel at Mount Sinai: "We will [first] do and [then] we will listen."[125] The first of HaShomer's "Ten Commandments" was: "Hebrew youth's greatest failing is in general craftiness, talk for the sake of talk, using high-flown and noncommittal words. Our people requires young people who are the same inside and outside, who are prepared to carry out their words *at every moment—in deed*."[126] A placard issued by the Tzeʿiri Tzion movement called on Jewish youth to courageously take up "the steel of action": "Our device for shaping life is *the deed*. Even after work, one must cast anchor in the port of deed and commence a greater labor with courage multiplied several times [that is, during times of "rest" one must continue to work even harder]. For one deed produces another, while the word is nothing but a game for silly children."[127]

The *halutzim* no longer required people of the word and the pen, asserted Eliezer Riger. On the contrary, they needed people who could grasp the mason's trowel, the hoe, the scythe, and the plow. If the Sanhedrin, the ancient Jewish court and legislature, were to be reestablished, it should tax speeches and articles and pay a stipend for silence. "We are overtired of being 'millionaires of moans and sighs,' millionaires of the word and of thought," he maintained.[128] Many *halutzim* believed that those who read a lot took too much leisure time and were unfit for work.[129] In a letter to his parents from Beitania, sent shortly after his aliya, Natan Ikar wrote that he was beginning to feel the mental effects of his transformation into a farmer. He no longer felt any interest in books or the written word. Work and the soil were his entire world.[130] In another letter, he claimed that the Jews had come to the Land in order to transform themselves from "the people of the book" into "the people of the soil." He was extremely angry at his friends who continued to read.[131] Tzvi Livneh of Nahalal testified that while he was still a boy, before his aliya, he had felt an urge to write and secretly composed poems, stories, and plays. But the minute he became a Zionist he understood that his goal was to turn the Jewish people into a working people by conquering labor. He then realized that writing was superfluous and would only interfere with achieving this goal. Sometime before his aliya, he burned all his notebooks.[132]

The Hebrew language was, therefore, a territory, a home inhabited by pioneer settlers. According to Yosef Aharonovich, only Hebrew could remove the stamp of "gypsyness" from the Jewish people. To him "gypsyness" indicated not only disconnection from historical time but also the lack of a place in the world. Restoring Hebrew as a spoken language marked a return to a place: "We feel in our souls the need to revive our land and our historical language and to live within them," he wrote.[133] "Here [in the Land] I breathed freely, my eyes opened," Yedidya Shoham wrote in his diary after reading Bialik's letters, written in Hebrew. "We experience a tragedy in our lives. Language is for us a tragedy. I know of only one solution: to live in Hebrew!"[134]

"The People of the Book": a Torah scroll after the Kishinev pogrom. Kishinev, 1903. From the Archives of the YIVO Institute of Jewish Research, New York

Language played such a central role in the boundary-creating aspect of pioneer desire for the Land of Israel that some gave revival of Hebrew precedence over revival of the Land, both conceptually and chronologically. "Who knows," Berl Katznelson wondered, "whether the Land of Israel is not an invention of the Hebrew language."[135] In a lecture in the summer of 1928, he argued that the battle for the Hebrew language was a principal, sometimes even the central, element of the national revival, because "there can be no redemption of the nation, neither spiritual nor material, if its language is not redeemed with it."[136] Hebrew, Haim Arlosoroff maintained, was the language born with the Israeli nation and the language "by which our nation was born."[137] In a letter, Shmuel Hugo Bergman described the joy that would overwhelm him just from his very presence in the Land. He felt he could never be sated by the "pure happiness" he felt at such moments.[138] But then he corrected himself: without knowing the language, it would be impossible to find a way into this world of the Land of Israel.[139]

A. D. Gordon too believed that in the special case of the Jewish people, revival of Hebrew was a necessary condition for revival of the Jewish nation in its land, and equal in value. "The nation will revive the language and the language will revive the nation," he wrote.[140] The connections between the language and the soul of the individual and of the nation were so profound and ineffable that if the national language died, the nation would die as well. It was no miracle, said Gordon, that so many Hebrew words had survived for hundreds and thousands of years. It was not simply because they had been used for religious purposes, or because persecutions had forced Jews to use Hebrew as a secret language. Rather, Hebrew words expressed the "uniqueness of the Jewish soul" in a way that no others could. He gave as examples *neshama* (soul), *emet* (truth), and *shalom* (peace). Revival of the Jewish people in their land made it fitting and essential that they reestablish the flow between language and soul: "Every word, every idiom, and every act of speech rooted and reborn in this way bear their fruit in season, in accordance with the extent and quality of the labor exerted at the time of their planting. This inner labor is necessarily, closely, and unremittingly connected with both national and human life, whose accessory the language is, influenced by them and influencing them, creating works according to them, in their mold, making its imprint, in its own image, on their creations."[141] "As long as we live," wrote Y. H. Brenner, "the Hebrew word is our soul, and without it we have no life."[142]

Given these beliefs and feelings about Hebrew, it is not surprising that the pioneers perceived the other languages spoken in the Land not simply as inappropriate but as actual defilements. The sound of foreign languages in the Land was like an idol in the sacred precinct, claimed Yosef Aharonovich. People who were prepared to give their lives for a piece of land, to preserve the nation's honor and for the preeminence of Hebrew, acted and died as martyrs, he said.[143] The Hebrew term for martyrdom, *kidush HaShem* (sanctification of God's name), should be understood here not only in its religious sense but also in a literal reading as "sanctification of the noun"—that is, the Hebrew word. Every language, Rachel Katznelson maintained, was in reality a repository of "national energy," and using the language expressed that energy. Speakers of Hebrew created, for themselves and for future generations, "a purer atmosphere of life": "Each word to which we have given feeling and thought has acted on someone, and that person cannot pronounce that word without feeling what we felt when we said it," she explained.[144] In terms of this ecological concept of language, Yiddish was a soporific language whose "air is too stuffy to breathe."[145]

"Pretty and pleasant is the *moshava*; its forest is also pretty, but it has few Jews. Very few. There are people there, thank God, not a few, but most of these people are alien to us and to our nation, and these foreigners fill the entire *moshava*."[146] This was how an inhabitant of Hadera portrayed the scene in 1908. He went on to describe the *moshava* as it should be, purged of foreign residents, foreign labor, and the sound of foreign languages. Hebrew would resonate and redefine the place. "The day will come," the inhabitant opined, "when Hadera will be full of

> And Russian speech shakes the quiet and placid air of the Land of Israel. Oriental harmony is tarnished by it. The heart shrinks. The soul recoils. . . .
>
> My nerves are on edge [when I hear the Russian language]. My voice is not heard from my lips outward . . . my head dizzies . . . it feels like it is held in pincers . . . I thought—any minute I will faint. I waited for the moment they [the Russian-speakers] left me and I fell on the earth. I embraced the soil tightly and emotionally, I sprawled on it and grasped it. My eyes closed, a heavy tear filled my heart, I wanted to let it out through my throat but I could not. . . .[147]
>
> —Meir Wilkansky, "In October Days," 1906–1911

Hebrew workers, and Hebrews will live in all the empty houses, and all the stables will be empty of Arabs. All Hadera, from one end to the other, will be filled with our people, and the Hebrew language, which is now heard only among the boys and girls, will be heard in every corner, and Hebrew laborers will bring a new life with them, and Hebrew song will be heard on the streets, and then the entire *moshava* will be ours."[148]

Word as Act: Language as Praxis

I have argued that pioneer language was a praxis in every sense of the word, just like labor and defense. And as the previous section demonstrates, the *halutzim* themselves perceived Hebrew as a praxis of the boundary-creating aspect of their desire for the Land. As I noted, scholars in a number of fields, particularly historians, have generally made a methodological distinction between the language of the *halutzim* as they spoke and wrote it and the world in which they lived and acted. These scholars' starting assumption is that pioneer language should be treated critically in historical writing. They see the *halutzim*'s language as full of rhetorical excess that must be pruned and purged if we seek to arrive at historical truth. However, this nominalist view overlooks both the desire of the *halutzim* and the status of their speech as a praxis.

A common claim of current scholarship is that this pioneer rhetorical excess, both quantitative and qualitative, produced a distorted picture of historical real-

> We will disseminate the language of our people in every place, we will make it echo among all the mountains, mixed with the rustle of the wind![149]
>
> —Meir Wilkansky, "Change of Values," 1906–1911

ity. Because of this "excessive" language, the pioneer enterprise was given disproportionate, even mythical weight in the Zionist narrative, while other narratives were downgraded or silenced. For example, Yehuda Nini, a historian who studied the settlement and displacement of the Yemenite Jews at Kinneret, argues that, practically speaking, there was no difference between the Ashkenazi and Yemenite pioneer enterprises.

Why, indeed, do we not recognize and remember Yemenite *halutziyyut*? The answer, according to Nini, involves not their actions but the way these actions were accepted (or rather not accepted) into the Zionist narrative. Both groups "made history," but the Ashkenazim gave massive and celebrated literary expression to their endeavor. There were almost as many Yemenite pioneer workers as Ashkenazi laborers at Degania and Kinneret, Nini points out. When the Yemenites arrived at Havat Kinneret, they began draining swamps and clearing thorny jujube trees. They worked at Kinneret, Degania, and Beitania, just like the Ashkenazim. But since they did not realize that they were making "national history," they did not write poetry or memoirs that could become part of a national epic. Thus, we lack poetic descriptions by them of the early days of draining swamps and pulling out weeds. Nini concludes, somewhat cynically, that hard labor and putting one's life at risk were apparently not enough to gain entry into the national epic and myth. That required someone to write the story down. Only then would the settlers' suffering and sacrifice take on historical significance.[150]

Similarly, Gur Alroey takes up the question of pioneer sources and language in his study of the Second Aliya. Zionist historical research, he argues, aggrandized and amplified the role of the *halutzim*. Only 1,000 to 2,000 of the 30 to 35,000 Jews who immigrated to Palestine during this period were "swamp-drainers, founders of communal settlements, Hebrew laborers and guards." All the rest were peddlers, craftsmen, farmers, small businessmen, and professionals who did not share the ideology of settling the Land and making the desert bloom. They were motivated by ostensibly "narrow" interests, seeking simply to make a living. As a whole, says Alroey, the period's arrivals were a heterogeneous group who worked hard and earned little, indigents who lived from hand to mouth in the precarious circumstances of large-scale population movement.[151]

Alroey attributes the historiographic bias (and deception) in favor of the *halutzim* and the relegation of the rest of the immigrants to the victory of the former in creating the Zionist narrative as well as to their highly developed historical and national consciousness. They presented themselves as epitomizing the Zionist idea with their bodies, spirits, and deeds and produced a huge, heterogeneous body of writings—memoirs, letters, diaries, and newspapers full of articles on a wide variety of subjects. These accessible sources have allowed scholars—myself included—to portray the era from an important and valuable but in the end limited point of view.[152]

Nini, Alroey, and other historians also claim that the pioneer enterprise was privileged in historiographic portrayals because the *halutzim* produced their own myth. Baruch Ben-Avram and Henry Near set out to explode the myth of the Third Aliya, which they assert was fashioned by the *halutzim* themselves while this wave of immigration was still in progress: "The Third Aliya did not wait very long [in contrast to the Second Aliya, whose myth emerged only at the end of the 1920s], since legends were created as the actions were in progress. The idealization of the *halutz* was accomplished by the *halutzim* themselves, both before their arrival and while they were working in the Land of Israel."[153]

I propose a different analysis. Nini, Alroey, and others make a qualitative distinction between types of praxes. They consider physical labor, defense, paving roads, and building settlements true, concrete praxes. But they see speech and writing about these praxes as acts with a different epistemological and ontological status—untrue, or at least manipulative, and as such outside the limits of the history in which they occurred: the history of the *halutzim*. This distinction is principally normative and academic and, in my opinion, mistaken.

What is the basis for these historians' distinction between working the land and creating the myth of working the land by, for example, writing a poem or history about it? After all, both working the land and writing the poem are pioneer praxes that exist within the pioneer world; neither comments on that world from the outside. The *halutzim* plowed the land, guarded it, spoke of their labor and their defense efforts, wrote poems and songs about these efforts, and by writing their own history created their own myth. My purpose in examining pioneer desire for the Land of Israel is to open up a way of understanding pioneer language as a praxis that is as legitimate and concrete as every other pioneer deed. The desire of the *halutzim* was a means of production. It produced the Land of Israel, the pioneer body, and the Hebrew language. And it also produced history, historiography, and the mythology of *halutziyyut*.

The sociologist Shmuel Noah Eisenstadt argues that never before the *halutzim* had so many volumes of polemic been written about such a multitude of issues by so few people in such a short time.[154] Pioneer language is a language of eruptions and gut-wrenching confessions, as we have seen here, both in its content and in its forms—personal and collective diaries, stories, poetry, and other genres. The classic examples of this effusiveness are collective diaries[155] and the works of A. D. Gordon. Here the *halutzim* use overwrought rhetoric not just to write *about* the Land but also *to write the Land of Israel*—to create their homeland through a speech act.[156] They used language to produce the image "Land of Israel," the metaphor "Land of Israel," the allegory "Land of Israel," the fantasy "Land of Israel," the myth "Land of Israel," and so on. As Yedidya Shoham wrote in his diary soon after arriving in Palestine in December 1920, "Now the deed has begun. The lyric poetry has become an epic."[157]

The *halutzim* who created—produced, as Deleuze and Guattari would put it—the Land of Israel in which we Israeli Jews live to this day also fashioned the language in which we imagine, think, speak, and write when we look at the Land, love it, conquer it, and refuse to give it up. We should not condemn this language as manipulative, and certainly not as untrue. The myth of the Land of Israel that the *halutzim* created is no less real than the Land itself. Their speech and writing were performative—their words produced rather than described the Land of Israel. This language, this myth, cannot be termed true or false, just as we cannot apply those terms to the furrow plowed in the earth.[158]

Novel critical approaches like those of Nini and Alroey miss the performative dimension of pioneer historiography and myth. Both the pen and the plow were tools that produced the Land of Israel. Just as the *halutzim* pierced the body-of-the-Land-without-organs with their plows and hoes to give expression and meaning to the soil, so their speech and writing pierced the limbless-body-of-exilic-time to set history in motion again. "The word itself was an important act in the Second Aliya," the author Ehud Ben-Ezer has correctly written, "no less than the hoe and working the land."[159]

Martin Buber claimed that in the writings of A. D. Gordon (and I would broaden this claim to include all pioneer speech), no distinction can be made between speech and being. Buber conceived Gordon's speech, his language, as part of his pioneer labor. Gordon knew what he did, Buber wrote—he knew that his labor was the human way of participating in cosmic life. "Gordon's knowledge is a faith and his faith is a life," Buber wrote. "Therefore his word is only one of the functions of his life, the one by which his life is expressed, by which this kind of life is expressed. His words will be preserved from one generation to another in indissoluble association with his memory."[160] Buber juxtaposes Walt Whitman, who with his language created the American pioneer myth, with Gordon, who personified the pioneer myth in his body and labor. Whitman sang the glory of the pioneers: "Fresh and strong the world we seize, world of labor and the march, / Pioneers! O pioneers!"[161] Gordon, in contrast, was himself a pioneer, and expressed in his being exactly what he was.

I have argued that with respect to the desire of the *halutzim* for the Land of Israel, no distinction should be made between concrete and rhetorical language (the nominalist paradigm) or between subjective-internal and objective-external experiences (the subjectivist-psychologistic paradigm). Such distinctions are pointless because pioneer desire itself opposed them. Consequently, there is no reason to make any historical or methodological distinction within the primary source material between, for example, letters and diaries of the period and the ostensibly fictional texts of poems and stories. These works of literature are an integral part of the pioneer desire for the Land of Israel, necessary components of pioneer praxis. Plowing the earth is no more or less important, "true," or concrete than a poem about the soil.

The pioneers, then, made pioneer history and historiography and created the myth of *halutziyyut* through labor, defense, paving roads, building settlements, and also by writing innumerable letters, personal diaries, collective diaries, memorial books, and works of poetry, fiction, and memoir. We can see this praxis of language in action when we recall the claim that the labor movement's hegemony during the period of the Yishuv and the state, at least until the 1970s, derived (among other factors) from its dominance not just in deed but also in documenting the deed, especially by comparison with the paucity of self-documentation by the revisionist Zionist right.[162] In 1928, Berl Katznelson gave a series of historical lectures at the first national seminar of the Socialist Youth organization under the rubric "An Outline of the History of the Labor Movement in the Land of Israel."[163] He opened his first lecture by declaring: "Know yourself." For every movement, as for every individual, he said, self-knowledge is the first condition for action.[164] And the writings of the *halutzim* created this self-knowledge.

It was doubtless the *halutz* David Ben-Gurion who fashioned the greatest myth in the history of the Zionist movement as a whole and the pioneer movement in particular.[165] In a letter to his father, Ben-Gurion wrote about the people of the First Aliya, who came to a desolate, empty, untamed land, the soil of which was naked, without grass, trees, or plants, a land where the air was burning and feverish. These pioneers worked, fought, fell, and rose up again. "Another twenty-five years will go by," Ben-Gurion wrote of himself and his generation, "and then our land will be one of the most fertile, most beautiful, happiest, and an old-new nation will blossom in this old-new Land, and then we will relate how we fevered and labored, trembled and dreamed."[166] The twenty-year-old Ben-Gurion asked his father to keep all his letters. "I would like," he wrote, "that a copy of each of my letters about the Land of Israel remain with me. But I cannot write the same thing twice, so I request that you at least keep all these letters at home, so they will not be lost. Years from now it will be important for me to know what I thought about the Land of Israel at every juncture and in each period."[167] Ben-Gurion revealed himself here as not just a maker of history but also a historiographer who documents himself, and a mythologist.

Eliezer Shohat argued that the *halutzim* actually wrote their history with their blood. Hundreds of years from now, he predicted, when a new generation arises in the Land of Israel and examines the pages of the pioneers' history, it will find in them much that is beautiful and sublime: "It will see that our fathers gained possession of their land and their freedom with all their hearts and all their blood. And it will draw great strength and great national vigor from those pages, and its heart will fill with national pride at the deeds of its forefathers, and great love for the Land and its fathers." Shohat, at the same time, feared that future generations might come across texts of another type. "But woe to us," he suggested, "if it finds in these pages only a few pennies for the Zionist collection boxes and the minutes of Zionist assemblies. In that case, it will close the history book with a dejected and drained spirit, and will recall with contempt its fathers, who could give no more to their land than this. That they handed over to others the sacred task of breathing new life into man."[168]

I will conclude with a depiction by M. Shweiger, a member of the Labor Battalion, of a younger generation gazing back at the *halutzim* from the future. He predicted that, a century hence, a teacher would lead his pupils to the area of Zionist settlements and show them, with a "magic lantern," scenes from the lives of their forefathers, members of the first Labor Battalion. This was written in October 1924.

> Scene 1: A broad valley covered in thorns and thistles. Myriads of rocks and the bones of dead beasts fill the entire valley.
>
> "What is that, teacher?" the children ask. "This is the place on which our blossoming Ein Harod now stands, at the time when our forefathers came from the exile to settle here."
>
> Scene 2: The sun appears over the horizon. Mars is in the east. All the stars have disappeared, except for the illuminating eye of the morning star twinkling in the east. On the same spot as in Scene 1 we already see signs of life. Five rows of tents are planted at the foot of the hill. Two men with rifles on their shoulders walk among the rows, their mouths open, as they beat long sticks on the tents. "What is this, teacher?" the children ask.
>
> "This is the camp in which our forefathers dwelt—the two men with the sticks are the night guards and now, in the morning, they are wakening the forefathers to work, beating with sticks on the tents and shouting, 'Wake up! Wake up! To work on the road!' The sleepers, deep in slumber, awake suddenly and in alarm."
>
> The children laugh and the teacher shows a new picture. . . .
>
> Scene 4: A broad valley strewn with piles of rocks. The same half-naked creatures [we saw before] straddle the piles and bring down hammers on the stones. The sun has come up. The workers sweat. . . .

Scene 6: After lunch. The day blazes like a furnace, a man covered in sweat and dust sits on a machine and plows. Suddenly Arabs appear on all sides, armed, large and small, with clubs, stones, knives, and pitchforks, acting as if they want to attack the plowing man. . . . The camp of the attackers approaches him and it looks as if they will soon tear him to shreds, but suddenly they all turn around and retreat in their tracks.

"What is this?" the children ask excitedly. "Those are the Arabs who wanted to frighten our forefathers from settling in this place, but they failed."[169]

Bibliography

Ackerman, Adam. "The Bible's Influence on the First Settlers and the Visionaries of the Idea of the Return to the Soil of the Homeland." In *Kivunim: The Journal of Zionism and Judaism*, 5, November 1979, 93–117. [Hebrew]

Ahad HaAm. *Collected Works of Ahad HaAm*. Jerusalem: Dvir and Hozaah Ivrith, The Jewish Publishing House, 1953. [Hebrew]

Aharonovich, Yosef. *Collected Works of Yosef Aharonovich*. 2 Vols. Tel Aviv: Am Oved, 1941. [Hebrew]

Ajzenstadt, Mimi, and Gabriel Cavaglion. "The Sexual Body of the Young Jew as an Arena of Ideological Struggle, 1821–1948." In *Symbolic Interaction*, 25, 1, 2002, 93–116.

Al Hasaf: Anthology on Life and Literature. Jerusalem: The Poʿalei Tzion Party in the Land of Israel, 1918. [Hebrew]

Almog, Oz. "Secular Religion in Israel." In *Megamot*, 37, 3, 1996, 314–339. [Hebrew]

———. *The Sabra: The Creation of the New Jew*. Tel Aviv: Am Oved, 1998. [Hebrew]

Almog, Shmuel. "From 'Muscular Jewry' to the 'Religion of Labor,'" *Zionism: Studies in the History of the Zionist Movement and of the Jewish Community in Palestine*, 9, 1984, 137–146. [Hebrew]

———. *Nationalism and Antisemitism in Modern Europe, 1815–1945*. Oxford: Pergamon, 1990.

———. *Nationalism, Zionism, Antisemitism: Essays and Studies*. Jerusalem: Hassifria Hatziyonit Publishing House of the World Zionist Organization, 1992. [Hebrew]

———. "Pioneering as an Alternative Culture," *Zion*, 58, 3, 1993, 329–346. [Hebrew]

———. "The Role of Religious Values in the Second Aliyah." In Shmuel Almog, Jehuda Reinharz, and Anita Shapira, eds. *Zionism and Religion*. Waltham, MA: Brandeis University, University Press of New England, 1998.

Alroey, Gur. "Suicide in the Second and Third Aliya Periods." In *Yahadut Zemanenu: Zionism, the State of Israel, and the Diaspora*, 13, 1999, 209–241. [Hebrew]

———. *Immigrants: Jewish Immigration to Palestine in the Early Twentieth Century*. Jerusalem: Yad Izhak Ben-Zvi, 2004. [Hebrew]

Ami Asaf. *Ami Asaf: A Selection of Articles, Discourses, and Letters*. Tel Aviv: Hamoshavim Movement, 1968. [Hebrew]

Amiran-Sapir, Revital. *Feminist Zionism*. A Thesis Submitted to the Degree of Master of Arts, Tel Aviv University, 1999. [Hebrew]

Anderson, Benedict. *Imagined Communities*. London: Verso, 1991.

Anthology of the Third Aliya at Kinneret on Its Fortieth Anniversary: 1920–1940. Kinneret: Kevutzat Kinneret, 1961. [Hebrew]

Arbel, Rachel, ed. *Blue and White in Color: Visual Images of Zionism, 1897–1947*. Tel Aviv: Beth Hatefutsoth/The Nahum Goldmann Museum of the Jewish Diaspora and Am Oved, 1997. [Hebrew]

Arlosoroff, Haim. *Collected Works of Haim Arlosoroff*. 6 Vols. Tel Aviv: A. J. Stybel, 1934. [Hebrew]

Avneri, Arieh L. *The Claim of Dispossession: Jewish Land Settlement and the Arabs, 1878–1948*. New Brunswick, NJ: Transaction Books, 1984.

Avineri, Shlomo. *The Making of Modern Zionism: Intellectual Origins of the Jewish State*. London: Weidenfeld & Nicolson, 1981.

Avronin-Abrahamson, Nehama. *Nehama Avronin-Abrahamson Diary*. Tel Aviv: Tammuz, 2000. [Hebrew]

Azaryahu, Maoz. "Water Towers: A Study in the Cultural Geographers of Zionist Mythology." In *Ecumene* 8, 3, 2001, 317–339.

Azaryahu, Maoz, and Aharon Kellerman. "Symbolic Places of National History and Revival: A Study in Zionist Mythical Geography." In *Transactions of the Institute of British Geographers*, 24, 1, 1999, 109–123.

Azmon, Yael, ed. *Will You Listen to My Voice? Representations of Women in Israeli Culture*. Jerusalem and Tel Aviv: Van Leer Jerusalem Institute and HaKibbutz HaMe'uhad, 2001. [Hebrew]

BaAvodah: Members' Booklet. Jaffa: Union of Farm Workers, 1918. [Hebrew]

Bachi, Roberto. "A Statistical Analysis of the Revival of Hebrew in Israel." In *Scripta Hierosolymitana*, 3, 1956, 179–247.

BaDerech. Vienna: The World Union of HaPoʿel HaTzaʿir and Tzeʿiri Tzion in Austria. [Hebrew]

BaGalil: News of the Office of the Moshavot Organization. Tiberias: Histadrut HaMoshavot. [Hebrew]

Baker, Harold D. "Obsessional and Hysterical Modes of National Identity." In *Journal for the Psychoanalysis of Culture and Society*, 2, 2, Fall 1997, 129–145.

Bar-Adon, Aaron. *S. Y. Agnon and the Revival of Hebrew*. Jerusalem: Bialik Institute, 1977. [Hebrew]

———. "The Contribution of the Second Aliya to the Revival of Hebrew: Perceptions and Reality." In *Proceedings of the Ninth World Congress of Jewish Studies*, Division D, 1, 1986, 63–70. [Hebrew]

———. "'The Founding Mothers' and Their Part in the Early Revival of Hebrew, 1882–1914." In *Language and Hebrew: Hebrew Journal for Language, Languages, and the Hebrew Language*, 3, May 1990, 5–26. [Hebrew]

Bartal, Israel. *Exile in the Homeland: Essays*. Jerusalem: Hassifria Hatziyonit Publishing House of the World Zionist Organization, 1994. [Hebrew]

———, ed. *The Second Aliya: Studies*. Jerusalem: Yad Izhak Ben-Zvi, 1997. [Hebrew]

Basok, Moshe, ed. *The Book of HaHalutz: An Anthology*. Jerusalem: The Jewish Agency, 1940. [Hebrew]

Beginning: Degania in Its First Decade, 1911–1921: From the Archive. Degania: no publisher, 1971. [Hebrew]

Bein, Alex. *The Return to the Soil: A History of Jewish Settlement in Israel*. Jerusalem: Youth and Hechalutz Department of the Zionist Organisation, 1952.

———. "'Der jüdische Parasit': Bemerkungen zur Semantik der Judenfrage." In *Vierteljahrshefte für Zeitgeschichte*, 13, 2, April 1965, 121–149.

Ben-Amitai, Levi. *The Stalks of Grain Within: A Collection of Songs*. Tel Aviv: A. J. Stybel, 1934. [Hebrew]

———. *Summer Fruit: Poems*. Tel Aviv: Am Oved, 1966. [Hebrew]

Ben-Artzi, Yossi. *Early Jewish Settlement Patterns in Palestine, 1882–1914*. Jerusalem: The Magnes Press, 1997.

Ben-Artzi, Yossi, Ruth Kark, and Ran Aaronsohn. "Khans or Estates? Sites Purchased for Jewish Colonies in Palestine, 1882–1914." In *Zionism: Studies in the History of the Zionist Movement and of the Jewish Community in Palestine*, 13, 1988, 263–284. [Hebrew]

Ben-Avi, Itamar. *Im Shahar Atzmautenu: Memoirs of the First Hebrew Child*. Jerusalem: The Public Committee for the Publication of the Writings of Itamar Ben-Avi, 1961. [Hebrew]

Ben-Avram, Baruch. "The Emergence of the Kevutza from the Aspiration of the Pioneers of the Second Aliya for Self-Employment." In *Cathedra: For the History of Eretz Israel and Its Yishuv*, 18, January 1981, 118–123. [Hebrew]

———. "The Kevutza and Indigenous Zionist Palestinian Collectivism." In *Cathedra: For the History of Eretz Israel and Its Yishuv*, 23, April 1982, 187–189. [Hebrew]

Ben-Avram, Baruch, and Henry Near. *Studies in the Third Aliya (1919–1924): Image and Reality*. Jerusalem: Yad Izhak Ben-Zvi, 1995. [Hebrew]

Ben-David, Benjamin. "Some Expressions of Longing for Zion (One Hundred Years of Aliya by the Jews of Bukhara)." In *Kivunim: The Journal of Zionism and Judaism*, 28, August 1985, 155–164. [Hebrew]

Ben-Eliezer, Uri. "State versus Civil Society? A Non-Binary Model of Domination through the Example of Israel." In *Journal of Historical Sociology*, 11, 3, September 1998, 370–396.

Ben-Gurion, David. *From Class into People*. Tel Aviv: Ayanot, 1955. [Hebrew]

———. *Early Writings*. Tel Aviv: no publisher, 1962. [Hebrew]

———. *The Letters of David Ben-Gurion*. 3 Vols. Tel Aviv: Am Oved and Tel Aviv University, 1971–1974. [Hebrew]

———. *Memoirs*. Tel Aviv: Am Oved, 1973. [Hebrew]

Ben-Gurion, David, and Izhak Ben-Zvi. *Eretz Israel in the Past and in the Present*. Jerusalem: Yad Izhak Ben-Zvi, 1979. [Hebrew]

Benjamin, R. (Yehoshua Radler-Feldman). *On the Borders: Essays and Articles*. Jerusalem: no publisher, 1922. [Hebrew]

Benjamini, Eliahu. *States for the Jews: Uganda, Birobidzhan, and Thirty-four Other Projects*. Tel Aviv: HaKibbutz HaMe'uhad and Sifriat Poalim, 1990. [Hebrew]

Ben-Porat, Amir. "Opportunity, Desire, and the Break into Palestine." In *Iyunim Bitkumat Israel: Studies in Zionism, the Yishuv, and the State of Israel*, 4, 1994, 278–298. [Hebrew]

Ben-Ya'akov, Yona, and Miriam Sion, eds. *The Purpose/Foundation of the First Settlers: Degania Alef, on Its Seventieth Anniversary, 1911–1981*. Degania Alef: Degania Alef, 1981. [Hebrew]

Ben-Yehuda, Eliezer, "The Dream and Its Fulfillment" [1917–1918]. In Eliezer Ben-Yehuda, *The Dream and Its Fulfillment: Selected Writings*. Jerusalem: Bialik Institute, 1978. [Hebrew]

Ben-Yehuda, Hemda. *The Happy Warrior: The Life of Eliezer Ben-Yehuda*. Jerusalem: Zion, 1932. [Hebrew]

———. *The Flag Bearer: The Life of Itamar Ben-Avi*. Jerusalem: Ben-Yehuda, 1944. [Hebrew]

Ben-Zion, Simcha. *Collected Works of Simcha Ben-Zion*. Tel Aviv: Dvir, 1960. [Hebrew]

Ben-Zvi, Izhak. *Eretz Israel under Ottoman Rule: Four Centuries of History*. Jerusalem: Bialik Institute, 1955. [Hebrew]

———. *Essays and Reminiscences*. Jerusalem: Yad Izhak Ben-Zvi, 1966. [Hebrew]

Ben-Zvi, Izhak, Yisrael Shohat, Mati Meged, and Yohanan Tverski, eds. *The HaShomer Book: Words of the Members*. Tel Aviv: Dvir, 1957. [Hebrew]

Berg, Nicolas. "Bilder von 'Luftmenschen': Über Metapher und Kollektivkonstruktion." In Dan Diner, ed., *Synchrone Welten: Zeitenräume jüdischer Geschichte*. Göttingen: Vandenhoeck & Ruprecht, 2005, 199–224.

Berkowitz, Michael. *Zionist Culture and West European Jewry Before the First World War*. Cambridge: Cambridge University Press, 1993.

———. *Western Jewry and the Zionist Project, 1914–1933*. Cambridge: Cambridge University Press, 1997.

———. *The Jewish Self-Image: American and British Perspectives, 1881–1939*. London: Reaktion Books, 2000.

Bernstein, Deborah S. *The Struggle for Equality: Women Workers in the Palestine Yishuv*. Tel Aviv: HaKibbutz HaMe'uhad, 1987. [Hebrew]

———, ed. *Pioneers and Homemakers: Jewish Women in Pre-State Israel*. Albany: State University of New York Press, 1992.

Biale, David. *Eros and the Jews: From Biblical Israel to Contemporary America*. Berkeley, CA: University of California Press, 1997.

Bialik, Hayim Nahman. *Songs from Bialik: Selected Poems of Hayim Nahman Bialik*. New York: Syracuse University Press, 2000.

Bistritzky, Nathan. *Days and Nights*. Tel Aviv: Sifriat Poalim, 1978. [Hebrew]

———. *The Hidden Myth*. Tel Aviv: Yachdav, 1980. [Hebrew]

Bloch, Ze'ev. *The Campaigns of the Kibbutz: Outline*. Merhavia: Sifriat Poalim, 1952. [Hebrew]

Bloom, Etan. "What 'The Father' Had in Mind? Arthur Ruppin (1876–1943), Cultural Identity, Weltanschauung, and Action." In *History of European Ideas*, 33, 2007, 330–349.

Blum, Shlomit. *The Women in the Labor Movement in the Second Aliya Period*. A Thesis Submitted to the Degree of Master of Arts, Tel Aviv University, 1980. [Hebrew]

Boyarin, Daniel. *Unheroic Conduct: The Rise of Heterosexuality and the Invention of the Jewish Man*. Berkeley, CA: University of California Press, 1997, 271–312.

Brener, Benjamin. *Reminiscences: 1911–1921*. Tel Aviv: Am Oved, 1978. [Hebrew]

Brenner, Yosef Haim. *Collected Works of Yosef Haim Brenner*. 4 Vols. Tel Aviv: HaKibbutz HaMe'uhad and Sifriat Poalim, 1977–1981. [Hebrew]

Brook, Marvin G. "Linkage of Oedipal Dangers and Mastery to Theodor Herzl's Zionism." In *Journal of Applied Psychoanalytic Studies*, 4, 2, April 2002, 171–184.

Buber, Martin. "Regeneration eines Volkstums" [1943]. In Martin Buber, *Der Jude und sein Judentum: Gesammelte Aufsätze und Reden*. Köln: Joseph Melzer Verlag, 1963, 249–271.

———. *On Zion: The History of an Idea*. Edinburgh: T. & T. Clark, 1985.

Bunzl, John, and Benjamin Beit-Hallahmi, eds. *Psychoanalysis, Identity, and Ideology: Critical Essays on the Israel/Palestine Case*. Boston: Kluwer, 2002.

Butler, Judith P. *Subjects of Desire: Hegelian Reflections in Twentieth-Century France.* New York: Columbia University Press, 1987.

Chetrit, Sami Shalom. *The Mizrahi Struggle in Israel: Between Oppression and Liberation, Identification and Alternative, 1948–2003.* Tel Aviv: Am Oved, 2004. [Hebrew]

Chowers, Eyal. "Time in Zionism: The Life and Afterlife of a Temporal Revolution." In *Political Theory*, 26, 5, October 1998, 652–685.

———. "The End of Building: Zionism and the Politics of the Concrete." In *The Review of Politics*, 64, 4, Fall 2002, 599–626.

Cogan, Mordechai, ed. *Ben-Gurion and the Bible: The People and Its Land.* Beer-Sheva: Ben-Gurion University of the Negev Press, 1989. [Hebrew]

Cohen, David. *To Their Land: The Pioneer Haggadah.* Jerusalem: M. Newman, 1973. [Hebrew]

Cohen, Uri S. *Survival of Death between the World Wars.* Tel Aviv: Resling, 2007. [Hebrew]

Dagan, Hagai. "The Concept of 'Homeland' and the Jewish Ethos: A Chronicle of Dissonance." In *Alpayim: Journal for Contemporary Thought and Literature*, 18, 1999, 9–23. [Hebrew]

Dayan, Deborah. *Happiness and Sorrow.* Tel Aviv: Masada and Hamoshavim Movement, 1958. [Hebrew]

Dayan, Shmuel. *Degania's First Quarter-Century.* Tel Aviv: A. J. Stybel, 1935. [Hebrew]

———. *Times of Vision and Siege (from My Diary, Testimonies, and Documents).* Tel Aviv: Masada and Hamoshavim Movement, 1953. [Hebrew]

———. *Nahalalim: The Story of Forty Years.* Tel Aviv: Masada and Hamoshavim Movement, 1961. [Hebrew]

Deleuze, Gilles, and Félix Guattari. *Anti-Oedipus: Capitalism and Schizophrenia.* Minneapolis: University of Minnesota Press, 1996.

De-Shalit, Avner. "From the Political to the Objective: The Dialectics of Zionism and Environment." In *Environmental Politics*, 4, 1, Spring 1995, 70–87.

Dror, Levi, and Israel Rosenzweig, eds. *The Book of HaShomer HaTzaʿir: The Movement from Its Beginning to After the Ghetto Uprisings, 1913–1945*, vol. 1. Merhavia: Sifriat Poalim, 1956. [Hebrew]

Edelstein, Ya'akov. "Ascents, Longings, and Grasping at Redemption (Two Hundred Years Since the Aliya of the Hasidim)." In *Kivunim: The Journal of Zionism and Judaism*, 28, August 1985, 145–153. [Hebrew]

Efrati, Nathan. "The Zionist Movement and the Revival of Hebrew." In *Leshonenu Laʿam: A Popular Journal for the Hebrew Language*, XLVIII, 3, April–June 1997, 89–134. [Hebrew]

———. *The Evolution of Spoken Hebrew in Pre-State Israel, 1881–1922.* Jerusalem: The Academy of the Hebrew Language, 2004. [Hebrew]

Efron, John M. *Defenders of the Race: Jewish Doctors and Race Science in Fin-de-Siècle Europe.* New Haven, CT: Yale University Press, 1994.

———. *Medicine and the German Jews: A History.* New Haven, CT: Yale University Press, 2001.

Eisen, Arnold M. *Galut: Modern Jewish Reflection on Homelessness and Homecoming.* Bloomington: Indiana University Press, 1986.

Eisenstadt, Samuel. *Our Living Hebrew Language.* Tel Aviv: Tekuma, 1967. [Hebrew]

Eisenstadt, Shmuel Noah. *Israeli Society: Background, Development, and Problems.* Jerusalem: The Hebrew University Magnes Press, 1967. [Hebrew]

———. *Israeli Society*. London: Weidenfeld and Nicolson, 1970, 1967.

Eisenstadt, Shmuel Noah, and Moshe Lissak, eds. *Zionism and the Return to History: A Reappraisal*. Jerusalem: Yad Izhak Ben-Zvi, 1999. [Hebrew]

Elam, Yigal. "Zionism and Patriotism." In Avner Ben-Amos and Daniel Bar-Tal, eds., *Patriotism: Homeland Love*. Tel Aviv: HaKibbutz HaMe'uhad, 2004, 29–59. [Hebrew]

Elazari-Volcani, Yitzhak. *Night Watches*. Tel Aviv: Tversky, 1950a. [Hebrew]

———. *Spheres*. Tel Aviv: Tversky, 1950b. [Hebrew]

Elboim-Dror, Rachel. *Yesterday's Tomorrow*. 2 Vols. Jerusalem: Yad Izhak Ben-Zvi, 1993. [Hebrew]

———. "'He Is Coming, from among Us Comes the New Hebrew': On the Youth Culture of the First Aliya." In *Alpayim: Journal for Contemporary Thought and Literature*, 12, 1996, 104–135. [Hebrew]

———. "The Ideal Zionist Woman." In Yael Azmon, ed., *Will You Listen to My Voice? Representations of Women in Israeli Culture*. Jerusalem and Tel Aviv: Van Leer Jerusalem Institute and HaKibbutz HaMe'uhad, 2001. [Hebrew]

Eliade, Mircea. *The Myth of the Eternal Return*. New York: Pantheon Books, 1954.

Eliav, Mordechai. *Eretz Israel and Its Yishuv in the 19th Century, 1777–1917*. Jerusalem: Keter, 1978. [Hebrew]

———, ed. *The First Aliya*. Jerusalem: Yad Izhak Ben-Zvi and Ministry of Defense, 1981. [Hebrew]

Elon, Amos. *The Israelis: Founders and Sons*. London: Weidenfeld & Nicolson, 1971.

———. *The Israelis: Founders and Sons*. Jerusalem: Schocken, 1972. [Hebrew]

Epstein, Yitzhak, "A Hidden Question" [Lecture Given at the Seventh Congress in Basel]. In *HaShiloah: A Monthly Journal of Literature, Scholarship, and Current Events*, 17, 97–102, July–December 1907, 193–206.

Erez, Yehuda, ed. *The Book of the Third Aliya*. 2 Vols. Tel Aviv: Ayanot and Am Oved, 1964. [Hebrew]

Even-Shoshan, Avraham. *The New Dictionary*. 4 Vols. Jerusalem: "Kiryat-Sefer," 1993. [Hebrew]

Even-Zohar, Basmat. *The Emergence of the Model of "The New Hebrew" in Modern Hebrew Literature: 1880–1930*. A Thesis Submitted to the Degree of Master of Arts, Tel Aviv University, 1988. [Hebrew]

Ever Hadany, Aharon, ed. *The Settlement of the Lower Galilee: Fifty Years of Its History*. Ramat-Gan: Masada and the Union of Farmers of the Lower Galilee. 1955?. [Hebrew]

Falk, Avner. *David, King of Israel: Psychoanalytic Biography of David Ben-Gurion*. Tel Aviv: Bar, 1987. [Hebrew]

———. *Herzl, King of the Jews: A Psychoanalytic Biography of Theodor Herzl*. Lanham, MD: University Press of America, 1993.

———. *A Psychoanalytic History of the Jews*. Madison, NJ: Fairleigh Dickinson University Press; London: Associated University Press, 1996.

Feinberg, Absalom. *Absalom: Papers and Letters of the Late Absalom Feinberg*. Jerusalem: Shikmona, 1975. [Hebrew]

Fichman, Ya'akov. *Members of the Generation: Storytellers, Poets, People*. Tel Aviv: Lador, Am Oved, 1952. [Hebrew]

Frankel, Rafael. "Ideological Motives in the Formation of the Kevutza during the Period of the Second Aliya." In *Cathedra: For the History of Eretz Israel and Its Yishuv*, 18, January 1981, 112–117. [Hebrew]

Fried, Yosef. *A Year in the Land of Israel (1908/9): Writings, Letters, and a Diary by a Member of the Second Aliya, Yosef Fried*. Ramat-Efal: Yad Tabenkin, 1985. [Hebrew]

Fuhrer, Ruth. "The Rise and Fall of the Pioneer Myth (Chapter in the History of Education in Israel, 1900–1983)." In *Kivunim: The Journal of Zionism and Judaism*, 23, May 1984, 5–23. [Hebrew]

Funkenstein, Amos. *Perceptions of Jewish History from Antiquity to the Present*. Tel Aviv: Am Oved, 1991. [Hebrew]

Gadon, Shmuel, ed. *The Paths of the Kevutza and the Kibbutz: A Collection of Accounts and Sources*. Tel Aviv: Ayanot and Am Oved, 1958. [Hebrew]

Gelber, Yoav. *Independence versus Nakba*. Or Yehuda: Kinneret, Zmora-Bitan, Dvir, 2004. [Hebrew]

Geller, Jay. "The Conventional Lies and Paradoxes of Jewish Assimilation: Max Nordau's Pre-Zionist Answer to the Jewish Question." In *Jewish Social Studies: History, Culture, and Society*, 1, 3, Spring 1995, 129–160.

Gelvin, James L. *The Israel-Palestine Conflict: One Hundred Years of War*. Cambridge: Cambridge University Press, 2005.

Genigar: 25 Years, 21.10.1922—13.10.1947. Genigar: Genigar, 1948. [Hebrew]

Gertz, Nurit. *Captive of a Dream: National Myths in Israeli Culture*. Tel Aviv: Am Oved, 1996. [Hebrew]

Gilman, Sander. *The Jew's Body*. New York: Routledge, 1991.

Ginossar, Pinhas. *Hebrew Literature and the Workers' Movement in Palestine in the Period of the Third Aliya (1918–1923)*. Thesis Submitted for the Degree of Doctor of Philosophy, Tel Aviv University, 1987. [Hebrew]

Ginossar, Pinhas, and Avi Bareli, eds. *Zionism: A Contemporary Controversy, Research Trends and Ideological Approaches*. Beer-Sheva: Ben-Gurion University of the Negev Press, 1996. [Hebrew]

Gluzman, Michael. "Longing for Heterosexuality: Zionism and Sexuality in Herzl's *Altneuland*." In *Theory and Criticism: An Israeli Forum*, 11, Winter 1997, 145–162. [Hebrew]

———. "'The Lack of Power—The Most Shameful Disease': Bialik and the Kishinev Pogrom." In *Theory and Criticism: An Israeli Forum*, 22, Spring 2003, 105–132. [Hebrew]

———. *The Zionist Body: Nationalism, Gender, and Sexuality in Modern Hebrew Literature*. Tel Aviv: HaKibbutz HaMe'uhad, 2007. [Hebrew]

Gonen, Jay Y. *A Psychohistory of Zionism*. New York: New American Library, 1975.

Gordon, Aharon David. *Collected Works of A. D. Gordon*. 5 Vols. Tel Aviv: The Central Committee of the HaPo'el HaTza'ir Party, 1925–1929. [Hebrew]

———. *Man and Nature*. Jerusalem: Hassifria Hatziyonit Publishing House of the World Zionist Organization, 1951. [Hebrew]

Goren, Jacob, ed. *Testimony of Victims of the 1903 Kishinev Pogrom As Written Down by Ch. N. Bialik and Others*. Tel Aviv: HaKibbutz HaMe'uhad and Yad Tabenkin, 1991. [Hebrew]

Gorny, Yosef. *From Rosh-Pina and Degania to Dimona: A History of Constructive Zionism*. Tel Aviv: Ministry of Defense, 1983. [Hebrew]

———. "The Miracle of the Mass Aliya." In Mordechai Naor, ed., *Immigrants/Olim and Transit Camps, 1948–1952: Sources, Summaries, Selected Events, and Supporting Material*. Jerusalem: Yad Izhak Ben-Zvi, 1986, 2–8. [Hebrew]

———. *Zionism and the Arabs, 1882–1948: A Study of Ideology*. New York: Oxford University Press, 2001.

Gothelf, Yehuda, and Avraham Cohen, eds. *The HaShomer HaTzaʿir Book: An Anthology for the Twentieth Anniversary of HaShomer HaTzaʿir 1913–1933*. Warsaw: Central Leadership of the HaShomer HaTzaʿir Organization, 1934. [Hebrew]

Granatstein, Yehiel. *The Students of the Baʿal Shem Tov in the Land of Israel: More Than Two Hundred Years since the Aliya of the Besht's Students and of the Maggid of Mezritch to the Land of Israel*. Tel Aviv: Maor, 1982. [Hebrew]

Grossman, David. *Present Absentees*. Tel Aviv: HaKibbutz HaMeʾuhad, 1992. [Hebrew]

Grosz, Elizabeth. *Jacques Lacan: A Feminist Introduction*. London: Routledge, 1991.

Gur-Arieh, Meir. *The Pioneers: A Collection of Silhouettes Cut by Meir Gur-Arieh*. Jerusalem: B'nai Bezalel, 1925. [Hebrew]

Gurevitch, Zali, and Gideon Aran. "The Land of Israel: Myth and Phenomenon." In *Studies in Contemporary Jewry*, 10, 1994, 195–210.

Gvat (The Martyrs of Pinsk Kevutza): Sources and Accounts. Ein Harod: Gvat in cooperation with the Poʿalei Eretz Israel Party Central Committee, 1937. [Hebrew]

HaAdama. Tel Aviv: "Ahdut HaAvodah." [Hebrew]

HaAhdut: A Weekly on the Affairs of the Workers and the Masses in the Land of Israel. Jerusalem: Poʿalei Tzion. [Hebrew]

HaAretz VeHaAvoda: Anthology of Literature, Labor, and Yishuv Affairs. Jaffa: The Central Committee of the HaPoʿel HaTzaʿir Party. [Hebrew]

Habas, Bracha, ed. *The Book of the Second Aliya*. Tel Aviv: Am Oved, 1947. [Hebrew]

Hacohen, Dvora. *Immigrants in Turmoil: Mass Immigration to Israel and Its Repercussions in the 1950s and After*. New York: Syracuse University Press, 2003.

Halpern, Ben, and Jehuda Reinharz. "The Cultural and Social Background of the Second Aliyah." In *Middle Eastern Studies*, 27, 3, July 1991, 487–517.

Hamitzer, Dan. "Ernst Pollack Died in Beitania." In *Monitin*, July 1981, 35, 89–93. [Hebrew]

Haramati, Shlomo. *Three First Teachers*. Jerusalem: Yad Izhak Ben-Zvi, 1984. [Hebrew]

———. *Members of the Ascent/Aliya: Senior Instillers of the Hebrew Language in Recent Generations, Their Contributions to the Hebrew Language and to Its Dissemination*. Tel Aviv: Yaron Golan, 1993. [Hebrew]

———. *Levites in the Temple of Hebrew: New Light on the Connection of Eight Famous Jewish People to Reborn Hebrew, in Writing and in Speech*. Tel Aviv: Yaron Golan, 1996. [Hebrew]

———. *Hebrew: From Language of Prayer to National Language*. Tel Aviv: Yaron Golan, 1997. [Hebrew]

Harshav, Benjamin. *The Meaning of Yiddish*. Berkeley, CA: University of California Press, 1990.

———. *Language in Time of Revolution*. Berkeley, CA: University of California Press, 1993.

The HaShomer Anthology: Documents, Memoirs, and Words of Appreciation Written by Veterans of HaShomer. Tel Aviv: Labor Archive, 1937. [Hebrew]

HaSolel: Voice of the Workers in Public Works. Ramat-Efal: Yad Tabenkin, 1991.

Hazan, Meir. "The Murder of Moshe Barsky: Transformations in Ethos, Pathos, and Myth." In *Israel Affairs*, 12, 2, April 2006, 284–306.

Hazleton, Lesley. *Israeli Women: The Reality Behind the Myths.* New York: Simon and Schuster, 1977.

Hertzberg, Arthur. *The Zionist Idea: A Historical Analysis and Reader.* New York: Harper & Row, 1966.

Hever, Hannan. "Representation and Ideology in the Eretz Israel Idyll of the Second Aliya." In *Theory and Criticism: An Israeli Forum*, 2, Summer 1992, 53–68. [Hebrew]

———. *Poets and Zealots: The Rise of Political Hebrew Poetry in Eretz Israel.* Jerusalem: Bialik Institute, 1994. [Hebrew]

———. *Toward the Longed-for Shore: The Sea in Hebrew Culture and Modern Hebrew Literature.* Jerusalem and Tel Aviv: Van Leer Jerusalem Institute and HaKibbutz HaMe'uhad, 2007. [Hebrew]

Hever, Hannan, Yehouda Shenhav, and Pnina Motzafi-Haller, eds. *Mizrahim in Israel: A Critical Observation into Israel's Ethnicity.* Jerusalem and Tel Aviv: Van Leer Jerusalem Institute and HaKibbutz HaMe'uhad, 2002. [Hebrew]

Hödl, Klaus. *Die Pathologisierung des jüdischen Körpers: Antisemitismus, Geschlecht und Medizin im Fin de Siècle.* Wien: Picus-Verlag, 1997.

Hoffmann, Haya. *Yemenite Jews in Eretz Israel as Reflected in Modern Hebrew Literature (1883–1948).* A Thesis Submitted to the Degree of Master of Arts, Tel Aviv University, 1982. [Hebrew]

Horowitz, Dan, and Moshe Lissak. *Origins of the Israeli Polity: Palestine under the Mandate.* Chicago: Chicago University Press, 1978.

———. *Trouble in Utopia: The Overburdened Polity of Israel.* Albany: State University of New York Press, 1989.

Horowitz, David. *My Yesterday.* Jerusalem: Schocken, 1970. [Hebrew]

Jabotinsky, Ze'ev. *Autobiography.* Jerusalem: Ari Jabotinsky, 1947. [Hebrew]

Judge, Edward H. *Easter in Kishinev: Anatomy of a Pogrom.* New York: New York University Press, 1992.

Jung, C. G. *Four Archetypes: Mother / Rebirth / Spirit / Trickster.* Princeton, NJ: Princeton University Press, 1973.

Kafkafi, Eyal. "Izhak Tabenkin's Ideology of Halutziyyut." In *Cathedra: For the History of Eretz Israel and Its Yishuv*, 48, June 1988, 125–144. [Hebrew]

Kamir, Orit. *Israeli Honor and Dignity: Social Norms, Gender Politics, and the Law.* Jerusalem: Carmel, 2004. [Hebrew]

Kamon, Azriel. *The Return to the Past: The Romantic Element and the Autochthonic Motif in the Yishuv in the Second Aliya Period, 1904–1914.* A Thesis Submitted to the Degree of Master of Arts, Tel Aviv University, 1989. [Hebrew]

Kaniel, Yehoshua. "Jewish Emigration from Palestine during the Period of the First and Second Aliyot (1882–1914)." In *Cathedra: For the History of Eretz Israel and Its Yishuv*, 73, September 1994, 115–138. [Hebrew]

———, ed. *The Second Aliya: Sources.* Jerusalem: Yad Izhak Ben-Zvi, 1997. [Hebrew]

Kark, Ruth, ed. *Redemption of the Land of Eretz Israel: Ideology and Practice.* Jerusalem: Yad Izhak Ben-Zvi, 1990. [Hebrew]

Karmi, Shlomo. *One People, One Language: The Revival of the Hebrew Language in an Interdisciplinary Perspective.* Tel Aviv: Ministry of Defense, 1997. [Hebrew]

Kashani, Reuven. "Expressions of Longing for Zion throughout the Generations." In *Kivunim: The Journal of Zionism and Judaism*, 20, August 1983, 107–117. [Hebrew]

Katriel, Tamar. *Dialogic Moments: From Soul Talks to Talk Radio in Israeli Culture*. Detroit: Wayne State University Press, 2004.

Katz, Yossi. *The "Business" of Settlement: Private Entrepreneurship in the Jewish Settlement of Palestine, 1900–1914*. Jerusalem: The Hebrew University Magnes Press, 1994, 1989.

Katznelson, Berl. *Collected Works of Berl Katznelson*. 12 Vols. Tel Aviv: Poʿalei Eretz Israel Party, 1945–1950. [Hebrew]

———. *B. Katznelson's Letters (1915–1918)*. 6 Vols. Tel Aviv: Am Oved, 1961–1984. [Hebrew]

———. *"The Second Aliya": Berl Katznelson's Lectures before the Socialist Youth*. Tel Aviv: Am Oved, 1990. [Hebrew]

Katznelson, Rachel. *Essays and Articles*. Tel Aviv: Am Oved, 1946. [Hebrew]

Katznelson-Shazar, Rachel. *The Person as He/She Is*. Tel Aviv: Am Oved, 1989. [Hebrew]

Kehilateinu: Pioneer Thinking, Doubts, and Longings. Jerusalem: Yad Izhak Ben-Zvi, 1998. [Hebrew]

Kellerman, Aharon. "Settlement Myth and Settlement Activity: Interrelationships in the Zionist Land of Israel." In *Transactions of the Institute of British Geographers*, 21, 2, 1996, 363–378.

Kellner, Yaʿakov. "The First Aliyot: Myth and Reality, Two Examples." In *Kivunim: The Journal of Zionism and Judaism*, 1, November 1978, 29–49. [Hebrew]

Keren, Michael. *Ben Gurion and the Intellectuals: Power, Knowledge, and Charisma*. DeKalb, IL: Northern Illinois University Press, 1983.

Keshet, Shula. *Underground Soul: Ideological Literature, The Case of the Early Kibbutz Novel*. Tel Aviv: Publications of the Porter Institute for Poetics and Semiotics, Tel Aviv University and HaKibbutz HaMeʾuhad, 1995. [Hebrew]

Kimmerling, Baruch. *Zionism and Territory: The Socio-Territorial Dimensions of Zionist Politics*. Berkeley, CA: Institute of International Studies, University of California, 1983.

Klausner, Yosef, ed. *Pinsker Book: Memorial Book on the Hundredth Anniversary of the Birth of Yehuda Leib Pinsker (1821–1921)*. Jerusalem: The Committee of the Society for the Settlement of the Land of Israel in Odessa, 1921. [Hebrew]

Klein, Melanie. "Love, Guilt and Reparation" [1937]. In Melanie Klein and Joan Riviere, *Love, Hate and Reparation*. London: The Hogarth Press and the Institute of Psycho-Analysis, 1962, 55–119.

Klier, John D., and Shlomo Lambroza, eds. *Pogroms: Anti-Jewish Violence in Modern Russian History*. Cambridge: Cambridge University Press, 1992.

Kolot: A Magazine. Warsaw: no publisher. [Hebrew]

Kuntres. Tel Aviv: The Zionist-Socialist Union of Workers in the Land of Israel, "Ahdut Ha-Avodah." [Hebrew]

Kushnir, Shimon. *An Echo from Gilboa: First Years in Emek Israel*. Tel Aviv: Ayanot, 1955. [Hebrew]

———. *Men of Nebo: From the Story of the Second Aliya*. Tel Aviv: Am Oved, 1968. [Hebrew]

Kuzar, Ron. *Hebrew and Zionism: A Discourse Analytic Cultural Study*. New York: Mouton de Gruyter, 2001.

Lacan, Jacques. "The Subversion of the Subject and the Dialectic of Desire in the Freudian Unconscious." In Jacques Lacan, *Écrits: A Selection*. New York, London: W. W. Norton & Company, 1977, 292–325.

Lamdan, Itzhak. *Collected Poems of Itzhak Lamdan*. Jerusalem: Bialik Institute, 1973. [Hebrew]

Lamm, Zvi. *The Educational Method of HaShomer HaTza'ir Youth Movement: The Story of Its Formation*. Jerusalem: The Hebrew University Magnes Press, 1998. [Hebrew]

Lang, Yosef. "The Revival of Hebrew in Rishon LeTzion, 1882–1914." In *Cathedra: For the History of Eretz Israel and Its Yishuv*, 103, March 2002, 85–130. [Hebrew]

———. *Speak Hebrew! The Life of Eliezer Ben Yehuda*. 2 Vols. Jerusalem: Yad Izhak Ben-Zvi, 2008. [Hebrew]

Laor, Yitzhak. *Narratives with No Natives: Essays on Israeli Literature*. Tel Aviv: HaKibbutz HaMe'uhad, 2000. [Hebrew]

Laqueur, Walter. *A History of Zionism: From the French Revolution to the Establishment of the State of Israel*. New York: Schocken Books, 2003.

Laskov, Shulamit. *The Biluim*. Jerusalem: Hassifria Hatziyonit Publishing House of the World Zionist Organization, 1981. [Hebrew]

———. *Yosef Trumpeldor: A Biography*. Jerusalem: Keter, 1995. [Hebrew]

Lavi, Shlomo. *The Aliya of Shalom Layish: A Story*. Tel Aviv: Am Oved, 1964. [Hebrew]

Levin-Talmi, Emma. *Tent Time: Kibbutz Stories*. Merhavia: Sifriat Poalim, 1949. [Hebrew]

Levy, Nissim. *The History of Medicine in the Holy Land: 1799–1948*. Tel Aviv: HaKibbutz HaMe'uhad; Haifa: The Bruce Rappaport Faculty of Medicine, 1998. [Hebrew]

Lieberson, Tehiya. *The Story of My Life*. Tel Aviv: Mifaley Tarbut Vechinuch, 1970. [Hebrew]

Lufban, Yitzhak. *Collected Works of Yitzhak Lufban*. Tel Aviv: Ayanot, 1954. [Hebrew]

Lyotard, Jean-François. *The Differend: Phrases in Dispute*. Minneapolis: University of Minnesota Press, 1988.

Mandel, George. "The Revival of the Language from a Socio-Linguistic Perspective." In *The Fourth European Hebrew Academic Conference for the Study of the Hebrew Language and Its Culture*. Jerusalem: World Hebrew Alliance, 1980, 62–65. [Hebrew]

Manor, Alexander. "Active Messianism: Maimonides as the Visionary of the Jewish People's Political Freedom (Marking 850 Years since His Birth)." In *Kivunim: The Journal of Zionism and Judaism*, 28, August 1985, 123–125. [Hebrew]

Margalit Stern, Bat-Sheva. *Redemption in Bondage: The Women Workers Movement in Eretz Israel, 1920–1939*. Jerusalem: Yad Izhak Ben-Zvi, 2006. [Hebrew]

MeBifnim: Kibbutz Ein Harod, vol. 1. Tel Aviv: HaKibbutz HaMe'uhad, via the Archive of the Bibliographic Institute and the Labor Archive, 1969. [Hebrew]

MeHayeynu: The Newspaper of the Yosef Trumpeldor Labor Battalion. Tel Aviv: Labor Archive, the Bibliographical Institute of HaKibbutz HaMe'uhad, and the Yosef Trumpeldor House (Tel Yosef), 1971. [Hebrew]

Michtav LaChaverim. Tel Aviv: The Zionist-Socialist Union of Workers in the Land of Israel, Ahdut HaAvodah. [Hebrew]

Milstein, Uri. *The Poems of Rachel: The Secret of Their Magic*. Ramat-Efal: Seridot, 1997. [Hebrew]

Miron, Dan, ed. *In the City of Slaughter: A Visit at Twilight, Bialik's Poem a Century After*. Tel Aviv: Resling, 2005. [Hebrew]

Mishory, Alec. *Lo and Behold: Zionist Icons and Visual Symbols in Israeli Culture*. Tel Aviv: Am Oved, 2000. [Hebrew]

Morgenstern, Arieh. *Messianism and the Settlement of Eretz Israel*. Jerusalem: Yad Izhak Ben-Zvi, 1985. [Hebrew]

Morris, Benny. *Righteous Victims: A History of the Zionist-Arab Conflict, 1881–2001*. New York: Vintage Books, 2001.

———. *The Birth of the Palestinian Refugee Problem Revisited*. Cambridge: Cambridge University Press, 2004.

———, ed. *Making Israel*. Ann Arbor: University of Michigan Press, 2007.

Mosse, George L. *Nationalism and Sexuality: Respectability and Abnormal Sexuality in Modern Europe*. New York: Howard Fertig, 1985.

———. *Fallen Soldiers: Reshaping the Memory of the World Wars*. New York: Oxford University Press, 1991.

———. "Max Nordau, Liberalism, and the New Jew." In *Journal of Contemporary History*, 27, 1992, 565–581.

———. *The Image of Man: The Creation of Modern Masculinity*. New York: Oxford University Press, 1996.

Myers, David N. *Re-Inventing the Jewish Past: European Jewish Intellectuals and the Zionist Return to History*. New York: Oxford University Press, 1995.

Nadav, Tzvi. *So We Began: From the Beginnings of the Life of Labor, of Defense, and of the Kevutza*. Tel Aviv: HaKibbutz HaMe'uhad, 1957. [Hebrew]

Naor, Mordechai, ed. *The Second Aliya, 1903–1914: Sources, Summaries, Selected Events, and Supporting Material*. Jerusalem: Yad Izhak Ben-Zvi, 1985. [Hebrew]

Naveh, Eyal, and Esther Yogev. *Histories: Toward a Dialogue with the Israeli Past*. Tel Aviv: Babel, 2002. [Hebrew]

Near, Henry. "Ideology, Anti-Ideology, and Historiography." In *Cathedra: For the History of Eretz Israel and Its Yishuv*, 18, January 1981, 124–129. [Hebrew]

———. "What Shaped the Kevutza: Ideology or Experience?" In *Cathedra: For the History of Eretz Israel and Its Yishuv*, 23, April 1982, 189–191. [Hebrew]

———. "The Terms of Collectivization: Terminology and Actuality in the History of the Kibbutz." In *Zionism: An Anthology on the History of the Zionist Movement and the Jewish Yishuv in the Land of Israel*, 13, 1988, 123–146. [Hebrew]

———. "Pioneers and Pioneering in the State of Israel: Semantics and Historical Developments, 1948–1956." In *Iyunim Bitkumat Israel: Studies in Zionism, the Yishuv, and the State of Israel*, 2, 1992a, 116–140. [Hebrew]

———. "Who Is a Pioneer? The Semantic Incarnations of Pioneer Terminology in the Labor Movement of the Land of Israel, 1917–1939." In *Tura: Studies in Jewish Thought*, 1992b, 228–248. [Hebrew]

Neumann, Erich. *The Great Mother: An Analysis of the Archetype*. New York: Pantheon Books, 1955.

Nini, Yehuda. *Kinneret's Yemenites: Their Settlement and Removal from the Land, 1912–1930*. Tel Aviv: Am Oved, 1996. [Hebrew]

Nordau, Anna, and Maxa Nordau. *Max Nordau: A Biography*. New York: The Nordau Committee, 1943.

Nordau, Max. *Zionistische Schriften*. Köln: Jüdischer Verlag, 1909.

———. *Max Nordau to His People: A Summons and a Challenge.* New York: Scopus, 1941.

———. *Zionist Writings,* vol. 1. Jerusalem: Hassifria Hatziyonit Publishing House of the World Zionist Organization, 1954. [Hebrew]

Nur, Ofer. "Sex, Eros, and Physical Labor: HaShomer HaTzaʿir and Psychoanalysis, 1918–1924." In *Zmanim,* 88, Autumn 2004, 64–73. [Hebrew]

Ofrat, Gideon. *Earth, Man, Blood: The Myth of the Pioneer and the Ritual of Earth in Eretz Israel Settlement Drama.* Tel Aviv: Cherikover, 1980. [Hebrew]

Oppenheimer, Franz. *Merchavia: A Jewish Co-operative Settlement in Palestine.* New York: Co-operative Society Erez-Israel, Head Office of the Jewish National Fund, and Jewish National Fund Bureau for America, 1914.

Ornan, Uzzi. "The Revival of Hebrew." In *Cathedra: For the History of Eretz Israel and Its Yishuv,* 37, September 1985, 83–94. [Hebrew]

The Paths of Development of Degania: A Story of Fifty Years. Tel Aviv: Davar, 1961.

Paz-Yeshayahu, Abigail. "Degania: The Road to Total Collectivization." In *Zionism: An Anthology on the History of the Zionist Movement and the Jewish Yishuv in the Land of Israel,* 17, 1993, 71–98. [Hebrew]

Pelah, Yitzhak. *Kiryat Anavim (Five Chapters): From the Life of Worker Farms on JNF Land.* Jerusalem: Jewish National Fund, Main Office, 1924. [Hebrew]

Peled, Rina. *"The New Man" of the Zionist Revolution: HaShomer HaTzaʿir and Its European Roots.* Tel Aviv: Am Oved, 2002. [Hebrew]

Peled, Yoav, and Adi Ophir, eds. *Israel: From Mobilized to Civil Society?* Jerusalem: Van Leer Jerusalem Institute and HaKibbutz HaMeʾuhad, 2001. [Hebrew]

Penkower, Monty Noam. "The Kishinev Pogrom of 1930: A Turning Point in Jewish History." In *Modern Judaism,* 24, 3, 2004, 187–225.

Penslar, Derek J. *Zionism and Technocracy: The Engineering of Jewish Settlement in Palestine, 1870–1918.* Bloomington: Indiana University Press, 1991.

———. *Israel in History: The Jewish State in Comparative Perspective.* London: Routledge, 2007.

Pinsker, Yehuda Leib. "Auto-Emancipation" [9.1892]. In Robert Chazan and Marc Lee Raphael, eds., *Modern Jewish History: A Source Reader.* New York: Schocken Books, 1974, 160–174.

Pirkei HaPoʿel HaTzaʿir. 13 Vols. Tel Aviv: Tversky, 1935–1939.

Portugali, Juval. *Implicate Relations: Society and Space in the Israeli-Palestinian Conflict.* Boston: Kluwer, 1993.

Poznansky, Menachem. *From the Life of Yosef Trumpeldor.* Jaffa: Histadrut, 1922. [Hebrew]

The Prague Convention of HaPoʿel HaTzaʿir from the Land of Israel and Tzeʿirei Tzion from Outside the Land. Prague: Gordonia Archive (file 1/145), 1920.

Presner, Todd Samuel. "'Clear Heads, Solid Stomachs, and Hard Muscles': Max Nordau and the Aesthetics of Jewish Regeneration." In *Modernism/modernity,* 10, 2, 2003, 269–296.

———. *Muscular Judaism: The Jewish Body and the Politics of Regeneration.* London: Routledge, 2007.

Rabinovich, A. Z., ed. *Yizkor . . . Monument to the Fallen Hebrew Workers of the Land of Israel.* Jaffa: no publisher, 1912. [Hebrew]

Rachel. *Flowers of Perhaps: Selected Poems of Rachel.* London: Menard Press, 1995.

Ram, Uri, ed. *Israeli Society: Critical Perspectives.* Tel Aviv: Breirot, 1993. [Hebrew]

———. *The Changing Agenda of Israeli Sociology: Theory, Ideology, and Identity*. New York: State University of New York Press, 1995.

Raz-Krakotzkin, Amnon. "Exile within Sovereignty: Toward a Critique of the 'Negation of Exile' in Israeli Culture." In *Theory and Criticism: An Israeli Forum*, 4, Fall 1993, 23–55. [Hebrew]

———. "Exile within Sovereignty: Toward a Critique of the 'Negation of Exile' in Israeli Culture (Part II)." In *Theory and Criticism: An Israeli Forum*, 5, Fall 1994, 113–132. [Hebrew]

Reinharz, Jehuda, and Anita Shapira, eds. *Essential Papers on Zionism*. New York: New York University Press, 1996.

Rogel, Nakdimon, ed. *The Tel Hai Affair: Documents of the Defense of Upper Galilee, 1919–1920*. Jerusalem: Hassifria Hatziyonit Publishing House of the World Zionist Organization, 1994. [Hebrew]

Rolnik, Eran J. "Oedipus in Palestine: The Migration of Psychoanalysis from Central Europe and Its Reception in Jewish Palestine." In *Zmanim*, 88, Autumn 2004, 44–62. [Hebrew]

———. *Freud in Zion: History of Psychoanalysis in Jewish Palestine/Israel, 1918–1948*. Tel Aviv: Am Oved, 2007. [Hebrew]

Roniger, Luis, and Michael Feige. "From Pioneer to *Freier*: The Changing Models of Generalized Exchange in Israel." In *European Journal of Sociology*, 33, 2, 1992, 280–307.

Rosen, Ora. *Changes in the Conditions and Status of Women in the Workers' Settlement: The Idea and Its Realization, a Comparison between Women in Collective and Individual Settlements*. A Thesis Submitted to the Degree of Master of Arts, Tel Aviv University, 1984. [Hebrew]

Roskies, David G. *Against the Apocalypse: Responses to Catastrophe in Modern Jewish Culture*. New York: Syracuse University Press, 1999.

Rotberg, Robert I., ed. *Israeli and Palestinian Narratives of Conflict: History's Double Helix*. Bloomington: Indiana University Press, 2006.

Ruppin, Arthur. *The Jews of Today: A Social-Scientific Research*. Odessa: Moriya, 1914. [Hebrew]

———. *Three Decades of Palestine: Speeches and Papers on the Upbuilding of the Jewish National Home*. Jerusalem: Schocken, 1936.

———. *Arthur Ruppin: Memoirs, Diaries, Letters*. London: Weidenfeld & Nicolson, 1971.

Sadan, Dov. *A Psychoanalytic Midrash: Studies in Brenner's Psychology*. Jerusalem: The Magnes Press, The Hebrew University, 1996. [Hebrew]

Saʿdi, Ahmad H., and Lila Abu-Lughod, eds. *Nakba: Palestine, 1948, and the Claims of Memory*. New York: Columbia University Press, 2007.

Sagiv, Assaf. "Zionism and the Myth of Motherland." In *Azure: Ideas for the Jewish Nation*, 5, Autumn 1998, 92–117.

Said, Edward W. *Orientalism*. New York: Vintage Books, 1994.

Sand, Shlomo. *Intellectuals, Truth, and Power: From the Dreyfus Affair to the Gulf War*. Tel Aviv: Am Oved, 2000. [Hebrew]

Schmelz, U. O., and R. Bachi. "Hebrew as Everyday Language of the Jews in Israel: Statistical Appraisal." In *Salo Wittmayer Baron: Jubilee Volume*. Jerusalem: American Academy for Jewish Research, 1974, 745–785.

Schnell, Izhak. "Nature and Environment in the Socialist-Zionist Pioneers' Perceptions: A Sense of Desolation." In *Ecumene*, 4, 1, 1997, 69–85.

Schweid, Eliezer. *The World of A. D. Gordon*. Tel Aviv: Am Oved, 1970. [Hebrew]

———. *The Land of Israel: National Home or Land of Destiny*. Rutherford, NJ: Fairleigh Dickinson University Press, 1985.

Sefer HaHaim: The Diary of Kevutzat Kiryat Anavim, 1920–1929. Jerusalem: Yad Izhak Ben-Zvi, 2001. [Hebrew]

Sefer Hakevutza: Kevutzat HaSharon 1922–1936, Pioneer Thinking, Doubts, and Longings. Jerusalem: Yad Izhak Ben-Zvi, 1996. [Hebrew]

Seidman, Naomi. "Lawless Attachments, One-Night Stands: The Sexual Politics of the Hebrew-Yiddish Language War." In Jonathan Boyarin and Daniel Boyarin, eds., *Jews and Other Differences: The New Jewish Cultural Studies*. Minneapolis: University of Minnesota Press, 1997a, 279–305.

———. *A Marriage Made in Heaven: The Sexual Politics of Hebrew and Yiddish*. Berkeley, CA: University of California Press, 1997b.

Sela-Levavi, Shirley. *Representations of Motherhood in Psychoanalytic Theories and in Hebrew Women's Literature*. A Thesis Submitted to the Degree of Master of Arts, Tel Aviv University, 2000. [Hebrew]

Selzer, Michael, ed. *Zionism Reconsidered: The Rejection of Jewish Normalcy*. London: Collier-Macmillan, 1970.

Shadmi, Eli, ed. *Sources for the Study of the History of HaShomer HaTzaʿir: Three Conventions and the Great Aliya, 1918–1921*. Givat Haviva: Center for the Documentation and Study of HaShomer HaTzaʿir, 2, March 1984a. [Hebrew]

———, ed. *Sources for the Study of the History of HaShomer HaTzaʿir: Toward Real and Sustainable Principles, 1920–1923*. Givat Haviva: Center for the Documentation and Study of HaShomer HaTzaʿir, 1, March 1984b. [Hebrew]

Shafir, Gershon. *Land, Labor, and the Origins of the Israeli-Palestinian Conflict, 1882–1914*. Cambridge: Cambridge University Press, 1989.

Shafir, Gershon, and Yoav Peled. *Being Israeli: The Dynamics of Multiple Citizenship*. Cambridge: Cambridge University Press, 2002.

Shaked, Gershon. "Literary Models and Models of Reality: Some Remarks concerning the Modern Hebrew Realistic Literature, 1920–1940." In *Cathedra: For the History of Eretz Israel and Its Yishuv*, 28, June 1983, 119–132. [Hebrew]

Shapira, Anita. *Futile Struggle: The Jewish Labor Controversy, 1929–1939*. Tel Aviv: HaKibbutz HaMeʾuhad, 1977. [Hebrew]

———. *Berl: The Biography of a Socialist Zionist: Berl Katznelson 1887–1944*. Cambridge: Cambridge University Press, 1985.

———. *Visions in Conflict*. Tel Aviv: Am Oved, 1988. [Hebrew]

———. *Land and Power: The Zionist Resort to Force, 1881–1948*. New York: Oxford University Press, 1992.

———. *New Jews, Old Jews*. Tel Aviv: Am Oved, 1997a. [Hebrew]

———. "The Origins of the Myth of the 'New Jew': The Zionist Variety." In *Studies in Contemporary Jewry*, 13, 1997b, 253–270.

———. "Ben-Gurion and the Bible: The Forging of an Historical Narrative?" In *Middle Eastern Studies*, 33, 4, 1997c, 645–674.

———. "Whatever Happened to the Negation of the Exile?" In *Alpayim: Journal for Contemporary Thought and Literature*, 25, 2003, 9–54. [Hebrew]

———. *Yigal Allon, Native Son: A Biography*. Philadelphia: University of Pennsylvania Press, 2007.

Shapira, Anita, and Derek J. Penslar, ed. *Israeli Historical Revisionism: From Left to Right*. London: Frank Cass, 2003.

Shapira, Anita, Jehuda Reinharz, and Jay Harris, eds. *The Age of Zionism*. Jerusalem: The Zalman Shazar Center, 2000. [Hebrew]

Shapira, Avraham. *The Kabbalistic and Hasidic Sources of A. D. Gordon's Thought*. Tel Aviv: Am Oved, 1996. [Hebrew]

Sharet, Yaʿakov, and Nachman Tamir, eds. *People of the Second Aliya: Memoirs*. 6 Vols. Tel Aviv: Histadrut Culture and Education Center in cooperation with Mifaley Tarbut Vechinuch, 1970–1974. [Hebrew]

Shatz, Tzvi. *On the Edge of Silence: Writings*. Tel Aviv: Mifaley Tarbut Vechinuch, 1967. [Hebrew]

Shavit, Zohar, ed. *The History of the Jewish Community in Eretz Israel since 1882: The Construction of Hebrew Culture in Eretz Israel*. Jerusalem: The Israeli Academy for Sciences and Humanities and The Bialik Institute, 1998. [Hebrew]

Shazar, Zalman. *Morning Stars: Memoirs and Essays*. Tel Aviv: Am Oved and Davar, 1950. [Hebrew]

Shiler, Eli, ed. *Sefer Zev Vilnay: Essays on the History, Archaeology, and Lore of the Holy Land, Presented to Zev Vilnay*. Jerusalem: Ariel, 1984. [Hebrew]

Shilony, Zvi. "Random Factors in the Creation of Degania." In Yossi Ben-Artzi, Israel Bartal, and Elchanan Reiner, eds., *Studies in Geography and History in Honour of Yehoshua Ben-Arieh*. Jerusalem: The Magnes Press, The Hebrew University, and The Israel Exploration Society, 1999, 408–437. [Hebrew]

Shimoni, Gideon. *The Zionist Ideology*. Waltham, MA: Brandeis University Press, 1995.

Shimonovitz, David. *Homeland: Essays and Stories*. Tel Aviv: Masada, 1947. [Hebrew]

Shlonsky, Avraham. *In the Wheel: Songs and Poems*. Tel Aviv: Davar, 1927.

Shoham, Yedidya. *Diary of Youth: The Early Days of the HaShomer HaTzaʿir Movement, Lvov 1917–Beit Alfa 1925*. Givat Haviva: Center for the Documentation and Study of HaShomer HaTzaʿir, 1987. [Hebrew]

Shohat, Eliezer. *On the Paths of Labor: Essays, Speeches, Letters*. Tel Aviv: Mifaley Tarbut Vechinuch, 1967. [Hebrew]

———. *Eliezer Shohat: About Him, His Path, in His Memory*. Tel Aviv: Mifaley Tarbut Vechinuch, 1973. [Hebrew]

Shohat, Ella. *Israeli Cinema: East/West and the Politics of Representation*. Austin: University of Texas Press, 1989.

Shorer, Haim, ed. *The Kishinev Pogrom of 1903*. Tel Aviv: World Federation of Bessarabian Jews, 1963. [Hebrew]

Shur, Shimon A. *Modern Hebrew ("Ivrit"): Ideology, Society, and Politics*. Haifa: The Herzl Institute for Research and Study of Zionism, 1999. [Hebrew]

———. *The Sword of Language: The Fights and Fighters of Modern Hebrew*. Haifa: The Herzl Institute for Research and Study of Zionism, 2003. [Hebrew]

Sicker, Martin. *Judaism, Nationalism, and the Land of Israel*. Boulder, CO: Westview Press, 1992.

Slutzki, Yehuda. *Short History of the Haganah*. Tel Aviv: Ministry of Defense, 1986. [Hebrew]

Smith, Anthony D. "The Question of Jewish Identity." In *Studies in Contemporary Jewry*, VIII, 1992, 219–233.

Smith, Charles D. *Palestine and the Arab-Israeli Conflict*. Boston: Bedford/St. Martin's, 2007.

Smoliar, Liron. *"In Every Generation": An Historical Perspective on the Kishinev Pogrom*. A Thesis Submitted to the Degree of Master of Arts, Tel Aviv University, 2003. [Hebrew]

Snir, Mordechai. *In Our Times: Articles and Essays on the Questions of the Nation and the Movement*. Tel Aviv: Am Oved, 1954. [Hebrew]

Stanislawski, Michael. *Zionism and the Fin de Siècle: Cosmopolitanism and Nationalism from Nordau to Jabotinsky*. Berkeley, CA: University of California Press, 2001.

Stein, Kenneth W. "A Historiographic Review of Literature on the Origins of the Arab-Israeli Conflict," *The American Historical Review*, 96, 5, December 1991, 1450–1465.

Sternhell, Zeev. *The Founding Myths of Israel: Nationalism, Socialism, and the Making of the Jewish State*. Princeton, NJ: Princeton University Press, 1998.

Stiman-Katz, Haya. *Early Hasidic Immigration to Eretz Israel*. Jerusalem: Yad Izhak Ben-Zvi, 1986. [Hebrew]

St. John, Robert. *Tongue of the Prophets: The Life Story of Eliezer Ben-Yehuda*. New York: Doubleday, 1952.

Sucharov, Mira M. *The International Self: Psychoanalysis and the Search for Israeli-Palestinian Peace*. New York: State University of New York Press, 2005.

Suchovolsky, Tzvi. *Man and His Labor*. Tel Aviv: Union of Farm Workers, Agricultural Center, 1973. [Hebrew]

Sufian, Sandra M. *Healing the Land and the Nation: Malaria and the Zionist Project in Palestine, 1920–1947*. Chicago: University of Chicago Press, 2007.

Tabenkin, Yitzhak. "The Defense and the 'HaShomer' during the Second Aliya" [1937]. In *Shorashim: Studies on the Kibbutz and the Jewish Labor Movement*, 1, 1979, 9–24. [Hebrew]

———. "The Political Parties and the Agricultural Workers Organization during the Second Aliya" [1937]. In *Shorashim: Studies on the Kibbutz and the Jewish Labor Movement*, 2, 1980, 7–24. [Hebrew]

———. "Beginnings of Socialist Zionism" [1937]. In *Shorashim: Studies on the Kibbutz and the Jewish Labor Movement*, 3, 1982, 7–36. [Hebrew]

———. "The Jewish Volunteer Movement during the First World War" [1937]. In *Shorashim: Studies on the Kibbutz and the Jewish Labor Movement*, 4, 1984, 7–28. [Hebrew]

———. "Identity and Difference among the Aliyot to the Land" [1937]. In *Shorashim: Studies on the Kibbutz and the Jewish Labor Movement*, 5, 1986, 11–26. [Hebrew]

Tal, Alon. *Pollution in a Promised Land: An Environmental History of Israel*. Berkeley, CA: University of California Press, 2002.

Teveth, Shabtai. *Ben-Gurion and the Palestinian Arabs: From Peace to War*. Oxford: Oxford University Press, 1985.

Theweleit, Klaus. *Male Fantasies: Women, Floods, Bodies, History*, vol. 1. Minneapolis: University of Minnesota Press, 1987.

———. *Male Fantasies: Psychoanalyzing the White Terror*, vol. 2. Minneapolis: University of Minnesota Press, 1989.

Troen, S. Ilan. *Imagining Zion: Dreams, Designs, and Realties in a Century of Jewish Settlement*. New Haven CT: Yale University Press, 2003.

Tsamir, Hamutal. "The Pioneers' Sacrifice, the Holy Land, and the Emergence of Women's Poetry in the 1920s." In Hannan Hever, ed., *A Moment of Birth: Studies in Hebrew and Yiddish Literatures, in Honor of Dan Miron*. Jerusalem: Bialik Institute, 2007, 645–673. [Hebrew]

Tzahor, Ze'ev. "Three Weeks in the Fall of 1917: From the Diary of Shmuel Yehudai." In *Cathedra: For the History of Eretz Israel and Its Yishuv*, 31, April 1984, 125–134. [Hebrew]

———. "Ben-Gurion's Mythopoetics." In *Israel Affairs*, 1, 3, Spring 1995, 61–84.

———. *The Shaping of the Israeli Ethos*. Tel Aviv: Am Oved, 2007. [Hebrew]

Tzemach, Shlomo. *First Year*. Tel Aviv: Am Oved, 1965. [Hebrew]

———. *Pages from a Notebook*. Jerusalem: Bialik Institute, 1972. [Hebrew]

———. *The Story of My Life, as Recorded by Ada Tzemach*. Jerusalem: Dvir, 1983. [Hebrew]

Tzur, Muki. *Doing It the Hard Way*. Tel Aviv: Am Oved, 1976. [Hebrew]

———. *By Turbulent Waters*. Tel Aviv: Am Oved, 1984. [Hebrew]

———, ed. *Higher Than Loneliness: Letters to and from A. D. Gordon*. Tel Aviv: HaKibbutz HaMe'uhad, 1998. [Hebrew]

Tzur, Muki, and Aharon Israeli, eds. *Kinneret: Haya and Ben-Zion Israeli*. Tel Aviv: Am Oved, 1985. [Hebrew]

Tzur, Muki, Tair Zvulun, and Hanina Porat, eds. *The Beginning of the Kibbutz*. Tel Aviv: HaKibbutz HaMe'uhad and Sifriat Poalim, 1981. [Hebrew]

Ufaz, Aviva. "The Portrait of a Shomer: Letters by Mendel Portugali." In *Cathedra: For the History of Eretz Israel and Its Yishuv*, 48, June 1988, 73–89. [Hebrew]

———. "The HaShomer Guard as Mirrored in Second Aliya Literature." In *Tura: Studies in Jewish Thought*, 1989, 214–223. [Hebrew]

———. "The World of Symbols in *Kehilateinu*. In *Cathedra: For the History of Eretz Israel and Its Yishuv*, 59, March 1991, 126–143. [Hebrew]

———. *Document and Fiction of the Third Aliya*. Tel Aviv: HaKibbutz HaMe'uhad, 1996. [Hebrew]

Ussishkin, Avraham Menachem. *The Ussishkin Book*. Jerusalem: Committee for Ussishkin's Book, 1934. [Hebrew]

Valfovsky, Menachem Zalman. *Songs and Poems*. Tel Aviv: Histadrut and HaKibbutz HaMe'uhad, 1953. [Hebrew]

Vital, David. *The Origins of Zionism*. Oxford: Oxford University Press, 1975.

———. *Zionism: The Formative Years*. Oxford: Oxford University Press, 1982.

———. *Zionism: The Crucial Phase*. Oxford: Oxford University Press, 1987.

Weiler, Yael. "The Fascinating World of HaShomer HaTza'ir." In *Cathedra: For the History of Eretz Israel and Its Yishuv*, 88, July 1998, 73–94. [Hebrew]

Weintraub, Richard. *Selected Works*. Merhavia: Al Hamishmar, 1976. [Hebrew]

Weisbord, Robert G. *African Zion: The Attempt to Establish a Jewish Colony in the East Africa Protectorate, 1903–1905*. Philadelphia: Jewish Publication Society of America, 1968.

Weiss, Meira. *The Chosen Body: The Politics of the Body in Israeli Society*. Stanford, CA: Stanford University Press, 2002.

Weitz, Yechiam, ed. *From Vision to Revision: A Hundred Years of Historiography of Zionism*. Jerusalem: The Zalman Shazar Center, 1997. [Hebrew]

Weitz, Yosef. *First Pages*. Tel Aviv: Gadish, 1958. [Hebrew]

Wilkansky, Meir. *To the Galilee, a Well We Have Dug*. Tel Aviv: Ministry of Defense, 1978. [Hebrew]

———. *In the Days of the Aliya*. Tel Aviv: Ministry of Defense, 1982. [Hebrew]

Winichakul, Thongchai. *Siam Mapped: A History of the Geo-Body of a Nation*. Honolulu: University of Hawaii Press, 1994.

The Words of Women Workers: Collection. Tel Aviv: Moʿetzet HaPoʿalot, 1930. [Hebrew]

Yaʿari, Avraham. *The Goodly Heritage: Memoirs Describing the Life of the Jewish Community of Eretz Yisrael from the Seventeenth to the Twentieth Centuries*. 2 Vols. Ramat-Gan: Masada, 1983. [Hebrew]

Yaʿari, Yehuda. *As a Glowing Light*. Jerusalem: Ogdan, 1969.

Yaʿari-Poleskin, Yaʿakov. *Dreamers and Fighters: Paintings and Notes from the Life and Activity of the Creators of the New Jewish Yishuv in the Land of Israel, 1871–1921*. Petah Tikva: S. Z. Gissin, 1922. [Hebrew]

Yaffe, Eliezer. *Collected Works of Eliezer Yaffe*. 2 Vols. Tel Aviv: Am Oved, 1947. [Hebrew]

Yaffe, S. D. *Paths in the Field: Memoirs*. Tel Aviv: Sifriat Hasade, 1959. [Hebrew]

Yanait-Ben-Zvi, Rachel. *We Ascend*. Tel Aviv: Am Oved, 1959. [Hebrew]

Yavnieli, Shmuel. *Journey to Yemen: On Assignment from the Land of Israel Office of the Zionist Organization, 1911–1912*. Tel Aviv: Poʿalei Eretz Israel Party, 1952. [Hebrew]

Yisraeli, Meir. *The First Hasidim in the Settlement of the Land of Israel*. Jerusalem: Rubin Mass, 1995. [Hebrew]

Yosef, Raz. *Beyond Flesh: Queer Masculinities and Nationalism in Israeli Cinema*. Piscataway, NJ: Rutgers University Press, 2004.

The Yosef Trumpeldor Labor Battalion: Anthology. Tel Aviv: Mizpah, 1931. [Hebrew]

Zagorodsky, Melech. *Manners of Settlement, Part I: Land of Gardens*. Jaffa: Raanania, 1919. [Hebrew]

Zakim, Eric. *To Build and Be Built: Landscape, Literature, and the Construction of Zionist Identity*. Philadelphia: University of Pennsylvania Press, 2006.

Zeira, Moti. "Shoshana, Valiant Girl, Where Are You?" In *Sdemot: The Literary Quarterly of the Kibbutz Movement*, October 1989, 111, 1–77. [Hebrew]

Zertal, Idith. *Israel's Holocaust and the Politics of Nationhood*. Cambridge: Cambridge University Press, 2005.

Zerubavel, Yaʿakov. *In Times of War and Revolution*. Tel Aviv: I. L. Peretz, 1966. [Hebrew]

Zerubavel, Yael. *Recovered Roots: Collective Memory and the Making of Israeli National Tradition*. Chicago: University of Chicago Press, 1995.

Zimmermann, Moshe. "Muscle Jews versus Nervous Jews." In Michael Brenner and Gideon Reuveni, eds., *Emancipation through Muscles: Jews and Sports in Europe*. Lincoln: University of Nebraska Press, 2006, 13–26.

Zipperstein, Steven. *Elusive Prophet: Ahad HaAm and the Origins of Zionism*. Berkeley, CA: University of California Press, 1993.

Notes

Chapter 1: Pioneers and Pioneerism

1 H. Libman, "From a Conversation," *MeBifnim*, 14, 25.5.1925, 275.

2 The discussion of desire offered in this book is influenced principally by the concept of desire as conceived by Hegel and his French followers and interpreters. For a review of this school's work, see Butler 1987.

3 Letter from Yosef Weitz to a friend in the exile [1.1910], in Weitz 1958, 152–153.

4 A. M. Kolar, in Ya'ari, ed., 1983, vol. 2, 928.

5 M. Karmi, "Segments," *HaAdama*, 1, 1919–1920, 200.

6 Even-Shoshan 1993, vol. 1, 394.

7 Ibid.

8 Berl Katznelson, "To the HeHalutz Movement" [1917], in Katznelson 1945, vol. 1, 51–60.

9 Cf. Letter from Berl Katznelson [1917], in Katznelson 1974, vol. 2, 378; letter from Berl Katznelson to the envoys of the Zionist movement [1918], in Katznelson 1974, vol. 2, 495–498.

10 Yosef Trumpeldor, "The Pioneer, His Nature and Destiny" [1918], in Basok, ed., 1940, 18–27.

11 Ben-Avram and Near 1995, 5–46; Near 1992b, 228–248; Henry Near, "Like All the Nations? Zionist Pioneering in International Context," in Shapira, Reinharz, and Harris, eds., 2000, 109–126. On the changes in the usage of the term after Israel's establishment, see Near 1992a, 116–140.

12 Letter from David Ben-Gurion to his father [19.10.1906], in Ben-Gurion 1971, vol. 1, 76.

13 Almog 1993, 329–346; Eisenstadt 1970, 17–19; Gorny 1983, 41–43; Ze'ev Tzahor, "The Consolidation of the Second Aliya's Leadership," in Naor, ed., 1985, 26–36; Muki Tzur, "The Second Aliya: Types of Immigrants and Their Socio-cultural Profile," in Bartal, ed., 1997, 282–293.

14 Gorny 1983, 39; Gorny 1986, 2–8. On critical views of this position, which aggrandizes the importance of the first Aliyot over the later ones, see Chetrit 2004, 42–71; Hacohen 2003; Hever, Shenhav, and Motzafi-Haller, eds., 2002.

15 Alroey 2004. For a parallel discussion of the Third Aliya, see Ben-Avram and Near 1995.

16 Ben-Avram and Near 1995, 17–22.

17 Katznelson 1990, 54.

18 For accounts of the nature of the change, see Ginossar and Bareli, eds., 1996; Morris, ed., 2007; Naveh and Yogev 2002; Peled and Ophir, eds., 2001; Ram 1995; Shapira and Penslar, eds., 2003; Penslar 2007.

19 Ben-David 1985, 155–164; Edelstein 1985, 145–153; Sicker 1992.

20 Schweid 1985, 57–58.

21 Gurevitch and Aran 1994, 197–199.

22 Dagan 1999, 20.

23 Berl Katznelson, "My Road to the Land" [5.4.1941], in Katznelson 1947, vol. 5, 375.

24 Letter from David Ben-Gurion to Shmuel Fuchs [2.1.1907], in Ben-Gurion 1971, vol. 1, 94.

25 Stiman-Katz 1986, 7–9. For more on the Hasidic aliya and settlement in the Land of Israel, see Granatstein 1982; Yisraeli 1995. On pre-Zionist immigration and settlement in the Land, see Ben-Zvi 1955; Eliav 1978; Morgenstern 1985.

26 Bartal 1994, 9–10.

27 Israel Bartal, "Exile in the Homeland," in Bartal 1994, 15–19.

28 On the First Aliya, see Eliav, ed., 1981, 2 vols.; Shmuel Ettinger and Israel Bartal, "The First Aliyah: Ideological Roots and Practical Accomplishments," in Reinharz and Shapira, eds., 1996, 63–93; Laskov 1981.

29 Alroey 2004, 122.

30 Dayan 1958, 11; E.[?] L. Yaffe in the name of the committee of the Galilee Union of Farmworkers, "On the Matter of Labor in the Galilee," *HaAhdut*, 31, 29.5.1914, 18; "Russian Members of Po'alei Tzion Migrate to the Land of Israel" [9.1904], in Kaniel, ed., 1997, 2; Mordechai Snir, "Homeland" [1920], in Snir 1954, 33; Yanait-Ben-Zvi 1959, 82.

31 Elon 1971, 106.

32 Berl Katznelson, "Hebrew Labor on the Tiberias-Tzemach Road" [2.11.1920], in Katznelson 1945, vol. 1, 318.

33 For political accounts and explanations of *halutziyyut*, see Ben-Avram 1981, 118–123; Ben-Avram 1982, 187–189; Yaacov Goldstein, "Self-Defense and Guarding: 'Bar-Giora' and 'HaShomer' in the Second Aliya," in Bartal, ed., 1997, 435–481; Yossi Goldstein, "Policy of the World Zionist Organization, 1904–1914," in Bartal, ed., 1997, 75–87; Halpern and Reinharz 1991, 487–517; Margalit Shilo, "The Role of the World Zionist Organization in Eretz Israel during the Second Aliya Period," in Bartal, ed., 1997, 88–103; Ze'ev Tzahor, "The Consolidation of the Second Aliya's Leadership," in Naor, ed., 1985, 26–36; Ze'ev Tzahor, "The Growth of Political Factions and Workers' Organizations," in Bartal, ed., 1997, 215–234.

For socioeconomic accounts and explanations of *halutziyyut*, see Avneri 1984; Blum 1980; Bloom 2007, 341–347; Nitza Druyan, "Oriental Jews in Eretz Israel during the Second Aliya Period," in Bartal, ed., 1997, 320–339; Dan Giladi, "Economy and Society during the Second Aliya," in Naor, ed., 1985, 4–25; Yehoshua Kaniel, "Members of the Second Aliya and the Sephardic Community," in Bartal, ed., 1997, 307–319; Katz 1994; Kimmerling 1983; Peled and Shafir 2002, 37–73; Penslar 1991, 41–149; Rosen 1984; Shafir 1989; Margalit Shilo, "The Women's Farm at Kinneret, 1911–1917: A Solution to the Problem of the Working Woman in the Second Aliya," in Bernstein, ed., 1992, 119–143; Margalit Stern 2006.

34 For geophysical accounts and explanations of *halutziyyut*, see Yehoshua Ben-Arieh, "Settlement in the Jordan Valley during the Second Aliya," in Naor, ed., 1985, 58–70; Ben-Artzi 1997; Ben-Artzi, Kark, and Aaronsohn 1988, 263–284; Shilony 1999, 408–437.

35 De-Shalit 1995; Schnell 1997; Tal 2002, 19–34.

36 For ideological accounts and explanations of *halutziyyut*, see Avineri 1981, 151–158;

Elboim-Dror 1993, 2 vols.; Elboim-Dror 2001, 95–115; Shmuel Ettinger, "The Ideology of the Second Aliya and the Socio-Political Ideology of Eastern European Jewry," in Bartal, ed., 1997, 3–10; Frankel 1981, 112–117; Halpern and Reinharz 1991, 487–517; Hertzberg 1966, 368–396; Near 1981, 124–129; Near 1982, 189–191; Shavit, ed., 1998; Shimoni 1995, 166–235.

For cultural accounts and explanations of *halutziyyut*, see Berkowitz 1993; Berkowitz 1997; Elboim-Dror 1996, 104–135; Rachel Elboim-Dror, "Creating the Educational Center in Eretz Israel," in Bartal, ed., 1997, 386–405; Peled 2002; Michael Grünzweig, "Hebrew in the Second Aliya Period," in Bartal, ed., 1997, 406–418; Michael Grünzweig, "The Status of Hebrew during the Second Aliya," in Naor, ed., 1985, 198–212; Avner Holtzman, "Self-Consciousness in the Literature of Eretz Israel during the Second Aliya," in Bartal, ed., 1997, 367–385; Yaacov Shavit, "Culture and Cultural Status: Basic Developments in Hebrew Culture during the Second Aliya Period," in Bartal, ed., 1997, 343–366; Muki Tzur, "The Second Aliya: Types of Immigrants and Their Socio-Cultural Profile," in Bartal, ed., 1997, 282–293.

37 For historical-religious accounts and explanations of *halutziyyut*, see Almog 1996, 314–339; Almog 1998, 237–250; Kashani 1983, 107–117; Manor 1985, 123–125.

38 Paz-Yeshayahu 1993, 71–98.

39 Ben-Avram 1981, 118–123; Ben-Avram 1982, 187–189; Near 1981, 124–129; Near 1982, 189–191.

40 For historical and historiographic discussions of the history of Zionism, see Bein 1952; Eisenstadt 1970; Ginossar and Bareli, eds., 1996; Horowitz and Lissak 1978; Horowitz and Lissak 1989; Laqueur 2003; Morris, ed., 2007; Peled and Ophir, eds., 2001; Peled and Shafir 2002; Penslar 2007; Ram, ed., 1993; Ram 1995; Reinharz and Shapira, eds., 1996; Selzer, ed., 1970; Shapira 1988; Shapira 1997a; Shapira and Penslar, eds., 2003; Shapira, Reinharz, and Harris, eds., 2000; Sternhell 1998; Vital 1975; Vital 1982; Vital 1987; Weitz, ed., 1997.

41 Shaked 1983, 119–132. Cf. Even-Zohar 1988; Ginossar 1987, 3 vols.; Avner Holtzman, "Self-Consciousness in the Literature of Eretz Israel during the Second Aliya," in Bartal, ed., 1997, 367–385; Keshet 1995; Ufaz 1989, 214–223.

42 Shaked 1983, 119.

43 Ginossar 1987, 3 vols.; Hever 1992, 53–68; Hever 1994; Keshet 1995.

44 For representations of *halutzim* and *halutziyyut* in political and social discourse, see Ben-Eliezer 1998, 370–396; Elboim-Dror 2001, 95–115. For a study of the representations of *halutzim* and *halutziyyut* in history books, see Fuhrer 1984, 5–23. For a study of the representations of *halutzim* and *halutziyyut* in museums, see Katriel 2004, 29–138. For studies on artistic representations of *halutzim* and *halutziyyut*, see Arbel, ed., 1997; Hoffmann 1982; Mishory 2000, 43–115; Ofrat 1980; Shohat 1989, 15–56; Yosef 2004, 1–47. For studies of the transformation of the concept itself, see Roniger and Feige 1992, 280–307. For studies on representations of *halutzim* and *halutziyyut* by the *halutzim* themselves, see Kellner 1978, 29–49.

45 Near 1988, 123–146.

46 Ufaz 1991, 126–143.

47 Smith 1992, 224.

48 Almog 1998, 35–38.

49 Ufaz 1996, 43–45.

50 Weiler 1988, 74, 80.

51 Ibid., 77–78, 88–94.

52 Sternhell 1998, 15–16.

Chapter 2: Desire and Rebirth

1 Letter from David Ben-Gurion to his father [13.5.1907], in Ben-Gurion 1971, vol. 1, 105; Dayan 1961, 108; Meir Wilkansky, "My First Day of Labor" [1906–1911], Wilkansky 1982, 14; Meir Wilkansky, "From the Time of the Aliya" [1906–1911], Wilkansky 1982, 130.

2 Tzipora Zeid, in Habas, ed., 1947, 530. Cf. A. M. Kolar, "From a Notebook of Memories," *HaAhdut*, 16, 26.1.1912, 12.

3 Letter from Ami Asaf [1922], in Ami Asaf 1968, 17; Yosef Baratz, in Gadon, ed., 1958, 77; Bernstein 1987, 20–24; Dayan 1935, 43, 99–103, 117; Habas, ed., 1947, 510, 683–684, 700; *Kehilateinu* 1998, 29, 30, 34, 37, 38, 46, 53, 74–75; Nadav 1957, 200–205; *The Paths of Development of Degania* 1961, 93–94; R. "Excerpts from the Diary of R., 1925–1937" [1925], in Bernstein, ed., 1992, 158–160; Shoham 1987, 24–25, 70, 128; Yisachar Sitkov, "Guard Tactics," in *The HaShomer Anthology* 1937, 194; Ufaz 1988, 77–88; Yanait-Ben-Zvi 1959, 138.

4 Elon 1971, 116–118. Cf. Bernstein 1987, 53–57; Elboim-Dror 2001, 108–110; Ufaz 1996, 38–45. Harshav 1993, 137; Hazleton 1977, 117–118; Tzur 1976, 36; Tzur, ed., 1998, 112, 114.

5 Hayuta Bussel, "Mankind's True Love," in Tzur, Zvulun, and Porat, eds., 1981, 71.

6 Esther Sturman, in Hazleton 1977, 118.

7 I adopt this critique of the Freudian project from Klaus Theweleit, who viewed it as desiccating psychological flow by imprisoning it in a topographical and structuralist model of the two psychological structures proposed by Freud: see Theweleit 1987, Theweleit 1989.

8 Biale 1997, 177, 183. Cf. Elboim-Dror 2001, 112–113; Kamir 2004, 168–170; Mosse 1985; Rolnik 2004, 46–53; Rolnik 2007, 17, 50–53; Tsamir 2007, 668–671; Weiss 2002, 21.

9 Nur 2004, 72–73.

10 Hazleton 1977, 93.

11 Gonen 1975, 18–19. For additional psychoanalytic studies, see Amiran-Sapir 1999; Sadan 1996. For additional psychoanalytic examination of the dawn of Zionism, see Brook 2002, 171–184; Falk 1993; Falk 1996, 667–702.

12 Schweld 1970, 22.

13 Falk 1987, 30.

14 Boyarin 1997, 271–312; Gluzman 1997, 145–162; Gluzman 2007; Yosef 2004, 1–47. For a broader discussion of the phenomenon, see Mosse 1985; Mosse 1996. Mosse also treats the Zionist project as "masculine"; see Mosse 1985, 151–154.

15 Seidman 1997a, 279–305. Seidman argues more broadly that Hebrew is "masculine" and Yiddish "feminine"; see Seidman 1997b.

16 In presenting Klein's approach, I am basing my discussion on her article "Love, Guilt, and Reparation" from 1937. See Klein 1962, 55–119.

17 Klein 1962, 103.

18 Ibid., 104.

19 Jung 1973, 7–44; Neumann 1955.

20 For a discussion on mythic time, see Eliade 1954.

21 Deleuze and Guattari 1996. On Deleuze and Guattari's concept of desire, see Butler 1987, 205–217.

22 Avraham Shlonsky, "Rushing," in Shlonsky 1927, 49.

23 Avraham Shlonsky, "Here," in Shlonsky 1927, 95.

24 Avraham Shlonsky, "Produce," in Shlonsky 1927, 105–106.

25 Avraham Shlonsky, "Soil," in Shlonsky 1927, 109.

26 Avraham Shlonsky, "Jezreel," in Shlonsky 1927, 122.

27 On the distinction among the three concepts, I am indebted to Jacques Lacan: see Butler 1987, 186–204; Grosz 1991, 59–67.

28 Lacan 1977, 312.

29 Yosef Aharonovich, "Old Arguments" [1914], in Aharonovich 1941, vol. 1, 186.

30 Ibid.

31 Letter from E-N [1.5.1920], in Erez, ed., 1964, vol. 1, 216; Moshe Arazi, in Erez, ed., 1964, vol. 2, 713; Yitzhak Ben-Zvi, "Our Intention" [1910], in Ben-Zvi 1966, 367; Letter from Yosef Trumpeldor to members of HeHalutz [3.12.1919], in Poznansky, ed., 1922, 210.

32 Shoham 1987 [3.5.1920], 147.

33 Azi.[?], "Around Ruhama," *HaAhdut*, 29, 25.3.1913, 21.

34 A. Ben-Barak [1921], in *Pirkei HaPo'el HaTza'ir*, 7, 1936, 91.

35 David Ben-Gurion, "Toward the Future" [4.4.1915], in Ben-Gurion 1955, 18.

36 Haim Arlosoroff, "The Social Nationalism of the Jews" [1919], in Arlosoroff 1934, vol. 3, 61.

37 Eliezer [1910], in *Pirkei HaPo'el HaTza'ir*, 1, 1935, 187.

38 Ya'akov Berkowitz, "The Words of Comrades at Assemblies" [4.9.1916], in *Beginning* 1971, 76.

39 Letter [10.8.1920], in Erez, ed., 1964, vol. 1, 222.

40 Ya'ari 1969, 205.

41 Dayan 1961, 59.

42 Nadav 1957, 121.

43 Letter from Ben-Zion Israeli to Meir Rotberg and Avraham Kahanovich [1910?], in Tzur and Israeli, eds., 1985, 75.

44 A. Reuveni, "The People of Beit Sela," *HaAhdut*, 10, 3.12.1918, 17.

45 Letter from Shimon Kushnir to Noah Naftulsky [1920?], Kushnir 1968, 198.

46 Z. L., "On the Banks of the Jordan," *Kuntres*, 2, 5, 26.4.1920, 19.

47 Ben-Yosef, "Letter from Rishon LeTzion," *HaAhdut*, 38–39, 26.7.1912, 36–37; "The Late Mordechai Starker[?]," *HaAhdut*, 11–12, 30.12.1914, 46; N-Y., "From a Private Letter by a Guard," *HaAhdut*, 19, 16.2.1912, 19; A. Reuveni, "The People of Beit Sela," *HaAhdut*, 10, 3.12.1918, 21; The Workers' *Kevutza* of Degania and the Moshavot Committee of Kinneret, "Protests in the Galilee," *HaAhdut*, 11–12, 26.12.1913, 37–38.

48 In the report by Gad Avigdorov on a trip to the north [probably early 8.1920], in Rogel, ed., 1994, 380.

49 *HaAhdut* editorial, "Our Comrades Are Falling. . . . Who Will Be Their Heirs?" [21.7.1911], in Kaniel, ed., 1997, 377.

50 Shmuel Dayan, "The Late Moshe Barsky" [26.12.1913], in Hazan 2006, 289.

51 Yosef Aharonovich, "A Voice from Outside" [1909], in Aharonovich 1941, vol. 1, 20; Haim Arlosoroff, "The Social Nationalism of the Jews" [1919], in Arlosoroff 1934, vol. 3, 61; Yitzhak Elazari-Volcani, "The Uniqueness of Selfhood" [1913], in Elazari-Volcani 1950b, 43–47.

Letters from David Ben-Gurion to his father, to Shmuel Fuchs, and to Menachem Ussishkin [1904, 1905, 1909], in Ben-Gurion 1971, vol. 1, 39, 47, 52, 138; R. Benjamin, "All Around" [1912], in Benjamin 1922, 225; Shmuel Dayan "Beginnings of Action" [20.12.1918], in Dayan 1953, 155; "The HaShomer HaTzaʿir Worldview" [1.1917], in Dror and Rosenzweig, eds., 1956, 42; Letters [1920, 1921], in Erez, ed., 1964, vol. 1, 216, 221, 231; P. Lipovetsky, "Labor Battalion," *MeHayeynu*, 1, 9, 1921–1922, 43; Letter from members of Degania to the parents of Moshe Barsky [1914], in *The Paths of Development of Degania* 1961, 70; "On the Way . . . ," *BaDerech*, 1–2, 31.12.1920, 2; Mordechai Snir, "Homeland" [1920], in Snir 1954, 32; Suchovolsky 1973, 89, 91.

52 Yehoshua Thon, "Devotion," in Rabinovich, ed., 1912, 20n.

53 Eliezer Yaffe, "Just 'Zion,' or Any Country?" [1906], in Yaffe 1947, vol. 2, 97.

54 David Ben-Gurion, "In Judea and the Galilee," in *The HaShomer Anthology* 1937, 261; Elon 1971, 109–110; David Gilad-Shmeterling, in Tzur, ed., 1998, 129; Habas, ed., 1947, 530, 674; Kushnir 1968, 48, 57; R. "Excerpts from the Diary of R., 1925–1937" [1925], in Bernstein, ed., 1992, 157; Letter from Zalman Rubashov to Rachel Katznelson-Shazar [1911], in Katznelson-Shazar 1989, 79–80; Suchovolsky 1973, 73, 90; Weitz 1958, 227–228; Yanait-Ben-Zvi 1959, 22, 58, 190, 322; Rachel Yanait-Ben-Zvi, "Foreword," in Ben-Zvi 1966, 6.

55 Menachem Zalman Valfovsky, "A Song to Sons-Without-Names" [1929], in Valfovsky 1953, 195–196.

56 Letter from Tzvi Shatz to Yosef Trumpeldor [10.1909], in Shatz 1967, 113.

57 Ibid.

58 Lieberson 1970, 10.

59 Yanait-Ben-Zvi 1959, 58.

60 Diary of Shoshana Bogen, "Pick the rose [shoshana] and bear it before you . . ." [1918?], in Zeira 1989, 53

61 Shmuel Yosef Agnon, "From Myself to Myself" [1976], in Shmuel Almog, "People and Land in Modern Jewish Nationalism," in Reinharz and Shapira, eds., 1996, 56.

62 For the psychoanalytic view of pioneer rebirth, see Falk 1996, 698. Cf. Sela-Levavi 2000, 92.

63 Letter from Yaʿakov Apter to Yosef Bussel [7.9.1918], in Tzur, ed., 1998, 256; David Gilad-Shmeterling, in Tzur, ed., 1998, 131; Sarah Chizik, "Selected from Her Memoirs and Letters," *HaAdama*, 2, 1920, 107.

64 R. Benjamin, "All Around" [1908], in Benjamin 1922, 203.

65 Zerubavel, "Lines," in Rabinovich, ed., 1912, 75. Cf. Absalom Feinberg, "Report to Mrs. Henrietta Szold" [10.1915], in Feinberg 1975, 373; Eliezer Yaffe, "The Foundation of the *Moshavei Ovdim*" [1919], in Yaffe 1947, vol. 1, 82.

66 Eliyahu Rappaport, "In a General Conversation," *Kehilateinu* 1998, 33.

67 Ibid., 33–34.

68 Letter from Ami Asaf [1924], in Ami Asaf 1968, 20.

69 Nadav 1957, 58, 103–104, 143.

70 For historical, historiographical, and methodological discussions of the "negation of the exile," see Raz-Krakotzkin 1993, 23–55; Raz-Krakotzkin 1994, 113–132; Eliezer Schweid, "The Rejection of the Diaspora in Zionist Thought: Two Approaches," in Reinharz and Shapira, eds., 1996, 133–160; Shapira 2003, 9–54; Gideon Shimoni, "The Theory and Practice of *Shlilat Hagalut* Reconsidered," in Shapira, Reinharz, and Harris, eds., 2000, 45–64.

71 Y. Reznichenko, "Foundation of the Labor Battalion," in *The Yosef Trumpeldor Labor Battalion* 1931, 11.

72 Y. Reznichenko, "Chapters of Life," in *The Yosef Trumpeldor Labor Battalion: Anthology* 1931, 273. Cf. Letter from Berl Katznelson to Haim Katznelson [5.9.1908], in Katznelson 1961, vol. 1, 69; Yaʿakov Zerubavel, "Arab Attacks on the Settlements of the Lower Galilee" [14.7.1911], in Kaniel, ed., 1997, 368.

73 Letter from Natan Ikar to his parents [2.2.1920], in Hamitzer 1981, 91.

74 Lieberson 1970, 12.

75 Elon 1971, 124–127.

76 David Shimonovitz, "Son of My Land: From the Notebook of a Wanderer" [1909–1919], in Shimonovitz 1947, 172.

77 Alroey 1999, 232; Ben-Zion 1960, v; Ben-Zvi, Shohat, Meged, and Tverski, eds., 1957, 108, 313; Erez, ed., 1964, vol. 2, 707, 793; "Index of Names," *Sefer HaKevutza* 1996 [1922–1936], 247–261; Katznelson 1961, vol. 1, 594n1; Kushnir 1968, 28, 45, 50, 62, 137; Rogel, ed., 1994, 125n4, 178n3; Shoham 1987 [25.1.1921], 161; Tzahor 1984, 125; Yanait-Ben-Zvi 1959, 187.

78 A. D. Gordon, "Our Labor from Now On," in Gordon 1926, vol. 2, 54; Letter from Tzvi Shatz to Anna, in Tzur 1984, 41. Cf. Letters from Yosef Trumpeldor to his friend Grisha [1909, 1911], in Poznansky, ed., 1922, 26, 30.

79 David Ben-Gurion, "At the Time of England's Declaration" [14.11.1917], in Ben-Gurion 1955, 38.

80 On Martin Buber, see Friedman 1991, Kirsch 2001.

81 Buber 1963, 249–250.

82 Ibid., 250.

83 Ibid., 251.

84 Ibid., 262.

85 Letter from David Ben-Gurion to his father [3.4.1913], in Ben-Gurion 1971, vol. 1, 266; Bistritzky 1980, 25; Yehuda Gothelf, "On the Nature of the Youth Movement" [1920], in Dror and Rosenzweig, eds., 1956, 59–60; Yosef Held, "In a General Conversation," *Kehilateinu* 1998, 76; Letter from Rachel Katznelson-Shazar to her brother Shmuel [1907?], in Katznelson-Shazar 1989, 52; Shoham 1987, 53, 71, 73, 75, 108, 111–112, 134, 137–139, 169–170; Letter from Eliezer Shohat to his wife [17.8.1923], in Shohat 1973, 142; The Tzeʿiri Tzion Center, "To Jewish Youth" [1919], in Dror and Rosenzweig, eds., 1956, 23–24; Yaʿari 1969, 212–213; Zerubavel, "Lines," in Rabinovich, ed., 1912, 76–77.

86 Yosef Aharonovich, "The Spirit and Matter in Zionism" [1913], in Aharonovich 1941, vol. 1, 107–108.

87 Horowitz 1970, 43, 46–47.

88 Letter from David Horowitz [1920/21], in Horowitz 1970, 87–88.

89 Letter from Haim Arlosoroff to his friend Kalev[?] Dugilatzky[?] [3.1.1916], in Arlosoroff 1934, vol. 6, 148. Cf. Letter from Eliezer Yaffe to his brother David, "To Uncle Yaffe" [4.11.1914], in Yaffe 1947, vol. 2, 159; Richard Weintraub, "The Ways of Youth" [1923], in Weintraub 1976, 17.

Chapter 3: Dissolving Boundaries

1 Dayan 1935, 42–43, 95; Dayan 1961, 14; Yehudit Edelman, in Habas, ed., 1947, 268; Letter from Berl Katznelson to his friends in Bobruisk [1911], in Katznelson 1961, vol. 1, 216; Kushnir 1955, 28; Yehuda Levitov [24.1.1921], in *Sefer HaHaim* 2001 [1920–1929], 25; Yosef Rabinovich [1920], in *Pirkei HaPo'el HaTza'ir*, 7, 1936, 72; Zerubavel, "Lines," in Rabinovich, ed., 1912, 74.

2 Eliezer Shohat, "National Creation and Accounts" [1911], in Shohat 1967, 22–23. Cf. Letter from Ami Asaf [1923], in Ami Asaf 1968, 19; Nahum Brodsky, "Community of Workers," *HaAdama*, 2, 1920, 25–34; Yitzhak Itzkovich, "To Aspire to Return to Earlier Ideals" [7.6.1913], in Kaniel, ed., 1997, 236; Letter from Berl Katznelson to Yisrael Katznelson [19.3.1911], in Katznelson 1961, vol. 1, 205–206, 207n2; Rachel Katznelson, "Sketches," in *The Words of Women Workers* 1930, 179–180; A. Likhterov, "On the Question of the Museum" [15.2.1921], in *Sefer HaHaim* 2001 [1920–1929], 27; Letter from Ze'ev Wakskratz[?] to a friend [1923], in Erez, ed., 1964, vol. 2, 501; Rachel Yanait, "From Toil to Labor," *Al Hasaf*, 1918, 7; Yosef Zelnik-Israeli [18.11.1921], in *Sefer HaHaim* 2001 [1920–1929], 67, 68; Ya'akov Zerubavel, "At the End of the Strike," in Zerubavel 1966, 75; Ya'akov Zerubavel, "Defense and Labor" [1911?], in Zerubavel 1966, 299.

3 Letter from Yosef Weitz to a friend in the exile [1.1910], in Weitz 1958, 152.

4 A. D. Gordon, "Letters from the Land of Israel" [1914?], in Gordon 1926, vol. 2, 231–232. Cf. Haim Arlosoroff, "The Social Nationalism of the Jews" [1919], in Arlosoroff 1934, vol. 3, 51–52.

5 Letter from Ami Asaf [1922], in Ami Asaf 1968, 17; Letter from Shmuel Dayan to Deborah Dayan [11.10.1919], Dayan 1961, 26–27; Kushnir 1955, 41; Letter from Shneor Spetchnik[?] to his brother Yehoshua [3.10.1919], in Rogel, ed., 1994, 64–65; Weitz 1958, 261.

6 Diary of David Gilad [1920], in *The Paths of Development of Degania* 1961, 279. Cf. Letter from David Ben-Gurion to his father [1.2.1908], in Ben-Gurion 1971, vol. 1, 116.

7 Weitz 1958, 185–186; Yanait-Ben-Zvi 1959, 33.

8 Mordechai Kushnir, "Said at an Inappropriate Time," *BaAvodah*, 1918, 84.

9 Yehudit Edelman, in Habas, ed., 1947, 268.

10 Eliyahu Karmieli, in Gadon, ed., 1958, 325. Cf. A. M. Kolar, "From a Notebook of Memories," *HaAhdut*, 16, 26.1.1912, 12.

11 Letter from Ami Asaf [1923], in Ami Asaf 1968, 18; Habas, ed., 1947, 171, 475, 503, 519, 542, 543, 698, 699, 701; *The HaShomer Anthology* 1937, 299–300, 430; Nadav 1957, 186; Tanhum Tanpilov, "To Be Workers," in Tzur, Zvulun, and Porat, eds., 1981, 89; Weitz 1958, 127; Ya'ari 1969, 166–167; Yanait-Ben-Zvi 1959, 8, 14, 17, 44, 153, 213.

12 Yanait-Ben-Zvi 1959, 45.

13 Pelah 1924, 10. Cf. David Kahana, "In a General Conversation," *Kehilateinu* 1998, 50.

14 Erez, ed., 1964, vol. 2, 705, 810; Letter from Yosef Fried to his wife [4.9.1908], in Fried 1985, 38.

15 Eliyahu Rappaport, "In a General Conversation," *Kehilateinu* 1998, 39.

16 Hazleton 1977, 91–94; Kamir 2004, 168–170.

17 Letter from David Ben-Gurion to his father [13.5.1907], in Ben-Gurion 1971, vol. 1, 106; Ever Hadany, ed., 1955?, 212; David Gilad-Shmeterling, in Tzur, ed., 1998, 129; Nadav 1957, 105; Shlomo Reichenstein, in Gadon, ed., 1958, 439–445; Weitz 1958, 250; Ya'ari 1969, 205, 206–207, 208.

18 David Ben-Gurion, "In Judea and the Galilee," in *The HaShomer Anthology* 1937, 262. Cf. Yosef Baratz, in Gadon, ed., 1958, 79; "The Company at Magdiel," in *Gvat* 1937, 173; David Gilad-Shmeterling, in Tzur, ed., 1998, 129.

19 Letter from David Ben-Gurion to Shmuel Fuchs [16.7.1904], in Ben-Gurion 1971, vol. 1, 22.

20 Letter from Yosef Aharonovich to a friend [1910], in Aharonovich 1941, vol. 1, 211; Bloch 1952, 55; Dayan 1935, 26; A. M. Kolar, in Habas, ed., 1947, 464.

21 Letter from Berl Katznelson to Leah Meron [1912], in Katznelson 1961, vol. 1, 423.

22 Eliyahu Rappaport, "In a General Conversation," *Kehilateinu* 1998, 33, 34.

23 Ibid., 34.

24 Mordechai Snir, "Homeland" [1920], in Snir 1954, 34.

25 Ben-Gurion and Ben-Zvi 1979, 228; R. Benjamin, "Leafs" [1905], in Benjamin 1922, 76; Comrade [1912], in *Pirkei HaPo'el HaTza'ir*, 7, 1936, 27; Letter from Shmuel Dayan to Deborah Dayan [26.9.1921], Dayan 1961, 53; David Gilad-Shmeterling, in Tzur, ed., 1998, 130; A. D. Gordon, "Letters from the Land of Israel" [1914?], in Gordon 1926, vol. 2, 228, 233, 234; Yitzhak Lufban, "The Socialism of the People" [1920], in Lufban 1954, 282; Mordechai Snir, "Said at an Inappropriate Time" [1918], in Snir 1954, 144; Ya'ari 1969, 164; Eliezer Yaffe, "For the Season in Professions" [1920], in Yaffe 1947, vol. 2, 187; Yanait-Ben-Zvi 1959, 82; Yavnieli 1952, 7; S. Yavnieli, "Transcript of the Words of the Supporters of the Proposal," *Al Hasaf*, 1918, 13; Y. Levi, in Genigar 1948, 168–169.

26 R. "Excerpts from the Diary of R., 1925–1937" [1925], in Bernstein, ed., 1992, 159.

27 Yitzhak Shweiger, "To a Brother in the Exile," *Kuntres*, 3, 14, 28.1.1921, 22.

28 Rachel, "Victims?" [1929], in Milstein, ed., 1997, 313.

29 Eliezer Yaffe, "Separated," in Yaffe 1947, vol. 2, 305.

30 Ibid., 306. Cf. Pelah 1924, 9; Tzvi Shatz, "On the Threshold" [1918], in Shatz 1967, 83–86.

31 Pelah 1924, 9.

32 Letter from David Ben-Gurion to the founding convention of the Histadrut, in the name of the alliance office of Po'alei Tzion [28.11.1920], in Ben-Gurion 1972, vol. 2, 43; Yitzhak Elazari-Volcani, "Moral" [1913], in Elazari-Volcani 1950b, 65–68; Yitzhak Lufban, "The Anniversary of the Jewish National Fund" [1927], in Lufban 1954, 29–31; Yehuda Yosepovich, "For the Explication of the Ways of the Yishuv," *HaAdama*, 1, 1919–1920, 709.

33 Haim Arlosoroff, "New Life" [1918], in Arlosoroff 1934, vol. 3, 13; David Ben-Gurion, "Crossroads" [11.1915], in Ben-Gurion 1955, 36; Dayan 1935, 57, 61–62; Yisrael Haderi, in Ya'ari, ed., 1983, vol. 2, 1227–1228; Shlomo Levitin, "At Dawn" [24.6.1930], in *The Yosef Trumpeldor Labor Battalion* 1931, 24.

34 Letter from Yosef Weitz to a friend in the exile [1.1910], in Weitz 1958, 151.

35 Bistritzky 1978, 150–151; Shapira 2007, 12; Yanait-Ben-Zvi 1959, 327.

36 For a discussion of the symbolism and imagery of water in Zionism, see Azaryahu 2001, 317–339; Hever 2007.

37 A. D. Gordon, "Letters from the Land of Israel" [1904], in Gordon 1926, vol. 2, 215. Cf. R. Benjamin, "All Around" [1908], in Benjamin 1922, 203.

38 Rachel, "On the Shores of Kinneret" [1929], in Milstein, ed., 1997, 302.

39 Nadav 1957, 58, 155.

40 Kushnir 1955, 42.

41 Tzvi Shatz, "To R-H, on the Fords of the Jordan" [1920], in Shatz 1967, 152.

42 Tzvi Shatz, "To R-H, on the Riverbank" [1920], in Shatz 1967, 157.

43 Tzvi Shatz, "To R-H, The Camp, Maʿabarot HaYarden" [1920], in Shatz 1967, 158.

44 Meir Wilkansky, "To the Galilee" [1907–1908], Wilkansky 1978, 85.

45 Avinoar, "At Kinneret, the Impressions of a Worker," *HaAhdut*, 25–26, 1.4.1912, 29.

46 Neta Harpaz, in Habas, ed., 1947, 226; Tanhum Tanpilov, "Relations between Newcomers and Veterans" [1919], in *Beginning* 1971, 85.

47 Meir Yaʿari. "We Are in the Land: Talk 1921," in Shadmi, ed., 1984a, 38. Cf. Yisrael Ben-Pinhas, "From a Kibbutz Diary," *Kehilateinu* 1998, 124–125.

48 Yanait-Ben-Zvi 1959, 49.

49 Dayan 1961, 130, 131; Kushnir 1968, 53.

50 Moshe Hallenberg, "In a General Conversation," *Kehilateinu* 1998, 70.

51 Nadav 1957, 59.

52 Letter from Michael Oved to the members of Kevutzat HaSharon, "Malaria Should Not Scare Us" [1925?], *Sefer HaKevutza* 1996, 89.

53 *The Paths of Development of Degania* 1961, 305–306; Menachem Zalman Valfovsky, "The Kinneret's Weep" [1922], "Autumn" [1922], "Songs of the Sea" [1923], in Valfovsky 1953, 125–126, 127, 128.

54 Shlomo Lavi, in Habas, ed., 1947, 94.

55 Letter from David Ben-Gurion to his father [13.5.1907], in Ben-Gurion 1971, vol. 1, 105; Dayan 1961, 108; Meir Wilkansky, "My First Day of Labor" [1906–1911], Wilkansky 1982, 14; Meir Wilkansky, "From the Time of the Aliya" [1906–1911], Wilkansky 1982, 130.

56 Zerubavel, "Lines," in Rabinovich, ed., 1912, 75. Cf. Avinoar, "At Kinneret, the Impressions of a Worker," *HaAhdut*, 25–26, 1.4.1912, 29; A son of the Galilee, "A Letter from the Lower Galilee," *HaAhdut*, 5–6, 19.11.1912, 34.

57 Ben-Shemni [1912], in *Pirkei HaPoʿel HaTzaʿir*, 1, 1935, 194.

58 Haim Arlosoroff, "New Life" [1918], in Arlosoroff 1934, vol. 3, 13.

59 David Ben-Gurion, "In Judea and the Galilee," in *The HaShomer Anthology* 1937, 263.

60 Israel Betzer, "The Cabin on the Other Side of the Jordan," in *The HaShomer Anthology* 1937, 95; Shimshon, "The Strike at Sejera," *HaAhdut*, 20, 27.2.1924, 18.

61 K. L. Silman, "From the Musings of the Heart," in Rabinovich, ed., 1912, 50.

62 Letter from Menachem Portugali to Tova Portugali [24.12.1913], *The HaShomer Anthology* 1937, 22. Cf. David Horowitz [1919], in Horowitz 1970, 75; "Korngold, Melamed, and Shweiger" [1909], in *Pirkei HaPoʿel HaTzaʿir*, 2, 1935, 264.

63 A. M. Kolar, "From a Notebook of Memories," *HaAhdut*, 16, 26.1.1912, 12; Yanait-Ben-Zvi 1959, 30; Yaʿakov Zerubavel, "Religious Hypocrisy and Hebrew Labor" [23.6.1911], in Kaniel, ed., 1997, 432.

64 Dayan 1935, 112.

65 "In the Working Land of Israel/On the Tiberias-Tzemach Road," *BaDerech*, 3–4, 31.1.1921, 32; Shimon Wolf, "In a General Conversation," *Kehilateinu* 1998, 44; Yaʿari 1969, 183–184.

66 Zerubavel, "Lines," in Rabinovich, ed., 1912, 76.

67 Letter from Ami Asaf [1923], in Ami Asaf 1968, 18; R. Benjamin, "Leafs" [1905], in Benjamin 1922, 76–77; Dayan 1961, 86; Ever Hadany, ed., 1955?, 202; Letter from Berl Katznelson to Hannah Katznelson [5.7.1912], in Katznelson 1961, vol. 1, 390; *The Paths of Development of Degania* 1961, 94; Letter from Eliezer Shohat to his wife [25.4.1922], in Shohat 1973, 127; Mordechai Snir, "Hardships of Absorption" [1920], in Snir 1954, 29; Weitz 1958, 133, 185–186; Yanait-Ben-Zvi 1959, 22, 24, 64.

68 Tzvia, "From My Journal: Night" [1924], *Sefer HaKevutza* 1996, 103.

69 Letter from Yosef Aharonovich to a friend [1910], in Aharonovich 1941, vol. 1, 211.

70 Absalom Feinberg, "Travel Journal" [4.9.1911], in Feinberg 1975, 191.

71 Rachel, "Victims?" [1929], in Milstein, ed., 1997, 312.

72 Hasia Drori, in Erez, ed., 1964, vol. 2, 515; Leah Herman-Gur Aryeh, "An Answer to the Question" [1922], in *Sefer HaHaim* 2001, 94; Lieberson 1970, 80–81, 82–83, 93, 122.

73 Tova Portugali, "On the Road," in *The HaShomer Anthology* 1937, 206.

74 R. Avishai, "Ayelet HaShahar," *BaGalil*, 6, 7.8.1919, 12.

75 Gideon Baratz, in Ben-Yaʿakov and Sion, eds., 1981, 13; Letter from David Ben-Gurion to Shmuel Fuchs [2.6.1904], in Ben-Gurion 1971, vol. 1, 6; Bistritzky 1978, 76–77, 99–100; Bistritzky 1980, 80–81; Dayan 1935, 66, 104; Elon 1971, 137; Ever Hadany, ed., 1955?, 198–199, 304; Menachem Haklai, in Erez, ed., 1964, vol. 2, 458; Habas, ed., 1947, 449, 701; Kushnir 1968, 30–31; Suchovolsky 1973, 56, 69; Letter from Yosef Trumpeldor to his friends D. and M. [8.8.1912], in Poznansky, ed., 1922, 47–48; Shlomo Tzemach, "Eliezer Shohat," in Shohat 1967, 11; Tzur, Zvulun, and Porat, eds., 1981, 115–116; Yaʿari 1969, 206.

76 Ben-Zvi, Shohat, Meged, and Tverski, eds., 1957, 97, 263; Dayan 1961, 128–130; Ever Hadany, ed., 1955?, 310; *The HaShomer Anthology* 1937, 23, 59, 71–72, 109, 121, 238–243, 331–332; Letter from Berl Katznelson to Haim and Yisrael Katznelson [10.5.1910], in Katznelson 1961, vol. 1, 144; *The Paths of Development of Degania* 1961, 314–316.

77 Tzipora Zeid, in Habas, ed., 1947, 531.

78 Alexander Zeid, in Habas, ed., 1947, 178.

79 Meir Spector, "On Guard in the Galilee and Judea," in *The HaShomer Anthology* 1937, 173.

80 Letters from David Ben-Gurion to his father and to Shmuel Fuchs [1904, 1909], in Ben-Gurion 1971, vol. 1, 22, 146; Brener 1978, 54–56; A. D. Gordon, "From My Trips on the Road" [1921], in Gordon 1928, vol. 4, 205; Elazar Halivni, "From a Kibbutz Diary," *Kehilateinu* 1998, 101; Hannah, "Letters of Pioneers," *BaDerech*, 3–4, 31.1.1921, 36; *The HaShomer Anthology* 1937, 222, 260; Letter from Shulamit Hayyut [27.10.1920], in Erez, ed., 1964, vol. 1, 230; Letters from Berl Katznelson to Haim Katznelson, Yisrael Katznelson, and Hannah Katznelson [1910], in Katznelson 1961, vol. 1, 141, 142; A. M. Kolar, "From a Notebook of Memories," *HaAhdut*, 16,

26.1.1912, 11–13; Kushnir 1968, 77; Shlomo Levitin, "Impressions from the Road," *MeHayeynu*, 1, 1, 29.7.1921, 4–5; Lieberson 1970, 93–94; Nadav 1957, 224–225; R. "Excerpts from the Diary of R., 1925–1937" [1925], in Bernstein, ed., 1992, 158–160; Weitz 1958, 227; Yosef, "Letters of Pioneers," *BaDerech*, 3–4, 31.1.1921, 37.

81 Letter from Yosef Aharonovich to a friend [1910], in Aharonovich 1941, vol. 1, 211.

82 Letter from Michael Oved to Tzvia, "I Work in Agriculture!" [1.5.1923], *Sefer HaKevutza* 1996, 49.

83 A. D. Gordon, "Letters from the Land of Israel" [1904], in Gordon 1926, vol. 2, 217.

84 Letter from David Ben-Gurion to his father [11.2.1908], in Ben-Gurion 1971, vol. 1, 115; R. Benjamin, "All Around" [1908], in Benjamin 1922, 207–208; Letters [no date, 1920, 1921], in Erez, ed., 1964, vol. 1, 224, 228, 231, 235, 240; Letter from Ami Asaf [1922], in Ami Asaf 1968, 17; Esther Becker, in Habas, ed., 1947, 510; Brener 1978, 51–52; Dayan 1961, 67; David Gilad-Shmeterling, in Tzur, ed., 1998, 129; Letter from Ben-Zion Israeli to Haya Israeli [9.8.1909], in Tzur and Israeli, eds., 1985, 64; Letter from Berl Katznelson to Hannah Katznelson [1910], in Katznelson 1961, vol. 1, 141; A. M. Kolar, "From a Notebook of Memories," *HaAhdut*, 16, 26.1.1912, 11–13; Lieberson 1970, 57; Mordechai Shenhavi, "Shumeriya" [22.4.1921], in Shadmi, ed., 1984a, 35; Nadav 1957, 100–101, 158–159.

85 Rachel Katznelson, "At Work" [1916], in Katznelson 1946, 250.

86 Member of Degania, in *The Paths of Development of Degania* 1961, 69.

87 M. Karmi, "Segments," *HaAdama*, 1, 1919–1920, 191.

88 Absalom Feinberg, "Travel Journal" [24.2.1912], in Feinberg 1975, 208.

89 R. Benjamin, "All Around" [1908], in Benjamin 1922, 205–206; Absalom Feinberg, "Travel Journal" [5.9.1911], in Feinberg 1975, 199.

90 R. Benjamin, "All Around" [1908], in Benjamin 1922, 203.

91 Meir Wilkansky, "To the Galilee" [1907–1908], Wilkansky 1978, 91.

92 David Shimonovitz, "Revenge," in Shimonovitz 1947, 34.

93 David Kahana, "In a General Conversation," *Kehilateinu* 1998, 50.

94 Letter from David Ben-Gurion to his father [19.10.1906], in Ben-Gurion 1971, vol. 1, 77; Ever Hadany, ed., 1955?, 186–187; Letter from Berl Katznelson to Haim and Yiṣrael Katznelson [10.5.1910], in Katznelson 1961, vol. 1, 144; Rachel Katznelson-Shazar, "On the 'Silent Era'" [1916], in Katznelson-Shazar 1989, 98–100; Tzalel, "Memoirs," in *The HaShomer Anthology* 1937, 145.

95 Cf. Shlomo Levitin, "Impressions from the Road," *MeHayeynu*, 1, 1, 29.7.1921, 4–5.

96 Letter from Shneor Spetchnik[?] to his brother Yehoshua [3.10.1919], in Rogel, ed., 1994, 65.

97 Letter from Yosef Aharonovich to a friend [1910], in Aharonovich 1941, vol. 1, 211–212; Avinoar, "At Kinneret, the Impressions of a Worker," *HaAhdut*, 25–26, 1.4.1912, 30; Ben-Zvi, Shohat, Meged, and Tverski, eds., 1957, 298, 299, 310; Brener 1978, 25–26; Dayan 1935, 42–43, 66–67, 70, 96–97, 114, 115–116, 166–168; Dayan 1961, 68–69; Gadon, ed., 1958, 62, 346; A. D. Gordon, "From My Trips on the Road" [1921], in Gordon 1928, vol. 4, 206; Hannah, "Letters of Pioneers," *BaDerech*, 3–4, 31.1.1921, 36; Yosef Held, "In a General Conversation," *Kehilateinu* 1998, 76; Letters [1920, 1921], in Erez, ed., 1964, vol. 1, 229, 235; *The Paths of Development of De-*

gania 1961, 23, 37, 41; *The Yosef Trumpeldor Labor Battalion* 1931, 30, 41–42, 141; Habas, ed., 1947, 266, 556–557; Nadav 1957, 35, 44, 51, 53, 55, 152, 154, 202; Letter from Eliezer Shohat to his wife [11.8.1923], in Shohat 1973, 142; Tzur, ed., 1998, 114, 237–248; Tzemach 1965, 228–231.

98 Letter from Yosef Aharonovich to a friend [1910], in Aharonovich 1941, vol. 1, 212.

99 Bloch 1952, 39–40.

100 Erez, ed., 1964, vol. 2, 679, 807; Nadav 1957, 88; Meir Wilkansky, "To the Galilee" [1907–1908], Wilkansky 1978, 40, 44, 73, 78–79; Weitz 1958, 161–162; S. D. Yaffe, in Habas, ed., 1947, 369; Yanait-Ben-Zvi 1959, 22, 24.

101 Letter from David Ben-Gurion to his father [19.10.1906], in Ben-Gurion 1971, vol. 1, 77.

102 A. Ben-Barak [1921], in *Pirkei HaPo'el HaTza'ir*, 7, 1936, 90.

103 Diary of David Gilad [1920], in *The Paths of Development of Degania* 1961, 280.

104 A-H, "Letters of Pioneers" [12.11.1920], *BaDerech*, 1–2, 31.12.1920, 46; Bistritzky 1978, 80–81, 142–143; H., "One Year" [23.10.1920], *Kehilateinu* 1998, 130; Letter from Natan Ikar to his parents [2.2.1920], in Hamitzer 1981, 91; Letter from Berl Katznelson to Leah Meron [3.2.1912], in Katznelson 1961, vol. 1, 312; Nadav 1957, 122, 204–205; *The Paths of Development of Degania* 1961, 9; Matityahu Stein, in Ben-Zvi, Shohat, Meged, and Tverski, eds., 1957, 306; Weitz 1958, 250; Yanait-Ben-Zvi 1959, 6, 22, 44, 108, 128, 165.

105 Letter from David Ben-Gurion to his father [1.10.1906], in Ben-Gurion 1971, vol. 1, 75.

106 Letters from David Ben-Gurion to his father [1906, 1907], in Ben-Gurion 1971, vol. 1, 77, 88, 89, 104.

107 Letter from Yosef Fried to his wife [4.9.1908], in Fried 1985, 38.

108 Tzvi Amrami, in Erez, ed., 1964, vol. 2, 468; R. Benjamin, "Leafs" [1905], in Benjamin 1922, 75.

109 Lieberson 1970, 57; Nadav 1957, 251; Weitz 1958, 250.

110 Rachel, A poem without a name [1927], in Milstein, ed., 1997, 99.

111 R. "Excerpts from the Diary of R., 1925–1937" [1925], in Bernstein, ed., 1992, 159.

112 Nesher Adler, "In a General Conversation," *Kehilateinu* 1998, 48.

113 Letter from Haim Arlosoroff to his mother and to all his loved ones [2.4.1921], in Arlosoroff 1934, vol. 6, 162.

114 Meir Wilkansky, "From the Time of the Aliya" [1906–1911], Wilkansky 1982, 132.

115 Letters from David Ben-Gurion to his father [1906, 1908], in Ben-Gurion 1971, vol. 1, 80, 83–84, 114–115; A. D. Gordon, "A Letter Not Sent in Time" [1912], in Gordon 1928, vol. 4, 247–248; *The HaShomer Anthology* 1937, 146, 168, 174–176; Letter [10.10.1920], in Erez, ed., 1964, vol. 1, 229; Letter from Menachem Portugali to Tova Portugali [17.1.1914], *The HaShomer Anthology* 1937, 25; Ya'ari 1969, 169–170, 174; Yanait-Ben-Zvi 1959, 15–16.

116 Yosef Weitz, "To the Galilee" [1912], in Weitz 1958, 141.

117 Dayan 1953, 240. Cf. N. Vatik, "At Tel Adash," *HaAhdut*, 19, 20.2.1914, 20.

118 Shimon Wolf, "In a General Conversation," *Kehilateinu* 1998, 43.

119 Nadav 1957, 120, 137, 138. Cf. Absalom Feinberg, "Travel Journal" [4.9.1911], in Feinberg 1975, 193–198; Shimon Wolf, "In a General Conversation," *Kehilateinu* 1998, 44; Zerubavel, "Lines," in Rabinovich, ed., 1912, 76–77.

120 Letter from Ami Asaf [1924], in Ami Asaf 1968, 22; Esther Becker, in Habas, ed., 1947,

509; Letter from David Ben-Gurion to his father [1.2.1908], in Ben-Gurion 1971, vol. 1, 115; Rachel Katznelson-Shazar, "On the 'Silent Era'" [1916], in Katznelson-Shazar 1989, 106–107; Nadav 1957, 74, 100–101, 233; Weitz 1958, 229; Yanait-Ben-Zvi 1959, 28, 83; Moshe Zlodin, in Ben-Zvi, Shohat, Meged, and Tverski, eds., 1957, 323.

121 Ya'akov Zerubavel, "With the Members of HaShomer at Tel Adash," in Zerubavel 1966, 140.

122 Nadav 1957, 100–101.

123 Pesya Abramson, "From the Letters of Pesya Abramson" [1916], in *The Words of Women Workers* 1930, 210.

124 Nesher Adler, "In a General Conversation," *Kehilateinu* 1998, 48; Ben-Zvi, Shohat, Meged, and Tverski, eds., 1957, 299, 335; Absalom Feinberg, "Travel Journal" [4.9.1911], in Feinberg 1975, 193–198; Letter from Menachem Portugali to Tova Portugali [3.1.1914], in Ufaz 1988, 88–89; Sharet and Tamir, eds., 1970, vol. 1, 202, 282; Suchovolsky 1973, 56, 69–70; Y. Tunis[?], in Habas, ed., 1947, 448; Yanait-Ben-Zvi 1959, 22, 28.

125 Letter from David Ben-Gurion to his father [1.2.1908], in Ben-Gurion 1971, vol. 1, 115.

126 Nadav 1957, 76.

127 A. D. Gordon, "A Letter Not Sent in Time" [1912], in Gordon 1928, vol. 4, 244.

128 Ibid., 245.

129 Ibid., 245–246. Cf. Eliezer Yaffe, "On Our Work in the Land of Israel" [1920], in Yaffe 1947, vol. 1, 52.

130 Yosef Aharonovich, "The Spirit and Matter in Zionism" [1913], in Aharonovich 1941, vol. 1, 106.

131 Letter from David Ben-Gurion to his father [11.2.1908], in Ben-Gurion 1971, vol. 1, 115; Kushnir 1955, 41; Yosef Malamud, in Ben-Zvi, Shohat, Meged, and Tverski, eds., 1957, 299; Nadav 1957, 158–159; Ya'ari 1969, 163; Yanait-Ben-Zvi 1959, 60, 101; Tzipora Zeid, in Habas, ed., 1947, 530; Zerubavel, "Lines," in Rabinovich, ed., 1912, 74.

132 S. Ben-Zvi, in Habas, ed., 1947, 471.

133 Dayan 1961, 131–132.

134 Rachel Katznelson-Shazar, "Year of 'Recapitulation of Youth'" [27.3.1915], in Katznelson-Shazar 1989, 108; Tzemach 1983, 66.

135 Letter from David Ben-Gurion to his father [16.12.1906], in Ben-Gurion 1971, vol. 1, 89.

136 S. Ben-Zvi, "Longing for Yom Kippur," in Tzur, Zvulun, and Porat, eds., 1981, 120; Mordechai Hadash, in Erez, ed., 1964, vol. 2, 803; Rachel Katznelson-Shazar, "On the 'Silent Era'" [1916], in Katznelson-Shazar 1989, 101; Moshe Kalvari, "Caught in Enchantment of Hebrew" [1916], in Habas, ed., 1947, 677–678; Yosef Malamud, in Ben-Zvi, Shohat, Meged, and Tverski, eds., 1957, 299; Nadav 1957, 139–140; Letter from Michael Oved to Tzvia, "I Work in Agriculture!" [1.5.1923], *Sefer HaKevutza* 1996, 50; Meir Wilkansky, "From the Time of the Aliya" [1906–1911], Wilkansky 1982, 119; Meir Wilkansky, "To the Galilee" [1907–1908], Wilkansky 1978, 89–90.

137 Avinoar, "At Kinneret, the Impressions of a Worker," *HaAhdut*, 25–26, 1.4.1912, 29–30.

138 Tahki, "From the Diary of a Kibbutz Member" [13.7.1922], in Gadon, ed., 1958, 346.

139 R. Benjamin, "All Around" [1908], in Benjamin 1922, 208.

140 Letter from Shmuel Dayan to Deborah Dayan [1922], Dayan 1961, 56.

141 Lieberson 1970, 35. Cf. Diary of Shoshana Bogen, "Nature" [1917–1918], in Zeira 1989, 47.

142 Yosef Held, "In a General Conversation," *Kehilateinu* 1998, 76.

143 Elon 1971, 129; Suchovolsky 1973, 81; Mary Yatziv, in Habas, ed., 1947, 569.

144 Letter from Ami Asaf [1922], in Ami Asaf 1968, 17.

145 Letter from Ami Asaf [1923], in Ami Asaf 1968, 18.

146 Gordon 1951, 51.

147 Yitzhak Tabenkin, in Habas, ed., 1947, 27. Cf. "The HaShomer HaTzaʿir Worldview" [1.1917], in Dror and Rosenzweig, eds., 1956, 43.

148 Yaʿakov Meir, in Habas, ed., 1947, 373.

149 Rachel Yanait-Ben-Zvi, in Ben-Zvi 1966, 127.

150 Letter from David Ben-Gurion to his father [1.2.1909], in Ben-Gurion 1971, vol. 1, 124. Cf. Ze'ev Bloch, "Kibbutz HaShomer HaTzaʿir Alef" [1940], in Dror and Rosenzweig, eds., 1956, 87.

151 Ackerman 1979, 93–117. On the influence of the Bible, see Shapira 1997, 645–674.

152 Yanait-Ben-Zvi 1959, 17.

153 Zalman Lifschitz, in Habas, ed., 1947, 387.

154 Ben-Eliav, "On Swellheadedness," *MeHayeynu*, 1, 15, 16.12.1921, 117; Ben-Zvi 1966, 87, 110, 130, 184, 186, 188; Yehuda Kopelovitch, "We Staked a Claim in the Valley," in *The Yosef Trumpeldor Labor Battalion* 1931, 66; Kushnir 1955, 30; Kushnir 1968, 77, 81; Yosef Weitz, "To the Galilee" [1912], in Weitz 1958, 143.

155 Letter from Yosef Fried to Naftali Shengil[?] [20.10.1908], in Fried 1985, 61.

156 Nadav 1957, 168; Yanait-Ben-Zvi 1959, 22.

157 Nadav 1957, 77.

158 Ben-Zvi 1966, 184, 188. Cf. Yitzhak Ben-Zvi, "On the Ruins of Samaria," *HaAhdut*, 18, 24.2.1911, 3–8; Yitzhak Ben-Zvi, "On the Ruins of Samaria," *HaAhdut*, 19, 3.3.1911, 3–8.

159 Rachel, "On the Shores of Kinneret" [1929], in Milstein, ed., 1997, 301, 302.

160 "A Packet of Letters from a Crazy Young Worker," in Tzur 1976, 118–119.

161 Letter from Michael Oved to the members of Kevutzat HaSharon, "Malaria Should Not Scare Us" [1925?], *Sefer HaKevutza* 1996, 89.

162 Elon 1971, 109–110.

163 Shlomo Levitin, "In the World of Creation," *MeHayeynu*, 1, 11, 7.11.1921, 62.

164 Ibid., 62–63.

165 Ibid., 63.

166 Bistritzky 1980, 12.

167 Ibid., 37.

168 Zalman Rubashov, "The Eternity of the Past," *HaAhdut*, 39–40, 8.8.1911, 14.

169 Ibid., 15.

170 Letter from Yedidya Shoham [12.8.1918], in Shoham 1987, 68.

171 Letter from Ben-Zion Israeli to Haya Israeli [1912], in Tzur and Israeli, eds., 1985, 99.

172 A. D. Gordon, "Hebrew University" [1913], in Gordon 1925, vol. 1, 117.

173 Yisachar Reiss, "The History of One *Kevutza*" [1918], in Dror and Rosenzweig, eds., 1956, 57.

174 Moshe Smilansky, "Heroism" [23.1.1920], in Rogel, ed., 1994, 416.

175 Rachel, "Rachel" [1926], in Raʿhel 1995, 26.

Chapter 4: Articulating the Physical Territory of the Land

1 Winichakul 1994.

2 My view of *halutziyyut* and Hebrew nationalism as presented here has been influenced by, among others: Baker 1997, 129–145; Gurevitch and Aran 1994, 195–210; Portugali 1993.

3 Nadav 1957, 17. Cf. Ze'ev Bloch, "In a General Conversation," *Kehilateinu* 1998, 61–62; Yehuda Levitov, "We Begin to Cover Ourselves with Hyssop" [20.7.1921], in *Sefer HaHaim* 2001, 45.

4 Yitzhak Ben-Zvi, "The Wandering of the Jews" [1.1907], in Ben-Zvi 1966, 341–342. Cf. Eliezer Yaffe, "The Foundation of the *Moshavei Ovdim*" [1919], in Yaffe 1947, vol. 1, 65–66.

5 L., "Toward the 'Soiled/Filthy Exiles,'" *HaAhdut*, 30, 22.5.1914, 1.

6 Alexander, "The Revival Below and the Revival Above," *HaAhdut*, 40–41, 7.8.1914, 5.

7 Letter from David Ben-Gurion to his father [7.11.1907], in Ben-Gurion 1971, vol. 1, 112.

8 Eliezer Yaffe, "Debates on the Question of the Program," in *The Prague Convention of HaPoʿel HaTzaʿir from the Land of Israel and Tzeʿirei Tzion from outside the Land* 1920, 37. Cf. Letter from Dov [2.1921], in Erez, ed., 1964, vol. 1, 227; A. D. Gordon, "A Letter Not Sent in Time" [1912], in Gordon 1928, vol. 4, 252; Letters from Yosef Trumpeldor to his friend Grisha [1908], in Poznansky, ed., 1922, 17; Yaʿakov Zerubavel, "Literary Conversations" [1911?], in Zerubavel 1966, 286.

9 Y. Gothelf, "Within Society and for Society" [1922?], in Gothelf and Cohen, eds., 1934, 81.

10 R. B., "Scraps of Old Conversations," *HaAdama*, 1, 1919–1920, 347.

11 "An Appeal by the Central Committee of the Union of HaPoʿel HaTzaʿir to All Young Zionists in the Exile" [1907–1908], in *Pirkei HaPoʿel HaTzaʿir*, 2, 1935, 158; Shemaryahu Ben-Mordechai, "We Will Prepare/Train Ourselves" [1.1919], in Dror and Rosenzweig, eds., 1956, 65; David Gilad-Shmeterling, in Tzur, ed., 1998, 132; Berl Katznelson, "In Memory of A.[?] Vitter[?]" [1919], in Katznelson 1945, vol. 1, 141; Katznelson-Shazar 1989, 89; Yitzhak Lufban, "Patience?" [1920], in Lufban 1954, 2; Nadav 1957, 9; "On the Way . . . ," *BaDerech*, 1–2, 31.12.1920, 1; Letters from Yosef Trumpeldor [1906, 1920], in Poznansky, ed., 1922, 8, 211–212; Tzemach 1983, 51; The World Union of HaPoʿel HaTzaʿir and Tzeʿiri Tzion, main office in Europe, "Communication. To All the Union's Organizations" [1921], *BaDerech*, 5–6, 28.2.1921, 7; Yaʿakov Zerubavel, "Literary Conversations" [1911?], in Zerubavel 1966, 287.

12 Michael Oved, "At the Season of the Year" [1925], *Sefer HaKevutza*, 67.

13 Eliezer Yaffe, "On Our Work in the Land of Israel" [1920], in Yaffe 1947, vol. 1, 49.

14 Yosef Aharonovich, "Facing the Disturbances" [1915], in Aharonovich 1941, vol. 1, 224. Cf. Zalman Rubashov, "The Eternity of the Past," *HaAhdut*, 39–40, 8.8.1911, 14–15.

15 David Ben-Gurion, "Toward the Future" [4.4.1915], in Ben-Gurion 1955, 14.

16 Berl Katznelson, "From Confusion" [1919], in Katznelson 1945, vol. 1, 139.

17 Alexander, "The Revival Below and the Revival Above," *HaAhdut*, 40–41, 7.8.1914, 5.

18 Group of youth from the Land of Israel, "Appeal" [1904], *HaAretz VeHaAvoda*, 1, 1913, 79. Cf. Mordechai Snir, "Homeland" [1920], in Snir 1954, 32.

19 Letters from David Ben-Gurion to his father and to Shmuel Fuchs [1904, 1906, 1913], in Ben-Gurion 1971, vol. 1, 22, 39, 66, 266.

20 Berl Katznelson, "From Confusion" [1919], in Katznelson 1945, vol. 1, 140; Berl Katznelson, "In Anticipation of the Time to Come" [1918], in Katznelson 1945, vol. 1, 73.

21 Mordechai Shenhavi, "Shumeriya" [22.4.1921], in Shadmi, ed., 1984a, 35.

22 Yehuda Levitov, "We Begin to Cover Ourselves with Hyssop" [20.7.1921], in *Sefer HaHaim* 2001, 47.

23 Tzvi Shatz, "On the *Kevutza*" [1920], in Shatz 1967, 91.

24 Yitzhak Elazari-Volcani, "From Home and from Elsewhere" [1919], in Elazari-Volcani 1950a, 74.

25 Ibid.

26 Eliezer Riger, "Assembly of HaShomer HaTzaʿir Counselors in Upper Trnava" [29–31.7.1918], in Shadmi, ed., 1984b, 10.

27 Harshav 1990, 11.

28 For a critical discussion of the Jewish/Zionist "return to history," see Eisenstadt and Lissak, eds., 1999; Eisen 1986.

29 David Shimonovitz, "Son of My Land: From the Notebook of a Wanderer" [1909–1919], in Shimonovitz 1947, 188.

30 Haim Arlosoroff, "The Social Nationalism of the Jews" [1919], in Arlosoroff 1934, vol. 3, 61.

31 Berl Katznelson, "My Road to the Land" [5.4.1941], in Katznelson 1947, vol. 5, 399.

32 On the different "territorialist" proposals, see Benjamini 1990; Weisbord 1968.

33 Ben-Zvi 1966, 55.

34 Ibid., 176.

35 Shmuel Almog, "People and Land in Modern Jewish Nationalism," in Reinharz and Shapira, eds., 1996, 59.

36 The writings of the *halutzim* are full of such expressions, so there is no point in citing sources. On the "empty land," see Elam 2004, 29–51; Raz-Krakotzkin 1993, 44–46.

37 Israel Betzer, "The Cabin on the Other Side of the Jordan," in *The HaShomer Anthology* 1937, 95; Mevi., "Kinneret," *HaAhdut*, 4, 18.11.1910, 23; Nadav 1957, 59.

38 S. Dik[?], "National Settlement," *HaAhdut*, 25, 10.4.1914, 12; Schweid 1985, 131–146.

39 Ben-Gurion and Ben-Zvi 1979, 227–228.

40 "A Diary from the Time of the Disturbances in the Lower Galilee" [1920], in *Beginning* 1971, 97–99; N-Y., "From a Private Letter by a Guard," *HaAhdut*, 19, 16.2.1912, 18–19; Thon [1911], in *Pirkei HaPoʿel HaTzaʿir*, 7, 1936, 49–51.

41 Yitzhak Hoz, "The Conquest of Merhavia," in *The HaShomer Anthology* 1937, 124.

42 El-R., "On the Questions of the Day," *HaAhdut*, 25, 10.4.1914, 3.

43 Yosef Baratz [1921], in *Pirkei HaPoʿel HaTzaʿir*, 7, 1936, 38; Yitzhak Ben-Zvi, "Our Intention" [1910], in Ben-Zvi 1966, 363; Letter from Dov [2.1921], in Erez, ed., 1964, vol. 1, 226; Group of youth from the Land of Israel, "Appeal" [1904], *HaAretz VeHaAvoda*, 1, 1913, 80; Katznelson

1990, 32; Letter from Berl Katznelson to Noah Naftulsky [1917], in Katznelson 1974, vol. 2, 368; N. P. Y., "A Letter from the Upper Galilee," *HaAhdut*, 16, 31.1.1913, 18; Tanhum Tanpilov, "The Horan Polemic 1912," in *Beginning* 1971, 27; Tanhum Tanpilov, "Records of the Degania Assembly," in Tzur, Zvulun, and Porat, eds., 1981, 53; Ze'ev Zamir, in Erez, ed., 1964, vol. 2, 456; Zemani [1912], in *Pirkei HaPo'el HaTza'ir*, 2, 1935, 59–60; Ya'akov Zerubavel, "Arab Attacks on the Settlements of the Lower Galilee" [14.7.1911], in Kaniel, ed., 1997, 366–367.

44 Shavti[?], "Letters of Pioneers" [30.10.1920], *BaDerech*, 1–2, 31.12.1920, 47.

45 Zerubavel, "Neighborly Relations," *HaAhdut*, 10, 11.12.1914, 1.

46 M. Ben-Levi, Letter from Migdal, *HaAhdut*, 18, 14.2.1913, 18; Berl Katznelson, "From within Labor" [28.12.1913], in Katznelson 1945, vol. 1, 32.

47 Yehuda Levitov, "We Begin to Cover Ourselves with Hyssop" [20.7.1921], in *Sefer HaHaim* 2001, 47.

48 Rachel Yanait, "The Question of Leaving and Its Economic Causes," *HaAhdut*, 30, 1.6.1911, 3.

49 Y. Reznichenko, "Foundation of the Labor Battalion," in *The Yosef Trumpeldor Labor Battalion* 1931, 11.

50 On the pioneer concept of "redemption," see Shmuel Almog, "Redemption in Zionist Rhetoric," in Kark, ed., 1990, 13–32; Henry Near, "Redemption of the Soil and of Man: Pioneering in Labor Zionist Ideology, 1904–1935," in Kark, ed., 1990, 33–47.

51 David Ben-Gurion, "Toward the Future" [4.4.1915], in Ben-Gurion 1955, 22.

52 Yosef Aharonovich, "On the Question of the Workers" [1912], in Aharonovich 1941, vol. 1, 53.

53 Oppenheimer 1914, 17.

54 Yosef Haftman, in Gadon, ed., 1958, 433–434.

55 R. Benjamin, "All Around" [1908], in Benjamin 1922, 205.

56 Mordechai Hadash, in Erez, ed., 1964, vol. 2, 802.

57 Ya'ari 1969, 165.

58 Over., Letter from Kfar Uria, *HaAhdut*, 16, 31.1.1913, 23.

59 Alroey 2004, 20–23. Alroey, who noticed this change, treats it as an expression of "the enlistment of the language for the purposes of the national movement," an approach that differs from my own; ibid. 23.

60 Rachel Yanait, in Elon 1971, 162.

61 Worker, "Letter from Merhavia," *HaAhdut*, 4, 7.11.1923, 18. Cf. Yosef Baratz [1925], in *Pirkei HaPo'el HaTza'ir*, 7, 1936, 41–42; N. Vatik, Letter from Metulla, *HaAhdut*, 20, 27.2.1914, 20; Tz. [1909], in *Pirkei HaPo'el HaTza'ir*, 7, 1936, 21.

62 It is worthy of note that this comment of Elon's was omitted from the English edition but appears in the Hebrew original; see Elon 1972, 178.

63 Noah Naftulsky, "They Paired Us Up on a Single Stretcher," in Tzur and Israeli, eds., 1985, 26.

64 Habas, ed., 1947, 246, 321, 463.

65 N. Vatik, Letter from Ramat Delaika, *HaAhdut*, 34, 30.6.1911, 17–18.

66 Ibid., 18.

67 Z. L., "On the Banks of the Jordan," *Kuntres*, 2, 5, 26.4.1920, 19–20.

68 Letter from Michael Oved to Tzvia, "I Work in Agriculture!" [1.5.1923], *Sefer HaKevutza*, 50. Cf. Diary of Moshe Greenwald [29.2.1920], in Rogel, ed., 1994, 269.

Sarah Chizik, "Selected from Her Memoirs and Letters" [1915, 1919], *HaAdama*, 2, 1920, 101, 103–104.

69 Habas, ed., 1947; Sharet and Tamir, eds., 1970–1974, vols. 1–6; Teveth 1985, 6–7.

70 Shlomo Kinnarti, "In Tent Camps," in *Anthology of the Third Aliya at Kinneret on Its Fortieth Anniversary* 1961, 39.

71 So many such examples exist of these associations that one could reasonably state that they appear in nearly every pioneer reference to the Arabs.

72 Zagorodsky 1919, 14.

73 David Ben-Gurion, "Toward the Future" [4.4.1915], in Ben-Gurion 1955, 18.

74 Ibid., 19.

75 Ibid. On Ben-Gurion's ambivalent attitude toward the local Arab population, see Teveth 1985.

76 I have borrowed the concept of "present absentees" from David Grossman; see Grossman 1992.

77 Ya'ari 1969, 208.

78 David Ben-Gurion, "Toward the Future" [4.4.1915], in Ben-Gurion 1955, 19.

79 Ben-Gurion and Ben-Zvi 1979, 192–206; Ben-Zvi 1966, 118–120; Shlomo Lavi, in Elon 1971, 165; Lieberson 1970, 31; Nadav 1957, 125; Yanait-Ben-Zvi 1959, 5, 17, 39–40, 66–67.

80 Epstein 1907, 193.

81 On Yitzhak Epstein, see Haramati 1984, 143–194; Haramati 1993, 81–126. On Epstein and his views about the Arab question, see Gorny 2001; Dowty 2001, 34–54.

82 Epstein 1907, 196.

83 Ibid., 193.

84 Ibid., 195.

85 Ibid. 195.

86 Ibid., 196.

87 Ibid., 201–202.

88 Ibid., 200.

89 Ibid., 204.

90 Other historians, of course, attribute the origins of the conflict to political, economic, ideological, and historical-religious factors, and date its inception differently—to the 1920s, with the rise of Palestinian nationalism; to 1948; or to 1967. For different theses on this matter, see Gelber 2004; Gelvin 2005; Gorny 2001; Morris 2001; Morris 2004; Rotberg, ed., 2006; Sa'di and Lughod, eds., 2007; Shafir 1989; Shapira 1992; Smith 2007. For psychoanalytic theses on the sources of the conflict, see Bunzl and Beit-Hallahmi, eds., 2002; Sucharov 2005. For a historical survey of the sources of the conflict, see Stein 1991, 1450–1465.

91 Letters from David Ben-Gurion to his father [1907, 1913], in Ben-Gurion 1971, vol. 1, 101, 257; Dayan 1961, 107; Kushnir 1955, 58.

92 Yosef Aharonovich, "The Idea of Labor" [1913], in Aharonovich 1941, vol. 1, 57.

93 Group of youth from the Land of Israel, "Appeal" [1904], *HaAretz VeHaAvoda*, 1, 1913, 79.

94 David Kahana, "In a General Conversation," *Kehilateinu* 1998, 51.

95 Tz. [1909], in *Pirkei HaPoʿel HaTzaʿir*, 7, 1936, 21.

96 Levi Ben-Amitai, "With the Furrow," in Ben-Amitai 1934, 8.

97 Yehudit Edelman, "From Judea to Samaria," in *The Words of Women Workers* 1930, 36.

98 Yaʿakov Pat, in Habas, ed., 1947, 479.

99 Kafkafi 1988, 125–126.

100 Letter from Shmuel Dayan to his son [1921], Dayan 1961, 61.

101 Rachel Katznelson-Shazar, "On the 'Silent Era'" [1916], in Katznelson-Shazar 1989, 100.

102 Emanuel Bar-Haim, in Gadon, ed., 1958, 451, 452; Ben-Nissan, "On the Road" [1921], in Dror and Rosenzweig, eds., 1956, 84.

103 Tzvi Lederer, "To the Road," *Kehilateinu* 1998, 97–98.

104 R., "On the Shores of Kinneret," *HaSolel*, 2, 29.1.1921, 77, 78.

105 Ben-Zion, "The Council of the Union of Farm Workers at Merhavia. Documentation. On the Condition of Labor," *Kuntres*, 17, 23.11.1919, 26–27.

106 Yosef Baratz [1921], in *Pirkei HaPoʿel HaTzaʿir*, 7, 1936, 40. Cf. Letter from Tanhum Tanpilov to Yaʿakov Apter [1920], in *Beginning* 1971, 105.

107 Haim Arlosoroff, "The Social Nationalism of the Jews" [1919], in Arlosoroff 1934, vol. 3, 52; M. Karmi, "Segments," *HaAdama*, 1, 1919–1920, 200; Kushnir 1955, 44; Yehuda Levitov [24.1.1921], in *Sefer HaHaim* 2001, 25; Y. Vidler[?], in Genigar 1948, 81–82; Eliezer Yaffe, "The Foundation of the *Moshavei Ovdim*" [1919], in Yaffe 1947, vol. 1, 70.

108 Hasia Drori, in Erez, ed., 1964, vol. 2, 515.

109 Dayan 1961, 132.

110 N. Yanshuf, Letter from Karkur, *HaAhdut*, 43, 22.8.1913, 19.

111 Pelah 1924, 4.

112 Levin-Talmi 1949, 127.

113 R. Benjamin, "All Around" [1908], in Benjamin 1922, 208; Yanait-Ben-Zvi 1959, 170; Eliezer Yaffe, "On Our Work in the Land of Israel" [1920], in Yaffe 1947, vol. 1, 52. Mordechai Kushnir, "Said at an Inappropriate Time," *BaAvodah*, 1918, 84; Asher Lotan, in Erez, ed., 1964, vol. 2, 825.

114 A. Shapira, "How We Began the Orchard Project," in Gothelf and Cohen, eds., 1934, 216, 217.

115 Yisrael Haderi, in Yaʿari, ed., 1983, vol. 2, 1228.

116 A. D. Gordon, "Letters from the Land of Israel" [1914?], in Gordon 1926, vol. 2, 227–229; Rachel, "Victims?" [1929], in Milstein, ed., 1997, 312.

117 Kushnir 1968, 86.

118 Zagorodsky 1919, 33.

119 Shmuel Dayan, in Yaʿari, ed., 1983, vol. 2, 1179; Letter from Eliezer Shohat to his wife [25.4.1922], in Shohat 1973, 131.

120 Yehuda Kopelovitch, "We Staked a Claim in the Valley," in *The Yosef Trumpeldor Labor Battalion* 1931, 66.

121 Haim Feinberg, "Memoirs," in *The HaShomer Anthology* 1937, 183. Cf. Yaʿakov Zerubavel, "Defense and Labor" [1911?], in Zerubavel 1966, 298, 300–301.

122 Yitzhak Ben-Zvi, "The Jews and Political Action" [30.12.1914], in Ben-Zvi 1966, 348–349.

123 Ben-Gorny [1911], in *Pirkei HaPoʿel HaTzaʿir*, 1, 1935, 112.

124 Yatza Vehazar [1912], in *Pirkei HaPoʿel HaTzaʿir*, 1, 1935, 114.

125 Tzvi Nadav, in Ben-Zvi, Shohat, Meged, and Tverski, eds., 1957, 89–90; Pele. [1913], in *Pirkei HaPoʿel HaTzaʿir*, 1, 1935, 123.

126 "Contract between the Council of the Rehovot *Moshava* and the Council of HaShomer, Section 16," in Ben-Zvi, Shohat, Meged, and Tverski, eds., 1957, 453.

127 Zalman Assushkin, "From Hadera to Hamra," in *The HaShomer Anthology* 1937, 126.

128 Ibid., 131–132, 134, 191.

129 Lieberson 1970, 88.

130 On the "beautiful death," see Lyotard 1988, 99–100. On the "beautiful death" in Zionism, see Bloom 2007, 346; Cohen 2007, 221–242.

131 Ben-Zion, "At Work," *Kuntres*, 3, 14, 28.1.1921, 28. Cf. Letter from Tanhum Tanpilov to Yaʿakov Apter [1920], in *Beginning* 1971, 105.

132 Ben-Eliav, "Our Demands," *MeHayeynu*, 1, 17–18, 6.1.1922, 140.

133 Alroey 1999, 231–237.

134 Berl Katznelson, "My Road to the Land" [5.4.1941], in Katznelson 1947, vol. 5, 388, 394.

135 L., "Comrades' Letters," *Kuntres*, 1, 16, 7.11.1919, 37.

136 Yitzhak Lufban, "Patience?" [1920], in Lufban 1954, 2.

137 Yitzhak Ben-Zvi, "The Jews and Political Action" [30.12.1914], in Ben-Zvi 1966, 349.

138 Letter from Yitzhak Ben-Zvi to Rachel Yanait-Ben-Zvi [23.9.1918], in Ben-Zvi 1966, 256–257.

139 R. Benjamin, "All Around," in Benjamin 1922, 314–315; Y. H. Brenner [1920], in Rogel, ed., 1994, 458; D. Cohen, "'The Guys,'" *Michtav LaChaverim*, 3, 72, 1921, 9; "Elusive Dawn," *Al Hasaf*, 1918, 102; Letter from Y. Kanevski[?] to the members of HeHalutz Movement in Constantinople [1920], in Erez, ed., 1964, vol. 1, 215; Rogel, ed., 1994, 278, 316, 434, 437, 438, 441, 446, 453, 458; S. Yavnieli, "Transcript of the Words of the Supporters of the Proposal," *Al Hasaf*, 1918, 13.

140 Letter from Yosef Trumpeldor to Samosha[?] [17.6.1906], in Poznansky, ed., 1922, 4–5.

141 Letter from Yosef Trumpeldor [13.6.1917], in Poznansky, ed., 1922, 201.

142 Ibid.

143 Letter from Yosef Trumpeldor to the defense committee of Ayelet HaShahar [4.1.1920], in Poznansky, ed., 1922, 217.

144 Letter from Yosef Trumpeldor to the defense committee of Ayelet HaShahar [9.2.1920], in Poznansky, ed., 1922, 231.

145 "Declaration for the Youth in the Land" [8.1.1920], in Rogel, ed., 1994, 153.

146 Eliezer Lubrani, "In Memoriam of My Brothers Who Fell in Galilee" [26.3.1920], in Shapira 1992, 100.

147 Zagorodsky 1919, 30–31. Cf. Efraim Rabinovich, "Getting to Know the Land's Natural Surroundings," *HaAdama*, 2, 1920, 170–178.

148 Ben-Gurion and Ben-Zvi 1979, 25, 26.

149 Lieberson 1970, 56.

150 Letter from Berl Katznelson to Haim Katznelson [1.11.1911], in Katznelson 1961, vol. 1, 279–280; Lieberson 1970, 56–57, 58, 61–63; Nadav 1957, 123–132; Suchovolsky 1973, 66–70; Yanait-Ben-Zvi 1959, 58.

151 Ze'ev Vilnay, "'Thou Shalt Love Thy Neighbor as Thyself,'" in Shiler, ed., 1984, 20.

152 Letter from David Ben-Gurion to his father [11.2.1908], in Ben-Gurion 1971, vol. 1, 114.

153 Moshe David Glicksman, in Habas, ed., 1947, 690.

154 Ben-Zvi 1966, 93.

155 Kushnir 1968, 112, 120.

156 Ben-Zvi 1966, 184.

157 Yanait-Ben-Zvi 1959, 218.

158 Lieberson 1970, 61.

159 Yanait-Ben-Zvi 1959, 45.

160 Letter from David Ben-Gurion to his father [26.7.1912], in Ben-Gurion 1971, vol. 1, 228.

161 Tzemach 1983, 77–91, 130–134.

162 Letter from Eliezer Shohat to his wife [2.3.1918], in Shohat 1973, 124.

163 "Haifa-Jadda Camp," *HaSolel*, 4, 15.4.1921, 167; Yehuda Reich, "The Quarry," *HaSolel*, 4, 15.4.1921, 162, 163, 164.

164 Ever Hadany, ed., 1955?, 219, 308–309; "Exhibition of Material for a Collection House in the Land of Israel," *Kuntres*, 1, 5, 27.6.1919, 39–41; Letter from Eliezer Shohat to his wife [5.5.1911], in Shohat 1973, 113; Tzemach 1983, 133; Ya'akov Zerubavel, "The Exhibition in the Galilee" [1912], in Zerubavel 1966, 308–313. Cf. A. Likhterov, "On the Question of the Museum" [15.2.1921], in *Sefer HaHaim* 2001, 26–29.

165 N. S., "Sejera," *Kuntres*, 1, 6, 4.7.1919, 36.

166 Azi.[?], Letter from Jamama, *HaAhdut*, 18, 14.2.1913, 16–17.

167 Ibid., 17.

168 Nadav 1957, 163, 164.

169 Ibid., 165.

170 Ibid., 152.

171 Ben-Eliav, "Our Demands," *MeHayeynu*, 1, 17–18, 6.1.1922, 141.

172 Dayan 1935, 20.

173 N. Vatik, Letter from Metulla, *HaAhdut*, 20, 27.2.1914, 20.

174 Oppenheimer 1914, 18.

175 "Arab Labor and Its Danger to the Yishuv" [10.1908], in Kaniel, ed., 1997, 359–360; Yitzhak Ben-Zvi, "Our Intention" [1910], in Ben-Zvi 1966, 365; Letter from Yosef Bussel in the name of *Kevutzat* Degania to Arthur Ruppin, "On New Buildings at the Permanent Site" [3.9.1911], in *Beginning* 1971, 15–16; Letter from A.[?].Y.[?] Golani, "A Year in Hadera" [1911], in Weitz 1958, 160; A. D. Gordon, "Letters from the Land of Israel" [1904], in Gordon 1926, vol. 2, 222; Letter from the HaShomer council to the council of Kfar Tavor [12.9.1913], in Ben-Zvi, Shohat, Meged, and Tverski, eds., 1957, 455; Letters from Berl Katznelson to Sarah Shmuckler, Leah Meron, and Meir Rotberg [1909, 1912], in Katznelson 1961, vol. 1, 118–125, 403; Rehovoti [1907], in *Pirkei HaPo'el HaTza'ir*, 1, 1935, 91; Suchovolsky 1973, 78–80; Letter from Yosef Trumpeldor to the de-

fense committee of Ayelet HaShahar [28.1.1920], in Poznansky, ed., 1922, 228–229; Z. L., "On the Banks of the Jordan," *Kuntres*, 2, 5, 26.4.1920, 19–20.

176 Yitzhak Elazari-Volcani, "Moral" [1913], in Elazari-Volcani 1950b, 65.

177 Eliezer Shohat, "National Creation and Accounts" [1911], in Shohat 1967, 22.

178 Ibid., 23.

179 Ibid., 22.

180 Letters from Berl Katznelson to Haim Katznelson and Yisrael Katznelson [5.1.1912], in Katznelson 1961, vol. 1, 305.

181 Yaffe 1959, 29. Cf. Worker, "Letter from Merhavia," *HaAhdut*, 4, 7.11.1923, 18; Yitzhak Elazari-Volcani, "Moral" [1913], in Elazari-Volcani 1950b, 64–65.

182 Ever Hadany, ed., 1955?, 301; Tzemach 1965, 105.

183 Ben-Zvi 1966, 120; Yaffe 1959, 29.

184 For a description of the incident, see Habas, ed., 1947, 275–276, 403, 422, 523–424; Ben-Zion Israeli, in Gadon, ed., 1958, 94; "It Happened in Lod" [1908], in *Pirkei HaPoʿel HaTzaʿir*, 2, 1935, 160–161; Katznelson 1990, 62; Lieberson 1970, 55; *The Paths of Development of Degania* 1961, 12–14; Sharet and Tamir, eds., 1970, vol. 1, 107–108. For another similar case, see Yona Horowitz, in Habas, ed., 1947, 208–209.

185 Tzemach 1965, 154–155; Tzemach 1983, 36.

186 Yosef Aharonovich, "The Conquest of Labor, or the Conquest of the Soil" [1908], in Aharonovich 1941, vol. 1, 7–18; Ben-Zvi 1966, 86–87; "On the Agenda: 'Redemption of the Land,'" *HaAhdut*, 13, 9.1.1912, 1–4.

187 Ben-Zvi, Shohat, Meged, and Tverski, eds., 1957, 117, 137, 272; *The HaShomer Anthology* 1937, 58, 67. On the origin of the slogan, see Anita Shapira, "Zionism and Power: Ethos and Reality," in Shapira 1988, 35.

188 Israel Shohat, "'HaShomer,'" in *The HaShomer Anthology* 1937, 433. Cf. Letter from David Canaany to Moshe Grossman [30/31.1.1920], in Rogel, ed., 1994, 198; Thon [1911], in *Pirkei HaPoʿel HaTzaʿir*, 7, 1936, 49.

189 Israel Shohat, "'HaShomer,'" in *The HaShomer Anthology* 1937, 434.

190 Avner [Ben-Zvi], "Di yafoʿer lektsyon" [14.4.1908], in Jonathan Frankel, "The 'Yizkor' Book of 1911: A Note on National Myths in the Second Aliya," in Reinharz and Shapira, eds., 1996, 435.

191 Ibid., 451n43.

192 M. Karmi, "Segments," *HaAdama*, 1, 1919–1920, 192–193, 195.

193 Yehoshua Thon, "Devotion," in Rabinovich, ed., 1912, 20.

194 The central committee of the Galilee Union of Farm Workers, *HaAhdut*, 10–11, 26.12.1913, 38; A letter by the HaShomer committee to Krause [14.11.1911], in Ben-Zvi, Shohat, Meged, and Tverski, eds., 1957, 451; Kushnir 1968, 75; "The Late Ben-Nahum," *HaAhdut*, 47–48, 25.9.1912, 29; A. Z. Rabinovich, "The Late Yaʿakov Plotkin," in Rabinovich, ed., 1912, 12; Matityahu Stein, in Ben-Zvi, Shohat, Meged, and Tverski, eds., 1957, 351; Rachel Yanait, "From Toil to Labor," *Al Hasaf*, 1918, 6; Yaʿakov Zerubavel, "Defense and Labor" [1911?], in Zerubavel 1966, 297; Yaʿakov Zerubavel, "The Strike at Sejera," in Zerubavel 1966, 71.

195 Kushnir 1968, 150.

196 "Yaʿakov Feldman," *HaAhdut*, 9, 12.12.1913, 27. Cf. Y. Zigel [1919], in *Pirkei HaPoʿel HaTzaʿir*, 7, 1936, 35.

197 Yaʿakov Zerubavel, "Defense and Labor" [1911?], in Zerubavel 1966, 300.

198 Letter from Yosef Nahmani to Haim Margaliot Kalvarisky [4.2.1920], in Rogel, ed., 1994, 206.

199 Yaʿakov Zerubavel, "Arab Attacks on the Settlements of the Lower Galilee" [14.7.1911], in Kaniel, ed., 1997, 367.

200 Zerubavel, "Lines," in Rabinovich, ed., 1912, 76.

201 HaPoʿel HaTzaʿir [1909], in *Pirkei HaPoʿel HaTzaʿir*, 2, 1935, 29; HaPoʿel HaTzaʿir [1913], in *Pirkei HaPoʿel HaTzaʿir*, 7, 1936, 30; Letter from members of Degania to the parents of Moshe Barsky [1914], in *The Paths of Development of Degania* 1961, 70; Yanait-Ben-Zvi 1959, 146; Zerubavel, "Lines," in Rabinovich, ed., 1912, 76.

202 Letter from Efraim Chizik to his brothers and sisters [4.3.1920], in Rogel, ed., 1994, 311–312.

203 Dayan 1953, 230.

204 Yaʿakov Meir, in Habas, ed., 1947, 376. Cf. Anonymous, "Internally and Externally," *MeHayeynu*, 2, 35, 1, 23.10.1922, 7; "First Convention of Volunteers in the Land of Israel" [15/16.2.1918], *Al Hasaf*, 1918, 90.

205 Kushnir 1968, 69.

206 Letter from Yosef Trumpeldor to his friend Grisha [12.10.1908], in Poznansky, ed., 1922, 21.

207 Ibid.

208 Yitzhak Elazari-Volcani, "This Way and That Way" [1913], in Elazari-Volcani 1950b, 29.

209 Yitzhak Elazari-Volcani, "The Uniqueness of Selfhood" [1913], in Elazari-Volcani 1950b, 44.

210 Ben-Zvi, Shohat, Meged, and Tverski, eds., 1957, 93, 100, 377; Ever Hadany, ed., 1955?, 248–250; Yehuda Kopelovitch, "We Staked a Claim in the Valley," in *The Yosef Trumpeldor Labor Battalion* 1931, 65; Rogel, ed., 1994, 284, 296; Thon [1911], in *Pirkei HaPoʿel HaTzaʿir*, 7, 1936, 50.

211 Letter from David Ben-Gurion to his father [25.3.1908], in Ben-Gurion 1971, vol. 1, 118.

212 Ibid.

213 *The HaShomer Anthology* 1937, 51, 124.

214 "New Victims," *HaAhdut*, 37, 21.7.1911, 1–2.

215 Letter from Yosef Trumpeldor to the defense committee of Ayelet HaShahar [10.1.1920], in Poznansky, ed., 1922, 222–223.

216 Letter from E-N [1.5.1920], in Erez, ed., 1964, vol. 1, 217; Letter from Ben-Zion Israeli to Haya Israeli [1910], in Tzur and Israeli, eds., 1985, 66; Letter from Eliezer Shohat to his wife [30.3.1911], in Shohat 1973, 112.

217 Thon [1911], in *Pirkei HaPoʿel HaTzaʿir*, 7, 1936, 51.

218 Anita Shapira, "Zionism and Power: Ethos and Reality," in Shapira 1988, 38.

219 Eliezer Yaffe, "Passages from My Diary" [1918], in Yaffe 1947, vol. 2, 145.

220 Ibid., 149.

221 Ibid., 151. Cf. Mordechai Snir, "Said at an Inappropriate Time" [1918], in Snir 1954, 142.

222 Shmuel Apter, Minutes of the assembly/council of the workers of the Galilee [18.10.1919], in Tzur and Israeli, eds., 1985, 141.

223 Sitkov, Minutes of the assembly/council of the workers of the Galilee [18.10.1919], in Tzur and Israeli, eds., 1985, 142.

224 Yosef Elkin, Minutes of the assembly/council of the workers of the Galilee [18.10.1919], in Tzur and Israeli, eds., 1985, 139.

225 "First Convention of Volunteers in the Land of Israel" [15/16.2.1918], *Al Hasaf*, 1918, 94. Cf. S. Yavnieli, "Transcript of the Words of the Supporters of the Proposal," *Al Hasaf*, 1918, 103.

226 A. D. Gordon, Minutes of the assembly/council of the workers of the Galilee [18.10.1919], in Tzur and Israeli, eds., 1985, 137–138. Cf. A. D. Gordon, "Our Labor from Now On," in Gordon 1926, vol. 2, 56–57; M. Karmi, "Segments," *HaAdama*, 1, 1919–1920, 195–197, 202.

227 Letter from Absalom Feinberg to Mendel Hankin [18.1.1909], in Feinberg 1975, 174; Ever Hadany, ed., 1955?, 202; The World Union of HaPoʿel HaTzaʿir and Tzeʿiri Tzion, main office in Europe, "Communication. To All the Union's Organizations" [1921], *BaDerech*, 5–6, 28.2.1921, 7; Zerubavel, "Lines," in Rabinovich, ed., 1912, 76; Yaʿakov Zerubavel, "Literary Conversations" [1911?], in Zerubavel 1966, 288.

228 Menachem Ussishkin, "Our Program" [1905], in Ussishkin 1934, 97.

229 R. Benjamin, "All Around" [1912], in Benjamin 1922, 220.

230 David Ben-Gurion and Alexander Heshin, "Yisker: Tsvayte Fargreserte Oyflage" [1916], in Jonathan Frankel, "The 'Yizkor' Book of 1911: A Note on National Myths in the Second Aliya," in Reinharz and Shapira, eds., 1996, 447.

231 Y. Kanievski, "The Tel Hai Era," *Michtav LaChaverim*, 3, 72, 1921, 15.

232 Mordechai Snir, "Said at an Inappropriate Time" [1918], in Snir 1954, 150.

233 Shimon Wolf, "In a General Conversation," *Kehilateinu* 1998, 41.

234 Letter from Berl Katznelson to Haim and Yisrael Katznelson [10.5.1910], in Katznelson 1961, vol. 1, 142.

235 Letter from Berl Katznelson to Yisrael Katznelson [19.3.1911], in Katznelson 1961, vol. 1, 205.

236 Shapira 1996, 228–236.

237 Anonymous, "From Our Lives," *MeHayeynu*, 1, 27, 10.4.1922, 281.

238 On the dimensions of *yerida* during the Second Aliya, see Kaniel 1994, 129–138. On the dimensions of *yerida* during the Third Aliya, see Ben-Avram and Near 1995, 5–46, 124–137, 189.

239 For a discussion of suicides in the Second and Third Aliyot, see Alroey 1999, 209–241; Tzur 1976, 27–44; Zeira 1989, 4–10. For diaries of *halutzim* who committed suicide, see Avronin-Abrahamson 2000; Zeira 1989, 1–77. For accounts of suicide cases, see "Alexander Brekner[?]," *HaAhdut*, 4, 10.11.1911, 23; Emanuel Bar-Haim, "Jerusalem," in *The Yosef Trumpeldor Labor Battalion* 1931, 141; Deganon [1913], in *Pirkei HaPoʿel HaTzaʿir*, 2, 1935, 67; Hamitzer 1981, 89–93; Habas, ed., 1947, 171, 702–705; Kushnir 1955, 36; *The Paths of Development of Degania* 1961, 105; Rogel, ed., 1994, 280; Shoham 1987, 176; Meir Spector, in Ben-Zvi, Shohat, Meged, and Tverski, eds., 1957, 258.

240 Alroey 1999, 210–212.

241 Letter from Haya Kastelanitz to Shlomo Kaplan, in Alroey 1999, 231.

242 Mordechai Snir, "Hardships of Absorption" [1920], in Snir 1954, 26.

243 Alroey 1999, 211–212.

244 Yosef Aharonovich, "Rachel Meizel" [1910], in *Pirkei HaPo'el HaTza'ir*, 2, 1935, 270.

245 Rachel Meizel's suicide note [1910], in Yosef Aharonovich, "Rachel Meizel" [1910], in *Pirkei HaPo'el HaTza'ir*, 2, 1935, 269.

246 Y.[?] Zamir's eulogy for Mordechai Wachsberg, in Alroey 1999, 226.

247 Letter from Anna to Tzvi Shatz [30.5.1913], in Tzur 1984, 38.

248 Letter from Yosef Fried to Yosef Rubinger [15.8.1908], in Fried 1985, 28.

249 Letter from Yosef Fried to his wife [21.6.1909], in Fried 1985, 82.

250 Letter from Yosef Fried to Shtreit[?] [27.6.1909], in Fried 1985, 85.

251 Letter from Yosef Fried to a friend [12.9.1909], in Fried 1985, 121.

252 Yitzhak Lamdan, "Bridge" [1924], in Lamdan 1973, 21.

253 Letter from Yosef Fried to his wife [18.9.1909], in Fried 1985, 127. Cf. Michael Sternberg, "The Land of Israel: From the Diary of One of the *Olim*," *Kolot*, 4, 1923, 131–133.

254 Dayan 1961, 72.

255 Letter from Eliezer Shohat to his wife [16.8.1923], in Shohat 1973, 142–143.

Chapter 5: Articulating the Pioneer Body

1 Katznelson 1990, 29–30; Shlomo Levitin, "At Dawn" [24.6.1930], in *The Yosef Trumpeldor Labor Battalion* 1931, 24; S. Yavnieli, "Transcript of the Words of the Supporters of the Proposal," *Al Hasaf*, 1918, 11; Zerubavel, "Lines," in Rabinovich, ed., 1912, 75. On the *luftmensch*, see Berg 2005, 199–224.

2 Mordechai Snir, "Said at an Inappropriate Time" [1918], in Snir 1954, 148. Cf. Menachem Elkind, "The Labor Battalion and Its Goals," *HaSolel*, 4, 15.4.1921, 159; Letter from Yosef Trumpeldor to Yehuda K-Tz. [4.8.1919], in Poznansky, ed., 1922, 204.

3 Letter to the members of Kevutzat Kiryat Anavim [1922], in *Sefer HaHaim* 2001, 102.

4 Letter from Yosef Trumpeldor to his friends D. and M. [8.8.1912], in Poznansky, ed., 1922, 47.

5 Alexander, "The Revival Below and the Revival Above," *HaAhdut*, 40–41, 7.8.1914, 5.

6 "The HaShomer HaTza'ir Worldview" [1.1917], in Dror and Rosenzweig, eds., 1956, 40, 41.

7 Letter from Yeshayah to Berl Katznelson [20.3.1909], in Katznelson 1945, vol. 1, 78.

8 A. D. Gordon, "The Congress" [1913], in Gordon 1925, vol. 1, 149.

9 On the Jew as a "parasitic" body, see Bein 1965, 121–149.

10 Haim Arlosoroff, "The Social Nationalism of the Jews" [1919], in Arlosoroff 1934, vol. 3, 44; Sarah Malkin, in Ya'ari, ed., 1983, vol. 2, 780; Letter from Yosef Trumpeldor to his sister [6.9.1906], in Poznansky, ed., 1922, 4–5; Tzemach 1983, 28, 44; Letter from Tzvia to the members of Kevutzat HaSharon, "A Letter from Nahalal to the *Kevutza*" [1923?], *Sefer HaKevutza* 1996, 55.

11 David Ben-Gurion, "Organizing the Workers of the *Moshavot*," *HaAhdut*, 28 29, 26.5.1911, 18; Letter from David Ben-Gurion to the Histadrut executive committee [24.9.1923],

in Ben-Gurion 1972, vol. 2, 167; S. Dik[?], "The Cooperative Moshav at Merhavia," *HaAhdut*, 29, 16.5.1914, 9; Menachem Elkind, "The Council of the Labor Battalion at Migdal" [17.6.1921], *HaSolel*, 240–241; S. Kaplinski, "The Question of the Farm Workers and the Groups," *HaAhdut*, 3–4, 23.10.1914, 12; Katznelson 1961, vol. 1, 429n21; Katznelson 1990, 28, 100; Letter from Berl Katznelson to Leah Meron [1912], in Katznelson 1961, vol. 1, 423; Yitzhak Lufban, "The Socialism of the People" [1920], in Lufban 1954, 283; Arthur Ruppin, "Mass Immigration and Finance" [1923], in Ruppin 1936, 107–120; Arthur Ruppin, "The Selection of the Fittest" [1919], in Ruppin 1936, 66–80; Suchovolsky 1973, 95; Ya'akov Zerubavel, "Defense and Labor" [1911?], in Zerubavel 1966, 299.

12 On the Jewish history of suffering and responses to it, see Roskies 1999. It is not of concern here whether the exilic Jew was actually passive; our subject is how the *halutzim* experienced the exile. For a critical discussion of the question of the passivity of the exilic Jew, see Amos Funkenstein, "Passivity as the Distinctive Trait of the Exile's Jews" [1982], in Funkenstein 1991, 232–242.

13 Ben-Zvi, Shohat, Meged, and Tverski, eds., 1957, 91, 102, 125–126; Sarah Chizik, "Selected from Her Memoirs and Letters" [1915], *HaAdama*, 2, 1920, 108–109; Letter from Shmuel Dayan to Deborah Dayan [15.2.1920], Dayan 1961, 25; Horowitz 1970, 68; Katznelson 1990, 38–39, 41; Letter from Berl Katznelson to Eliyahu Golomb [11.2.1918], in Katznelson 1974, vol. 2, 417; L., "Comrades' Letters," *Kuntres*, 1, 16, 7.11.1919, 37; "On the Agenda," *HaAhdut*, 8, 9.12.1912, 1–4; "Our Spilt Blood," *Kuntres*, 1, 4, 13.6.1919, 14–15; A.[?] R., "In Our Hebrew World," *HaAhdut*, 34, 20.6.1913, 8–10; Sharet and Tamir, eds., 1970, vol. 1, 10, 20, 35, 74, 105–106, 111, 295; Letter from Hasia Tartakowa[?] to A. D. Gordon [17.2.1921], in Tzur, ed., 1998, 53–54; Letters from Yosef Trumpeldor [1904, 1905, 1906, 1908, 1910, 1917, 1919, 1920], in Poznansky, ed., 1922, 3, 7, 19, 29, 202, 206, 211–212; Tzemach 1983, 29–30, 41, 50.

14 In Penkower 2004, 187.

15 Almog 1990, 56–61; Goren, ed., 1991, 9–49; Judge 1992; Penkower 2004, 187–225; Shorer, ed., 1963; Tzur, ed., 1998, 53n1. On the reception of the pogrom, see Smoliar 2003. On anti-Jewish pogroms in modern Russian history, see Klier and Lambroza, eds., 1992.

16 Berl Katznelson, "My Road to the Land" [5.4.1941], in Katznelson 1947, vol. 5, 383, 391.

17 Shoham 1987 [24.11.1918], 95.

18 Ibid.

19 Tzur, ed., 1998, 53n1.

20 Ya'akov Zerubavel, "'The Eternal Jew,'" in Zerubavel 1966, 64.

21 On the poem "City of the Killings," see Miron, ed., 2005; Smoliar 2003, 109–129.

22 Letter from Haim Arlosoroff to his friend Kalev[?] Dugilatzky[?] [29.5.1918], in Arlosoroff 1934, vol. 6, 155.

23 Gluzman 2003, 105–132; Goren, ed., 1991; Shorer, ed., 1963, 25–80; Smoliar 2003, 91–93.

24 Hayim Nahman Bialik, "City of the Killings" [July–September 1904], in Bialik 2000, 2.

25 Katznelson-Shazar 1989, 31–32.

26 Rachel Katznelson-Shazar, "I Want to Be an Invited Guest!" [1909–1911], in Katznelson-Shazar 1989, 61.

27 Rachel Katznelson-Shazar, "On the 'Silent Era'" [1916], in Katznelson-Shazar 1989, 98.

28 Baruch Zuckerman, "From the Horrors of Those Days [from a Letter by Comrade Baruch Zuckerman to His Wife, Comrade Nina]," in *Gvat* 1937, 17.

29 Ibid., 18.

30 For an account of the history of the "Jewish problem" as a history of the "problem of the Jewish body," see Efron 1994, 123–174; Efron 2001, 105–150; Gilman 1991; Hödl 1997; Presner 2007.

31 Almog 1993, 329–346.

32 Eliezer Riger, "The Revival of Strength" [6.1918], in Shadmi, ed., 1984b, 18.

33 Ibid., 19.

34 On Pinsker, see Klausner, ed., 1921. On Max Nordau, see Nordau and Nordau 1943.

35 Yehuda Leib Pinsker, opening speech at the Katowitz Congress [6.11.1884], in Pinsker 1951, 68–69.

36 Max Nordau, address at the First Zionist Congress [29.8.1897], 71.

37 Max Nordau, "Was Bedeutet das Turnen für uns Juden" [7.1902], in Nordau 1909, 383.

38 Max Nordau, "Muskeljudentum" [6.1900], in Nordau 1909, 379–380.

39 Ibid., 380.

40 Almog 1984, 137–146. On Nordau and his concept of the "muscular Jew" in historical context, see Geller 1995, 129–160; Mosse 1992, 565–581; Presner 2003, 269–296; Stanislawski 2001, 19–97; Zimmermann 2006, 13–26.

41 Habas, ed., 1947; Sharet and Tamir, eds., 1970–1974, vols. 1–6.

42 Hasia Drori, in Erez, ed., 1964, vol. 2, 514. Cf. S. Kaplinski, "The Question of the Farmworkers and the Groups," *HaAhdut*, 3–4, 23.10.1914, 14.

43 A. D. Gordon, "The Congress" [1913], in Gordon 1925, vol. 1, 167.

44 Letter from Berl Katznelson to Yisrael Katznelson [13.11.1911], in Katznelson 1961, vol. 1, 294.

45 Letter from David Ben-Gurion to his father [8.11.1906], in Ben-Gurion 1971, vol. 1, 83.

46 Tzemach 1965, 91.

47 Letter from Yosef Weitz to a friend in the exile [1.1910], in Weitz 1958, 151.

48 Ibid.

49 Azi.[?], "Letter from Jamama," *HaAhdut*, 18, 14.2.1913, 19; Ben-Zvi, Shohat, Meged, and Tverski, eds., 1957, 87, 91, 104, 134, 299, 455; *The HaShomer Anthology* 1937, 58, 291, 432; Kaniel, ed., 1997, 376, 388; "Yosef Saltzman," *HaAhdut*, 7, 28.11.1913, 24; Tzvi Neshri, in Habas, ed., 1947, 199–201; Yanait-Ben-Zvi 1959, 144.

50 HaPoʿel HaTzaʿir [1913], in *Pirkei HaPoʿel HaTzaʿir*, 7, 1936, 30.

51 Ben-Yosef, "Letter from Rishon LeTzion," *HaAhdut*, 38–39, 26.7.1912, 36–37; *The HaShomer Anthology* 1937, 171, 112; Meir Spector, "On Guard in the Galilee and Judea," in *The HaShomer Anthology* 1937, 171. On hostilities between Jews and Arabs during this period, see Slutzki 1986, 11–125; Teveth 1985, 3–85.

52 Matityahu Stein, in Ben-Zvi, Shohat, Meged, and Tverski, eds., 1957, 307.

53 Letter from Avraham Hartzfeld to the members of the Central Committee of the Union of Farm Workers [1/2.3.1920], in Rogel, ed., 1994, 280.

54 Ajzenstadt and Cavaglion 2002, 102–104; Berkowitz 1993, 99–118. On the "new Jew" or "new man," see Shapira 1997b, 253–270.

55 Ef. Libenson, "To the Founding Assembly" [7.11.1921], in *Sefer HaHaim* 2001, 58.

56 Letters from David Ben-Gurion to the HeHalutz Organization in Bulgaria and to the Histadrut Executive Committee [1922, 1923], in Ben-Gurion 1972, vol. 2, 100, 164–168; Katznelson 1961, vol. 1, 48–49n3; Y. M., "BeHalutz, 'The HeHalutz Farm,'" *Michtav LaChaverim*, 2, 22.8.1919, 27–28; Peled 2002, 93–112; Shoham 1987, 19, 152; Letter from Yosef Trumpeldor to friends [10.6.1912], in Poznansky, ed., 1922, 42–43. For a discussion of HaShomer HaTzaʿir's educational methods, see Lamm 1998. For a historical account of the process of making the Jews productive, see Shmuel Almog, "Productivization, Proletarization, and Hebrew Labor," in Almog 1992, 139–168.

57 Berl Katznelson, "My Road to the Land" [5.4.1941], in Katznelson 1947, vol. 5, 388, 391.

58 Shoham 1987 [24.5.1920], 152.

59 Ibid., 153.

60 Horowitz 1970, 30.

61 "An Appeal by the Central Committee of the Union of HaPoʿel HaTzaʿir to All Young Zionists in the Exile" [1907–1908], in *Pirkei HaPoʿel HaTzaʿir*, 2, 1935, 158; Benjamin, "Toward the New Year," *Kuntres*, 3, 1, 8.10.1919, 4; Lieberson 1970, 108.

62 Letter from David Ben-Gurion to the Trade Unions Center of the Jewish National Workers Alliance in America, New York [24.7.1923], in Ben-Gurion 1972, vol. 2, 132.

63 Ef. Libenson, "For the Days 20–21 Tammuz" [26/27.7.1921], in *Sefer HaHaim* 2001, 48.

64 Katznelson 1990, 55–56, 60–61.

65 Tzemach 1965, 86, 97–98, 107.

66 Letter from David Ben-Gurion to his father [8.2.1907], in Ben-Gurion 1971, vol. 1, 101; Sarah Chizik, "Selected from Her Memoirs and Letters" [1915], *HaAdama*, 2, 1920, 103; Dayan 1961, 86, 102, 134; Letter [17.1.1921], in Erez, ed., 1964, vol. 1, 224; Letters from Berl Katznelson, in Katznelson 1961, vol. 1, 122–123, 135n31, 211, 218; "Letters of Pioneers," *BaDerech*, 7–8, 31.3.1921, 32; Lieberson 1970, 38, 53; *The Paths of Development of Degania* 1961, 243; Rachel Shapira, "From a Kibbutz Diary," *Kehilateinu* 1998, 106; Letter from Shneor Spetchnik[?] to his brother Yehoshua [3.10.1919], in Rogel, ed., 1994, 64–65; Letter from Yosef Trumpeldor to his friend Grisha [19.10.1911], in Poznansky, ed., 1922, 38; Yanait-Ben-Zvi 1959, 322.

67 Diary of Yedidya Shoham [21.8.1920], in Shadmi, ed., 1984a, 21.

68 Letter from Menachem Portugali to Tova Portugali [28.5.1913], *The HaShomer Anthology* 1937, 19.

69 Yitzhak Elazari-Volcani, "Modes of Building" [1919], in Elazari-Volcani 1950a, 33.

70 Letter from Hannah Katznelson to Rachel Katznelson [18.7.1918], in Zeira 1989, 60.

71 *The Paths of Development of Degania* 1961, 167.

72 Letter from Tzvia to the members of Kevutzat HaSharon, "A Letter from Nahalal to the *Kevutza*" [1923?], *Sefer HaKevutza* 1996, 56.

73 A. D. Gordon, "Work" [1911], in Gordon 1925, vol. 1, 98.

74 Aliza Shidlovsky, in Habas, ed., 1947, 558; Meir Wilkansky, "Tilling/Hoeing" [1906–1911], Wilkansky 1982, 69.

75 Arieh Avatihi, in Erez, ed., 1964, vol. 2, 680; Tzemach 1965, 224.

76 Eliezer Yaffe, "Communication #2" [1914], in Yaffe 1947, vol. 1, 15.

77 Letter from Berl Katznelson to Hannah Katznelson [5.7.1912], in Katznelson 1961, vol. 1, 388. Katznelson offers many details of his experience as a worker: see Katznelson 1961, vol. 1, 48–49, 58–59, 65, 68–70, 111–113, 175–176, 220–221, 272, 279–280, 290–292, 294–295, 312, 422–423, 532, 543.

78 Letter from Shulamit Hayyut [27.10.1920], in Erez, ed., 1964, vol. 1, 230.

79 Yisachar Reiss, "The History of One *Kevutza*" [1918], in Dror and Rosenzweig, eds., 1956, 56. Cf. "An Appeal by the Central Committee of the Union of HaPo'el HaTza'ir to All Young Zionists in the Exile" [1907–1908], in *Pirkei HaPo'el HaTza'ir*, 2, 1935, 159.

80 Meir Ya'ari, "Hands, First and Foremost" [1918], in Dror and Rosenzweig, eds., 1956, 48.

81 Yitzhak Ben-Zvi, "Our Intention" [1910], in Ben-Zvi 1966, 370.

82 Yosef Haftman, "Quarry," in Gur-Arieh 1925, 5.

83 David Ben-Gurion, "The Question of Unity" [22.2.1919], in Ben-Gurion 1962, 74, 76; A. Likhterov, "On the Question of the Museum" [15.2.1921], in *Sefer HaHaim* 2001, 27; Shoham 1987 [15.10.1918], 77; Ya'akov Zerubavel, "Defense and Labor" [1911?], in Zerubavel 1966, 298.

84 A. D. Gordon, "A Bit of Introspection" [1911], in Gordon 1925, vol. 1, 86.

85 A. D. Gordon, "Work" [1911], in Gordon 1925, vol. 1, 97–98.

86 Lieberson 1970, 102.

87 *The Paths of Development of Degania* 1961, 248.

88 Letter from Golda Meyerson [13.12.1921], in Erez, ed., 1964, vol. 1, 241.

89 Member of Degania, in *The Paths of Development of Degania* 1961, 58.

90 Mordechai Hadash, in Erez, ed., 1964, vol. 2, 807.

91 Katznelson 1961, vol. 1, 273n3n4n5; Berl Katznelson, "To the HeHalutz Movement" [1917], in Katznelson 1945, vol. 1, 55.

92 Letter from Berl Katznelson to Hannah Katznelson [8.9.1911], in Katznelson 1961, vol. 1, 272.

93 Letter from Berl Katznelson to Hannah Katznelson [5.7.1912], in Katznelson 1961, vol. 1, 388.

94 M. Y., "The Botanical Exhibition of Efraim Rabinovich," *Kuntres*, 3, 4, 22.10.1920, 24.

95 Pelah 1924, 3, 9.

96 Nadav 1957, 135.

97 Letter from Berl Katznelson to Hannah Katznelson [5.7.1912], in Katznelson 1961, vol. 1, 388.

98 Nadav 1957, 122.

99 Ibid., 135. Cf. *The HaShomer Anthology* 1937, 184, 191–192, 244–259.

100 Shoshana Bluwstein, in Ya'ari, ed., 1983, vol. 2, 817–818.

101 Haim Tartakower, "The Role of HaPo'el HaTza'ir in the Movement to Redeem Our People," *BaDerech*, 7–8, 31.3.1921, 10.

102 Mordechai Snir, "Hardships of Absorption" [1920], in Snir 1954, 23.

103 Letter from Yosef Aharonovich to a friend [1910], in Aharonovich 1941, vol. 1, 212.

104 Meir Wilkansky, "From the Time of the Aliya" [1906–1911], Wilkansky 1982, 128.

105 Shoham 1987 [13.1.1919], 108.

106 Dayan 1935, 61–62.

107 Meir Wilkansky, "My First Day of Labor" [1906–1911], Wilkansky 1982, 25.

108 Cf. Katznelson 1990, 69.

109 Dayan 1961, 12; Yosef Aharonovich, "Marxism" [1926], in Aharonovich 1941, vol. 1, 218; Tzemach 1965, 158, 201, 207, 214, 215–216, 223–224.

110 A. D. Gordon in a letter from Berl Katznelson to Sarah Shmuckler and Leah Meron [at the end of Yom Kippur, 1910], in Katznelson 1961, vol. 1, 111.

111 In Zalman Lifschitz, in Habas, ed., 1947, 389.

112 Berl Katznelson, "From within Labor" [28.12.1913], in Katznelson 1945, vol. 1, 28.

113 Meir Wilkansky, "Tilling/Hoeing" [1906–1911], Wilkansky 1982, 62.

114 *The Paths of Development of Degania* 1961, 246.

115 Yaʿakov Shmueli, in Erez, ed., 1964, vol. 2, 818.

116 S. Ben-Zvi, in Habas, ed., 1947, 472.

117 Nahum Brodsky, "Community of Workers," *HaAdama*, 2, 1920, 25.

118 M. Bdolach, in Erez, ed., 1964, vol. 2, 709; Kushnir 1968, 100, 119; Lieberson 1970, 54; Shlomo Reichenstein, in Gadon, ed., 1958, 444; Weitz 1958, 185–186.

119 Tzur, Zvulun, and Porat, eds., 1981, 48.

120 Shoshana Bluwstein, in Yaʿari, ed., 1983, vol. 2, 818.

121 Kushnir 1968, 100, 119; Suchovolsky 1973, 65; Weitz 1958, 185–186.

122 S. D. Yaffe, in Habas, ed., 1947, 368.

123 S. D. Yaffe, in Habas, ed., 1947, 367.

124 Katznelson 1990, 93.

125 Tzemach 1983, 21.

126 Yisrael Kadishman in Habas, ed., 1947, 293; Katznelson 1961, vol. 1, 403n1.

127 Letter from Yosef Weitz to his father [24.7.1908], in Weitz 1958, 133–134.

128 Simcha Ben-Zion, "The Levites" [7.2.1909], in Ben-Zion 1960, 366.

129 Tanhum Tanpilov, "Relations between Newcomers and Veterans" [1919], in *Beginning* 1971, 85.

130 Dayan 1935, 45; Tzvi Nadav, "From My Memoirs," in *The HaShomer Anthology* 1937, 335–336; Yaʿakov Pat, in Habas, ed., 1947, 479; Suchovolsky 1973, 96.

131 David Ben-Gurion, "In Judea and the Galilee," in *The HaShomer Anthology* 1937, 262.

132 Nadav 1957, 88.

133 Weitz 1958, 136.

134 Nadav 1957, 91, 92.

135 Haim Rosenfeld, in Muki Tzur, "The Second Aliya: Types of Immigrants and Their Sociocultural Profile," in Bartal, ed., 1997, 290.

136 Dayan 1961, 59–60.

137 Israel Giladi, in Slutzki 1986, 33.

138 Letter from Shulamit Hayyut [27.10.1920], in Erez, ed., 1964, vol. 1, 230.

139 Michael Oved, "What Will Our Ideal Be?" [1926], *Sefer HaKevutza* 1996, 138–139.

140 Eliyahu Rappaport, in Erez, ed., 1964, vol. 2, 800.

141 Ben-Zvi, Shohat, Meged, and Tverski, eds., 1957, 91, 117, 150; *The HaShomer Anthology* 1937; "The HaShomer Plan" [4.1909], in Kaniel, ed., 1997, 370–371; Nadav 1957, 190–191.

142 Letter from Yitzhak Ben-Zvi to Shlomo Kaplinsky [4.6.1918], in Ben-Zvi 1966, 253.

143 Letter from Yitzhak Ben-Zvi to Rachel Yanait-Ben-Zvi [6.9.1918], in Ben-Zvi 1966, 254.

144 Letters from David Ben-Gurion to Paula [1918], in Ben-Gurion 1971, vol. 1, 347, 350, 351, 353, 362, 368–369.

145 Meir Spector, "On Guard in the Galilee and Judea," in *The HaShomer Anthology* 1937, 168.

146 Aryeh Shahar, in Sharet and Tamir, eds., 1970, vol. 1, 385.

147 Dayan 1961, 101–102; Nadav 1957, 189; Shapira 1992, 71–72.

148 Ben-Gurion 1973, 38; *The HaShomer Anthology* 1937, 146, 218; Moshe Sher, in Ben-Zvi, Shohat, Meged, and Tverski, eds., 1957, 132.

149 M. Bdolach, in Erez, ed., 1964, vol. 2, 709; Letter from Haim Bretschneider [11.6.1920], in Erez, ed., 1964, vol. 1, 219; Ever Hadany, ed., 1955?, 306; Letter from Natan Ikar to his parents [2.2.1920], in Hamitzer 1981, 91; P. Lipovetsky, "Labor Battalion," *MeHayeynu*, 1, 9, 1921–1922, 43; One from the commune, "The First Two Years" [1920], in Gadon, ed., 1958, 60; A. S., "On Guard," *Kuntres*, 20, 9.1.1920, 10–11; Yanait-Ben-Zvi 1959, 137.

150 Ben-Zvi, Shohat, Meged, and Tverski, eds., 1957, 86, 118, 119, 263, 369, 370, 372, 375, 377; Ever Hadany, ed., 1955?, 192–193, 209, 211, 243–244, 290; Tzipora Zeid, in Habas, ed., 1947, 533–534.

151 On the "society of dignity" in the Zionist context, see Kamir 2004.

152 Letter from David Ben-Gurion to his father [9.5.1909], in Ben-Gurion 1971, vol. 1, 129.

153 Letter from David Ben-Gurion to his father [15.10.1909], in Ben-Gurion 1971, vol. 1, 145.

154 Ever Hadany, ed., 1955?, 151.

155 Ben-Zvi, Shohat, Meged, and Tverski, eds., 1957, 113, 118; Letter from Berl Katznelson to Haim and Yisrael Katznelson [10.5.1910], in Katznelson 1961, vol. 1, 144; Yanait-Ben-Zvi 1959, 137; Alexander Zeid, in Habas, ed., 1947, 172.

156 Meir Spector, "On Guard in the Galilee and Judea," in *The HaShomer Anthology* 1937, 174.

157 Ben-Gurion 1973, 38.

158 Ever Hadany, ed., 1955?, 295–296; Lavi 1964, 52, 60.

159 Matityahu Stein, in Ben-Zvi, Shohat, Meged, and Tverski, eds., 1957, 310.

160 M. Lvovsky, in Habas, ed., 1947, 711. Cf. Brener 1978, 30.

161 Yehudit Horowitz, in Ben-Zvi, Shohat, Meged, and Tverski, eds., 1957, 362; Ya'akov Meir, in Habas, ed., 1947, 362.

162 "Ya'akov Feldman," *HaAhdut*, 9, 12.12.1913, 27. Cf. Ben-Zvi, Shohat, Meged, and Tverski, eds., 1957, 91, 93, 98, 133, 308; Ever Hadany, ed., 1955?, 225; Israel Giladi, "Memoirs from the Life of Yehezkel Nisanov," *HaAhdut*, 20–21, 15.3.1911, 19–20; Mamshi and Shin [1908–1909], in *Pirkei HaPo'el HaTza'ir*, 2, 1935, 26; "Yehezkel Nisanov," *HaAhdut*, 18, 24.2.1911, 1–2.

163 Haya Kroll, "A Few Moments," in *The HaShomer Anthology* 1937, 210.

164 Diary of Moshe Greenwald [29.2.1920], in Rogel, ed., 1994, 270.

165 Nadav 1957, 182. Cf. Yisachar Sitkov, "Guard Tactics," in *The HaShomer Anthology* 1937, 190.

166 Letter from David Ben-Gurion to his father [27.1.1907], in Ben-Gurion 1971, vol. 1, 99;

Ben-Zvi, Shohat, Meged, and Tverski, eds., 1957, 97, 102, 296, 376; Letter from Berl Katznelson to Hannah Katznelson [1910], in Katznelson 1961, vol. 1, 141.

167 Simcha Ben-Zion, "On Guard (from the Recent Past)," in Ben-Zion 1960, 343.

168 Meir Spector, "On Guard in the Galilee and Judea," in *The HaShomer Anthology* 1937, 174.

169 Haya Kroll, "A Few Moments," in *The HaShomer Anthology* 1937, 210.

170 Mordechai Yigal, in Ben-Zvi, Shohat, Meged, and Tverski, eds., 1957, 102.

171 Ben-Eliav, "Our Demands," *MeHayeynu*, 1, 17–18, 6.1.1922, 140; Letter from David Ben-Gurion to his father [22.8.1911], in Ben-Gurion 1971, vol. 1, 160; Bistritzky 1978, 79, 154–155, 157; Menachem Haklai, in Erez, ed., 1964, vol. 2, 458; Letter from Berl Katznelson to Sarah Shmuckler [7.12.1917], in Katznelson 1974, vol. 2, 400; *Kehilateinu* 1998, 49, 54, 62, 69; Kushnir 1955, 39–40; *The Paths of Development of Degania* 1961, 246; Letter from P-N [24.12.1920], in Erez, ed., 1964, vol. 1, 227; Mordechai Snir, "Said at an Inappropriate Time" [1918], in Snir 1954, 148; Moshe Zaludin, "In Smoke and in Poverty," in *The HaShomer Anthology* 1937, 224.

172 Rachel, "On the Shores of Kinneret" [1929], in Milstein, ed., 1997, 302.

173 A. D. Gordon, "Irrational Solution" [1909], in Gordon 1925, vol. 1, 29.

174 A. D. Gordon, "Letters from the Land of Israel" [1914?], in Gordon 1926, vol. 2, 230–231.

175 Ibid., 233.

176 Shulamit Ron-Polani, "Until There Are Calluses," in Tzur, Zvulun, and Porat, eds., 1981, 171.

177 Nadav 1957, 153–154. On the history of the disease in the Land of Israel, see Levy 1998, 478–494; Sufian 2007; Zakim 2006, 54–90.

178 Dayan 1935, 58–59; Habas, ed., 1947, 195, 197, 206, 212, 245; Letter from Michael Oved to the members of Kevutzat HaSharon, "Malaria Should Not Scare Us" [1925?], *Sefer HaKevutza* 1996, 89–90; Diary of Yedidya Shoham [21.8.1920], in Shadmi, ed., 1984a, 22; Weitz 1958, 156; Letter from Tzvi to his parents [7.5.1920], in Erez, ed., 1964, vol. 1, 218.

179 Rachel, "On the Shores of Kinneret" [1929], in Milstein, ed., 1997, 302.

180 Yanait-Ben-Zvi 1959, 118.

181 Baruch Ben-Yehuda, "The Heat Was Unbearable," in Tzur, Zvulun, and Porat, eds., 1981, 99.

182 Hannah Katznelson-Nesher, in Sharet and Tamir, eds., 1970, vol. 1, 243; Yehudit Edelman, "From Judea to Samaria," in *The Words of Women Workers* 1930, 35. Levi Ben-Amitai, "In Malaria," in Ben-Amitai 1934, 14–16; Ya'ari 1969, 201–204.

183 David Ben-Gurion, "In Judea and the Galilee," in *The HaShomer Anthology* 1937, 261. Cf. M. Segalov, in Habas, ed., 1947, 292–293; Ya'akov Shmueli, in Erez, ed., 1964, vol. 2, 818–819.

184 Letter from David Ben-Gurion to his father [13.5.1907], in Ben-Gurion 1971, vol. 1, 106. Cf. Letter from Shmuel Dayan to Deborah Dayan [4.1.1921], in Dayan 1961, 57; Hannah Katznelson-Nesher, in Sharet and Tamir, eds., 1970, vol. 1, 242–243; Lieberson 1970, 88.

185 On A. D. Gordon, see Schweid 1970. On Yosef Trumpeldor, see Laskov 1995.

186 Erez, ed., 1964, vol. 1, 9, 10, 12, 13, 25, 28, 31, 33, 41, 55, 107–112, 114, 145, 146, 161, 198, 199, 215–216, 230, 234, 256, 279, 289, 291, 315, 321, 325–327, 329, 330, 333, 346, 361; Erez, ed., 1964, vol. 2, 455–457, 459, 485, 497, 498, 581, 632, 642, 801, 851, 883, 904, 905, 907; Habas, ed., 1947, 251, 386, 440, 547, 563, 719, 741, 747.

187 Letter from Yosef Trumpeldor to his father [20.1.1905], in Poznansky, ed., 1922, 2.

188 Cohen 1973, 31, 45.

189 Jabotinsky 1947, 205–206.

190 Pinsker 1974, 163.

191 Ibid.

192 Ibid., 171.

193 Ibid., 171.

194 Max Nordau, "Die Aufgaben des Zionismus" [1898], in Nordau 1909, 323.

195 Ibid., 327–328.

196 Max Nordau, "The Only Solution to the Jewish Question" [1900], in Nordau 1954, 194.

197 Letter from David Ben-Gurion to Shmuel Fuchs [16.7.1904], in Ben-Gurion 1971, vol. 1, 22; Letter from Yitzhak Ben-Zvi to Rachel Yanait [11.12.1916], in Ben-Zvi 1966, 232; E.[?] L. Yaffe in the name of the committee of the Galilee Union of Farm Workers, "On the Matter of Labor in the Galilee," *HaAhdut*, 31, 29.5.1914, 18; Letter [3.6.1920], in Erez, ed., 1964, vol. 1, 221.

198 Eliezer Yaffe, "The Dry Bones: Listen!" [1906], in Yaffe 1947, vol. 2, 91–92.

199 A. D. Gordon, opening speech [15.5.1920], in Gordon 1926, vol. 2, 36.

200 A. D. Gordon, "Letters from the Land of Israel" [1914?], in Gordon 1926, vol. 2, 274.

201 Haim Arlosoroff, "The Social Nationalism of the Jews" [1919], in Arlosoroff 1934, vol. 3, 51, 52.

202 A. D. Gordon, "Letters from the Land of Israel" [1914?], in Gordon 1926, vol. 2, 239.

203 Ibid., 243, 244; A. D. Gordon, "A Letter Not Sent in Time" [1912], in Gordon 1928, vol. 4, 250–253.

204 Yavnieli 1952, 41.

205 Mordechai Snir, "Hardships of Absorption" [1920], in Snir 1954, 20, 28.

206 Ruppin 1914, 18.

207 Ibid., 123.

208 A.[?] R., "In Our Hebrew World," *HaAhdut*, 34, 20.6.1913, 8.

209 Ibid., 9.

210 Ibid.

211 HaPo'el HaTza'ir [1907], in *Pirkei HaPo'el HaTza'ir*, 1, 1935, 57.

212 David Ben-Gurion, "'One Law'" [1.4.1912], in Ben-Gurion 1962, 60.

213 A. D. Gordon, opening speech [15.5.1920], in Gordon 1926, vol. 2, 35. Cf. P., "After the Council of HaPo'el HaTza'ir in the Land of Israel," *BaDerech*, 5–6, 28.2.1921, 9.

214 Letter from Absalom Feinberg to his father, Yisrael Feinberg [14.10.1907], in Feinberg 1975, 176–177.

215 Ben-Zvi 1966, 41.

216 Ibid., 42.

217 A. D. Gordon, "Letters from the Land of Israel" [1914?], in Gordon 1926, vol. 2, 268–269.

218 Ibid., 244.

219 A. D. Gordon, opening speech [15.5.1920], in Gordon 1926, Vol. 2, 37

220 Yosef Aharonovich, "A Voice from Outside" [1909], in Aharonovich 1941, vol. 1, 19, 20.

221 Ibid., 20.

222 Haim Arlosoroff, "The Social Nationalism of the Jews" [1919], in Arlosoroff 1934, vol. 3, 61.

223 Elisha, "Our Roles," *MeHayeynu*, 1, 13, 1921, 88.

224 Mordechai Snir, "Said at an Inappropriate Time" [1918], in Snir 1954, 150.

225 From the Seventh General Congress of HaPoʿel HaTzaʿir [1912], in *Pirkei HaPoʿel HaTzaʿir*, 2, 1935, 190.

226 A. D. Gordon, "Our Labor from Now On," in Gordon 1926, vol. 2, 54.

227 Ruppin 1914, 187.

228 Yosef Aharonovich, "The Spirit and Matter in Zionism" [1913], in Aharonovich 1941, vol. 1, 108. Cf. Berl Katznelson, "In Anticipation of the Time to Come" [1918], in Katznelson 1945, vol. 1, 64.

229 A.[?] Tratkover, "The Value of the Enterprise" [1921], in Ben-Avram 1981, 123.

230 David Shimonovitz, "Son of My Land: From the Notebook of a Wanderer" [1909–1919], in Shimonovitz 1947, 178–179.

Chapter 6: Pioneer Language

1 Letters from David Ben-Gurion to his father [1907, 1908], in Ben-Gurion 1971, vol. 1, 106, 115–116; Ben-Sarah [1910], in *Pirkei HaPoʿel HaTzaʿir*, 1, 1935, 71–72; Dayan 1935, 38; Letter from Dov [2.1921], in Erez, ed., 1964, vol. 1, 226; Katznelson 1990, 52, 109–110; Berl Katznelson, "My Road to the Land" [5.4.1941], in Katznelson 1947, vol. 5, 398; Lieberson 1970, 58–59; Feibel Tanpilov, in Habas, ed., 1947, 441; Tzemach 1965, 65; Tzemach 1972, 131; Tzemach 1983, 33; Worker, "Letter from Merhavia," *HaAhdut*, 4, 7.11.1923, 20.

2 For Berl Katznelson on this subject, see Katznelson 1990, 20–21, 30–31. The revival of the Hebrew language is a rich and complex subject. In this book I discuss the desire of the *halutzim*—that is, their perceptions of themselves—and for that reason I do not offer a historical, historiographical, and methodological account of this matter. For such an account, see Bar-Adon 1990, 5–26; Efrati 1997, 89–134; Efrati 2004; Karmi 1997; Kuzar 2001; Lang 2002, 85–130; Ornan 1985, 83–94; Chaim Rabin, "The National Idea and the Revival of Hebrew," in Reinharz and Shapira, eds., 1996, 745–762; Shur 1999.

3 Tzemach 1972, 131–132.

4 Ben-Zvi 1966, 107–108.

5 Yosef Aharonovich, "Old Arguments" [1914], in Aharonovich 1941, vol. 1, 187–188. Cf. Mordechai Snir, "Homeland" [1920], in Snir 1954, 34.

6 Letters from David Ben-Gurion to his father [1906], in Ben-Gurion 1971, vol. 1, 75, 86; Haramati 1996, 143–144; Letter from Natan Ikar to his parents [2.2.1920], in Hamitzer 1981, 91; Pesach Lipovetsky, in Habas, ed., 1947, 313–314; Yanait-Ben-Zvi 1959, 7–8, 10; Tzemach 1965, 77–78.

7 Natan Hofshi, in Habas, ed., 1947, 240.

8 Letter from Shulamit Hayyut [27.10.1920], in Erez, ed., 1964, vol. 1, 229.

9 Ben-Yehuda's status as the "reviver of the Hebrew language" is controversial. On the question, see Kuzar 2001, 41–136. On Eliezer Ben-Yehuda, see Lang 2008, 2 vols.; St. John 1952.

10 Ben-Yehuda 1978, 130.

11 In Ben-Yehuda 1944, 13.

12 Ben-Avi 1961, 12–14, 17–22, 24–25; Ben-Yehuda 1932, 70–71; Ben-Yehuda 1944, 7, 11–13; Ben-Yehuda 1978, 130–132.

13 Ben-Avi 1961, 46–47; Ben-Yehuda 1932, 88–90; Ben-Yehuda 1944, 33–35; Ben-Yehuda 1978, 130–132.

14 Ben-Avi 1961, 27.

15 Ibid., 32–33.

16 Ibid., 42–43.

17 Ben-Yehuda 1978, 56–57, 65, 74, 82–83, 84–86, 94, 96, 100–101, 131, 132.

18 Ibid., 129–130, 132.

19 Bar-Adon 1977, 71n18, 84–90; Bar-Adon 1986, 63–66; Efrati 2004, 108–126; Eisenstadt 1967, 62–67; Michael Grünzweig, "Hebrew in the Second Aliya Period," in Bartal, ed., 1997, 406–418; Michael Grünzweig, "The Status of Hebrew during the Second Aliya," in Naor, ed., 1985, 198–212; Haramati 1996, 175–176; Haramati 1997, 193–201; Harshav 1993, 108–109.

20 Bar-Adon 1986, 70.

21 Harshav 1993, 110–111; Shur 1999, 21; Shur 2003, 50.

22 Bachi 1956, 186–189, 192–195, 197–199; Schmelz and Bachi 1974, 746–750, 760.

23 Bachi 1956, 187–188; Bachi and Schmelz 1974, 749–750.

24 On the attitudes of HaPoʿel HaTzaʿir toward Yiddish and Hebrew, see Shur 2003, 13–50.

25 Y. [?] R., "Language and the Worker," *HaAhdut*, 12, 4.1.1914, 4–7.

26 On the attitudes of Poaʿlei Tzion toward Yiddish and Hebrew, see Shur 2003, 51–83.

27 On the attitudes of the Independents and Ahdut HaAvodah toward Yiddish and Hebrew, see Shur 2003, 84–105.

28 "BeHalutz," *Kuntres*, 1, 15, 24.10.1919, 26; Letters from David Ben-Gurion to the HeHalutz Organization in Bulgaria and to the Histadrut Executive Committee [1922, 1923], in Ben-Gurion 1972, vol. 2, 100, 164–168; Haramati 1996, 174–175; Katznelson-Shazar 1989, 88–89; Kushnir 1968, 29, 45; Sharet and Tamir, eds., 1970, vol. 1, 20–21, 74, 171, 176–177, 235, 255, 261, 331; Shoham 1987, 7, 12, 13–14, 19, 26, 28, 35, 36, 38, 39, 43, 46, 48, 57, 63, 73, 116, 122, 140, 147; Manya Shohat, "The Collective," in *The Words of Women Workers* 1930, 4; Letters from Yosef Trumpeldor [1908, 1913, 1919], in Poznansky, ed., 1922, 20, 22, 51, 209; Yanait-Ben-Zvi 1959, 58; Tzemach 1983, 10–12, 16–18.

29 Ben-Gurion 1973, 7. Cf. "Yishai Adler and His Family," in Sharet and Tamir, eds., 1970, vol. 1, 34–35.

30 Letters from David Ben-Gurion to his father and to Shmuel Fuchs [1904, 1905, 1908], in Ben-Gurion 1971, vol. 1, 32–33, 58, 116; Tzemach 1983, 22, 28, 61.

31 Ben-Gurion 1973, 79; Letters from David Ben-Gurion to his father, to Shmuel Fuchs, and to Paula [1905, 1906, 1910, 1911, 1914, 1918], in Ben-Gurion 1971, vol. 1, 55, 65, 150, 167, 295, 380, 389, 398, 400, 411.

32 Letters from David Ben-Gurion to his father [1920, 1921], in Ben-Gurion 1972, vol. 2, 24, 54, 90; The Will of David Ben-Gurion [4.7.1918], in Ben-Gurion 1973, 104.

33 Letter from David Ben-Gurion to Shlomo Kaplinsky [24.4.1923], in Ben-Gurion 1971, vol. 2, 125.

34 A-H, "Letters of Pioneers" [12.11.1920], *BaDerech*, 1–2, 31.12.1920, 46; S. Dayan [1911], in *Pirkei HaPoʿel HaTzaʿir*, 1, 1935, 237; A.[?] Y.[?] Golani [1908–1909], in *Pirkei HaPoʿel HaTzaʿir*, 1, 1935, 223; Lieberson 1970, 51–52.

35 Tzemach 1972, 133–134; Yosef Weitz, "To the Galilee" [1912], in Weitz 1958, 143.

36 Harshav 1990, 22–23.

37 David Ben-Gurion, in Shur 2003, 83.

38 Rachel Katznelson, "The Council of the Union of Farm Workers at Merhavia. Documentation. The Work of Culture," *Kuntres*, 18, 11.12.1919, 29.

39 Dayan 1935, 38.

40 Bar-Adon 1977, 87; Ever Hadany, ed., 1955?, 181, 185; Kushnir 1968, 98, 139; L., "At work, Kinneret," *Kuntres*, 20, 9.1.1920, 29; Shur 2003, 48–49.

41 Kushnir 1968, 139.

42 Berl Katznelson, "My Road to the Land" [5.4.1941], in Katznelson 1947, vol. 5, 399. For more on Katznelson's Hebrew, see Berl Katznelson, "My Road to the Land" [5.4.1941], in Katznelson 1947, vol. 5, 378, 382–383, 386–388, 392, 394; Letter from Berl Katznelson to Yisrael Katznelson [13.11.1911], in Katznelson 1961, vol. 1, 294.

43 Yosef Aharonovich, "Who Won?" [1914], in Aharonovich 1941, vol. 1, 182.

44 Ruppin 1971, 96–97.

45 Letter from David Ben-Gurion to the Civilian Secretary of the Government of Palestine, Government House [31.12.1922], in Ben-Gurion 1972, vol. 2, 119; Yaʿakov Zerubavel, "Pages of a Diary from 1915" [1915], in Zerubavel 1966, 87–88.

46 Alexander Heshin, "Chapters from a Diary" [7.8.1910], in Kaniel, ed., 1997, 32.

47 Shoham 1987 [4.1.1919], 105.

48 Ibid. [29.4.1920], 147.

49 Ibid. [30.6.1920], 156.

50 Letter from Eliezer Shohat to his wife [22.3.1922], in Shohat 1973, 128.

51 Moshe Smilansky, in Habas, ed., 1947, 695.

52 Ever Hadany, ed., 1955?, 300.

53 Tzemach 1972, 133–134.

54 Yael Gordon, in Habas, ed., 1947, 547–548.

55 Elon 1971, 110–111; Kushnir 1968, 139–140.

56 Noah Tamir, in Habas, ed., 1947, 684–685.

57 Tzemach 1972, 134.

58 Tzemach 1983, 24.

59 Feibel Tanpilov, in Habas, ed., 1947, 441.

60 Mary Yatziv, in Habas, ed., 1947, 566–567.

61 Katznelson 1961, vol. 1, 459–460n20–25; Kaznitzki[?], in Erez, ed., 1964, vol. 2, 790; Kushnir 1968, 98.

62 "At Work, by the Culture Committee," *Kuntres*, 1, 3, 28.5.1919, 27–30; "At Work, Lessons for Teachers of the Workers," *Kuntres*, 1, 15, 24.10.1919, 30–31; Letter from Yitzhak Ben-Zvi to Rachel Yanait-Ben-Zvi [6.9.1918], in Ben-Zvi 1966, 254; Eliezer Kroll, in Ben-Zvi, Shohat, Meged, and Tverski, eds., 1957, 273; Shur 2003, 32–34; Suchovolsky 1973, 114; D. Tz., "In the Battalions, Rafah," *Kuntres*, 1, 4, 13.6.1919, 36; Tzemach 1983, 38; Tzvi, "From the Life of Workers in Rehovot" [20.11.1913], in Kaniel, ed., 1997, 105–106; Ufaz 1988, 76; Yosef Weitz, "To the Galilee" [1912], in Weitz 1958, 143; B. Y. [1910], in *Pirkei HaPo'el HaTza'ir*, 1, 1935, 105–106; Y. B. Z., "From the Councils of Public Works," *Michtav LaChaverim*, 3, 72, 1921, 25.

63 "At Work, by the Culture Committee," *Kuntres*, 1, 3, 28.5.1919, 27–30; "The Council of the Union of Farm Workers at Merhavia. Documentation. The Work of Culture," *Kuntres*, 18, 11.12.1919, 28–33; A. D. [1913], in *Pirkei HaPo'el HaTza'ir*, 1, 1935, 217; Dayan 1935, 38; "Haifa-Jadda Camp," *HaSolel*, 4, 15.4.1921, 167; HaPo'el HaTza'ir [1914], in *Pirkei HaPo'el HaTza'ir*, 1, 1935, 275; Letters from Natan Ikar to his parents [1920], in Hamitzer 1981, 91; Rachel Katznelson-Shazar, "On the 'Silent Era'" [1916], in Katznelson-Shazar 1989, 95–99; Y. Levitov [1920], in *Pirkei HaPo'el HaTza'ir*, 7, 1936, 138–139; Shur 2003, 30–31; Tzemach 1983, 68; Ze'ev Zamir, in Erez, ed., 1964, vol. 2, 456.

64 Haramati 1996, 179–186; Berl Katznelson, "In Anticipation of the Time to Come" [1918], in Katznelson 1945, vol. 1, 84–86; Berl Katznelson, "The *Kuntres* Said" [1919], in Katznelson 1945, vol. 1, 148; Berl Katznelson, "To the HeHalutz Movement" [1917], in Katznelson 1945, vol. 1, 58–60; Kushnir 1968, 153.

65 Haramati 1996, 148–149, 154–155.

66 Ben-Zvi 1966, 118–120; Ben-Zvi, Shohat, Meged, and Tverski, eds., 1957, 85, 87, 375; Neta Harpaz, in Habas, ed., 1947, 225; *The HaShomer Anthology* 1937, 51, 149–150; Shoham 1987 [14.8.1920], 161; Tzemach 1983, 67.

67 Neta Harpaz, in Habas, ed., 1947, 229.

68 Ibid.

69 Ibid., 230.

70 Levi Ben-Amitai, "To Degania," in Ben-Amitai 1966, 32.

71 Ibid., 230.

72 Ibid., 231. Cf. Rachel Katznelson, "Language Migrations" [1918], in Katznelson 1946, 9–22.

73 Berl Katznelson, "Ahdut HaAvodah" [21.2.1919], in Katznelson 1945, vol. 1, 120.

74 Haramati 1996, 179.

75 Ibid., 179–180.

76 Rachel Katznelson, "Language Migrations" [1918], in Katznelson 1946, 9–22. On Berl Katznelson's proposal, see letter from Berl Katznelson to the Jerusalem vegetable *kevutza* [15.6.1918], in Katznelson 1974, vol. 2, 552, 555n20.

77 Berl Katznelson, "The *Kuntres* Said" [1919], in Katznelson 1945, vol. 1, 149.

78 Ruppin 1914, 186.

79 David Gilad-Shmeterling, in Tzur, ed., 1998, 131.

80 Mordechai Snir, "A. D. Gordon" [1920], in Snir 1954, 17.

81 Congress of the Teachers' Union, "Love of the Hebrew Language and Working the Soil"

[9.1905], in Kaniel, ed., 1997, 274–275; executive committee, "Ahdut HaAvodah Publishers," *Kuntres*, 1, 5, 27.6.1919, 3–5; Yanait-Ben-Zvi 1959, 40.

82 L. N., "Matters Before the Teachers' Assembly: 1. The Yishuv and Education," *Kuntres*, 3, 1, 8.10.1919, 29.

83 Zalman Shazar, "Her Scattered Light," in Shazar 1950, 181.

84 Ibid., 182.

85 Weitz 1958, 227.

86 A. Chen, "Principal Matters," *Kolot*, 1, 1923, 23.

87 Harshav 1990, 39, 61–73. Cf. Alexander, "The Revival Below and the Revival Above," *HaAhdut*, 40–41, 7.8.1914, 8.

88 Rachel Katznelson, "Language Migrations" [1918], in Katznelson 1946, 21.

89 Alexander, "The Revival Below and the Revival Above," *HaAhdut*, 40–41, 7.8.1914, 8.

90 Rachel Katznelson, "Language Migrations" [1918], in Katznelson 1946, 22.

91 Ibid., 10.

92 Ibid., 11, 15–17.

93 Shoham 1987 [30.9.1917], 32.

94 Moshe Kalvari, "Caught in Enchantment of Hebrew" [1916], in Habas, ed., 1947, 680.

95 Letter from Berl Katznelson to Hannah Katznelson [1910], in Katznelson 1961, vol. 1, 141.

96 Tzvi Shatz, "To R-H, on the Fords of the Jordan" [1920], in Shatz 1967, 156.

97 Eliezer Yaffe, "To Clarify the Concepts in Our Profession" [1917], in Yaffe 1947, vol. 2, 186.

98 Yosef Haim Brenner, "Pages" [1.1906], in Brenner 1981, vol. 3, 108.

99 Z. Feller, "Members' Letters: Language and Labor," *Michtav LaChaverim*, 2, 22.8.1919, 10.

100 Yitzhak Elazari-Volcani, "The Uniqueness of Selfhood" [1913], in Elazari-Volcani 1950b, 44.

101 Ibid., 45.

102 Ibid. Cf. Alexander, "The Revival Below and the Revival Above," *HaAhdut*, 40–41, 7.8.1914, 3–13; "The Ten Commandments of HaShomer" [1916], in Gothelf and Cohen, eds., 1934, 14.

103 Haramati 1996, 182–186; Nathan Shifris, in Habas, ed., 1947, 197.

104 N. S., "Sejera," *Kuntres*, 1, 6, 4.7.1919, 36; M. Y., "The Botanical Exhibition of Efraim Rabinovich," *Kuntres*, 3, 4, 22.10.1920, 25.

105 N. S., "Sejera," *Kuntres*, 1, 6, 4.7.1919, 36.

106 Dayan 1961, 80.

107 R. Benjamin, "All Around" [1908], in Benjamin 1922, 206; Akiva Ettinger, in Erez, ed., 1964, vol. 2, 460; Ever Hadany, ed., 1955?, 219; *Pirkei HaPo'el HaTza'ir*, 7, 1936, 22, 214, 216, 236; Worker, "Degania as One Big Family" [9.1.1912], in Kaniel, ed., 1997, 189.

108 Yosef Shapira, "At the Margins of the Book," in Shohat 1973, 240.

109 Meir Wilkansky, "My First Day of Labor" [1906–1911], Wilkansky 1982, 14.

110 Eliezer Yaffe, "The Foundation of the *Moshavei Ovdim*" [1919], in Yaffe 1947, vol. 1, 95.

111 Mandel 1980, 62–65.

112 Tzemach 1983, 43–44, 45. Cf. Ben-Hava [1912], in *Pirkei HaPoʿel HaTzaʿir*, 1, 1935, 203; "The HaShomer HaTzaʿir Worldview" [1.1917], in Dror and Rosenzweig, eds., 1956, 40; L., "At Work, Kinneret," *Kuntres*, 20, 9.1.1920, 29; Sarah Malkin, "A Reality That Darkened the Beautiful World We Built for Ourselves" [3.1912], in Kaniel, ed., 1997, 100; Hadassah Rosenblit, "Memories from Safed" [1918], in Habas, ed., 1947, 574.

113 Letter from the Central Committee of the Social Democratic Hebrew Workers' Party in the Land of Israel, "Communication 3," *HaAhdut*, 9, 12.12.1913, 18.

114 Dayan 1935, 95. Cf. "The HaShomer HaTzaʿir Worldview" [1917], in Gothelf and Cohen, eds., 1934, 20.

115 Yehuda Levitov [24.1.1921], in *Sefer HaHaim* 2001, 23.

116 Dayan 1935, 95.

117 Zalman Lifschitz, in Habas, ed., 1947, 389–390.

118 M. Karmi, "Segments," *HaAdama*, 1, 1919–1920, 202.

119 Letter from Eliezer Yaffe to his brother David, "To Uncle Yaffe" [4.11.1914], in Yaffe 1947, vol. 2, 159.

120 Suchovolsky 1973, 18.

121 Executive committee, "On the Death of a Comrade," *Kuntres*, 26, 19.2.1920, 2. Cf. Yitzhak Shweiger, "Inscribe It [in Your Memories] . . . !," *MeHayeynu*, 1, 13, 1921, 87.

122 Chowers 1998, 676–678; Chowers 2002, 599–626.

123 Tzahor 2007, 21.

124 Ben-Zvi 1966, 42; Hannah Katznelson-Nesher, in Sharet and Tamir, eds., 1970, vol. 1, 306; Yehuda Levitov [1921, 1922], in *Sefer HaHaim* 2001, 45, 63; "On Guard" [1917], in Dror and Rosenzweig, eds., 1956, 31–32; Eliezer Riger, "The Revival of Strength" [6.1918], in Shadmi, ed., 1984b, 7; Eliyahu Rosenbaum, "The Way of HaShomer in the Land: Opening Remarks for the First Issue of *HaShomer*" [1917], in Gothelf and Cohen, eds., 1934, 22; Haim Tartakower, "The Role of HaPoʿel HaTzaʿir in the Movement to Redeem Our People," *BaDerech*, 7–8, 31.3.1921, 10.

125 Berl Katznelson, "To the HeHalutz Movement" [1917], in Katznelson 1945, vol. 1, 54.

126 "The Ten Commandments of HaShomer" [1916], in Gothelf and Cohen, eds., 1934, 14.

127 Tzeʿiri Tzion Center, "To Jewish Youth" [1919], in Dror and Rosenzweig, eds., 1956, 24.

128 Eliezer Riger, "The Revival of Strength" [6.1918], in Shadmi, ed., 1984b, 17.

129 Yardeni [1909–1910], in *Pirkei HaPoʿel HaTzaʿir*, 2, 1935, 36.

130 Letter from Natan Ikar to his parents [3.5.1920], in Hamitzer 1981, 91.

131 Letter from Natan Ikar to his parents [3.6.1920], in Hamitzer 1981, 93.

132 Tzvi Livneh, in Sharet and Tamir, eds., 1970, vol. 1, 259.

133 Yosef Aharonovich, "Old Arguments" [1914], in Aharonovich 1941, vol. 1, 187.

134 Shoham 1987 [15.10.1918], 77.

135 Dov Sadan attributes this statement to Katznelson. See Shlomo Karmi, "The Revival and Healing of the Language: Stages, Goals, Conditions, Principles of Action, and 'Early' and 'Late' from a Chronological and Causative Point of View," in Karmi 1997, 222, 235n10. On Katznelson's view of Hebrew, see "First Communication from the Third Convention," by Berl Katznelson [1.1913], in Katznelson 1961, vol. 1, 450–451.

136 Berl Katznelson, "The Nemeses of Our Language" [1928], in Katznelson 1946, vol. 3,

293. Cf. The Workers' *Kevutza* of Degania and the Moshavot Committee of Kinneret, "Protests in the Galilee," *HaAhdut*, 10–11, 26.12.1913, 37–38.

137 Haim Arlosoroff, "The Social Nationalism of the Jews" [1919], in Arlosoroff 1934, vol. 3, 75. Cf. Yosef Aharonovich, "The Hall of Hebrew Culture" [1909], in Aharonovich 1941, vol. 1, 164–165.

138 Letter from Hugo Bergman [7.1920], in Erez, ed., 1964, vol. 1, 220.

139 Ibid.

140 A. D. Gordon, "Hebrew Speech" [1920], in Gordon 1928, vol. 4, 235.

141 Ibid., 238–239.

142 Y. H. Brenner, in Fichman 1952, 79.

143 Yosef Aharonovich, "On the Language of Instruction at the Technion" [1914], in Aharonovich 1941, vol. 1, 176, 177.

144 Rachel Katznelson, "Language Migrations" [1918], in Katznelson 1946, 13.

145 Ibid., 15.

146 Hagolani [1908], in *Pirkei HaPoʿel HaTzaʿir*, 1, 1935, 219–220.

147 Meir Wilkansky, "In the Days of October" [1906–1911], Wilkansky 1982, 44, 45.

148 Hagolani [1908], in *Pirkei HaPoʿel HaTzaʿir*, 1, 1935, 220.

149 Meir Wilkansky, "Transvaluation of Values" [1906–1911], Wilkansky 1982, 44, 34.

150 Nini 1996, 93, 103, 110, 127.

151 Alroey 2004, 7, 11, 77, 116–125.

152 Ibid., 16–17.

153 Ben-Avram and Near 1995, 43.

154 Eisenstadt 1970, 17–18. It is worthy of note that this comment of Eisenstadt's was omitted from the English edition. It appears in the Hebrew original; see Eisenstadt 1967, 13.

155 *HaSolel* 1991; *Kehilateinu* 1998 [1922]; *MeHayeynu*; *Sefer HaHaim* 2001 [1920–1929]; *Sefer HaKevutza* 1996 [1922–1936].

156 I have borrowed this expression from Yitzhak Laor's book: Laor 2000.

157 Shoham 1987 [6.12.1920], 170.

158 For a critical treatment of the pioneer myth, see Alroey 2004, 20–23, who addresses the myth of the *Roslan*; Katriel 2004, 112–138, who addresses the myth of Beitania; Rogel, ed., 1994, 25–29; Anita Shapira, "Zionism and Power: Ethos and Reality," in Shapira 1988, 42–44; Zertal 2005, 9–25; Zerubavel 1995, 39–47, who addresses the Tel Hai myth; Sand 2000, 174–202, who addresses the mythos of pioneer language; Hazan 2006, 284–306, who addresses the death of *halutzim* in general and the case of Moshe Barsky specifically; Sagiv 1998, 92–117, who addresses the myth of "birth from the Land"; Azaryahu and Kellerman 1999, 109–123; Kellerman 1996, 363–378, who addresses the mythic geography of the Land of Israel. For a critical discussion of this view of Israeli myths, see Gertz 1996; Naveh and Yogev 2002. Cf. Myers 1995. For a broader critical discussion of the concept of the modern national myth, see Anderson 1991; Mosse 1991.

159 Ehud Ben-Ezer, "The Second Aliya through the Mirror of Its Literature," in Naor, ed., 1985, 186.

160 Buber 1985, 157.

161 Ibid.

162 Tzahor 2007, 38, 57–58, 169–171.

163 Katznelson 1990. Compare this with Tabenkin's lectures on the history of the Jewish labor movement in the exile and in the Land of Israel, which he gave in the summer of 1937 at the Kibbutz HaMe'uhad seminar at Ein Harod: Tabenkin 1979, 9–24; Tabenkin 1980, 7–24; Tabenkin 1982, 7–36; Tabenkin 1984, 7–28; Tabenkin 1986, 11–26. Also see Shmuel Almog, "The Second Aliya: Self-Image and Modern Interpretation," in Bartal, ed., 1997, 38–59; Mordechai Naor, "HaShomer: The Myth Was Born during the Second Aliya," in Naor, ed., 1985, 101–110.

164 Katznelson 1990, 17.

165 Cogan, ed., 1989; Keren 1983, 100–117; Shapira 1997, 645–674; Tzahor 1995, 61–84.

166 Letter from David Ben-Gurion to his father [13.5.1907], in Ben-Gurion 1971, vol. 1, 106.

167 Letter from David Ben-Gurion to his father [19.10.1906], in Ben-Gurion 1971, vol. 1, 79.

168 Eliezer Shohat, "National Creation and Accounts" [1911], in Shohat 1967, 25. Cf. D. Cohen, "'The Guys,'" *Michtav LaChaverim*, 3, 72, 1921, 8.

169 M. Shweiger, "And It Happened at the End of Days," *MeHayeynu*, 1, 11, 7.11.1921, 69–70.

Index